EXPLORING SOCIAL POLICY IN THE 'NEW' SCOTLAND

Edited by Gerry Mooney and Gill Scott

First published in Great Britain in June 2005 by

The Policy Press
University of Bristol
Fourth Floor
Beacon House
Queen's Road
Bristol BS8 1QU
UK

Tel +44 (0)117 331 4054
Fax +44 (0)117 331 4093
e-mail tpp-info@bristol.ac.uk
www.policypress.org.uk

British Library Cataloguing in Publication Data
A catalogue record for this book is available from the British Library.

Library of Congress Cataloging-in-Publication Data
A catalog record for this book has been requested.

ISBN 1 86134 594 1 paperback

A hardcover version of this book is also available

Gerry Mooney is Staff Tutor in Social Sciences and Senior Lecturer in Social
Policy at The Open University (Scotland). **Gill Scott** is Professor of Social Inclusion
and Equality at Glasgow Caledonian University and Director of the Scottish Poverty
Information Unit.

Cover design by Qube Design Associates, Bristol.
Front cover: photograph taken from a demonstration by striking nursery nurses at the
Scottish Parliament in Edinburgh, 11 March 2004; kindly supplied by Duncan Brown.
Printed and bound in Great Britain by MPG Books, Bodmin.

Contents

Acknowledgements

As ever with a book such as this, a number of people 'behind the scenes' have contributed in different but very important ways. We are very grateful to our colleagues at The Open University (in Edinburgh and in Milton Keynes) and at Glasgow Caledonian University who have offered their support and advice. In particular, Gerry would like to thank Jenny Robertson at The Open University in Edinburgh for her unfailing help and also her willingness to photocopy 'yet another' article or 'press cutting' for him. Special thanks from Gill to colleagues at the Scottish Poverty Information Unit who provided support and suggestions for clarity at the beginning of the project. We are both very grateful to Laura Wilson in the School of Law and Social Sciences at Glasgow Caledonian for her work in preparing the final typescript and also to Duncan Brown for providing us with an excellent photograph of striking nursery nurses in early 2004 for the book cover. Györgyi Túróczy was also a great source of support and helped us immensely in sorting out references, and so on. At The Policy Press, Rowena Mayhew, Dawn Rushen, Laura Greaves and their colleagues have also been a source of much encouragement, support and good advice.

Thanks must go to the referees who gave very helpful comments on the proposal for the book and helped clarify our thoughts on the direction of the book as a whole. We are also very grateful to all the authors for working to a very tight schedule, for their willingness to meet the exacting requirements for each chapter that we laid down and for their continuing enthusiasm for a critical analysis of social policy in Scotland.

Finally, work on this book took up time that might have been devoted to more relaxing pursuits and to time with our respective families. So, from Gerry to Ann and Hilary and from Gill to Mick, thanks for everything.

List of contributors

Margaret Arnott is Senior Lecturer in Political Science at Glasgow Caledonian University.

Usha Brown was Research Fellow at the Scottish Poverty Information Unit, Glasgow Caledonian University, between 1996 and 2004.

Hazel Croall is Professor of Criminology at Glasgow Caledonian University.

Philomena de Lima is a Development Officer/Researcher at UHI PolicyWeb, UHI-Millennium Institute, Inverness.

Iain Ferguson is Senior Lecturer in Social Work at the Department of Applied Social Science, University of Stirling.

Morag Gillespie is Research Fellow at the Scottish Poverty Information Unit, Glasgow Caledonian University.

Charlie Johnstone is Lecturer in Sociology at the University of Paisley.

Alex Law is Lecturer in Sociology at the University of Abertay Dundee.

Ailsa McKay is Lecturer in Economics at Glasgow Caledonian University.

Chris McWilliams is Lecturer in Urban Studies, School of the Built Environment, Heriot-Watt University, Edinburgh.

Gerry Mooney is Staff Tutor in Social Sciences and Senior Lecturer in Social Policy in the Faculty of Social Sciences at The Open University (Scotland).

Lynne Poole is Lecturer in Social Policy at the University of Paisley.

Gill Scott is Professor of Social Inclusion and Equality and Director of the Scottish Poverty Information Unit at Glasgow Caledonian University.

Carol Tannahill is Project Manager of the Glasgow Centre for Population Health and is an Honorary Senior Lecturer with the University of Glasgow, a Fellow of the Faculty of Public Health, and since 1998 has acted as a Consultant to the World Health Organisation Centre for Urban Health.

Themes and questions

Gerry Mooney and Gill Scott

Introduction

Devolution raises important questions for the study of social and welfare policy. Not only does it open up the potential for new forms of governance to emerge, but there is much expectation also that devolution (as an emerging development in different nation states) will provide for the production of diverse forms of social policies that can be transferred across national boundaries and frontiers. This volume will be of value to those who are interested in exploring how territorial differences in the political, economic and social make up of the UK impact on social policy. There is little doubt that the contemporary social policy environment in the UK has changed significantly in the last three decades. The end of a welfare consensus in the 1980s, the changing economic position of the country, and shifts in social and political composition have all been recognised as significant factors in the development of policy. Much has been made of such factors in exploring divergences in welfare between countries (Alcock and Craig, 2001). Less attention has been paid to how such factors affect regions within countries, yet in an era of devolution and claims for territorial justice, such analysis becomes important (Walsh, 1995; Tomaney, 2002). It is particularly important when competing expectations exist about the potential impact of devolution.

Welfare in federal regimes, such as the US and Germany, are seen by some as maintaining inequalities between states and reducing the capacity of some to support the poor (Clasen and Freedman, 1994; Steiger, 2004). By contrast, devolution in Scotland was welcomed as a way to improve welfare and social policy, not as a means of minimising standards and entitlements. Donald Dewar, who was to become the first First Minister in the new Scottish Parliament, commented:

> Too many Scots are excluded, by virtue of unemployment, low skills levels, poverty, bad health, poor housing or other factors from full participation in society.... This Government is determined to take action to tackle exclusion, and to develop policies, which will promote

a more inclusive, cohesive and ultimately sustainable society. (D. Dewar,
in *The Herald*, 3 February 1998)

In this book, we hope to explore what has happened in particular areas of social
policy and welfare against such contrasting views and consider what lessons
devolution in Scotland holds for policy analysts and public sector agencies. In
producing this book we have been concerned from the outset to avoid an inward-
looking, parochial discussion. The questions and issues that are raised throughout
the book are important for the comparative analysis of social policy in the context
of devolved government and beyond, opening up questions about how
comparative social policy should be advanced.

A 'new' Scotland?

We thought long and hard about the title of this collection, especially with
regard to the notion of a 'new' Scotland. The idea of a *new* Scotland, of a *golden-
age* post-devolution, has been a recurring theme in discussions of political processes,
attitudes and policies since 1999 (see Paterson et al, 2001; Hassan and Warhurst,
1999, 2002b; Curtice et al, 2002; Bromley et al, 2003). As Hassan and Warhurst
(2002a, p 7) observe, devolution promised an era characterised by a 'new politics',
with greater participation and involvement of more Scots, and a policy-making
agenda that was more closely in tune with 'Scottish needs'. This in turn reflects
wider social, economic, political and cultural changes in Scottish society in recent
decades (see Bechhofer and McCrone, 2004; Paterson et al, 2004). These two
elements of what Hassan (1998, p 9) has elsewhere referred to as "the new
politics thesis" emphasise that Scotland has become a 'better place' in recent
times, a more confident, diverse and pluralist society, typified by a recently emerged
cultural renaissance. However, in questioning the extent to which such a picture
is characteristic of much of Scottish civil society, Hassan also argues that devolution
and the re-establishment of a Scottish Parliament offer up the potential for new
forms of political participation and collaboration to be developed.

While rejecting some of the claims made about the new Scotland, Hassan and
Warhurst are, along with many others it must be said, seduced to some degree by
the idea of a *new Scotland*, the potential for a new politics to emerge and also by
particular interpretations of some recent changes in Scottish society. On the
opening page of their 2002 edited collection, for instance, they claim that:

> Scotland is slowly becoming a different place from the rest of the
> UK: a society and body politic with a different set of priorities, debates
> and policies. (Hassan and Warhurst, 2002a, p 5)

While going on to acknowledge that "at least this is the way it is meant to be",
this discourse of change both underpins and permeates the new Scotland notion
in all its varied guises. Hassan and Warhurst here point to a picture of a changed

society that extends beyond the boundaries of political attitudes and processes to encompass far more widespread and significant transformations in recent Scottish society. In this respect, they have suggested a 12-point strategy for the development of a 'new Scots social democracy' for the early 21st century in which, while maintaining the egalitarianism and collectivism of 'old social democracy', we can find a commitment to entrepreneurialism, to the consumers and users of public services (and against the vested 'producer interests' of trade unions) and to new forms of governance (Hassan and Warhurst, 2002a, pp 20-1).

Much of this is not too far removed from key aspects of New Labour's discourses of 'modernisation' and 'reform', or indeed with elements of Third Way thinking (see Chapters One and Two in this collection). And here, the discourse of a 'new' Scotland, we would argue, has a much wider and even more problematic meaning and resonance, resting as it does on a contentious interpretation of recent social and economic changes. That there have been far-reaching changes in Scottish society in recent decades there is widespread agreement, though all too often the uneven, partial and contradictory nature of many of these has not been acknowledged to an extent that is surely merited. In 2001, social scientists from Edinburgh University claimed on the back of a study of social and political attitudes in Scotland that:

> There is currently a real sense in Scotland that everything is changing; that nothing can be taken for granted..... The country is going through the closest to a social revolution that can be found in a developed western democracy. (Paterson et al, 2001, p 167)

More recently, members of the same research centre have been to the fore again in advancing their claim that Scottish society has undergone far-reaching change. In a two-page spread in *The Scotsman* on 15 May 2004, Edinburgh University sociologists Frank Bechhofer and David McCrone, under the headline 'Scotland 2004: Why we've never had it so good', refer to their study 'Living in Scotland' as presenting "a truly astonishing picture of a Scotland which has transformed dramatically even since adults in their mid-twenties were born" (Johnston et al, 2004).

In claiming that the Scotland of the early 2000s is "barely recognisable as the same place" of the early 1980s, Paterson et al (2004, p 149) focus on demographic, household, employment and other changes to advance their argument. What tend to be obscured here are the profound continuities with the past, particularly in relation to the highly unequal social relations of power that characterise Scottish society. In claiming in their feature in *The Scotsman*, referred to above, that "for eight out of ten people, Scotland is a better place to live than 25 years ago", Bechhofer et al (2004) are in danger of misunderstanding and underestimating the significant continuities in terms of inequality, polarisation and division that make recent social policy in Scotland look like the beginning rather than end of necessary attempts to address key issues for the future welfare of Scottish citizens

– attempts that are also having unforeseen, contradictory and often negative outcomes. To be fair, the authors do recognise that Scotland remains an unequal society. To quote Paterson et al (2004, p 151) again:

> Nevertheless, one would require truly rosy spectacles not to see a much darker side. Amidst this largely benevolent change, Scottish society is seriously divided and stratified. The basis of stratification has changed somewhat, and the size of the disadvantaged segments of society has shrunk, but the nature and experience of the resulting exclusion may, if anything, have worsened.

However, what is being implied here is that poverty and related forms of disadvantage are almost marginal or residual features of contemporary Scottish society rather than the lived experience of a substantial proportion of the population. And in using the highly problematic terminology of a 'darker side', there is a failure to understand the processes that lead to polarisation and inequality, that there is a relationship between the accumulation of wealth and the accumulation of poverty. We do not have space here to unpack some of the other claims made here about re-stratification, or in other places about the declining significance of social class, or regarding what are argued to be beneficial employment changes. Instead, we note that the analysis of social and economic change is, like the devolved Scotland itself, a much argued over and debated matter.

Another version of the new Scotland thesis is presented by Gordon Brown and Douglas Alexander MP. Here the 'new' Scotland is seen to be a crucial part of a 'new' Britain under construction by New Labour in Westminster. They map a vision of this new (or renewed) Britain on the basis of shared values, ideas and institutions, not least the post-war Beveridgean welfare state: the UK welfare state of the NHS, of UK National Insurance (Brown and Alexander, 1999). In this 'new Unionism', the political dichotomy that faces the electorate in Scotland is essentially a clear-cut choice between the Scottish National Party's 'separatist' independence and the continuing commitment to social justice and to the welfare state. Again, unfortunately we do not have the space to discuss this new Unionism in much detail, save to note that Brown and Alexander, while highlighting that the postwar welfare system was part of a UK-wide settlement (see also Keating, 2002; Stewart, 2004a, 2004b), neglect to tell us just how far New Labour has fought to distance itself from key aspects of this settlement, in the process completely reworking the idea of social justice itself.

The relevance for all of this for our discussion and analysis of developments in social and welfare policy in Scotland today is only too clear. It raises important questions about the type of society, public services and welfare system that we want to see developing in Scotland in the future, issues to which we return in the concluding chapter of this book. Claims about a new Scotland feed directly contentious claims that public and social policy in Scotland after devolution has been fundamentally transformed (see Mooney and Poole, 2004):

> The English once fled to Gretna Green to get married in a hurry. Now there are other enticements drawing them north. Scotland is becoming a social magnet, attracting English people who want better care for their elderly, better university education with grants and no student fees, higher levels of hospital staffing, improved ratios of teachers to pupils in schools. And it's no longer a matter of taking the high or the low road north: Scotland just has better roads. (Fraser and Cusick, 2001)

This kind of hyperbole feeds the surprisingly uncritical commentary that has tended to characterise much of the discussion of social policy in Scotland in the early years of the 21st century while simultaneously helping to generate yet another in a long and very undistinguished line of myths that all too often feature in accounts of Scottish society. Such myths cohere around claims that in some ways 'the Scots' are more inclined to be collective, social democratic, egalitarian and that these inherent values, that insulate 'them' against Thatcherism, now work to protect them from some of the more radical of New Labour/ Blairite policies (a theme picked up also in Chapter One of this book). For example, one contributor to a two-day feature in *The Guardian* in November 2003, on public services in Scotland, felt compelled to write that:

> The Scottish people are collaborative by nature and they don't want bogus organisational entities forced on them, they want one NHS and all want to feel part of that one national endeavour and public service. (McIndoe, 2003)

Elsewhere, one academic commentating on developments in social work following devolution, claimed that there is a:

> greater public ownership of welfare in Scotland than in England. In middle class and professional circles you do not think twice about owning up to being a social worker for fear of a diatribe about delinquents, inadequate parents, neglectful social workers and dependent scroungers. (Cheetham, 2001, pp 625-6)

While acknowledging that "there is much to be done in all fronts" in relation to poor housing, poverty and morbidity, Cheetham (2001, p 626) goes on to argue that:

> what is recognised, perhaps more in Scotland than elsewhere in the UK, is that welfare policies, traditions and services are essential in

> diminishing the sorrowful state of affairs. Sam Galbraith, the first Scottish Minister responsible for Health and Social Work put it nicely: 'Welfare is part of the way Scotland does its business'.

The idea that Scottish society is imbued with a distinctive set of political and social attitudes has long been a subject of much debate and speculation. There has been extensive research on attitudes to welfare in Scotland that have concluded that attitudinal and political differences north and south of the border differ only marginally. The one issue that appears to distinguish Scotland and England (if less so Scotland and some of the northern English regions) relates to greater support in Scotland for the redistribution of income and wealth (see Paterson et al, 2001; Curtice et al, 2002). However, with the announcement in July 2004 that First Minister Jack McConnell had accepted the principle of private funding for state schools (see *The Herald*, 9–10 July, 31 August 2004), and in a major about-turn that Foundation Hospitals and greater consumer choice would be a feature of Scotland's health service in the near future (see *Sunday Herald*, 4 July 2004), it would appear that the 'Scottish people' are not entirely immune from 'bogus organisational entities' referred to by McIndoe above!

The idea of a 'new' Scotland is also being constructed in other ways and here the Scottish Executive plays a major role. Scottish politicians, especially from the Labour Party, are not averse to drawing upon perceived ideologies and myths about Scottish civil society, particularly concerning its egalitarian and collectivist tendencies. However, such myths are also often constructed as 'old-fashioned' attitudes, particularly when they are viewed as a hindrance to the Scottish Executive's key goal of imagining the new Scotland as a vibrant' and 'dynamic' economy in which enterprise can flourish. Such a vision is central to the 2003 Partnership Agreement between Scottish Labour Party and the Scottish Liberal Democrats, the governing coalition in the Scottish Executive (Scottish Executive, 2003) where the pursuit of social justice and social inclusion is founded upon a strategy of 'growing the Scottish economy'. Elsewhere, there is a commitment to improving public services and the promotion of consumer choice, issues that have come to be central to the ensuing debate around welfare and public services in Scotland.

In all of this, the new Scotland is constructed first and foremost, in the language of the Scottish Executive, as a 'smart, successful Scotland', with greater emphasis on wealth creation as opposed to wealth redistribution. These issues are explored more fully by Alex Law in Chapter Two (see also Raco, 2002, 2003), but here we simply draw attention to some of the ways in which New Labour in Scotland has striven to marry 'old' and 'new' Scotland. In the words of former Minister and current Member of Scottish Parliament (MSP) Wendy Alexander (quoted in Joshi and Wright, 2004, p 15):

> Our conviction is that Scotland has a remarkable set of assets on which to build. So long as we are not beholden to our past Scotland

can become a test bed for a unique mixture of both the American
spirits of enterprise and of European solidarity.

Any attempt to grapple with change is accompanied by efforts to re-present and
reconstruct the past, in ways that simultaneously both illuminate and obscure
particular relations and processes. Arguably, however, here we have a new myth
in the making: Scotland as a country in which the apparent contradiction between
enterprise and welfare, competitiveness and cohesion has been resolved.

In seeking to undermine some of the myths that are in the process of being
cemented about the 'new' devolved Scotland, we are also problematising and
questioning the use of all too pervasive and homogenising notions such as 'the
Scots' and indeed 'Scotland' in the sense of 'Scotland going its own way with
education policy', or 'Scotland operating with a different set of values' (see, for
example, Greer, 2003, p 213, in relation to health policy).

The discourse or idea of a 'new Scotland' is highly contentious. It is problematic
in our view as it works to not only obscure and marginalise the continuing
legacies of the past, but also in the process to construct and present opposition to
recent policy changes as almost a relic of another (almost forgotten) world. The
choice of an image from the 2004 Scotland-wide nursery nurses strike for the
front cover of this volume was no accident but a reflection that developments in
social and welfare policy in Scotland today do not occur in isolation from wider
social inequalities, nor do they simply generate a passive response. Against claims
highlighted above that 'we've never had it so good', Scotland is today a society
characterised by deep-seated disadvantage and a marked social polarisation. Such
a claim is hardly new. However, as many of the chapters in this book show,
inequalities and contestations of policy direction remain a significant aspect of
the devolved Scotland. In a major comparative study of the 1991 and 2001
census, researchers from Sheffield University found that Glasgow continues to
be the poorest city in the UK, but that deprivation was increasing faster there
than in any other part of Scotland (Dorling and Thomas, 2004). While there are
a number of specific factors that might help to explain Glasgow's position here,
the same researchers also concluded that wealth inequalities and the number of
households living in poverty had increased between 1991 and 2001.

Social policy in the 'new' Scotland: towards 'Scottish solutions'?

There are a number of different factors that have led to this book being produced.
In part, it reflects research undertaken by many of the contributors on different
aspects of social and welfare policy in Scotland today, and the need for this to be
brought together in a single volume. It is evident from the different chapters
contained here that the Scottish Executive has been extremely active across
different fields of welfare and social policy since devolution in 1999. As one

former minister to the Scottish Executive, and current Labour MSP, expressed this:

> After more than 300 years without a parliament, the pace has been quicker than for centuries. But without the parliament little of this progress would have happened. Imagine where we would have been now if, in 1997 as in 1979, Scotland had hesitated about home rule. (W. Alexander, in *Scotland on Sunday*, 30 June 2002)

Of course, prior to devolution, many areas of social policy in Scotland fell under the jurisdiction of the Scottish Office, notably in relation to education, housing and health care provision (see also Chapter One of this book). In other areas, such as criminal justice, the distinctive legal system that exists in Scotland compared with other areas of the UK has been historically reflected in Scottish-specific policies; for example, in relation to youth justice, an issue taken-up by Hazel Croall in Chapter Seven. Further, there was extensive administrative difference prior to the constitutional reform brought about through and by devolution itself.

However, devolution *promised* greater divergence in policy between Scotland and other areas of the UK. We say 'promised' because, at the time of writing this (mid-2004), arguably it would be fair to say that the jury is out on how far these promises have been met. A repeated claim of those supporting devolution in the late 1990s was that it would allow the development of distinctively 'Scottish solutions for Scottish problems' (Stewart, 2004a, 2004b). To quote Donald Dewar (1998):

> We have a proud tradition in Scotland of working to tackle social division. We have developed innovative responses to social problems, many of which are now being promoted within the UK as models of good practice. We have a body of people ... who are committed to creating a fairer society in Scotland. And in the not too distant future we will have a Scottish Parliament, which will give us the opportunity to develop Scottish solutions to Scottish needs, and to bring the arm of government closer to the needs of the people. Devolution matters. It will let us take the decisions that matter here in Scotland. It is an end in itself: but it is a means to other ends, and none more important than the creation of a socially cohesive Scotland. (Scottish Office Press Release, 3 November)

While the idea of 'Scottish solutions' has become something of a mantra for Scottish ministers, those familiar with New Labour's approach to social policy will quickly see, in this comment from Dewar, a discursive approach which is largely borrowed from New Labour in Westminster. Key here is the mobilisation of notions of social cohesion, and by implication social inclusion and exclusion (discussed in Chapters One and Two in this volume; see also Levitas, 1998; Fairclough, 2000). These have become as important to the Scottish Executive approach to social policy as they are to New Labour's wider social policy reforms (see Mooney and Johnstone, 2000; Brown et al, 2002).

There is an important question raised by this which revolves around the extent to which social policy in Scotland is following a divergence path or, as a consequence of pressures from the government in Westminster, from the constraints imposed by the 1998 Scotland Act, the 'Scottish Devolution' Act, or from other factors such as global economic developments, one that demonstrates trends towards convergence with other parts of the UK. For the contributors to this book, this necessitates the adoption of a critical approach that engages with the actuality of social policy developments in Scotland and that seeks to locate them in a wider social, economic and political context. This book, then, reflects the desire that many of us have to offer a critically informed commentary upon, and analysis of, social policy in post-devolution Scotland. Indeed, several of us would go further and argue that one of the most disappointing aspects of academic commentary on devolution thus far is that much of it seems to accept, in a rather uncritical way, Scottish Executive pronouncements about what it is doing in relation to social policy. While links between academic research and policy making are of course to be applauded when this is appropriate, there has as yet been relatively little in the way of critical academic commentary on Scottish social policy that seeks to analyse this in relation to the underlying discourses deployed by the Scottish Executive and New Labour in Scotland and that takes account of the crucial issues of wider economic and social inequalities and social divisions. We return to this later in this Introduction.

Social policy in post-devolution Scotland

Scottish devolution offered greater opportunity and potential for policy divergence between Scotland and the rest of the UK. As we write this, one year into the term of the second reconvened Scottish Parliament, and five years following devolution itself, it could be argued that it is still too early to tell how far policy divergence (or convergence) is likely. However, there are already clearly established signs as to the future direction of social policy in Scotland. These allow us to offer some insights on the policy objectives of the Scottish Executive. It is also important to recognise the constraints that also impinge, to varying degrees, on the scope of the Scottish Parliament to enact divergent policies. As Keating (2002) and Parry (2002), among others, have noted, the financial interdependence between Holyrood (the site of the Scottish Parliament) and Westminster and the power of the Chancellor of the Exchequer in London to decide upon the block grant given to Edinburgh are obvious cases in point. Then there is the matter of devolved and reserved powers. Section 5 of the 1998 Scotland Act reserved 11 key areas of government policy making to Westminster, including employment, social security, immigration, trade and industry and industrial relations. This means that, in relation to immigration and asylum policy, for example, two key policy developments, the 1999 Immigration and Asylum Act and the 2002 Immigration, Asylum and Nationality Bill, frame policy in these areas as much in Scotland as in the rest of the UK (see Ferguson and Barclay, 2002). Health care, housing, social work, local government and criminal justice, among other matters, were fully devolved to the Scottish Parliament (see Keating, 2002, pp 16-17). Further, and less well known, is the existence of the Sewell Convention. Named after Lord Sewell, who was a key player in the passage of the Scotland Bill through the House of Lords in 1998, this was a pivotal component of the devolution settlement for Scotland (see Bell, 2004). It allows the Westminster Parliament, with the approval of Holyrood, to develop policies and implement legislation even in those policy areas that are designated as devolved responsibilities. (This will be explored more fully in Chapter One of this book.)

Of the many important areas of social policy making that have already received considerable political and academic attention since Scottish devolution, two in particular stand out: free personal care for older people, and the financing of students in higher education. Both are widely interpreted as highlighting the divergent path that the Scottish Parliament is following in relation to key areas of social welfare and, given this, we briefly summarise the important elements of each here.

The Scottish Executive introduced free personal and nursing care for older people on 1 July 2002, under the 2002 Community Care and Health (Scotland) Act. While this policy has been called one of 'devolution's major successes' (McCabe, 2004), it has something of a controversial history. In 1999, the Majority Report of the Royal Commission on Long-Term Care (the Sutherland Commission) recommended that those principles underpinning the NHS (that is, funded by taxation, based on need, free at the point of use) should apply also to nursing and personal care, and thus all costs should be covered by the state (Stewart, 2004b, p 126). Both the Scottish Executive and the UK government, with reference to the Commission's Minority Report, first rejected the full implementation of this conclusion. It stated that the costs of such a policy were underestimated, a significant increase in demand was predictable, and that the universality of the policy would not target and benefit those groups among older people who were deemed to be most needy. However, in Scotland, the Scottish Parliament's Health and Community Care Committee called for full implementation while voluntary and professional organisations were also campaigning for the policy's introduction. In the Scottish Executive coalition partners, the Liberal Democrats also threatened revolt if the policy was not enacted. Following this the incoming First Minister, Henry McLeish, announced a policy reversal and in January 2001, despite the disapproval of Westminster, a political decision was made to fund personal and nursing care for older people irrespectively of their personal financial situation.

While this has since been portrayed as a uniquely 'Scottish solution', it is important to acknowledge that support for this policy was UK-wide. As successive attitude surveys indicated, public opinion on the issue was much the same in both Scotland and England: 89% in Scotland and 84% in England agreed that the main responsibility for residential care of older people lies with the government. Eighty-two per cent in Scotland and 84% in England expressed the opinion that more government spending was required to support those caring for sick or older people (Paterson et al, 2001, p 125). This indicates that the issue of personal care itself was not solely 'Scottish'. However, devolution made it possible for the Scottish Executive to choose a different solution from that of England and to provide universal free personal care as opposed to the selective, means-tested care that featured South of the Border. The key aim of the policy is to provide security and dignity for older people and to help them stay in their homes and communities. The importance of the latter is enhanced by the fact that the Scottish tradition of employing greater resources on institutional care is challenged by demographic change, notably that Scotland's population is increasingly ageing. According to the Scottish Executive, in 2001 15% of the population was aged 65+ and by 2031 this rate would rise to 24% (Stewart, 2004b, p 126).

The policy provides £145 per week towards personal care for people aged 65+ in care homes and £65 per week towards nursing care if required. Old people living in their own homes receive personal care from their local authorities free of charge. In June 2004 there were 48,700 people receiving free care, the majority of them living in their own homes (40,531). The uptake of free personal care increased by 15% in care homes and by 74% in own homes between 2002 and 2004 (Scottish Executive Press Release, 2004). The number of clients given free nursing care rose by 15% over the same period. There are significant regional differences, however, both in expenditure and in relation to the increase in client numbers (for example, in Fife a 200% increase in personal care clients in care homes has been recorded, while in Dumfries and Galloway there has been a 40% decrease).

Policies for the funding of students in higher education in Scotland have also taken a different path from elsewhere in the UK. Since autumn 2000, Scottish students on full-time higher education courses have not been required to pay tuition fees up front. The issue of student finances emerged in Scotland as early as the first elections for the devolved government in 1999. Concerns addressed by this debate were common all over the UK, however. With education being firmly in the control of the Scottish Parliament (and often at the heart of Scottish national identity), fees and loans were generally regarded as undermining the principles of equality of access (Paterson, 2003, p 171). Higher and further education was also given a key role in the devolved government's commitment to social inclusion and lifelong learning. In 2001, a new scheme introduced grants for students from low-income families. The allocation and amount of grants depend on the students' or their families' financial situation and their aim is to reduce the amount of loans students need to take up to support themselves. The new Graduate Endowment scheme is the students' contribution to fund these bursaries. After they have completed their course and started to earn, they have to pay an amount fixed at the time of their entry to the university at a rate proportionate to their earnings (currently £2,154). Some students are exempt from this contribution due to personal circumstances (for example, lone parents or students with disabilities). The system of student loans was also maintained, the amount available depending on income. There are additional grants and loans allocated to mature students, lone parents or disabled students.

However, in this case, policy was somewhat out of step with public opinion. The British Social Attitudes survey in 2001 showed in both Scotland and England there was general support for means-tested fees and that students should contribute somehow to their education depending on their financial situation (63% in Scotland and 57% in England). In both countries, only one third shared the view that no student should pay (Bromley et al, 2003, p 10). The Scottish Executive's distinctive solution of abolishing up-front fees and introducing endowment contributions for some students was supported only by 11% (Curtice et al, 2002, p 205). Opinions on grants were closer to the government's position. Almost everybody agreed in Scotland and in England that grants had to be restored, and two thirds thought that they should be means-tested (Paterson et al, 2001, pp 148-9).

There have been further concerns about the funding of higher education. The cost of the reforms was estimated to reach £50 million by 2004 (Trench, 2001). Abolishing tuition fees carried a danger of Scottish universities becoming under-funded and finding it harder to compete with English universities in relation to the recruitment of high-quality teaching staff. As the endowment scheme applies only to students who entered a course after 2001, it will take a longer period to develop a substantial fund for the bursaries.

However, there have already been some positive signs. Participation in higher education by the age of 21 in Scotland reached 50% in 2000, while it was around 30% in England (Paterson et al, 2001, pp 148-9), although the socioeconomic background of the student population has remained fairly steady, with voices raised that the current system of finance is doing little to promote higher educational opportunities among the more severely disadvantaged sections of the population.

In relation to both student finance and personal care for older people, there has been much debate and controversy about the effectiveness of each policy. Both within and outside Scotland, these two issues have been widely discussed in relation to what they say about the scope and direction of social policy in the context of devolution. While, as we can see here, there are very obvious signs of difference between the approach of the Scottish Executive and other governments' in the UK, there are also common issues and questions of financing, about selectivity/universality and about the impact that such policies have in a divided social landscape.

Themes and questions

The dominant approach to social policy adopted in this book is one that seeks to explore social and welfare policy in its broadest sense, relating developments in social policy innovation to wider questions of social relations, social divisions and social inequalities. We are concerned here to offer both a politics of Scottish social policy, and a politics of 'social problems' in Scotland. In so doing it is recognised that there are contrasting and competing ways of making sense of such issues, but we have been keen to avoid a simple 'concern' with 'social problems' without seeing these as part of a wider set of social relations, a highly unequal set of social relations. Thus, to borrow from C. Wright Mills (1959, p 226):

> Do not allow public issues as they are officially formulated, or troubles as they are privately felt, to determine the problems that you take up for study.

Devolution has created a new policy environment in Scotland, albeit one in which the enduring legacies of the past are all too evident. Thus, we can see strong continuities in the role that the media and other powerful groups play in shaping the scene to which policies are developed in response. Three examples will suffice here. While the media in Scotland have not been fully paid up members of the anti-immigration bandwagon, that has been a feature of large sections of the press media based in England in the early 2000s, nonetheless there have been numerous 'scare' stories about the negative impact that asylum seekers have on Scottish society. As we have seen, claims have been made that the new Scotland is a culturally mixed place, open to new ideas, people and lifestyles – a place of diversity. However, this has not prevented the Roman Catholic Church in Scotland, together with some Christian Fundamentalist groups, embarking on a crusade against 'non-traditional' lifestyles and the teaching of sex education in schools, issues that some sections of the media have been keen to highlight, not always in progressive ways. And then we have the recurring concerns with juvenile 'delinquency'. In 2003 in particular there was something of a moral panic in 'middle Scotland', fuelled by both the media and New Labour politicians, that anti-social behaviour had become the 'scourge' of Scottish society, particularly in relation to youth crime. In the devolved Scotland, as much as in the Scotland of pre-1999, we should not underestimate the power that certain groups have in defining, constructing and reproducing 'social problems' (Clarke and Cochrane, 1998).

Wright Mills (1959) argues that to fully appreciate how 'public issues' come to be constructed and defined, the wider social context must be central to the investigation. Understanding the structural context is essential, we argue, if we are to provide an informed discussion of social policy in post-devolutionary

Scotland. Of central importance for the analysis of social and welfare policy in general is a commitment to critical engagement and interrogation of claims made by policy makers, politicians and by governments at all levels. In different ways and from different standpoints, the chapters that comprise this book share an approach that seeks to offer:

- an evaluation and analysis of social policies in their respective field;
- an examination of the 'newness' of social policy in the 'new' Scotland by considering pre- and post-devolution social policies;
- an exploration of convergence and divergence between social policy in post-devolutionary Scotland and the rest of the UK;
- an analysis of social inclusion, social inequalities and social divisions as they relate to and impact on the relevant social policy site; and
- some assessment of what needs to be done and what needs have yet to be met in relation to the relevant social policy areas.

The central thrust of the book will be its analytical approach. It is recognised, of course, that there is no single approach that is mobilised across the entire collection. Different authors will adopt different perspectives in their chapters, but all share a commitment to providing a critically informed discussion of developments in Scottish social policy. This is achieved in part by addressing a series of questions:

- the extent to which policy developments in a particular area of social policy represent a continuation from or divergence from policies pre-devolution;
- the degree to which there is increasing Scottish policy distinctiveness – or convergence between different parts of the UK, post-devolution;
- what particular social needs remain to be met in the relevant social policy site.

The question of the distinctiveness of social policy in Scotland in comparison with England and Wales since devolution is a theme that underpins many of the chapters and individual authors have approached this in different ways, some by offering a Scotland versus UK-wide comparison, others by considering Scotland against England and/or Wales. Throughout, a primary concern has been to challenge some of the myths about social policy in the 'new' Scotland and to explore the question, is devolution doing what people thought it would do in relation to social policy?

Structure of the book

It is important that we acknowledge from the start that this book does not seek to 'cover' every aspect of social and welfare policy in Scotland since devolution. There is no separate chapter on housing policy, although issues closely related to housing are explored in Chapter Six in particular. Likewise, we do not discuss geographical inequalities in Scotland per se in a single chapter, although such issues do emerge in a number of the chapters. Space allowing, we would have been inclined to include a chapter on regional policy in Scotland (perhaps also encompassing land reform) in ways that connect both to social policy concerns. Unfortunately, constraints of space mean that there is no chapter on the experiences of welfare workers, or welfare users or on the role of the voluntary sector in the devolved Scotland. Instead, we have opted for those sites of welfare wherein the Scottish Parliament has arguably been most active and, given our concern with social divisions and inequalities, we thought it important to have chapters that explored matters of equality, gender and ethnicity in Scotland today, while issues relating to social class emerge in many of the discussions.

Chapters One and Two offer an overview of developments in social policy in Scotland since devolution, with Chapter Two explicitly linking these with strategies for developing the Scottish economy. They also highlight the dominant ideologies and discourses that inform social policy in contemporary Scotland arguing that neoliberalism, as elsewhere in the UK, is the dominant shaping influence. Chapter One provides a valuable start to the text by developing an in-depth analysis of changes in governance that devolution promised and delivered in Scotland and Wales. It examines the extent of divergence across a range of policy areas north and south of the border and concludes that 'modernisation' has meant much the same – a neoliberal agenda and the incorporation of non-radical voices. It argues that a failure to deliver on the promises of wider governance stems from political will and existing political alliances both sides of the border as much as limitations in the devolution settlement.

Chapter Two covers many important issues that are increasingly central to debates on social policy today but which have arguably been much neglected in the literature. Alex Law's analysis here of welfare nationalism, social justice and entrepreneurship extends the analysis of limitations to policy divergence through its focus on a welfare orthodoxy that gives primacy to market/business interests despite assertions that social justice lies at the heart of New Labour's thrust in Scotland. Law sees the power this ideology exerts as deriving from the way in which networks of political, business and media interests have formed and reformed since devolution. He goes on to argue that pro-business assumptions exert as great a pressure in Scotland as Blair's government and that the possibility of welfare nationalism is a long way from being realised.

In Chapter Three, Gill Scott, Gerry Mooney and Usha Brown draw back from this rather pessimistic notion, that devolution can produce little change in the conditions that social policy has traditionally addressed. Rather, it examines how far the social justice agenda has made a difference to the extent and nature of poverty in Scotland. The chapter outlines the social and economic factors that have put some groups at greater risk of poverty and goes on to critically examine policies designed to promote work as a route out of poverty and those designed to reduce the risks of poverty faced by children. Its main argument is that considerable experience in developing policy interventions at devolved level has occurred, albeit largely determined by the threat that social exclusion poses to an economically successful Scotland. At the same time, like Chapter One, it also argues that much still needs to be done and that a successful anti-poverty programme would have to be much wider in scope and demands public support as well as policy shifts.

The next two chapters highlight how process and policy changes since devolution have structured the response to the fragmented and differentiated nature of Scottish society identified earlier in Chapter One. In Chapter Four, Ailsa McKay and Morag Gillespie examine whether a distinctive social policy agenda, with reference to women, has emerged in Scotland and points to the important part played by women themselves in influencing policy strategies. High hopes existed for a more gender-equitable Scotland after devolution. The chapter concludes, however, that while women have made a difference in how the 'new' Scotland operates, the difference the 'new' Scotland has made to women is not yet so transparent. By contrast, according to Philomena de Lima in Chapter Five, a lack of political representation in the process of policy formulation remains a problem for minority ethnic groups. Nevertheless, de Lima argues that devolution has opened up new, if sometimes contradictory, opportunities to address racism and discrimination in ways that did not occur before. De Lima is optimistic that a greater chance of addressing the social exclusion of minority ethnic groups now exists.

Since devolution in 1999, there has been a continual stream of initiatives in the whole range of social policy for which the Scottish Administration has responsibility. Authors of the final five chapters of this book evaluate the significance of these changes for particular sites of welfare. They all point to a level of legislative and organisational change that reinforces the idea that there have been 'Scottish solutions to Scottish problems'. In Chapter Six, Charlie Johnstone and Chris McWilliams single out the development of social inclusion partnerships as a Scotland specific response to the problems of cities and urban deprivation. In Chapter Seven, Hazel Croall highlights what she sees as a move towards more populist agendas in the areas of criminal and youth justice at the same time as stressing the continuation of a clearly Scottish 'welfarism' within criminal justice policy.

In Chapter Eight, Carol Tannahill argues that there are particular factors relating to patterns of health and ill-health in Scotland that necessitates the further development of Scottish-specific policies. In particular the 'Scottish effect', as it has been called, is manifested in a life expectancy rate that is lower than the rest of the UK and much of Continental Western Europe and in the wide gap in health and morbidity between rich and poor. The latter serves to remind us once again, that Scotland is far from being an homogeneous land.

While highlighting the specificity of policy in Scotland, these three writers point to a convergence in approaches north and south of the border. In Chapter Nine, Iain Ferguson offers a critical assessment of the growing crisis in social work. He attributes the crisis to the growing domination of managerial and market-based approaches that underlie New Labour's delivery of welfare. Two main points characterise his argument. First, he argues that the domination of a neoliberal agenda in welfare leads to a less than adequate response to the deprivation and exclusion experienced by the least powerful in the 'new' Scotland. Second, he points to an undermining of welfare professionals as a result of recent policy developments.

Margaret Arnott's discussion leads to different conclusions regarding the divergence in Scottish social policy and the role of professionals in her analysis of a different policy sector. She argues strongly that the long history of a separate and distinctive educational establishment in Scotland is underpinned by and reinforces the professional power of educationalists in different ways to England. She also sees this as leading to a different way of addressing social inequality and social exclusion through schools and local authority education departments. Nevertheless, she sees this diversity as increasingly constrained by the move towards closer integration of economic and social policy that was identified earlier in the book. Arnott has chosen to focus on a particularly important area of Scottish education – and one that is arguably much more significant than the question of student tuition fees that we review above – comprehensive schooling. Political and popular support for comprehensive schooling is a cornerstone of Scotland's education system and is much more pronounced than in England. Indeed, some commentators have argued that this is much more significant than differences between Scotland and England in relation to tuition fees (Bromley et al, 2003, p 11). It is an issue that has also from time to time threatened to highlight potentially significant differences between the approach of the Scottish Executive and the Westminster government in relation to the promotion of 'choice' and 'diversity' in public service provision (*The Herald*, 4 December 2004).

In the book's Conclusion, we return to examine what lessons these different policy arenas hold for policy analysts in Scotland and beyond. In particular, we highlight the unevenness of developments in and across different sites/policy areas in Scotland and how policies reflect and impact on social divisions/ differentiation. We also return to examine what conclusions the contributors lead us to make on questions of convergence/divergence post-devolution before discussing what a future policy agenda that addresses issues of governance and inequality might look like.

Further resources

Ferguson, I., Lavalette, M. and Mooney, G. (2002) *Rethinking welfare*, London: Sage Publications.

McCrone, D. (2001) *Understanding Scotland*, (2nd edn), London: Routledge.

Powell, M. (ed) (1999) *New Labour, New welfare state?*, Bristol: The Policy Press.

Powell, M. (ed) (2002) *Evaluating New Labour's welfare reforms*, Bristol: The Policy Press.

Sweeney, T., Lewis, J. and Etherington, N. (eds) (2003) *Sociology and Scotland: An introduction*, Paisley: Unity Publications.

On the web ...

ESRC Devolution and Constitutional Change Programme	www.devolution.ac.uk
The Herald (and *Sunday Herald*)	www.theherald.co.uk
Institute of Governance	www.institute-of-governance.org
Joseph Rowntree Foundation	www.jrf.org.uk
The Scotsman (and *Scotland on Sunday*)	www.scotsman.co.uk
Scottish Centre for Research on Social Justice	www.scrsj.ac.uk
Scottish Council Foundation	www.scottishpolicynet.org.uk
Scottish Executive	www.scotland.gov.uk
Scottish Human Services (SHS) Trust	www.shstrust.org.uk
Scottish Left Review	www.scottishleftreview.org
Scottish Parliament	www.scottish.parliament.uk

References

Adams, J. and Robinson, P. (2002) *Devolution practice: Public policy differences within the UK*, London: Institute of Public Policy Research.

Alcock, P. and Craig, G. (eds) (2001) *International social policy: Welfare regions in the developed world*, London: Palgrave.

Bechhofer, F. and McCrone, D. (2004) 'Why we've never had it so good', *The Scotsman*, 15 May.

Bell, I. (2004) 'Who picks up the Bills?', *Sunday Herald*, 6 June.

Bromley, C., Curtice, J., Hinds, K. and Park, A. (eds) (2003) *Devolution – Scottish answers to Scottish questions?*, Edinburgh: Edinburgh University Press.

Brown, G. and Alexander, D. (1999) *New Scotland new Britain*, London: The Smith Institute.

Brown, U., Scott, J., Mooney, G. and Duncan, B. (eds) (2002) *Poverty in Scotland 2002: People, places and policies*, London/Glasgow: Child Poverty Action Group/Scottish Poverty Information Unit.

Cheetham, J. (2001) 'New Labour, welfare and social work and devolution: a view from Scotland', *British Journal of Social Work*, vol 31, pp 625-8.

Clarke, J. and Cochrane, A. (1998) 'The social construction of social problems', in E. Saraga (ed) *Embodying the social*, London: Routledge, pp 3-42.

Clasen, J. and Freedman, R. (1994) *Social policy in Germany*, London: Harvester Wheatsheaf.

Curtice, J., McCrone, D., Park, A. and Paterson, L. (2002) *New Scotland, new society?*, Edinburgh: Edinburgh University Press/Polygon.

Dorling, D. and Thomas, B. (2004) *People and places: A 2001 Census atlas of the UK*, Bristol: The Policy Press.

Fairclough, N. (2000) *New Labour, new language?*, London: Routledge.

Ferguson, I. and Barclay, A. (2002) *Seeking peace of mind: The mental health needs of asylum seekers in Glasgow*, Stirling: Department of Applied Social Science, University of Stirling.

Fraser, D. and Cusick, J. (2001) 'The land of milk and honey', *Sunday Herald*, 14 January.

Greer, S. (2003) 'Policy divergence: will it change something in Greenock?', in R. Hazell (ed) *The state of the nations 2003: The third year of devolution in the United Kingdom*, London, UCL Constitution Unit, pp 195-214.

Hassan, G. (1998) *The new Scotland*, London: The Fabian Society.

Hassan, G. and Warhurst, C. (eds) (1999) *A different future*, Glasgow/Edinburgh: The Big Issue in Scotland/Centre for Scottish Public Policy.

Hassan, G. and Warhurst, C. (2002a) 'Future Scotland: the making of the new social democracy', in G. Hassan and C. Warhurst (eds) *Tomorrow's Scotland*, London: Lawrence and Wishart, pp 5-25.

Hassan, G. and Warhurst, C. (eds) (2002b) *Tomorrow's Scotland*, London: Lawrence and Wishart.

Johnston, I., McCrone, D. and Bechhofer, F. (2004) 'Scotland 2004: why we've never had it so good', *The Scotsman*, 15 May, pp 18-19.

Joshi, H.E. and Wright, R.E. (2004) *Population replacement and the reproduction of disadvantage* (The Allander Series: Starting life in Scotland in the new millennium), Glasgow: Fraser of Allander Institute, University of Strathclyde.

Keating, M. (2002) 'Devolution and public policy in the United Kingdom: convergence or divergence?', in J. Adams and P. Robinson (eds) *Devolution in practice*, London: IPPR, pp 3-21.

Levitas, R. (1998) *The inclusive society*, London: Macmillan.

McCabe, T. (2004) www.scotland.gov.uk/News/Releases/2004/09/28111008 (accessed 25 November 2004).

McIndoe, R. (2003) 'In good health', in 'Border difference', *The Guardian*, 5 November.

Mooney, G. and Johnstone, C. (2000) 'Scotland divided: poverty, inequality and the Scottish parliament', *Critical Social Policy*, vol 20, no 2, pp 155-82.

Mooney, G. and Poole, L. (2004) '"A land of milk and honey"? Social policy in Scotland after devolution', *Critical Social Policy*, vol 24, no 4, pp 458-83.

Parry, R. (2002) 'Delivery structure and policy development in post-devolution Scotland', *Social Policy and Society*, vol 1, no 4, pp 315-24.

Paterson, L. (2003) *Scottish education in the twentieth century*, Edinburgh: Edinburgh University Press.

Paterson, L., Bechhofer, F. and McCrone, D. (2004) *Living in Scotland: Social and economic change since 1980*, Edinburgh: Edinburgh University Press.

Paterson, L., Brown, A., Curtice, J., Hinds, K., McCrone, D., Park, A., Sproston, K. and Surridge, P. (2001) *New Scotland, new politics?*, Edinburgh: Edinburgh University Press/Polygon.

Raco, M. (2002) 'Risk, fear and control: deconstructing the discourses of New Labour's economic policy', *Space and Polity*, vol 6, no 1, pp 25-47.

Raco, M. (2003) 'The social relations of business representation and devolved governance in the United Kingdom', *Environment and Planning A*, vol 35, pp 1853-76.

Royal Commission on Long-Term Care, The (1999) *With respect to old age: Long-term care – Rights and responsibilities* (Sutherland Report), Cm 4192-I, London: The Stationery Office.

Scottish Executive (2003) *A partnership for a better Scotland: Partnership agreement between the Scottish Labour Party and Scottish Liberal Democrats*, Edinburgh: Scottish Executive.

Steiger, D. (2004) *Eradicating child poverty in Scotland in an era of devolution*, London: Foreign and Commonwealth Institute.

Stewart, J. (2004a) '"Scottish solutions to Scottish problems"? Social welfare in Scotland since devolution', in N. Ellison, L. Bauld and M. Powell (eds) *Social Policy Review 16*, Bristol: The Policy Press/Social Policy Association, pp 101-20.

Stewart, J. (2004b) *Taking stock: Scottish social welfare after devolution*, Bristol: The Policy Press.

Tomaney, J. (2002) 'The evolution of regionalism in England', *Regional Studies*, vol 37, no 7, pp 721-31.

Trench, A. (ed) (2001) *The state of the nations: The second year of devolution in the United Kingdom*, London: Imprint Academic.

Walsh, K. (1995) *Territorial justice and citizenship*, Birmingham: INLOGOV.

Wright Mills, C. (1959) *The sociological imagination*, Oxford: Oxford University Press.

ONE

Governance and social policy in the devolved Scotland

Lynne Poole and Gerry Mooney

This chapter explores the experiences of British and Scottish social policy making and welfare provision since devolution. It challenges the claims of a new Scottish society and social policy by a UK-wide comparison of recent developments. The chapter also critically evaluates the Scottish Executive's achievements in social policy, highlights the possibilities and limitations of devolution and examines the potential for a more distinctively Scottish social policy making. The following topics are included:

- New Labour and the 'modernisation' of governance and public services: continuities and discontinuities with the past;
- welfare partnerships and devolution as governance;
- New Labour and devolution: constitutional, procedural and financial developments;
- the distinctiveness of Scottish social policy: convergence and divergence in different social areas;
- comparison between Scottish and Welsh social policy and practice; and
- the modernisation of public services in a devolutionary context: constraints and tensions.

Introduction

This chapter provides an overview of developments in social policy in Scotland since devolution. In doing so it explores the road to the 1997 Referendum (Scotland and Wales) Act and the impact of the reopening of a Scottish Parliament in 1999 with particular reference to social welfare. However, in examining recent experiences in Scottish policy and polity, this chapter seeks to move beyond a summary of both policy documents and the promises of the Scottish Executive and Scottish Parliament in order to uncover the underlying assumptions, themes and tensions that are emergent in Scottish social policy making in the devolutionary context. Here we are interested in exploring the reality of Scottish devolution rather than claims made at a rhetorical level, and in challenging common-sense claims about 'Scottishness', the 'social democratic impulse' north of the border and parochial assumptions and descriptions about 'the Scots' and

Scotland. Hence, we take as our starting point a recognition of the diversity and contestation that exist in Scotland and an awareness of the social divisions and inequalities that are in evidence in Scottish society. Such a position enables us to subject claims of a distinctively Scottish social policy to critical scrutiny, particularly when seen in the context of broader New Labour agendas throughout the UK.

The main aims of this chapter are:

- to provide the background to recent social policy developments in Scotland, highlighting The Scotland Act of 1998 and the issue of reserved and devolved powers; and
- to explore the possibilities for a distinctively Scottish social policy in the context of devolution by comparing developments north of the border with those in the rest of Britain.

The chapter comprises four main sections. We begin by exploring the question of whether or not we are witnessing a 'new' approach to governance under New Labour in the name of societal 'modernisation' and 'national renewal'. From this we then examine the concept of governance and the claim that we are witnessing a shift towards new modes and processes of governing in Britain under New Labour which centre on the activation and inclusion of networks in policy making and the delivery of provision through partnerships on the one hand and a devolutionary strategy on the other. We note that for Conservative and New Labour governments since 1979, shifts in governance strategies have been bound up with a political commitment to change both the culture of public services and methods and processes adopted in the construction and delivery of welfare provision, a central concern of this chapter.

Placing recent developments in the spheres of governance and public service provision in the broader devolutionary framework enables us to critically assess the possibilities for a divergence between social policy and welfare provision in Scotland and the rest of Britain. Hence, in the second part of the chapter, we outline the main constitutional developments since 1999, charting the balance between devolved matters and reserved powers, as well as the use of the Sewell Convention. This section also explores briefly the emergence of both a 'new' policy process and a 'new' politics within this devolutionary context and highlights the main *constitutional* possibilities and limitations of devolution and the *potential* for a more distinctively Scottish social policy.

Following this, the focus shifts to a discussion of the early years of devolution, charting the main achievements of the Scottish Parliament in the sphere of social policy thus far. Here we consider how far these relate to social policy developments in the rest of Britain and the extent to which the Scottish Parliament has delivered specifically 'Scottish solutions for Scottish problems' (Scottish Executive, 1999, 2003; Stewart, 2004a, 2004b).

In the light of findings presented in this section, the final part of the chapter focuses on the gap between the potential for social policy divergence in Scotland

and a reality that falls far short of a distinctively Scottish approach to welfare. It is argued that a number of constraining factors are at work: the inherent limitations of the devolution settlement; New Labour's broader 'modernising' agenda; the fragmented, diverse and divided nature of Scotland (as England and Wales), represented by the concepts of a patriarchal and racially structured capitalism (Williams, 1989) and the spatially divided nation; and the issue of political will on the one hand and of popular action, resistance and allegiances on the other.

The chapter ends with a summary of the key arguments and draws together our conclusions based on the first five years of devolutionary governance in Scotland.

New Labour, governance and the 'modernisation' of public services

This section explores questions of governance, societal 'modernisation' and 'national renewal' through a focus on the development of networks, partnerships and a devolutionary strategy under the post–1997 New Labour governments.

'Modernisation' and 'national renewal'

At the heart of the New Labour project is a stated commitment to 'modernisation', a strategy which can be seen to involve the 'modernisation' of public services on the one hand (Powell, 1999; Clarke et al, 2000; Newman, 2001) and the 'modernisation' of the modes and structures of governance on the other (Bochel and Bochel, 1998; Newman, 2001; Glendinning et al, 2002). This strategy emerges in the context of a number of interrelated claims about 'globalisation' – constructed as "a single, uncontradictory, uni-dimensional phenomenon" (Hall, 1998, p 11) which gives rise to inevitable outcomes everywhere and is uncontrollable by nation states either individually or as a collective force (Watson and Hay, 2003) – and the needs of a 'modern' economy.

Also important for New Labour is the development of a 'national renewal' agenda that seeks to tackle the problems of a democratic and accountability deficit and an exclusive approach to governance, all of which came to be closely associated with the Conservative governments of 1979-97. In this period, it was widely argued that the government increasingly lost its legitimacy as it 'worked against the grain', refusing to listen to and include key stakeholders and, consequently, failing to deliver not only the right 'solutions' to the 'problem' of public services but also on the principles of democracy and accountability. New Labour, then, keen to build on its legitimacy after the 1997 General Election, committed itself to open, accountable and inclusive government – to be a government that consults and listens from day one. For example, the White Paper, *Modernising government* (Cabinet Office, 1999), committed New Labour to developing a more 'joined-up', 'strategic' approach to policy making which would involve the government drawing a broader range of stakeholders and networks into the policy process through the activation of new partnership arrangements. In this way, it sought to present itself as 'a safe pair of hands' in which to place the future of public services and the 'interests of society', and in doing so perhaps even de-politicise its decision making (see Newman, 2001).

However, the idea of 'national renewal' is also about a reorientation of policy and a (re)prioritising of certain objectives over others, both in the Scottish and broader British context. This centres on the elevation of business interests, economic and skills development, competitiveness and innovation over what we can call 'welfare narratives' which emphasise the social democratic principles of equality and social justice. In Scottish political circles, this has been presented as the need to construct an 'entrepreneurial' Scotland in the face of increased global competition (see Chapter Two of this book; Raco, 2002). Of course, claims of a stronger social democratic orientation in Scotland, with an emphasis on social justice, inclusion and egalitarianism, for example, have long been contested. Moreover, there is evidence to suggest that whatever influence such narratives *might* have had in the past, they have declined in importance in the post-devolution period, challenged by a more pro-business and entrepreneurial narrative. This is perhaps most clearly demonstrated in the recent speeches of key politicians and political commentators, and in recent education policies emerging from the Scottish Parliament. We return to this theme later in this chapter.

While the range of tools utilised by successive New Labour governments in the quest for 'modernisation' and 'national renewal' is broad, the focus here will be on what are arguably two of the main strategies employed in the pursuit of 'modernisation':

- the construction of 'partnerships' in a range of forms, incorporating responsibilised stakeholders; and
- devolution, accompanied by a 'new' politics that is seen to bring key groups on board.

Both can be seen in broad terms as representing 'new' forms of governance and both are arguably crucial to the legitimisation of government action insofar as they show it to be working in the interests of consumers, tax payers and voters. These strategies, of course, are not employed in isolation and, as we shall see in later sections of this chapter, a number of 'old' weapons have found their way into the New Labour armoury – not least marketisation, managerialisation and individual responsibilitisation, all of which were central to the neoliberal project of the post-1979 Conservative governments. The employment of both 'new' and 'old' strategies can be seen as part of a New Labour emphasis on 'what works'. This idea speaks to a pragmatic concern with the effectiveness of policy and practice as well as efficiency and thus to a move beyond a simple replication of neoliberal strategies (see also Clarke, 2004, for a discussion of the 'subordinated' strands of New Labour thinking that mark it out as different from the neoliberalism associated with the Thatcher and Major governments). Indeed, it is the concept of the 'Third Way' that has been used most regularly to capture the ways in which Prime Minister Blair's party has worked to carve a path between the traditions of 'old' Labour, reflected in the welfare settlements of the postwar period, and those of the New Right, rooted in a commitment to market-based/led solutions (Blair, 1998). Hence, embodied in this conceptualisation of the Third Way is an appeal to both continuities and discontinuities with the past.

Having explored briefly the concepts of 'modernisation' and 'national renewal' from a New Labour perspective, we can now turn our attention to consider in more detail both partnership and devolution within a governance framework.

There is a growing social policy literature on governance that explores, among other things, the role of welfare partnerships in the New Labour project (see, for example, Newman, 2001; Glendinning et al, 2002; Daly, 2003). And, while to date rather less attention has been paid to the place of devolution in that project from a social policy perspective (Parry, 1997, 2002a, 2002b), in the sections that follow we will examine the importance of both developments. This will enable us to take the discussion forward to consider the Scottish dimension and, more specifically, whether we are seeing the construction of a distinctively Scottish social policy.

New Labour and welfare partnerships as governance

It has been argued, that in the search for acceptable modes of welfare production and delivery, a number of governance strategies have been employed by British governments over time. Indeed, in the social policy arena, governance theory has as its starting point the claim that bureaucratic hierarchies dominated in the period of post-war welfare 'settlement', these being increasingly displaced by markets under the post-1979 Conservative governments (Glendinning et al, 2002). Moreover, it has been argued that more recently, market-based/orientated modes are being surpassed in importance by networked modes of governance, of which partnerships are an integral part (Clarke and Glendinning, 2002, p 35).

While partnerships are clearly not exclusively the tools of New Labour, it has been argued that the growth in their relative importance can be viewed as part of a shift in "the governance systems and processes of modern societies" (Clarke and Glendinning, 2002, p 34). Similarly, pure forms of governance and control do not really exist in practice in a welfare context – as illustrated by the tendency for social policy commentators to draw on Le Grand and Bartlett's (1993) concept of the 'quasi-market' to capture market-*like* formations (Powell and Exworthy, 2002) – and "different modes of governance, including those based on markets, hierarchies and networks, are likely to co-exist, with different institutional combinations in specific nations" at any one time (Newman, 2001, p 13). Nevertheless, it has been suggested that a consideration of the increasing significance of network-like modes of governance, such as partnerships (a sort of 'quasi-network'), "as part of a broader transition to new modes of governing statutory welfare services" (Clarke and Glendinning, 2002, p 34) is useful insofar as it captures the distinctiveness of New Labour's approach when compared to those of the 'old' Left and New Right. Indeed, for Daly (2003), the concept of governance is a useful one for social policy analysts as it provides a framework in which the main developments under New Labour (managerialism, partnerships, and so on) can be situated. In short, it has a 'descriptive value' and allows a comparison of organisational 'settlements', past and present.

So while New Labour continue to draw on bureaucratic hierarchy and market-type modes of governance, associated with 'old' Left and New Right respectively, they also speak of a Third Way of providing an "acceptable mode of welfare production and delivery" (Rummery, 2002, p 230), which fits more neatly with its stated commitment to processes of inclusive 'modernisation' which keep the public 'on-side'. As Daly notes (2003, p 120, drawing on the work of Benington and Donnison, 1999), a key objective of the Third Way is

> to shift the centre of gravity of governance away from the bureaucratic state and the private market towards civil society and its informal networks and communities.

Or at least so the rhetoric goes. Again we can identify clear continuities with the past coupled with important breaks from it.

New Labour and devolution as governance

Newman (2002, p 349) has noted that there are "different tiers and spheres of governance (local, regional, national, transnational)". Hence, devolution can be seen as a 'new' form of governance involving different stakeholders, partners and networks at the regional and national levels. Importantly for the Blair project, devolution can be a tool in the activating of particular communities, giving them increased voice. This in turn can be viewed as a significant tool for any government interested in increasing its legitimacy and speaking to the democratic and accountability deficits associated with the Thatcher and Major governments, particularly in Scotland and Wales where the Conservative Party has failed to do well electorally (Chaney et al, 2001; Paterson et al, 2001; Chaney and Drakeford, 2004).

While New Labour has not, broadly speaking, sought to take a nationalist stance on the Scottish and Welsh question, they have perhaps seen devolution as a 'new' mode of governance that can be presented in their own terms; that is, in terms of offering a decentralisation of power which brings policy making closer to the people, increases their voice and speaks more directly to their choices and interests (Chaney et al, 2001; see also the 1997 White Papers *A voice for Wales* and *Scotland's Parliament*).

We should note at this point that this period did not mark the beginning of the Labour Party's flirtation with devolution – more of which later in this chapter.

Nevertheless, in this period, devolution was represented as an intrinsic part of the New Labour project.

New Labour, new governance?

Having briefly outlined the argument that partnerships as quasi-networks and devolution are key features of a shift towards a 'new' governance, it is necessary to pause and consider some of the limits of the governance framework for social policy commentators, many of whom have expressed caution about overstating the argument. For example, Clarke and Glendinning (2002) have cautioned that, to date, the development of partnerships and networked forms of governance has, at best, been uneven and partial. Moreover, they have argued that making them mandatory in many cases, and encouraging their formation through both incentives and penalties, as New Labour has done, leaves the issue of partnership effectiveness unaddressed – the long recognised tensions of "working across organisational, budgetary, contractual and professional boundaries" remain unresolved (Clarke and Glendinning, 2002, p 41).

Furthermore, the practice of partnership formation sits uneasily with the tendency of government to centralise power and closely regulate, even control, the devolution of roles and responsibilities. This is especially clear when we consider the setting of targets and government/business priorities and the squaring of them with the principles of partnership autonomy and community participation. What we are often left with, then, are attempts to restrict membership to those deemed by government and powerful groups to be 'fit' partners (Ling, 2000) and to restrict autonomy through "central direction and resource control" (Clarke and Glendinning, 2002, p 46).

So, while the networking angle conjures up the notions of dynamism, flexibility, increased horizontal relations, stakeholder inclusion and so on (see Rhodes, 1997, 2000), such developments may well be working to *increase* government control – what Newman (2001) calls a "steering" rather than "enabling" approach and what Rummery (2002, p 233) refers to as "a more centralised control of welfare governance".

Just as there are limits to the claims made by the supporters of a 'new' governance delivering a different type of polity and policy process rooted in partnerships, so too are there problems with seeing devolution through rose-coloured spectacles. In the case of devolution, again we have seen unevenness, albeit for a number of different reasons, some of which are historical. And just as there is tension between the drive for partnerships on the one hand and the authoritarian impulses of government on the other, we can also see tensions between a centralised polity, whereby the Prime Minister's office closely controls the business of the Cabinet, Parliament and the party, and the decentralisation of some degree of political power through the opening of a Scottish parliament and Welsh Assembly (Newman, 2001; see also Keating, 2002, p 2). We shall explore this issue in more detail in later sections of this chapter where we discuss the constraints on the Labour-led governments in Scotland and Wales.

Notwithstanding the difficulties increasingly associated with the use of the concept of governance in social policy, as noted earlier in this chapter, we feel that it is a useful tool for our purposes, as long as it is used with caution. As Newman (2002, p 353) writes:

> A concern with the dynamics of policy process itself, set in the context of contemporary theories of governance, power and the state, is essential for those seeking to analyse and understand what is going on in social policy.

Moreover, it helps us to fit specific developments, such as the activation of partnerships and processes of devolution, into a wider schema and situate them within New Labour's broader 'modernisation' and 'national renewal' projects.

We do, of course, also need to take care that in drawing on the idea of a *new* governance we still give due emphasis to those aspects of New Labour's 'modernising' agenda that represent important continuities with 'old' modes and approaches. By this we mean its continued application of marketisation, managerialisation and individual responsibility. As we shall see in later sections of this chapter, New Labour, north and south of the border, have been conspicuous in their enthusiasm for commodifying public services in the interests of opening up new markets for business and the private sector and applying market-based 'solutions' to public service 'problems' as a matter of principle/ideology as opposed to pragmatism (Whitfield, 2001; Mooney and Poole, 2002, 2004).

Having explored partnership and devolution in a governance framework and argued that claims that we are witnessing a 'new' approach to governance under New Labour should be treated with caution in the light of clear continuities with past approaches, it is necessary to turn our attention to the main constitutional developments since 1999 and the emergence of both a 'new' policy process and a 'new' politics within this devolutionary context. In focusing principally on Scottish devolution, albeit making comparisons with the experiences in Wales where appropriate, the following section of the discussion highlights the main *constitutional* possibilities and limitations of devolution and the *potential* for more distinctively Scottish social policy.

New Labour and devolution

Historically, the 1536 and 1543 Acts of Parliament were crucial to the process of union between England and Wales, Scotland becoming part of this union much later, following the Acts of 1706 and 1707. However, despite this union, there developed a growing recognition of the need for more devolved structures to address the specific interests of, and conditions in, Scotland and Wales (see Stewart, 2004a, 2004b). For example, in 1885 the Scottish Office was resurrected and grew in terms of its functions until, by the 1960s, the Secretary of State was expected to take an interest in all matters affecting Scotland and five main departments had been created to deal with issues of development, education, industry, health policy and so on, as applicable to Scotland. Furthermore, the Balfour Commission on Scottish Affairs, reporting in 1954, sought to ensure that Scottish business was dealt with in Scotland and that Scottish interests were represented at Westminster. Indeed, joint business and policy issues were dealt with through economic and social committees on which there was Scottish representation. Scottish-specific legislation was usually dealt with in separate Scottish parliamentary committees, thus minimising the influence of non-Scottish MPs. Hence a 'Scottish sub-system' grew up marking a gradual administrative devolution in Scotland (Bogdanor, 1999).

However, while Scotland enjoyed its own legal system and its own arrangements for handling executive business, it continued to have no separate parliament to which the Scottish executive could be held directly accountable. And it was to this deficit that Labour's 1974 White Paper *Democracy and devolution: Proposals for Scotland and Wales* (Cmnd 5732) spoke. This document called for directly elected assemblies in Scotland and Wales, with the Scottish Assembly being granted executive and legislative, and the Welsh Assembly only executive, powers. A first-past-the-post electoral system was proposed. The assemblies would be block-grant financed with no revenue raising powers. The post of Secretary of State would remain and there would be no reduction in the numbers of Scottish and Welsh MPs at Westminster. However, devolution in England was to be postponed (Bogdanor, 1999). In time, this paper was to form the basis of the 1978 Scotland and Wales Act, although the act was not implemented as a result of the 40% rule incorporated into the 1979 referendum arrangements that was not met in Scotland, and due to the rejection of the act by the Welsh electorate. Hence, the first Thatcher government repealed it (Bogdanor, 1999).

Ironically, the next push for devolution came *in response* to Thatcherism, following a period of Conservative 'minority' rule and the emergence of what was widely perceived to be a democratic deficit in Scotland and Wales, made worse, according to Bogdanor (1999), by the government's efforts to restrict Scottish-only activity in Parliament and the party's subsequent failure to return a single MP for a Scottish constituency in 1997 (see also Pilkington, 2002). In 1989, the Scottish Constitutional Convention was set up with the aim of translating what was perceived as widespread support for devolution into concrete proposals. Two reports, *Towards Scotland's Parliament* (Scottish Constitutional Convention, 1990) and *Scotland's Parliament, Scotland's right* (Scottish Constitutional Convention, 1995) followed and were to form the basis of the 1998 Act following John Smith's embrace of the devolution agenda and Tony Blair's subsequent adoption of Smith's two-question strategy.

Scottish devolution and New Labour

The 1997 Referendum (Scotland and Wales) Act ensured that a popular mandate for devolution would be achieved before any devolution act was passed through the House of Commons. This was, of course, secured as 74.3% of those voting in Scotland supported devolution and 63.5% agreed that the Parliament be given tax-raising powers in the form of an income tax base rate leeway of three pence in the pound (Bogdanor, 1999; see also Paterson et al, 2001). In Wales, support for devolution (this time without tax-raising and primary legislative powers) was more muted, with only 50.1% voting in favour (Bogdanor, 1999). The Scottish vote paved the way for policy devolution, at least potentially (Keating, 2001), although this was never on the cards in Wales, where devolution is more limited in scope (see Chaney and Drakeford, 2004).

The devolution package was presented in such a way as to emphasise the New Labour-orientated discourses of inclusion, democratic accountability, partnership, cooperation and a decentralising of power. However, in reality, devolution presented problems insofar as it represented a constitutional change that sought to reconcile the principle of self-government in domestic affairs in Scotland with the maintenance of Westminster parliamentary supremacy. This involved a rethinking of government as "a series of interdependent layers, each with its own rights and responsibilities" (Bogdanor, 1999, p 1), something, as we noted earlier in this chapter, that does not sit easily with centralised polity and authoritarian government.

While the primary legal framework for Scotland continues to be determined at Westminster, with the Scottish Parliament as subordinate, there are clear Britain-wide implications arising out of the power of the latter to pass primary legislation in devolved areas and the 'new' policy process and politics that have increasingly come to be associated with devolution.

Focusing first on the issue of primary legislation and devolved powers, a single list of reserved matters was drawn up granting the Scottish Parliament the right only to make laws within its own areas of competence: Section 5 of the 1998 Scotland Act reserved 11 key areas to Westminster including employment, social security, trade and industry while health, education, housing, social work, local government and law among other fields were devolved (see Keating, 2002, pp 16-17 for a full listing). Moreover, the right of Westminster to make laws for Scotland remained and this presented a further potential constraint on Scottish policy makers. Should Westminster decide to exercise its supremacy, it could, in theory, continue to dominate Scottish policy making. In recognition of this potential, the Sewell Convention was put in place to protect the Scottish Parliament from the undue use of Westminster powers over Scotland (Bogdanor, 1999). It allows the Westminster Parliament (with Holyrood approval) to develop and implement legislation in those policy areas that are not reserved and hence are implicitly devolved, only after consultation and agreement. However, in practice, the use of Sewell resolutions has taken a rather unexpected turn: in the first two and a half years of the reconvened Scottish Parliament, such resolutions were passed a total of 31 times compared to just 30 Holyrood acts passed in the same period (Hassan and Warhurst, 2002, pp 14-15). And, up until February 2003, the Scottish Parliament had agreed to 39 Sewell motions. Notwithstanding the use of Sewell, however, should the Scottish Parliament refrain from falling back on the safety net of Westminster, not least in order to pacify New Labour and respond to the more inclusive policy process north of the border, there is a clear *potential* for policy divergence in all areas of responsibility devolved to it.

Concordats are another check on the devolution process insofar as they are drawn up to set out clearly the relationship between Westminster and the Scottish Parliament and Welsh Assembly where roles and responsibilities are divided between the different bodies but the actions of each have consequences for the others. These are non-statutory and are not legally binding but nevertheless spell out the relationship between different institutions of government and the expectations and requirements of the different parties. More specifically, they are designed to ensure that the devolved institutions do not overstep the mark (Bogdanor, 1999, pp 205-9).

Turning to the issue of a 'new' politics, with the introduction of the additional-member system of proportional representation (Bogdanor, 1999, pp 221-7) the power of the two main political parties – New Labour and the Conservative Party – was potentially threatened. The first and subsequent elections to the Parliament saw an increase in smaller party representation – the Greens and Scottish Socialist Alliance/Party, to name but two, took their place alongside the Scottish Nationalists and the Liberal Democrats as oppositional voices. Indeed, in both the 1999 and 2003 elections, New Labour was forced into a coalition with the latter, creating increased possibilities for policy divergence (Parry, 2002a).

In addition, under these new arrangements the power of Scottish committees has grown. The Scottish Parliament draws more actors into the policy process – Scottish organisations, Scottish branches of British groups and Scottish groups affiliated to British federations – and thus empowers them, to a certain extent, to influence policy decisions. However, as Keating (2001) notes, this shift in role from one of principally lobbying for a Scottish voice and share of resources to more varied activities in an open system where groups may be competing against each other for the attention of the policy makers and a share of the money available, is something of a challenge for those involved and to notions of a 'Scottish interest'. Nevertheless, once again the *potential* for a divergence of Scottish policy is apparent.

There is also scope for a divergence of social policy in the form of new provision. In theory, the Scottish parliament can legislate for additional welfare rights for the Scottish population. One such example of this is the case of free personal care for older people. The Scottish rather than Westminster Parliament enacted this in 2002 following the 'majority' recommendations of the Sutherland Commission (Royal Commission on Long-Term Care, 1999) on the future of long-term care. However, with respect to the care issue, there has been heated debate regarding the funding of long-term care for older people that almost led to the break-up of the coalition (Woods, 2002, pp 43-5). Costing an estimated £125 million per year, the UK Treasury allocated 'Scottish Block' budget was not increased to pay for it – the Treasury is clearly reluctant to grant additional funds to finance Scottish-specific welfare policies that open up an inequality of entitlement between Scottish and English residents. However, the Scottish Parliament refused to use its revenue-raising powers, relying instead on resources being diverted from some other areas including cancer care services. Clearly this issue is already testing the limits of divergence, as finance raised from a common tax base to fund different levels of entitlement in Scotland and England creates political opposition and leaves politicians with undesirable choices to make as no additional funds are forthcoming from the Treasury in support (Keating, 2001; Pollock et al, 2001). Indeed, several local authorities have been reported as considering resorting to means testing older people amid claims that 25% of councils do not have sufficient funds to meet the cost of this 'flagship' social policy (*The Herald*, 13 November 2002). These practical difficulties capture the tensions that exist between the increased scope for policy differentiation through devolution on the one hand and the pressure to retain key features of the old system and/or mirror English policy on the other.

Similarly, the potential for social policy divergence in a devolutionary context is also conditioned by the financial provisions of the Barnett Formula, introduced in 1980 to regulate public expenditure increases over time and to ensure that the Scottish share did not continue to rise proportionally through claims of increased need, for example. Since devolution, it is the role of the Scottish Parliament to decide how to spend its block funding – how to define its priorities, how much will be passed on to local authorities and so on. Since 1992, attempts have been underway to ensure a convergence of spending levels per head of population, known as the 'Barnett squeeze'. This entails reducing the percentage increase in Scottish expenditure as a proportion of English increases. While continued decreases in the Scottish population will offset convergence (Bogdanor, 1999), any decisions in Westminster to cut levels of public expenditure, or more precisely slow down the rate of increase in expenditure, will impact on Scotland too. Levels of public expenditure will be cut proportionately, leaving the devolved bodies to decide where and what to cut. The only option open to the Scottish parliament, should it wish to resist a decline in revenue, is to use its tax-raising powers. And, given that an increase of up to three pence in the pound is modest in terms of the additional monies that could be generated, even this option is a limited one (Bogdanor, 1999). The Barnett Formula, then, is a significant factor in constraining policy divergence.

Having explored the potential for a distinctive Scottish social policy to emerge, while highlighting those constitutional, procedural and financial factors that may facilitate or prevent such a potential being realised, we can now turn our attention to the experiences of devolution in Wales in order to compare the two settlements.

Welsh devolution and New Labour

In this section, we briefly explore the terms of Welsh devolution as it provides an interesting comparative study with Scotland, particularly in relation to the limits and potentials of devolution and the role of ideology and political will in modern policy making (an issue to be discussed later in this chapter).

As noted earlier in this chapter, and in contrast to the Scottish case, the Welsh Assembly was introduced following a very slim popular mandate in the 1997 referendum. Nevertheless, the 1998 Government of Wales Act led to the development of a Welsh executive forum. Low turnout at the first assembly elections reinforced the shaky grounding of the assembly and resulted in a minority Labour government in the first instance, although following the coalition agreement of October 2000 the Liberal Democrats were brought on board and, after the 2003 elections, Labour were able to govern without the aid of a coalition partner, albeit with a majority of one (Chaney and Drakeford, 2004, p 122).

The Welsh Assembly has fewer powers than the Scottish Parliament. It is only empowered to develop secondary or subordinate legislation in its areas of competence, principally education, health, housing and the personal social services (for a full listing, see Keating, 2002). Secondary legislation, in essence, is that which fills in the details of a framework defined by Acts of Parliament.

It should be noted that primary legislation for England and Wales is likely to differ in some respects. For example, for Wales it will need to be loose enough as to ensure a role for secondary legislative changes, whereas for England this approach would probably be seen to give too much discretion to the departments and their ministers (Bogdanor, 1999). Moreover, the assembly is also likely to exert a pressure on Westminster where primary legislation affects it. The case of long-term care for older people is again illustrative, this time because Sutherland was rejected by Westminster, a decision that applies in Wales too but was not greeted warmly by the assembly, which has since mounted a challenge to English policy makers. That said, non-statutory concordats exist to ensure that the principle of cooperation between the two bodies is maintained, so there may well be limits in practice to what the assembly can do even in terms of lobbying. (Of course, these concordats work both ways, and should the assembly perceive Westminster to be under-consulting with it, they may work in favour of the former.) As it stands, then, changes to primary laws have to be approved by Westminster (Keating, 2001, p 2) and the assembly has been granted no revenue raising powers. Nevertheless, the Welsh Assembly has enough powers in key areas of welfare for Chaney and Drakeford (2004, p 124) to refer to it as a "social policy Assembly for Wales" and to indicate the very real potential for policy divergence in these devolved areas of responsibility.

The more limited powers of the Welsh Assembly are perhaps a reflection of historical realities – unlike Scotland, prior to devolution Wales did not have independent institutions intact and had been constructed as a 'non-historic' nation, without the institutions of statehood by some commentators and, perhaps more importantly, many policy makers at Westminster. The need for a Wales-specific organisation was first recognised as early as 1907 when a Welsh Department of the Board of Education was set up (overseeing Welsh education practice and the development of language policy, for example), marking the beginnings of the "process of administrative decentralization" (Bogdanor, 1999, p 158) and eventually resulting in the establishment of 17 departmental administrative units by the 1950s and the appointment of a Secretary of State for Wales and a Welsh Office in 1964. However, independent institutions – as represented by the Scottish legal system, for example – were missing in the Welsh context (Bogdanor, 1999). Nevertheless, issues of democracy and accountability associated with the Thatcher years also applied in Wales so it was to get its opportunity for devolution, like Scotland, with the coming of the first Blair government.

In common with the Scottish case, Wales is also financed via the block grant, is at the mercy of the 'Barnett squeeze' (although Bogdanor, 1999, argues that recent changes have benefited Wales in public expenditure terms) and has the same electoral system in place. However, notwithstanding the potential for divergence in some key areas of policy making noted earlier in this chapter, given the limitations of Welsh devolution and the absence of a parliament, one could reasonably expect the opportunities for policy divergence in Wales to be significantly less than in Scotland (an issue to which we return later in this chapter). But before turning our attention to the question of a Welsh and Scottish social policy specificity, it is important to chart the impact of devolution on England and the English regions, albeit briefly.

Devolution, England and New Labour

In this section, we briefly explore the impact of devolution on England and the English regions in order to highlight the challenges the new constitutional settlement presents south of the border. For reasons of space, we limit ourselves to a short discussion of what has been termed the 'West Lothian Question'. This revolves around the dilemma of whether or not to allow Scottish MPs to vote on English domestic affairs. Given that the Scottish domestic affairs are now the responsibility of the Scottish Parliament and its Executive, and decisions cannot be directly influenced by English MPs, a constitutional political imbalance has emerged from the process of devolution. This can be illustrated with reference to the Foundation Hospitals Bill presented to the Westminster Parliament in March 2003. In Scotland, Foundation Hospitals were initially rejected (seemingly only to be accepted in July 2004 following a political U-turn). However, support for the policy in England from Scottish Labour MPs was crucial in ensuring its passage through Westminster (Mooney and Poole, 2004). This highlights the tensions arising from the fact that the devolution settlement gives Scottish MPs, as a collective force, more say in the affairs of say the northern English regions than their own MPs and representatives have, the English regions currently having neither territorial ministers nor assemblies of their own.

This imbalance has been addressed only partially to date through the Devolution Act and the 1997 White Paper, *Building partnerships for prosperity* (DTI, 1997). This document led to the setting up of nine Regional Development Agencies (RDAs) – indirectly elected regional chambers rooted in local authorities – and a city-wide local authority in London with a directly elected mayor, albeit with relatively few powers, thus, according to Bogdanor (1999), representing more of an upper tier of local government than anything more radical. In addition, the *possibility* of more Regional Assemblies in England being developed was enabled by the Devolution Act, should there be a demand for them in the future (although this policy received a set-back in October 2004 when voters in North East England rejected plans for a Northern Assembly). And finally, the number of Scottish and Welsh MPs in Westminster was reduced as part of the devolution settlement. However, the new constitutional settlement in England, it would appear, is as of yet unfinished.

Having outlined the main constitutional developments since 1999 and the key features of the 'new' policy process and polity within a Scottish devolutionary context, the discussion now moves on to explore the argument that despite devolution opening up the *possibility* of a more distinctively Scottish Social Policy, the real experience of devolution has not delivered anything as radical as Scottish social policy specificity.

The early years of devolution: 'Scottish solutions to Scottish problems'?

This section focuses on the early years of Scottish devolution and charts the main achievements of the Scottish Parliament in the sphere of social policy to date. It goes on to consider how far these relate to social policy developments in the rest of Britain and to what extent the Scottish Parliament has delivered a distinctively Scottish social policy.

Scottish devolution: achievements and constraints

Renewed interest in the issue of Scottish distinctiveness and social policy divergence has, of course, been sparked by Scottish devolution (see, for example, Stewart, 2004a, 2004b). This is seen by some to have opened up space for a distinctively *Scottish* social policy, which builds on the differences in the organisation, delivery and finance of welfare in Scotland prior to devolution. As Keating (2001) notes, there has always been a significant degree of administrative devolution in Scotland (and Wales). However, we want to argue that, just as the extent of that Scottish administrative distinctiveness has sometimes been over-stated (see for example, Ozga, 1999, 2000; Breitenbach and MacKay, 2001; Curtice et al, 2002), so too has the extent to which a more distinctive Scottish social policy will *necessarily* develop in the context of devolution and the rise of New Labour (Stewart, 2004b). Indeed the Scottish Executive's claims that it is developing 'Scottish solutions for Scottish problems' (Scottish Executive, 1999, 2003) is open to contestation, particularly when we consider the record of the Scottish Executive and Parliament to date.

Parry (2002b, p 7) claims that, while there have been several pieces of legislation passed in Edinburgh, there have really only been three *major* policy divergences: long-term care, student tuition fees, and teachers' pay, each deriving from what he terms 'coalition pressure' from Scottish Labour's Liberal Democrat partners (Parry, 2002a, p 322). And even with these there are ongoing controversies. The problems of implementing Sutherland's recommendations on free long-term care for older people, funded out of general taxation and written into the Scottish legislatory framework in 2002 via the Community Care and Health (Scotland) Act (Hazell, 2003), have already been highlighted. In addition, as was highlighted in this book's Introduction, with regard to the issue of Higher Education finance, it is true that the Scottish Executive now pays student fees 'up-front', but as these have to be repaid once a graduate is earning £10,000+ per annum, it is misleading to claim that tuition fees have been 'abolished' in Scotland (Rees, 2002, p 111). The maintenance grant issue has been largely sidestepped, with students complaining in greater numbers about the increasing levels of debts they are incurring. There is also the complicating factor of the traditional four-year honours degree structure that has a larger financial impact on students in Scotland with potentially negative consequences for Scottish Higher Education in general. Combined, these have arguably worked as a disincentive to some people from poorer working-class backgrounds from entering Further and Higher Education.

Turning to the McCrone pay settlement for teachers, agreed in 2001 (Scottish Executive, 2001), central is the trade-off between increased pay on the one hand and changed working practices and increased working hours on the other. In essence, the teachers' settlement in Scotland is a managerialist tool for ensuring flexibility within the state education system. The additional contracted hours of work have been presented as an opportunity for teachers to access increased professional development and training opportunities and to say goodbye to working at home given that the number of hours worked is now capped, at least in theory. However, the full impact of McCrone is not yet clear and early reports suggest that the deal is not as positive as it has perhaps been presented by the media insofar as teachers continue to work additional hours at home, not least as a result of large class sizes and increased responsibilities, and the full compliment of terms and conditions of work for teachers has not yet been entirely agreed upon (see, for example, the Professional Association of Teachers website, www.pat.org.uk).

There *are* other areas of divergence that appear to be emerging as the second term of the Labour–Liberal Democrat coalition gets under way following the Scottish General Elections in May 2003. For example, the *Partnership Agreement* (Scottish Executive, 2003) between the coalition partners promises the reform of league tables. It also flags-up the need to review both the curriculum and testing within the comprehensive system, in line with a recent Education

Committee report (see McCrone, 2003) and perhaps a reflection of Liberal Democrat priorities. However, it is unlikely to lead to any radical departures that might work to destabilise the settlement between England and Scotland.

The initial rejection of Foundation Hospitals appeared to represent another marked difference in policy. However, the fact that Labour MPs played a key role in getting the legislation through Westminster for implementation in England raised the question as to what extent the Scottish government could maintain its resistance to them spreading north of the border, particularly where the long-term commitment of New Labour politicians is lacking (see Mooney and Poole, 2004). Indeed the U-turn on this issue in July 2004 and the renewed emphasis on 'consumer choice' in the Scottish NHS laid bare the tensions inherent in attempting to forge a distinctively Scottish policy in the devolutionary context. Moreover, a whole host of other health policies will continue to be replicated in Scotland (see Scottish Executive, 2003). And, while there have been differences in the pace of change in Scotland and England regarding the NHS, with a slow erosion of the purchaser/provider split south of the border compared to an immediate abolition in the north (Timmins, 2001), the difference is largely one of pace and *not* substance (see Chapter Seven of this book). Citing the work of Greer (2003), Stewart (2004b, pp 125-6) argues that "in Scotland, the government pursues Private Finance Initiatives (PFIs) for less ideological reasons, and it shows", and refers to "Scottish scepticism about the role of the private sector in both health and education" (Stewart, 2004b, p 15). He further claims that 'the Scots' are reluctant to embrace private solutions and have historically made rather less of opportunities for private health care and education. However, we would argue that in doing so he misses a crucial point: privatisation agendas are not only embodied in the provision of private services but also in the involvement of the private sector and business interests in the provision of core public services (see Mooney and Poole, 2005, in relation to housing). It has been estimated that public services in Scotland have been mortgaged to the tune of £25+ billion, through the Scottish Executive's fondness for assorted PFI/Public Private Partnerships (PPP) programmes (*Sunday Herald*, 13 June 2004). In the summer of 2004, there was a series of conflicting messages from First Minister McConnell and other Scottish Ministers on the need for the Executive to commit to key Blairite reforms including, as we noted earlier, Foundation Hospitals, while in relation to secondary school education there have been suggestions that, as in parts of England, 'successful entrepreneurs' will be encouraged to fund specialist 'beacon' schools (see articles in *Sunday Herald*, 4 July 2004; *The Scotsman*, 5 and 10 July 2004; *The Herald*, 30-31 August 2004). That Scotland, alongside England, provides a plethora of opportunities for the emerging British edu-business sector and private care providers to increase their involvement and investment in welfare provision, is difficult to deny in the face of the mounting evidence (see Pollock et al, 2001; Mooney and Poole, 2005), reflecting a growing convergence, as opposed to divergence of policy in key areas.

In criminal justice, the picture is also one of increased convergence in the context of a 'moral panic' around 'anti-social' behaviour and youth crime (reflected in the controversy around the so-called 'neds' culture in autumn 2003 and the subsequent passing of an Antisocial Behaviour Bill in June 2004). This has led to a commitment to pilot English-style Youth Courts, to review the children's hearing system again, introduce parent orders and build on the anti-social behaviour orders introduced in 1999 to include under-16-year-olds and the wider use of electronic tagging. Many of these developments are embodied in the 2003 Criminal Justice (Scotland) Act.

Elsewhere we continue to see similar policies emerging north and south of the border, for example, in mental health the 2003 Mental Health (Care and Treatment) (Scotland) Act reflects British-wide trends, and while Scotland was quicker off the mark regarding the Repeal of Section 2A/28, despite its social conservatism, England has now followed suit and introduced 'civil union' and adoption/fostering rights for gay men and lesbians, showing that convergence can be a two-way process (Keating, 2001).

On a more general level, perhaps one of the most stark examples of continued policy convergence north and south of the border is the case of PPPs, which have been imposed on policy makers in Scotland and England, illustrating the power of the Treasury to promote certain initiatives as the 'only show in town' (Pollock et al, 2001). The PFI (the forerunner to PPPs), launched in November 1992 by the Conservative government, was based on the idea that public sector capital projects were increasingly inefficient and costly and the *assumption* that the private sector, with its inherent efficiency and superior managerial skills (and borrowed capital), could be brought in to build and/or refurbish schools and hospitals, maintain and operate them (albeit excluding core business in the first instance) and lease them to the local authority over a period of up to 30 years through a binding contract. Central was the assumption that private interests, driven by the profit motive, could be steered by public service agendas and that stakeholders could be made socially responsible. And yet it appears that the only safeguard here is the ability of the lessee to fine the consortia (the partners) should it fail to meet specified outcomes built into the contract. Indeed, that PPPs have not delivered on a range of measures has already been well documented (see, for example, Whitfield, 1999, 2000, 2001; Pollock et al, 2001; Audit Scotland, 2002; Audit Commission, 2003).

Nevertheless, New Labour's broader public services 'modernisation' agenda *across* Britain has at its heart an emphasis on PPPs and an increased role for market-based solutions to poorly performing public services. Indeed, PPPs are clearly the *preferred* option for New Labour, so much so that the requirement introduced in 1994 that PFI be shown to be impracticable *before* a traditional approach to public service financing can be considered, remains in place (Kerr, 1998). Moreover, finance from central government takes the form of 'PFI' credits, embodying a lack of real choice regarding 'modernisation' routes despite the lack of evidence that PPPs are always the best policy option available (IPPR, 2001). And, even though the cost of PPP/PFI routes to the modernisation of public service infrastructure is greater than funding capital projects via traditional routes, partnerships between the public and private sector have come to form the centrepiece of Scotland's as well as England's 'modernising' programme for schools and hospitals and are part of a broader New Labour agenda to reinvent and present itself as the 'party of business'. For example, First Minister Jack McConnell, speaking at the Scottish Labour Party conference in early 2004, argued that Scottish New Labour needed to root itself more firmly in a pro-business culture, repositioning itself further away from its historical "obsession with public services" (*The Herald*, 28 February 2004). He was quoted as saying, "For too long Scottish politics has been dominated by a consensus that public services came before enterprise and growth", reflecting the Scottish coalition governments' commitment to a modern knowledge-based, indeed knowledge-driven, economy which places economic growth and supporting business as their top priorities (Scottish Executive, 1999, 2003; see also Raco, 2002). These issues are explored more fully in Chapter Two.

Of course, given the specific relationship between Scottish New Labour and the public sector unions in particular (see later in this chapter), McConnell has been careful to be seen to keep other stakeholders on board. For example, the 2002 protocol between the Scottish Trades Union Congress (STUC) and the Scottish Executive provides for new employees working alongside transferred staff to be on terms and conditions 'no less favourable' than transferred staff (Unison, 2003, p 19) and the concordat signed on 15 April 2002, arguably gave the STUC and Unison a greater say in government policy. Nevertheless, the thrust of policy and its implementation is clearly shared north and south of the border, despite the devolution settlement and despite the fact that in a MORI poll 91% of Scots (compared with 78% in Britain as a whole) agreed in principle that private companies should be kept out of public services (Labour Research, 2002).

Having explored some of the main achievements and limitations of Scottish social policy making and highlighted the high degree of convergence between Scottish and English social policy under New Labour, we can now turn our attention to the experience of devolution in Wales and, in doing so, draw out some comparative evidence for consideration.

Comparing social policy and practice: Scotland and Wales

In this section, we return to the experiences of Wales in the post-devolution period and explore the social policy achievements of the Welsh Assembly in more detail in order to demonstrate the importance of the role of ideology and political will in the making of a distinctive welfare system that departs from the English one in important ways. The aim is to chart the outcomes to date of Welsh policy making after 1999 and, in doing so, to show that other factors outside the terms of the constitutional settlement are important in driving forward an agenda that is not dominated by New Labour thinking.

It is particularly interesting to note that, while one would imagine an even more limited pattern of divergence between England and Wales than England and Scotland, given the inherent limitations of the Welsh devolution settlement, a number of commentators have suggested that a rather different reality is in evidence (Woodward, 2001; Davies, 2003; Chaney and Drakeford, 2004). Indeed, despite its limited powers, the Welsh Assembly has delivered a policy agenda that differs from England (and Scotland) in key ways (Davies, 2003). Its achievements include:

- free prescriptions for under-25s, a price freeze for all other groups and a commitment to free prescriptions for all the 2003 Manifesto;
- free eye tests for high risk groups;
- free bus passes for older and disabled people with a commitment to extend the free public transport principle in the 2003 Manifesto;
- free school milk for infants;
- the abolition of testing for seven-year-olds with a review of testing for 11- and 14-year-olds promised in 2003 Manifesto;
- the abolition of secondary school league table publication. As Jane Davidson, Minister for Education and Lifelong Learning in the Welsh Assembly, argued:

> What good does it do a community to know that, no matter how well that school is achieving against its own targets year on year, it is not achieving the same as a community down the road which has far more affluent parents? (Woodward, 2001, p 2)

- the introduction of new student grants for all Welsh students wherever in the UK they study in 2002;
- the replacement of New Labour's Best Value regime with a Programme for Improvement in Wales, involving local authorities' self-assessment of their position and performance and possible routes for improvement. Such an approach, according to Davies (2003), focuses on achievements as opposed to adopting the latest political fads and, for Woodward (2001) reflects a commitment to education authority and Trade Union involvement to ensure a strategic approach, a level playing field over time with a decrease in differences between schools and the inclusion, as opposed to the by-passing, of all stakeholders (especially those who are representative and democratically accountable) and not just those deemed 'fit' by powerful groups and government. Indeed, the 'Protocol' agreed with the Trades Unions in Wales goes beyond that in Scotland which only covers PPPs (Davies, 2003).

Additional promises were also made in 2003, including:

- an end to home care charges for disabled people;
- free breakfasts for all primary school children;
- a rejection of top-up fees. Again Jane Davidson's comments have been informative of the assembly's stance:

> I do not see it as an issue benefiting our sector in Wales when one of our biggest agendas is about widening participation. (Woodward, 2001, p 2)

- a rejection of specialist school status and a reliance on the private sector in education (Davies, 2003), deemed by Jane Davidson to be "untested measures" (Woodward, 2001, p 2) which present a risk to education.

Of course, we need to take care not to get carried away with the achievements and pronouncements of the Welsh Assembly. Like Scotland, Wales is constrained in important respects by the Treasury. For example, PFI/PPPs have featured in Wales, this being the procurement route of preference for the Treasury, significantly reducing the choices available to Welsh politicians. However, they have not been embraced with the enthusiasm of Labour politicians north of the border (Davies, 2003; Chaney and Drakeford, 2004). Moreover, the Welsh Assembly has not been shy in challenging Westminster, even in 'reserved' areas. For example, in May 2002 the Welsh Assembly voted unanimously to challenge Westminster on free personal care for older people funded out of general taxation (Hazell, 2003).

Given that the Richard Commission on the future of the Welsh Assembly and the devolution settlement reported back in March 2004, recommending the reform of the assembly, principally through the development of a separate legislature and executive in Wales, with the legislature empowered to pass primary legislation in devolved areas, the introduction of tax-varying powers and the introduction of a Single Transferable Vote system of proportional representation, all by 2011 (Richard Commission, 2004), it seems likely that Welsh policy divergence will grow in significance should its recommendations be embraced.

We can thus argue that despite the greater power of the Scottish Parliament when compared to the Welsh Assembly, a straightforward pattern of policy choices is not readily apparent. Indeed, it appears from the evidence to date that while the construction of 'Scottish solutions to Scottish problems' has been limited, the application of a specifically 'Welsh' policy has been more fruitful. In the final section of this chapter we focus on the possible explanations for this unexpected outcome.

Modernising public services in a devolutionary context: constraints and tensions

This part of the chapter focuses on the gap between the potential for social policy divergence in Scotland and a reality that falls far short of a distinctively Scottish approach to welfare. It highlights the other main factors and actors that are exerting an influence on the performance of devolved bodies, arguing that a number of constraints, some without the terms of the constitutional settlement, are at work. The discussion is organised around five themes:

• the inherent limits of the devolution settlement;
• the broader New Labour context;
• political will;
• popular resistance and political alliances; and
• the fragmented and differentiated nature of Scottish society.

The inherent limits of the devolution settlement

It is clear from the discussion so far that the 'reserved powers' listed in Section 5 of the 1998 Scotland Act work to limit even the *potential* for divergence to only some policy areas. Numerous examples illustrate this: social security policy is decided at Westminster for the whole of the UK; provision for refugees across Britain is framed by two Westminster-led policy documents (the 1999 Immigration and Asylum Act and the 2002 Immigration, Asylum and Nationality Bill) (see Ferguson and Barclay, 2002); and so on. (See subsequent chapters of this book for further examples). Moreover, as noted earlier, the use of the Sewell Convention also works to constrain the Scottish Parliament in important ways. Originally designed to safeguard Scottish autonomy in devolved areas, Sewell Resolutions have nevertheless been used in practice to hand over power to Westminster on some key issues of policy. Another limiting or constraining factor is the pressure exerted by The Treasury. This has, *to a major degree,* reduced the Scottish Government's scope for action (Adams and Robinson, 2002). The example of PPPs/PFI is illustrative given that the Treasury imposed fiscal rules in Scotland as in England that promoted the use of private finance across the public sector, as noted earlier in this chapter.

In addition, in an attempt to maintain a unified British market, for example, concordats are used to prevent 'market distortions', again limiting the range of policies adopted or considered. These have been used to regulate the relationship between the Scottish Parliament and Westminster, often in ways which emphasise the requirements of the latter.

And, given that the whole of Britain shares a welfare social contract in broad terms, uneven entitlement across the nations is difficult to square with a British tax structure that has not been varied by the Scottish Parliament to date. The Cubie Report on university finance and the Sutherland Report on long-term care for older people perhaps reflect the challenge policy divergence presents to policy makers North and South of the Border, both of which drew a response that provided for no new money from The Treasury and ensured that the Parliament was left with the options of either reallocating resources within the Barnett settlement or raising taxes (Keating, 2001).

Nevertheless, we would argue that *more* devolution is not necessarily the answer. Put crudely, the Parliament has as yet not used all of the powers it has, such as its tax-varying powers, nor has it been slow to give Westminster a significant voice in devolved matters. Moreover, the Welsh case demonstrates that achievements can be secured even where the devolution settlement is even more limited than in Scotland.

The broader New Labour context

Notwithstanding the different polity that has emerged in Scotland (and Wales), which has resulted in more diverse voices without the three main English parties having a say in the policy process, the current dominance of New Labour in Scotland, as lead partner, has had serious consequences for the development of a Scottish social policy, undermining the political will to chase alternatives to the Blair orthodoxy.

It has been argued that current First Minister Jack McConnell, like Henry McLeish before him, is a fully signed up member of New Labour. His pursuit of New Labour outcomes – 'what works', 'best value', partnership, PPPs and market-led solutions to the problem of public service provision and performance, the development of business opportunities and the prioritising of Scottish economic development – has served to confirm his New Labour credentials. While he may have diluted the tone of many of his pronouncements in the interests of bringing key stakeholders, such as the STUC, on board, giving them "a specific role in consultation" (Taylor, 2002, p 135) over the future of public services, he is clear that the private sector will play a key role in Scottish public service provision. Indeed, it seems that differences between England and Scotland are exaggerated in the language of politics in order that a specifically Scottish route be perceived to be followed by the public and to counter the potential challenge of those to the 'left' of Scottish Labour. Yet, as Taylor (2002) argues, looking beyond the rhetoric, many key characteristics of policy and practice are, in fact, shared by England and Scotland.

Moreover, Scottish Labour Party autonomy can be seen as problematic from a party perspective, undermining the very essence of an institution based on shared core values and principles. And, while Blair has stated that policy divergence north and south of the Border is perfectly acceptable where it is a logical response to real differences between the two nations, he has also claimed that there are no real tensions between New Labour in England and Scotland (*The Scotsman*, 5 November 2002) as Scottish New Labour have fully taken on board the 'modernising public services' agenda, sometimes in what appear to be diverse ways but *always* reflecting the broader New Labour commitment to change and its basic principles of reform. Indeed, as noted earlier in this chapter, the Sewell Convention ensures this in some cases, used almost routinely to pass power back to Westminster to legislate on 'sensitive' matters for the whole of Britain. In these instances, Scottish MSPs are denied the chance to scrutinise legislation as it develops despite the fact that amendments from the bill stage may have been significant (Taylor, 2002).

A question of political will?

Clearly from the discussion of Welsh Assembly achievements earlier in this chapter, political will is important in pushing the limits of the devolution settlement. Indeed, Davies (2003) argues that, while claims of "Welsh exceptionalism", including the dominance of the Labour movement in Wales, the size of public sector and the degree of reliance upon it for welfare and work, the well-rooted tradition of collective action and the smallness of the country making networking and collaboration easier, carry some weight, it is *ideological difference* and a *political will* to pursue different priorities and reform routes to those pushed by Blair's New Labour that have proved crucial. Indeed, the so-called 'exceptional' qualities of Wales are broadly shared by Scotland which has not achieved such a level of policy divergence, thus lending weight to Davies' argument that ideology and political will matter. Clearly it is in relation to policy initiatives and divergence in the area of public services that such an ideologically driven approach has been most fruitful – the commitment to citizenship rights, to equality of outcome, to social solidarity over individualism, to the citizen over the consumer, all mark Welsh Labour out as not very 'new' and have resulted in a range of universalist policies and a commitment to collectivism long since abandoned in England. And while "Current arrangements permit only marginal departures from the Downing Street script", Davies (2003) argues that:

> Welsh Labour's deviations on public services point in interesting directions: away from consumerism, competition, targets and 'co-payments', and towards new partnerships with local government and unions and an insistence on equality and universality.

Chaney and Drakeford (2004) lend further weight to this line of argument, suggesting that if one takes an approach which looks beyond legal, constitutional and budgetary powers towards questions of ideological frameworks and actions it is possible to begin to *explain* policy comparisons between England and Wales, and, for us, Scotland, England and Wales. Indeed, Chaney and Drakeford also argue that Welsh Labour is committed to the granting of unconditional citizenship rights, resulting in a range of universal, free-at-the-point-of-use services, as noted earlier in this chapter. Moreover, the principle of equality, and equality of outcome in particular, over choice has shaped numerous social policies, not least the assembly's critique of and resistance to Foundation Hospitals which are seen to advantage some already privileged consumers over others and to elevate choice of the few over equality of service and access for all. A commitment to cooperation over competition is also crucial for these authors in explaining Welsh social policy developments – the active participation of interest groups and an engagement with numerous new consultative networks have been strongly encouraged in relation to a range of policies such as the Strategy for Older People in Wales (WAG, 2003). Of course, as Chaney and Drakeford note, not all post-1999 policies emerging from the assembly demonstrate all the core characteristics of the ideological framework of Welsh Labour but there is plenty of evidence, it would seem, to support the argument that divergence of policy is significantly facilitated by its existence and the political will to apply principled thinking to the policy-making arena.

So, there are alternatives, but there needs to be a political will to pursue them in the face of New Labour dominance. Of course, in the Welsh case we should note the importance of legitimacy building – the assembly was only very marginally supported by the electorate and for Welsh Labour to get a majority after the 'hung' assembly experience of the early days it arguably needed to produce a range of policies that reflected the electorate's priorities. So electoral survival is also a significant factor, and, in the case of Welsh Labour, attention to such issues paid off with a very slim majority government in 2003, as noted earlier in this chapter.

Where alternative routes have been pursued in Scotland, they have largely resulted from what Parry (2002a) calls "coalition pressures" and not from a conviction politics. In 2002, the political will to *make a Scottish social policy* was found to be sorely lacking when the Free School Meals Bill (calling for universal free school meals across the entire Scottish school system) was presented to the Parliament and was resoundingly defeated by a combination of New Labour, Liberal Democrat and Conservative MSPs (see Brown and Phillips, 2002). This deficit, then, has significantly constrained the drive for a Scottish social policy specificity.

Popular resistance and political alliances

In addition to the constraining effects of the south-looking Scottish Labour Party, it is also important to examine the political allegiances that are in evidence in Scotland. Indeed, Scottish politics is characterised by particular political allegiances that also work to constrain divergence pressures – one important example is the specific nature of Scottish Trades Unions–Scottish Labour relations (see Mooney and Poole, 2004). The interdependence of these groups can be seen to have diluted organised resistance and counter-discourse formation in post-devolution Scotland, again demonstrating that social policy divergence and the development of a Scottish social policy cannot be taken for granted – the potential is arguably there, but there are institutional limitations as well as a number of wider constraints.

Nevertheless, we must note that a degree of resistance to New Labour agendas in Scotland has nevertheless been in evidence, around public service closures, such as the Govanhill pool in Glasgow (Mooney and Fyfe, 2004), and against poor pay and conditions as was the case with the nursery nurses dispute across Scotland during the first few months of 2004 (Mooney and McCafferty, 2005). There is also growing public anger across the country around the reorganisation of hospital and acute care provision in many of Scotland's health board areas (see *The Herald*, 6 September 2004). In fact, we might usefully consider the extent to which there have been, and continue to be, attempts to reconstruct and protect the public realm from the 'bottom up' or at the grassroots level in the face of what John Clarke (2004, p 27) has called the "dissolution of the public" from the top down.

Conclusion: a divided and differentiated Scottish society

Policy making in Scotland, as elsewhere, needs to be seen in the wider context of a patriarchal and racially structured capitalist society (see Williams, 1989). Recognising this enables us to be critical about claims about 'Scottish solutions to Scottish problems' that embody the assumption of an undifferentiated Scotland with a shared set of interests and priorities. Scotland is an unequal and fragmented country with class, social and spatial divisions making it difficult to talk about 'the Scots' in an unproblematic way.

As we have argued elsewhere (Mooney and Poole, 2002, 2004), divisions and inequalities are in evidence in relation to schooling and educational attainment, housing provision, conditions and ownership, in terms of health status and treatment opportunities and with regard to poverty, opportunity and material wealth (see also Paterson et al, 2004). These divisions are not only divisions of class and gender, but also around racial and ethnic difference, age, sexual orientation and physical and mental ability. Although it is relatively early days, there is to date little evidence to support the claim that institutional and political differences have *transformed* the social relations. The often claimed 'collectivity' of 'the Scots' (claims that are not supported by the available research in this area, see Paterson et al, 2001; Curtice et al, 2002) has not shaped policy outcomes in any significantly different way.

There are also marked geographical divisions in contemporary Scotland. Hence, it simply does not make sense to speak of a Scottish 'national interest' and set of priorities when the needs, perceptions and attitudes of those living in the Highlands, the Islands, the Central Belt and the Borders and the large council estates and leafy suburbs may differ considerably. Put simply, Scotland is a spatially divided nation and there has been little in the way of a sustained attack on such divisions and inequalities either in Scotland or in England.

In this chapter, we have sought to open up the debate around devolution, highlighting its limits and potentials as well as its achievements to date. In doing so, we have raised a number of questions about the Scottish system of welfare in the post-1999 period and begun to challenge the often taken for granted notion of a 'new' Scotland working towards a distinctively Scottish social policy to meet the needs and priorities of the Scottish population. Moreover, while we have taken care to recognise the *potential* for Scottish social policy specificity in the context of devolution, we have at one and the same time tempered this with a discussion of those constraining factors that have so far worked to limit the achievements of the Scottish Parliament in important ways, often resulting in further policy convergence between England and Scotland and a replicating of New Labour assumptions, policies and priorities north of the border.

In sum, there is at the time of writing (mid-2004) already evidence that a range of factors are facilitating the development of some 'Scottish solutions', not least the role of the Liberal Democrat partners in the governing coalition, who have pushed for a rejection of university fees and an embrace of free personal care for older people, the smaller parties represented by the Scottish electoral system and the voices of those speaking from the margins. However, we also need to take care not to overstate the extent of policy divergence as well as to acknowledge the wider implications it has for other services and their financing in Scotland. Moreover, there is also clear evidence of a number of factors and actors pulling the agenda back in line with that at Westminster and limiting the scope for radical social policy departures over time, a tendency that currently seems stronger in Scotland than Wales, despite the more limited devolution settlement in the latter. Perhaps, as Parry (2002a, p 322) claims, it is only in *different* political circumstances, where the principle governing groups differ in Scotland and England, that we will see the domestication of power to the Scottish Executive being a vehicle for significant policy change. Certainly there needs to develop a political will to actually utilise the powers available to policy makers north of the border and the ideological vision to carve out an alternative agenda to that broadly prescribed by Blair and New Labour with its emphasis on market solutions, individual responsibility and private interests.

Further resources

Chaney, P. and Drakeford, M. (2004) 'The primacy of ideology: social policy and the first term of the National Assembly for Wales', in N. Ellison, L. Bauld and M. Powell (eds) *Social Policy Review 16*, Bristol: The Policy Press/Social Policy Association, pp 121-42.

Keating, M. (2002) 'Devolution and public policy in the UK: divergence or convergence?', in J. Adams and P. Robinson (eds) *Devolution in practice*, London: IPPR, pp 3-21.

Whitfield, D. (2001) *Public services of corporate welfare: Rethinking the nation state in the global economy*, London: Pluto.

On the web ...

National Assembly for Wales	www.wales.gov.uk
Scottish Executive	www.scotland.gov.uk
Scottish Parliament	www.scottish.parliament.uk

References

Adams, J. and Robinson, P. (2002) *Devolution in practice: Public policy differences within the UK*, London: IPPR.

Audit Scotland (Accounts Commission) (2002) *Taking the initiative – Using PFI contracts to renew council schools*, Edinburgh: Audit Scotland.

Audit Commission (2003) *PFI in schools: The quality and cost of building and services provided by early PFI schemes*, London: Audit Commission.

Benington, J. and Donnison, D. (1999) 'New Labour and social exclusion: the search for a Third Way – or just gilding the ghetto again?', in H. Dean and R. Woods (eds) *Social Policy Review 11*, Luton: Social Policy Association, pp 45-70.

Blair, T. (1998) *Third Way: New politics for the new century* (Fabian Pamphlet 588), London: The Fabian Society.

Bochel, C. and Bochel, H. (1998) 'The governance of social policy', in E. Brunsdon, H. Dean and R. Woods (eds) *Social Policy Review 10*, London: Social Policy Association.

Bogdanor, V. (1999) *Devolution in the United Kingdom*, Oxford: Oxford University Press.

Breitenbach, E. and MacKay, F. (eds) (2001) *Women and contemporary Scottish politics*, Edinburgh: Polygon.

Brown, U. and Phillips, D. (2002) *'Even the tatties have batter': Free nutritious meals for all children in Scotland*, Glasgow: Child Poverty Action Group Scotland.

Cabinet Office (1999) *Modernising government*, Cm 4310, London: The Stationery Office.

Chaney, P. and Drakeford, M. (2004) 'The primacy of ideology: social policy and the first term of the National Assembly for Wales', in N. Ellison, L. Bauld and M. Powell (eds) *Social Policy Review 16*, Bristol: The Policy Press/Social Policy Association, pp 121-42.

Chaney, P., Hall, T. and Pithouse, A. (eds) (2001) *New governance, new democracy? Post-devolution Wales*, Cardiff, University of Wales Press.

Clarke, J. (2004) 'Dissolving the public realm? The logics and limits of neo-liberalism', *Journal of Social Policy*, vol 33, no 1, pp 27-48.

Clarke, J. and Glendinning, C. (2002) 'Partnerships and the remaking of welfare governance', in C. Glendinning, M. Powell and K. Rummery (eds) *Partnerships, New Labour and the governance of welfare*, Bristol: The Policy Press, pp 33-50.

Clarke, J., Gewirtz, S. and McLaughlin, E. (2000) (eds) *New managerialism, new welfare?*, London: Sage Publications.

Curtice, J., McCrone, D., Park, A. and Paterson, L. (eds) (2002) *New Scotland, new society?*, Edinburgh: Polygon.

Daly, M. (2003) 'Governance and social policy', *Journal of Social Policy*, vol 32, no 1, pp 113-28.

Davies, S. (2003) 'Inside the laboratory: the new politics of public services in Wales', *Catalyst*, August (www.catalystforum.org.uk/pubs/paper17.html).

DTI (Department of Trade and Industry) (1997) *Building partnerships for prosperity*, Cmnd 3814, London: The Stationery Office.

Ferguson, I. and Barclay, A. (2002) *Seeking peace of mind: The mental health needs of asylum seekers in Glasgow*, Stirling: Department of Applied Social Science, University of Stirling.

Glendinning, C., Powell, M. and Rummery, K. (2002) (eds) *Partnerships, New Labour and the governance of welfare*, Bristol: The Policy Press.

Greer, S. (2003) 'Policy divergence: will it change something in Greenock?', in R. Hazell (ed) *The state of the nations 2003: The third year of devolution in the United Kingdom*, London: Constitution Unit, University College London, pp 195-214.

Hall, S. (1998) 'The great moving nowhere show', *Marxism Today* (Special Issue), November/December.

Hassan, G. and Warhurst, C. (2002) (eds) *Tomorrow's Scotland*, London: Lawrence and Wishart.

Hazell, R. (ed) *The state of the nations 2003: The third year of devolution in the United Kingdom*, London: Constitution Unit, University College London.

IPPR (Institute of Public Policy Research) (2001) *Building better partnerships*, London: IPPR.

Keating, M. (2001) 'Devolution and public policy in the United Kingdom: divergence or convergence?', Paper presented at 'Devolution in Practice' seminar, IPPR, London, 29 October.

Keating, M. (2002) 'Devolution and public policy in the UK: divergence or convergence?', in J. Adams and P. Robinson (eds) *Devolution in practice*, London: IPPR, pp 3-21.

Kerr, D. (1998) 'The PFI miracle', *Capital and Class*, vol 64, pp 17-27.

Labour Research (2002) 'Scottish hurtle down PFI road', *Labour Research*, April.

Ling, T. (2000) 'Unpacking partnership: the case of health care', in J. Clarke, S. Gewirtz and E. McLaughlin (eds) *New managerialism, new welfare?*, London: Sage Publications, pp 82-101.

McCrone, D. (2003) 'Scottish Parliament: key events' (www.institute-of-governance.org/onlinepub/mccrone/keyevents_0902.html).

Mooney, G. and Fyfe, N. (2004) *Active communities of resistance: Contesting the Govanhill pool closure in Glasgow, 2001-2002*, Social Policy Association Annual Conference, 'From Third Way to Which Way?', Nottingham, 13-15 July.

Mooney, G. and McCafferty, T. (2005) '"Only looking after the weans"? The Scottish nursery nurses strike, 2004', *Critical Social Policy*, vol 25, no 2, pp 223-39.

Mooney, G. and Poole, L. (2002) *Is Scotland different? New Labour and privatisation in Glasgow*, Social Policy Association Annual Conference, 'Localities, Regeneration and Welfare', Middlesbrough, 16-18 July.

Mooney, G. and Poole, L. (2004) '"A land of milk and honey"? Social policy in Scotland after devolution', *Critical Social Policy*, vol 24, no 4, pp 458-83.

Mooney, G. and Poole, L. (2005) 'Marginalised voices: resisting the privatisation of council housing in Glasgow', *Local Economy*, vol 20, no 1, pp 27-39.

Newman, J. (2001) *Modernizing governance*, London: Sage Publications.

Newman, J. (2002) 'Putting the "policy" back in social policy', *Social Policy and Society*, vol 1, no 4, pp 347-54.

Ozga, J. (1999) 'Two nations? Education and social inclusion-exclusion in Scotland and England', *Education and Social Justice*, vol 1, pp 44-50, 64.

Ozga, J. (2000) 'Education: New Labour, new teachers', in J. Clarke, S. Gewirtz and E. McLaughlin (eds) *New managerialism, new welfare?*, London: Sage Publications, pp 222-35.

Parry, R. (1997) 'The Scottish Parliament and social policy', *Scottish Affairs*, vol 20, Summer, pp 34-46.

Parry, R. (2002a) 'Delivery structure and policy development in post-devolution Scotland', *Social Policy and Society*, vol 1, no 4, pp 315-24.

Parry, R. (2002b) 'Social policy in Scotland after devolution: what is happening?', *SPA News*, May/June, pp 6-9.

Paterson, L., Bechhofer, F. and McCrone, D. (2004) *Living in Scotland: Social and economic change since 1980*, Edinburgh: Edinburgh University Press.

Paterson, L., Brown, A., Curtice, J., Hinds, K., McCrone, D., Park, A., Sproston, K. and Surridge, P. (2001) *New Scotland, new politics?*, Edinburgh: Edinburgh University Press.

Pilkington, C. (2002) *Devolution in Britain today*, Manchester: Manchester University Press.

Pollock, A., Shaol, J., Rowland, D. and Player, S. (2001) *Public services and the private sector: A response to the IPPR*, London: Catalyst.

Powell, M. (1999) (ed) *New Labour, new welfare state? The third way in British social policy*, Bristol: The Policy Press.

Powell, M. and Exworthy, M. (2002) 'Partnerships, quasi-networks and social policy', in C. Glendinning, M. Powell and K. Rummery (eds) *Partnerships, New Labour and the governance of welfare*, Bristol: The Policy Press, pp 15-32.

Raco, M. (2002) 'Risk, fear and control: deconstructing the discourses of New Labour's economic policy', *Space and Polity*, vol 6, no 1, pp 25-47.

Rees, G. (2002) 'Devolution and the restructuring of post-16 education and training in the UK', in J. Adams and P. Robinson (eds) *Devolution in practice*, London: IPPR, pp 104-14.

Rhodes, R.A.W. (1997) *Understanding governance*, Buckingham: Open University Press.

Rhodes, R.A.W. (2000) 'Governance and public administration', in J. Pierre (ed) *Debating governances: Authority, steering and democracy*, Oxford: Oxford University Press.

Richard Commission (2004) 'Report' (www.richardcommission.gov.uk/content/template.asp?ID=/content/finalreport/index-e.asp).

Royal Commission on Long-Term Care, The (1999) *With respect to old age: Long-term care – Rights and responsibilities* (Sutherland Report), Cm 4192-I, London: The Stationery Office.

Rummery, K. (2002) 'Towards a theory of welfare partnerships', in C. Glendinning, M. Powell and K. Rummery (eds) *Partnerships, New Labour and the governance of welfare*, Bristol: The Policy Press, pp 229-45.

Scottish Constitutional Convention (1990) *Towards Scotland's Parliament*, Edinburgh: Convention of Scottish Local Authorities.

Scottish Constitutional Convention (1995) *Scotland's Parliament: Scotland's right*, Edinburgh: Convention of Scottish Local Authorities.

Scottish Executive (1999) 'A partnership for Scotland: a programme for government' (www.scotlibdems.org.uk/docs/coalitionhtm).

Scottish Executive (2001) *A teaching profession for the 21st century: Agreement reached following the recommendations made in the McCrone Report*, Edinburgh: Scottish Executive.

Scottish Executive (2003) 'A partnership for a better Scotland: partnership agreement' (www.scotland.gov.uk/library5/government/pfbs-00.asp).

Scottish Office (1997) *Scotland's Parliament*, Cm 3658, Edinburgh: HMSO.

Stewart, J. (2004a) '"Scottish solutions to Scottish problems"? Social welfare in Scotland since devolution', in N. Ellison, L. Bauld and M. Powell (eds) *Social Policy Review 16*, Bristol: The Policy Press/Social Policy Association, pp 101-20.

Stewart, J. (2004b) *Taking stock: Scottish social welfare after devolution*, Bristol: The Policy Press.

Taylor, B. (2002) *Scotland's Parliament: Triumph and disaster*, Edinburgh: Edinburgh University Press.

Timmins, N. (2001) *The five giants: A biography of the welfare state* (2nd edn), London: HarperCollins.

Unison (2003) *What is wrong with PFI in schools?*, London: Unison.

WAG (Welsh Assembly Government) (2003) *Strategy for older people in Wales*, Cardiff: WAG.

Watson, M. and Hay, C. (2003) 'The discourse of globalisation and the logic of no alternative: rendering the contingent necessary in the political economy of New Labour', *Policy & Politics*, vol 31, no 3, pp 289-305.

Welsh Office (1997) *A voice for Wales*, Cm 3718, London: HMSO.

Whitfield, D. (1999) 'Private finance initiative: the commodification and marketisation of education', *Education and Social Justice*, vol 1, no 2, pp 2-13.

Whitfield, D. (2000) 'The third way for education: privatisation and marketisation', *Forum*, vol 42, no 2, pp 82-5.

Whitfield, D. (2001) *Public services of corporate welfare: Rethinking the nation state in the global economy*, London: Pluto.

Williams, F. (1989) *Social policy: A critical introduction*, London: Polity.

Woods, K.J. (2002) 'Health policy and the NHS in the UK 1997-2002', in J. Adams and P. Robinson (eds) *Devolution in practice,* London: IPPR, pp 25-59.

Woodward, W. (2001) 'Great Wales', *Education Guardian*, 2 October.

TWO

Welfare nationalism: social justice and/or entrepreneurial Scotland?

Alex Law

This chapter locates current debates around social policy in Scotland in the context of economic, social and political change in the latter half of the 20th century. Taking the notion of 'welfare nationalism', it is argued that Scottish welfare nationalism is a distinctive part of a wider British welfare nationalism that accompanied the Keynesian/Beveridgean welfare state in the post-1945 period. In considering the extent to which this has been undermined in recent times, this chapter also explores the new welfare consensus emerging around New Labour's 'third way' themes of social justice and competitiveness/ entrepreneurialism.

Among the issues explored in this chapter are:

- welfare nationalism in post-Second World War Scotland;
- the extent to which welfare nationalism has been eclipsed by a more pro-market, neoliberal approach centred around an ideology of modernisation, competitiveness and the knowledge economy; and
- the influence of business and corporate networks on policy making in the devolved Scotland.

Introduction

In his book, *Where there is greed*, Gordon Brown (1989) ridiculed claims that Margaret Thatcher's Conservative governments of the 1980s had engineered an enduring economic miracle and everlasting national prosperity. Brown had little difficulty in showing that, in contrast, the huge state revenues accrued from North Sea oil were squandered on lavish tax breaks for the rich, the creation of a permanent pool of unemployed labour and subsidised a costly privatisation programme. Moreover, Thatcher's messianic faith "that business always knows best and markets work most efficiently when least regulated" resulted in "a huge transfer of resources from the poor to the rich" (Brown, 1989, pp 6-7). Not only were such inequalities socially unjust, but they were also economically inefficient. In response, Brown called for "a new supply side socialism", since only socialist policies could ensure social justice *and* economic growth:

> At its best socialism has always been concerned with production and not only distribution, with our basic case that unbridled capitalism is inefficient as well as unfair and economic intervention is not just moral but more productive....Efficiency and fairness depend on each other. (Brown, 1989, pp 9–10)

As Chancellor of the Exchequer for successive New Labour governments, Brown renounced interventionist policies and accepted a broad neoliberal framework for economic policy that precisely views 'unbridled capitalism' as producing both efficiency and social justice. Of course, this all depends on what is actually meant by 'social justice', which is, as we will see, a rather elusive term that can be filled with contradictory meanings (Mooney and Scott, 2003).

As MP for a Scottish constituency, Brown always made a special point of discussing the multiple ways that Conservative policies affected Scotland adversely. He was particularly incensed that "the legitimate aspirations of the Scots for an Assembly" were thwarted repeatedly by Thatcherite Scottish Ministers:

> With a Scottish Assembly there would have been no poll tax, no opt-out schools or opt-out hospitals, and no buses or electricity privatisation. Nowhere is the denial of democracy more obvious than in the case of Scotland. Nowhere is the response of the majority of people – and their support for elementary democratic rights – now more clear. (Brown, 1989, pp 182)

Rather than 'supply-side socialism', New Labour in both Scotland and the UK kept faith with Thatcherite 'supply-side capitalism' and presided over worsening material inequalities across the UK in the late 1990s and 2000s. Not that New Labour simply borrowed everything wholesale from Conservative ideology: New Labour has gone to great lengths to differentiate itself on the basis of its egalitarian aspirations and commitment to 'social justice'. Anything more directly redistributive would prove counter-productive since it will frighten off affluent tax payers from supporting New Labour's social agenda (Lister, 2001). In this way, the perils of Old Labour welfare reformism informs the Third Way politics of recuperation, whereby any radically redistributive measure will merely play straight into the hands of the New Right and only end up affirming the unequal market conditions that it wishes to oppose. Some middle term, a 'third way', was needed to mediate the extremes of the market and state welfare. 'Social justice' provides an inoffensive means of wafting a gentle aroma of egalitarian intentions over the stale odour of pronounced market inequalities.

Self-fulfilling appeals to the objective reality of market forces instruct New Labour's social policies. With the advent of a Scottish Parliament in 1999, the inequities of marketisation and privatisation that Brown once railed against have been allowed to stand and, in cases like the Private Finance Initiatives (PFIs)/Public Private Partnerships (PPPs) and Housing Stock Transfers, have been taken much further than previous Conservative governments. Scotland is governed by an alliance of New Labour and the Liberal Democrats who share a broad consensus about the appropriate roles for the state and the market with the mainstream parties notionally to their left, the Scottish National Party (SNP), and to their right, the post-Thatcherite Conservative Party. While differing in matters of degree, mainly around how to implement 'market-friendly' choices in welfare provision, ideologically the main parties do not differ in kind. All agree that any aspirations for social welfare must be tempered with the new 'realities' of changed economic, social and political conditions. On this basis, it has been possible to construct a new orthodoxy for a highly circumscribed and selective role for the state as merely 'enabling' rather than as the core producer and provider of the full panoply of welfare services.

This chapter addresses the changing ways that welfare, nation and political economy are mediated in the 'New' Scotland. It sets out to develop a critical political economy of welfare nationalism in order to contextualise some of the more detailed analyses of particular areas of social policy in Scotland dealt with in later chapters of this book. It describes how the peculiar form of Scottish 'welfare nationalism' developed historically as twin to British 'welfare nationalism'. Welfare nationalism refers to the specific role played by nationalism as a force for political mobilisation in the negotiation of state welfare (Paterson, 1994; McEwen, 2002). When provided by state-controlled institutions, welfare services articulated a powerful form of social integration and helped domesticate class struggle. In turn, the promissory note of state welfare legitimises the forms of state power over and material inequalities within a territorially bounded community. As Michael Mann (1996, p 297) evocatively said:

> Citizens – often led by labour movements – became true zoo animals, dependent on and emotionally attached to their national cages.

To the extent that the postwar British state appeared to honour its commitment to welfare provision and full male employment nationalist demands for a separate Scottish state had little political resonance. At the same time, a distinct Scottish national identity was mobilised across the political spectrum by the perpetual framing of welfare and economic questions in terms of protecting a distinctive 'Scottish national interest'. The British welfare state's dual role of territorial integration and legitimation of class inequalities was jeopardised in the 1960s and the 1970s by worsening unemployment and fiscal crisis. Many Scots rejected the Thatcherite solution of privatisation and state welfare austerity. Any crisis of state welfare could be resolved less by the supposed technical efficiency of markets than by an increase in popular democracy framed by a distinctive Scottish national identity. Moreover, the neoliberal restructuring of capital fed into demands for a parliament to protect Scotland's vital 'national interests' by out-performing rival locations. I finally consider the emerging institutional discourses and structures in Scotland as the social policy horizon becomes increasingly framed by competitive 'entrepreneurialism' and 'social cohesion' as forlorn attempts to mediate the apparent antinomies of devolution and globalisation. First, the terms of this antinomy as New Labour adopted it before and during the first term of the Scottish Parliament are set out.

Serving two masters? Social justice and neoliberal economy

Welfare policies are always premised upon assumptions about the relationship between global and national economies. While key instruments of social policy have been devolved to Scotland (as described in Chapter One of this book), macroeconomic policy is retained at the UK level beyond the direct reach of the Scottish Executive. Many of the functions formerly undertaken by the Scottish Office were passed on to the Scottish Parliament as 'devolved powers' including: economic development; financial support for Scottish business; promotion of trade and exports; inward investment; tourism; energy; administration of the European Structural Funds; and transport. Although these devolved responsibilities fall well short of the economic powers of standard nation-states, the new Parliament possesses considerable room for manoeuvre to reshape the economic landscape in Scotland. So far, it has chosen to remain faithful to the economic framework set by the UK Chancellor. Here social justice is framed as subordinate to and a platform for the needs of national economic performance.

The central tenets of this new welfare orthodoxy around social justice and economic competitiveness were set out by the John Smith–inspired Commission on Social Justice (CSJ), *Social justice: Strategies for national renewal* (CSJ, 1994). While the CSJ was at pains to distance its prognosis from that of Thatcherite neoliberalism, it conspired with the key neoliberal claim that a profound social, economic and political revolution had taken place in the last 25 years. Such was the depth of change that the goals of the 'traditional left' of public ownership and redistributive taxation had become an irrelevant chimera.

> *We have no option* but to engage with the three great revolutions – economic, social and political – which are changing our lives, and those of people in every other industrialized country. (CSJ, 1994, p 14; emphasis added)

First, 'the economic revolution' is assumed to be a global revolution. International financial flows, foreign direct investment, transnational institutions have turned national sovereignty into little more than a political fiction. Since the forces of global market competition are far from benign, the state needs to equip its 'human capital' to compete by facilitating worker-management partnerships in high-value 'inclusive enterprises'. Second, a 'social revolution' is argued to have occurred. With a falling and ageing population, more diverse, mobile and less hierarchical, the welfare state is argued to have become anachronistic to the new structure of social needs. While the CSJ (1994, pp 28) "do not accept the common assertion that class is dead" and hold no brief for right wing discourses of a 'feckless underclass', class is redefined in terms of "social and economic *exclusion* – from work, transport, politics, education, housing, leisure facilities". Third, 'the political revolution' referred to a new era of 'political openness' and 'participation and democracy' in the face of the collapse of 'the old certainties' of Stalinism, Keynesianism and Thatcherism, and fed in to the same pressures that were leading towards constitutional change. Government in the UK was viewed as too remote, centralised and paternalist. Thatcherism falsely tried to model citizenship after that of the individual as consumer while at the same time attacking public service workers and their trade unions.

Ten years on and such assumptions about dramatic and irresistible economic, social and political change underwrite the New Labour approach to social welfare in Scotland and the UK. As a prognosis of changing empirical realities, however, the claims for 'revolution' in each sphere have been the subject of trenchant critique, which there is no space to rehearse here (see Ferguson, et al, 2002, ch 8). Even such an enduring phenomenon as social class is made amenable to New Labour remedies by defining it mainly in terms of poverty and deprivation. Class is thereby reduced to an ambiguous condition of 'social exclusion' (Levitas, 1998; Mooney and Johnstone, 2000). In his speech to the Scottish Centre for Research in Social Justice, First Minister Jack McConnell is explicit that the notion of social justice that he wants to see adopted in the New Scotland is an instrumentalist one:

> Our commitment to social justice is *not an end in itself, but a means to an end.* We are *not in the business of creating services for the poor.* We are in the business of creating positive change for the long-term by *opening up opportunities* – for all. (McConnell, 2002, p 7; emphasis added)

Whatever social justice is taken to refer to, it is understood by New Labour in exclusively utilitarian terms, as a social means to an economic end, rather than an economic means to widen and enrich social ends. By 2004, the Scottish Executive's 'social justice milestones' were failing and replaced by 'closing the opportunity gap targets' designed to measure the skills and attributes needed to get socially marginalized groups into paid employment. As the Communities Minister, Margaret Curran, put it:

> This is not just about being nice to people who are disadvantaged. It is in the economy's interest and benefits us all to tackle these problems. (quoted in Naysmith, 2004, p 10)

McConnell (2002, p 9), in his Social Justice speech, goes on to state that community regeneration "is regeneration to secure social justice. Regeneration as the means to the end". To follow this chain of reasoning is to see the shadow of Benthamite social policy in the thought of New Labour: regeneration is a means to the end of social justice; social justice is a means to creating entrepreneurial individuals; as 'human capital' commodified (co-modified) individuals are a means to social cohesion; finally, social integration is a means to economic competitiveness. The ultimate goal of urban regeneration, public services, and social justice then is to create a new entrepreneurial selfhood that will consistently create market advantage and ruthlessly seize opportunities to beat-off cut throat market competition. Social justice is acceptable because it is defined in advance as demanded by market necessities. Social needs, in contrast, rarely rate a mention in New Labour rhetoric, perhaps because the non-monetary equality inherent in the concept of 'social need', expressed in terms of personal autonomy and physical health, is universal, objective and primary and does not depend for its legitimacy on market criteria.

Neoliberal capitalism is naturalised by New Labour as the limit point of all human activity and potentiality. Claims for political 'openness' and 'participation' have become under New Labour, both at the UK and the Scottish levels, managed exercises in pushing through a narrow business-friendly agenda. Business is felt by New Labour to bring a more neutral, hardheaded sense of market 'objectivity' to bear on otherwise contentious and subjective political decisions. This has the advantage for politicians to selectively shift political responsibility from themselves to the overriding necessity of market signals. Meanwhile, perhaps most notoriously, New Labour's globalisation discourse of intensified world competition and placeless economic change is mobilised to justify flexible and compliant labour forces. 'Supply-side socialism' thus appears to involve training labour power in the virtues of lifelong self-flexibility to adapt knowledge, skills and personality instrumentally to the vicissitudes of labour market demands. Such claims about a distinctively Scottish welfare system therefore rest largely on a shared ideological framework between Holyrood and Westminster about what kind of economic and welfare systems are practicable and realistic within a neoliberal global order. With the split in responsibilities for much welfare provision and economic policies between a devolved Scottish Executive and the UK state some of the contradictions between welfare and economy may well become more pronounced.

This is not to deny that Scotland has been subject to some differences in welfare provision, as Chapter One of this book demonstrated. The Scottish Executive appears to have a closer relationship with the welfare state trade unions and the Scottish Trades Union Congress than is the case at the UK level. Nor has Scotland been subject to such deeply contentious policies in England as the Foundation Hospitals proposal and front-loaded top-up fees in Higher Education. Despite such important differences, policy in Scotland, like the UK, share more similarities than dissimilarities. At the time of writing, the further entrenchment of Blairist welfare reforms such as Foundation Hospitals are being actively considered by the Scottish Labour Party policy forum for inclusion in the 2007 Scottish Election Manifesto. Of course, a trend towards welfare homogeneity may be something imposed on any state working within an overarching neoliberal consensus. For instance, there has been no attempt by any of the major parties to fund improved services by increasing the rate of direct taxation in Scotland within the 3% margin permitted by the new constitution since September 2002. Then the SNP abandoned its 'Penny for Scotland' slogan, coined for the 1999 General Election, in favour of the insipid slogan 'Release our Potential'. Instead, economic priorities determine social needs rather than the other way around. As Scottish New Labour and the Scottish Liberal Democrats stated in their coalition statement "the challenge of a global society" needs to be faced squarely in order to create "a Scotland where enterprise can flourish":

> Growing the economy is our top priority. A successful economy is the key to our future prosperity and a pre-requisite for building first-class public services, social justice and a Scotland of opportunity. (Scottish Executive, 2003)

Such unanimity on the primacy of market realities is also rooted in the persistence of an undemocratic, postwar sub-state apparatus in Scotland. Half-hidden, half-ignored, a distinct administrative apparatus centred on the Scottish Office carried out the practical framing and implementation of policies in what it perceived to be 'the Scottish national interest' (Bond et al, 2003). However, rather than the consensus-seeking welfare bureaucracy defending 'Scotland's national interest', today the national interest is identified with how well the 'enabling' Scottish mini-state competes with other locations to settle global capital in Scotland, offsetting a minimum of social responsibilities as so much obstructive regulation while supplying an optimum level of cost-efficient, trained human capital. Perhaps the single most repeated claim for the relationship between welfare and the economy in the 'New' Scotland is that the undemocratic nature of the British Welfare State has now been reformed to make it more accountable and responsive to social needs. However, this merely defers the fundamental question: can the new arrangements in Scotland simultaneously serve two masters – social justice *and* neoliberal political economy?

Welfare nationalism in Scotland

Keynesianism became hegemonic precisely because capital accumulation could no longer be left to the caprice of market disorder. It was understood that the primary aim of the economy was full male employment. As a nationalist compromise in class struggle, this formed the bedrock of what T.H. Marshall (1950) termed 'social citizenship'. The central presupposition of British social citizenship was that national integration would ameliorate class struggle so long as the market operated efficiently for the male 'breadwinner' to provide for his immediate family and only exceptionally need to call upon state support when sick, between jobs or in retirement. At the heart of social citizenship has always been the dual goal of national cohesion and economic competitiveness. While the 1945-51 Labour government entered mythology as a radical social democratic project intent on transforming capitalism, its legacy was much more pragmatic and functional. As the Scottish economic historian, Bruce Lenman (1977, p 243), put it:

> It is not too unfair to describe the policy of the Labour government as essentially a mixture of liberal social reform, state welfare, and enlightened capitalism if one assumes that an enlightened capitalist is prepared to accept state control of certain industries, especially when the alternative is collapse. One snag about this approach is that it can easily make nonsense of market economies without providing any real alternative.

If social democracy helped to stave-off economic collapse in postwar Scotland, it did so with ambitions to bring a certain kind of geographical justice to the depressed regions of Britain as part of the nationalist promise of social citizenship. Britain's declining regions would be integrated closer into the workings of the national economy in order to prevent widespread unemployment in economically peripheral areas. In this way, the British welfare nationalism emanating from the social citizenship of the central UK state would be bolstered by the social cohesion of communities and regions. Only Scotland was not merely an administrative unit; it was also a nation in an age when the idea of 'self-determination' of nations was still thought to be a feasible democratic option.

Paradoxical as it may seem, while classical social citizenship was supposed to create a binding form of integral *British* welfare nationalism, it helped spawn a distinct form of semi-autonomous *Scottish* welfare nationalism (McEwen, 2002). Lindsay Paterson (1994, p 21) argues that as the British welfare state was put under the technocratic control of experts in Scotland it became subject to the politics of nationalist contention as both undemocratic and inefficient:

> Part of the controversy in Scotland about self-government is whether greater [democratic] participation has to be at the expense of maintaining the level of welfare which Scotland has enjoyed as part of what is still one of the materially richest states in the world....The protest takes two forms, and in this respect Scotland is following a common European pattern. The one is a protest in the terms that the welfare state has claimed for its own – that the system is not, any longer, delivering the material goods that it once did. The other is a claim for participation, a defiance of technocratic rule by experts.

This was the outgrowth of an 'official nationalism' that formed the ideological core of the 'middle opinion' of Scottish Office functionaries. Welfare nationalism was one way of relieving the interwar threat of Bolshevism as a solution to impoverished social conditions in Scotland. From the 1930s, Scottish Secretaries of State, pre-eminently Walter Elliott from the Right and Tom Johnston from the Left, carved out a sphere of influence for the Scottish Office to frame what counted as the Scottish 'national interest'. Nationalist demands for separate government could be displaced so long as the British state was successfully pressurised by Scottish technocrats to practically tackle unemployment, poor housing or disease.

Middle-class professionals thus captured the bureaucratic welfare state in Scotland, reinforcing technical efficiency over democratic participation as the primary criteria for judging the success or otherwise of the welfare state. This lack of democracy was justified by a supposedly distinctive Scots education in a social ethic of service to the rest of the population:

> The middle class could feel that they owned the Scottish state because they managed it. Indeed, whole new segments of that class were produced in the new state institutions such as health, education, social work and the nationalized industries. (Paterson, 1994, p 113)

The new welfare nationalism of the Scottish middle classes was consolidated by the social democratic consensus and the long economic boom. The aspirations of the bureaucratic welfare state were largely the same as those of the middle class. Educationalists, social workers, health professionals and urban planners could find high-status employment in the welfare state due to the social value placed on their technical and managerial expertise. Scope existed to implement social reforms from above, with a managerial emphasis on how reforms were implemented rather than on the nature of the reforms themselves. What Moore and Booth (1989) call a 'negotiated order' emerged, carving out a degree of Scottish administrative autonomy within the unitary UK state apparatus. Scotland, therefore, possessed both a functioning network of bureaucrats and a defined national identity around which claims about welfare nationalism could be mobilised. A highly-developed network encompassing welfare professionals, planners, trade union officials, business managers, civil servants, and other worthy groups like the churches grew up around Scottish Office patronage. By the 1980s, for instance, it was estimated that the Scottish Secretary appointed around 4,000 positions to bodies concerned with economic issues such as the Scottish Development Agency (Moore and Booth, 1989). Positioned at the centre of this web of quasi-state patronage, the Scottish Office was courted by 'middle opinion' to form a Keynesian consensus on what constituted the Scottish national interest. Quasi-state functionaries and institutional personnel thus shared a broadly consensual political belief system, technocratic labourism. The core personnel in the Scottish bureaucratic welfare state intermingled socially within a shared face-to-face milieu. This network was summed up by a journalist in the late 1970s:

> [T]hey all know each other – a tight circle of politicians, businessmen, civil servants, lawyers, trade unionists, churchmen, academics, and a

nostalgic sprinkling of titled gentry. They fix the nation's agenda. (Baur, cited by McCrone, 1992, p 137)

Consensual 'middle opinion' of the welfare middle classes readily responded to and helped define demands for increasing the autonomy of Scottish control over social policy implementation within the framework of Scotland as an equal and voluntary partner in the UK state. Above all, Scottish welfare nationalism was sustained more widely in the population less by Scottish institutions themselves than by the everyday interaction with welfare professionals like teachers, nurses, dentists, opticians, social workers, housing officers, and so on. As Paterson (1994, p 181) put it, welfare nationalists, "whether official or oppositionist, have created a world of dense Scottishness which creates a feeling of natural allegiance in nearly everyone who has been brought up here, or who has lived here for any appreciable length of time".

It was this sense of administrative autonomy that the Thatcher and Major governments eroded. Thatcher adopted an absolutist view of the UK state as a wholly sovereign entity, which simply ignored the Scottish middle class standpoint of the UK as an equal and voluntary partnership of nations. Those bodies that survived were increasingly staffed by local business interests sympathetic to the Thatcherite project of deregulation, privatisation, marketisation and entrepreneurial individualism. Local government, although under a weak form of democratic accountability, found its powers further reduced while at the same time unelected quangos spread over the skin of the policy network to manage and disburse public money. Welfare professionals in Scotland resented being sidelined from decision making and policy implementation, and the opportunities for advancement that such positions used to represent:

> The middle classes saw themselves as the guardians of the welfare state; any threat to their hegemony was interpreted as a threat to Scotland itself. Thus Thatcher did not have to be deliberately anti-Scottish for her policies to be received as such. Her reforms impinged on specifically Scottish institutions because she wanted to end what she saw as the suffocatingly consensual way in which Britain had been governed since 1945.... In Scotland, this laid the government open to the accusation of politicising the devolved administration, especially health and education; and that charge is the gravest that can be levelled in the lexicon of technocracy. (Paterson, 1994, p 169)

All this exposed the underlying contradiction that the welfare-dependent middle classes could protest at the 'politicisation' of the administrative structures that they had previously run themselves as a matter of political preference! For the embattled middle classes, many of whom by the 1980s were migrating from a working class background by way of the 1960s and 1970s expansion of the university sector, Thatcherite attacks on the Scottish mini-welfare state were at once personal, sectional and national. Thatcherism not only failed to arrest decline and revive material prosperity but its fundamental lack of democratic credentials in Scotland became identified with the intolerable absence of democratic legitimacy for the Thatcherite project as a whole.

Too much emphasis is placed by accounts of welfare nationalism such as Paterson's on the way that national identity is reproduced by middle class professionals and politicians (see also McEwen, 2002). National identity is not generated solely by the enunciated politics of nationalist campaigning over the state's allocation of welfare resources. It also understates the subterranean processes by which national identity is reproduced ideologically to make sense of everyday life, not least by the demands of mass communications (Law, 2004). Moreover, the boundary separating welfare nationalism from what might be called 'warfare nationalism' is not hermetically sealed. As Michael Mann (1996, p 298) put it:

> The modern nation-state remains a uniquely intense conception of sovereignty. Militarism, communications infrastructures, economic, social and familial regulation, and intense feelings of national community have been fused into a single caging institution.

Hence, the intra-state welfare framing of national identity is kept permanently available as 'hot nationalism' to mobilise populations for violent inter-state politics (Billig, 1995). Against abstract citizenship theorists such as Jurgen Habermas (1996, p 291), who argued that welfare nationalism would create a pluralist 'real nation' against the myth of the integral homogenous nation where 'each citizen can perceive, and come to appreciate, citizenship as the core of what holds people together', welfare nationalism always contains the danger of reactionary, exclusive communitarianism as the basis of civil society. Legitimate and deserving 'insiders' within the national community, especially if defined by ancestry or birth, may express a 'just' claim on state support while the needs of resident 'outsiders' like immigrants, asylum seekers and economically marginal groups are rendered undeserving and illegitimate. Hence, there exists gross unevenness within the apparently smooth spaces of territorially based welfare nationalism.

In the Scottish context, far from being intrinsically identified with Scottish national identity, attitudinal data consistently shows that the middle class are less intensively 'Scottish' as opposed to 'British' than working-class Scots (McCrone, 2001). Welfare nationalism was reproduced less by face-to-face contact with middle-class professionals than by the material improvements that the welfare state conferred on Scots (McEwen, 2002). As the UK state reneged on the promise of social citizenship and social needs were placed increasingly under the atomised conditions of market simulation, which electoral mechanisms proved to be inadequate defences against, notions of binding British-wide welfare nationalism broke down. If the professional middle classes had been viewed by the broad population as the legitimate protectors of 'the Scottish national interest' and, in this way, national identity in Scotland was defined as something closely bound to social democracy and the social benefits of the welfare state, then the abject failure to materially, rather than symbolically, resist Thatcherism through the 1980s and 1990s might suggest that such groups forfeited their right to see themselves as the special envoys of welfare nationalism. Indeed, as Paterson (1996, p 246) notes in a survey of 20th century education,

> Scottish nationalism of the period since the 1960s has been as much a critique of the elites which have ruled Scotland in the Union since 1945 as of the current constitutional arrangements.

In other words, why should middle class groups assume national-popular leadership over a society whose level of material welfare they singularly failed to protect for more than 30 years? The Poll Tax, for instance, was introduced by the Conservative government partly in response to demands from middle-class constituencies in Scotland and was eventually defeated through popular protest and a grassroots campaign of illegality at the local and the UK levels, a popular politics of resistance to which the 'managed autonomy' of the Scottish mini-welfare state was wholly irrelevant, where they did not in fact actually oppose what they viewed as non-constitutional methods. If a sense of Scottish distinctiveness became more intense it may be due more to the way that the basic avenue to social reproduction through the regulated sale of commodified labour power has become destabilised and that exposure to market power was exacerbated by the reorganisation of the British welfare state. Here economic change intersects with the reformed welfare state to construct the harsh realities that welfare appeals to 'the national interest' were once supposed to alleviate.

From welfare nation to entrepreneurial Scotland?

Economic planning became a central plank of welfare nationalism in postwar Scotland. It attempted to fill the space vacated by the restructuring of Scottish capitalism. Although Keynesian regional policy became increasingly discredited from the 1970s onwards, in Scotland it was a material factor in preventing a repeat of the disorderly market dislocation of the interwar years. Despite this, the more regional policy failed to deliver full employment and 'even' development within the terms of Scottish autonomy inside the UK, the more it gave sustenance to 'unofficial' forms of welfare nationalism in Scotland. In conditions of failing to meet social needs, the critique of the undemocratic and unrepresentative middle-class professional layer became more insistent from both the Left and the Right.

Business organisations like the Confederation of British Industry (CBI) in Scotland channelled a large proportion of its resources into lobbying the Scottish Office and consulted routinely with the Scottish Trades Union Congress (STUC). Regional policies gave a further centrifugal impetus to welfare nationalism in Scotland. Whether measured by output, productivity or employment, staple industries in Scotland like textiles, coal, metals, heavy engineering and shipbuilding were already in deep decline before the 1940s, well before the term 'post-industrial' was minted (Scott and Hughes, 1980). Economic nationalism, brought to a pitch in the 1970s by the discovery of North Sea oil under the SNP's inaccurate slogan, 'It's Scotland's Oil' (Harvie, 1994), was further invigorated by a series of plant closures in Scotland in the 1980s – the vehicle factories at Bathgate and Linwood, the aluminium smelter at Invergordon, the steel plants at Gartcosh and Ravenscraig – largely products of 1960s regional policy, as well as the flight of multinational capital of Caterpillar at Uddingston, Timex in Dundee, and Hoover in Cambuslang. Closures and the threat of plant rundown resulted in broad alliances to wage unsuccessful defensive campaigns to protect 'the Scottish national interest'. Just as galling to welfare nationalists were repeated claims by Conservative Scottish Ministers that Scots had become welfare 'subsidy-junkies', with public spending in Scotland supposedly being subsidised by the more vigorous economy of South East England (Rosie, 2000).

Privatisation and deregulation altered the relationship between capital and the welfare state. Margaret Thatcher despaired of the Scots forgetting the supposedly native traditions of Adam Smith, self-help, enterprise and entrepreneurship and remaining the ungrateful, docile supplicants of entrepreneurial wealth creators based elsewhere (Bond et al, 2003). Ian Lang (1994, p 234), Conservative Scottish Minister, could argue that a new loan scheme for small businesses in Scotland was "built firmly on the traditions of Scottish thrift and enterprise". Such national traditions would come to be endorsed by Gordon Brown and Jack McConnell under the sheen of neoliberal hegemony. In contrast, Tom Nairn (2000, p 239) claimed that the Scottish response to 'free-range enterprise' merely reinforced the fusion of Scottish national identity with a craven, parochial, consensus-seeking timidity, which avoided any political challenge to the UK state itself:

> Sometimes this Caledonian institutionalism has been carelessly identified with 'socialism', and sometimes with an imagined native (or even clannic) propensity towards the collective. These supposed traits are then depicted as the cause of an anti-individualism in Scottish society – distrust of success and personal wealth, and unwillingness to take initiative. During the period of Thatcherism this kind of critique naturally gained in popularity. As one government after another tried to make capitalism more popular, and to instil an entrepreneurial outlook, it became tempting to ascribe their failure to some sort of inherited recalcitrance or incapacity.

Such complaints of a genetic anti-entrepreneurial spirit continue to be heard in the devolved Scotland. Carol Craig (2003), self-styled missionary for Scottish entrepreneurialism, bemoans the state of national dependency on old-fashioned Scottish welfarism, impeding the release of a native spirit of free market capitalism and self-help.

Thatcherite politicians resented the role played by state bureaucrats and especially trade union functionaries within the administrative apparatus. Part of the struggle to frame neoliberalism as a hegemonic ideology was to replace the state discourse of 'development' with market discourses of 'enterprise' and to make welfare provision a matter of increasing individual responsibility. In Scotland, this was signalled by the setting-up of Scottish Enterprise (SEN) in the late 1980s at the behest of CBI Scotland (Danson, et al, 1990). The main body responsible for economic development, the Scottish Development Agency, was merged with the Training Agency to form SEN, while the Highlands and Islands Development Board became Highlands and Islands Enterprise. Local Enterprise Companies (LECs) became responsible for economic policy in specific localities. Publicly funded private companies, the LECs, were to be governed by a board, at least two thirds of whom were appointments from local businesses that lacked even the very modest democratic accountability of local government.

In opposition to Conservative rule, key bodies in the Scottish network created the Scottish Constitutional Convention in 1989 to campaign for a Scottish Parliament. This brought together MPs, local authorities, the churches, STUC, women's groups and the Federation of Small Businesses, all of whom asserted that they were, of course, merely acting on behalf of the interests of the Scottish people (see Paterson, 1998, p 3). As James Kellas (1992, p 221) summarised the complexion of the Convention:

> All in all, an impressive array of the "great and the good" within the Liberal-Labour-nationalist establishment, ... underpinned by the hard and practical men (and some women) of the Labour Party, local authorities (mainly the same people), the STUC and so on.

Thus an unelected body assumed the mantle of campaigning against the 'democratic deficit' of Scotland being governed by a party it did not elect! As Paterson (1994, p 176) notes:

> In many respects, the appearance of this rhetoric is ironic. The Convention was a supreme instance of the Scottish corporatist process at work, its results based on an inscrutable process of consensual decision-making concealed by the 1980s rhetoric of popular sovereignty.

Larger business interests, represented by CBI Scotland, were deeply hostile to devolution in any form. Instead they supported both Conservative Party hostility to the Convention and continued Tory rule at the Scottish Office, that is, until they were summarily deposed in 1997. Conservatives like the MP Allan Stewart feared that a Scottish Parliament would lead inevitably to the break-up of the United Kingdom, providing a "secure Socialist power base from which to challenge Westminster", and that it found its strongest supporters among Scottish welfare nationalists "who have mismanaged many councils, driven rates up and business out, disastrously mishandled housing policy" (Stewart, 1987, p 155). By the mid-1990s, the last Conservative Scottish Minister, Michael Forsyth, went on an ideological offensive against a Scottish Parliament, focusing upon what he called the 'Tartan Tax', the proposed power to vary taxation by up to 3%. This would merely undo the Conservative's 'great project' of a neoliberal 'prosperous new millennium' for Scotland:

> During the 1980s an attempt was made to breathe life into the corpse [of devolution] by leftist politicians hoping to ring-fence Scotland's collectivist and interventionist establishment and protect it from the free market reforms of the Conservative government. That was the new motive for advocating a Scottish parliament: socialism in one country. (Forsyth, 1995, p 246)

However, Forsyth's belated attempt to engage in 'intense consultation' in order to head-off the pressure for a Scottish Parliament and impending Conservative Party electoral liquidation made some concessions to Scotland's 'collectivist and interventionist establishment', although admittedly many of them were well on the way to meeting Forsyth half-way along the neoliberal road:

> One of the people who was most helpful to me during my consultation exercise of the past three months was Campbell Christie, General Secretary of the STUC. Revitalise the Scottish Economic Council, he suggested: strengthen it and use it to enable people to participate in Government policy making. Good idea, Campbell, I said. (Forsyth, 1995, p 251)

Despite the supposedly anti-entrepreneurial values of Caledonian welfarism, entrepreneurial discourses have since become hegemonic in the devolved institutions, at the heart of which is the New Labour machine.

Yet, this image of the small-scale, energetic entrepreneur defies the continuing reality of the central role played by large-scale institutional capital and the public sector in Scotland and the deep inter-dependencies that exist with the rest of the UK economy and polity. Modern Scotland has always been and remains economically integrated with the rest of the UK. More than half of total Scottish exports are for the rest of the UK, which in turn supplied the bulk of imports into the Scottish economy (Hood, 1999, p 39). The relatively open Scottish economy is a function of small national scale and the failure of economic autarchy in the UK to stimulate a 'growth pole' in Scotland around which dynamic local capitals could cluster. One effect was to induce multinational capital to settle some branch-plant activities as Scotland became a screwdriver destination on the western fringe of the markets of continental Europe. What this strategy did accomplish was to plug Scotland deeper into the international division of labour, especially the Atlantic division of labour, more so than Britain as whole. Even more so than local productive units, multinationals act as a bridgehead for importing the effects of economic crisis. High levels of 'external control' open-up and integrate local production into wider processes of global economic turbulence as capital readjusts investment and supply decisions and restructures production. Multi-national capital flight was only grounded temporarily by confrontations with organised labour, most spectacularly in the cases of the 1987 Caterpillar work-in and the Timex lock-out in the early 1990s.

In terms virtually identical to New Labour's Scottish Executive, Conservative Scottish Ministers, like Ian Lang (1994, p 235), were only too happy to emphasise the benefits of neoliberal Unionism for mediating the global economy:

> In the realm of business, our great financial institutions stand on the threshold of a new prosperity and success, thanks to this [Conservative] Government's drive to knock down barriers to trade and commerce and their ability to grab with both hands the immense opportunities that are available to all over Europe. The double benefits of Scotland's skills and environment allied with the UK's sound economic management, low corporate taxation and low inflation, are combining to attract inward manufacturing investment as never before.

Lang's prognosis of 'a new prosperity' was not widely perceived at the time to be accurate or meaningful in Scotland. The number of plant closures and openings in the 1990s and early 2000s broadly cancelled each other out. However, only a few years later, New Labour politicians in the devolved Scotland would repeat the same 'business-friendly' rhetoric almost word for word. Indeed, an economic policy based on inward investment only seemed to compound the structural weakness of exposure to multinational capital and the shifting priorities of the new international division of labour. Such a strategy does not reverse the priorities of a low-wage economy but feeds off it. Hence, multinational investment is concentrated in certain parts of Central Scotland, where large pools of low-wage labour power can be tapped into (Peat and Boyle, 1999a).

Nor is it the case that Thatcherism was bad news for the whole of Scotland equally. While workers, their trade unions and the users of public services protested against privatisation and marketisation, some capitals headquartered in Scotland benefited considerably from the already available and functioning capital that privatisation forcibly redistributed. Scottish firms like Stagecoach, Scottish Power and the Royal Bank of Scotland absorbed other capitals through take-over, buy-out or merger in recently deregulated markets and exercised 'external control' elsewhere in the UK and throughout the world (Peat and Boyle, 1999b, p 94). In 1999, Perth-based Stagecoach bought North America's second largest bus operator Coach USA for £1.1 billion and planned to cut the highly unionised workforce from 12,000 to 7,500 (Bridgland, 2000). Stagecoach's chairman-owner Brian Soutar also attempted to intervene ideologically to 'lead' Scottish society by bankrolling the campaign against the repeal by the Scottish Parliament of homophobic legislation, the notorious Section 28 (Brown, 2000). In contrast to the concealed, staid, consensual world of welfare bureaucrats, Soutar is the epitome of the new enterprising Scottish national interest: outward-looking, growing from a local base, prospering from taking advantage of Tory bus deregulation, placing orders with Scottish suppliers, even reciting Burns at the annual STUC conference. However, on the other hand, this patriotic Soutar cannot be separated from the reactionary Soutar who evinces homophobic prejudices and religious pieties while attacking trade unions and workers' jobs and conditions in Scotland as well as the rest of the UK and North America.

The lie of the land: business capture and the Scottish Executive

Although the Conservatives declined electorally and failed to prevent the Scottish Parliament, the neoliberal agenda that they helped to initiate now defines economic and welfare discourses in Scotland. Businesses are pushing at an open door as they lobby to reframe the Scottish national interest as their own interest. As the new Parliament was brought into existence amid claims of its refreshing 'openness' to scrutiny, monitoring and access, two rival tendencies within the Scottish Labour Party emerged to shape how welfare and policy discourses in the media were disseminated and managed (Schlesinger et al, 2001). On the one hand, there was a wilting commitment to traditional right wing labourism and civil-service secrecy, as epitomised by Donald Dewar, the late First Minister. On the other hand, a coalition of mainly young Scottish New Labour modernisers, much less enamoured by paternalistic discourses of public service, prefer a more 'open' approach to information, so long as it is carefully managed in the style of New Labour 'spin'. This latter group were closer in spirit to the enthusiasm for public relations shown by Michael Forsyth's politicised use of the Scottish Office Information Directorate in the mid-1990s. With Donald Dewar's death, the style of the Scottish Executive came to mirror that of New Labour more closely.

Politics, business and media were rewired to the Scottish Parliament. A new network of commercial lobbyists descended upon Edinburgh to greet the new opportunities opened up by devolution. These were joined by a concerted effort by previously antipathetic business leaders, public affairs directors and associations like CBI Scotland, who set up a Holyrood watchdog body to promote business interests and whose regular economic briefings institutionalised their access to MSPs. The Scottish Parliament Business Exchange was created in 2001 by the Chief Executive of the Scottish Parliament, Paul Grice, and its Presiding Officer, David Steel (Miller, 2002). Its board is composed of five MSPs and ostensibly allows MSPs to be 'educated' about business while participants from multinational corporations, lobbyists and enterprise quangos 'shadow' MSPs. While it is officially promoted as a platonic affair based on mutual understanding, there is no code of conduct to prevent businesses abusing the access provided by their obliging host

MSPs. Within the Executive itself, the Information Directorate was re-branded as the Scottish Executive Media and Communications Group, a name change that "smacks more of a commercial PR outfit than of a public service" (Schlesinger et al, 2001, p 271). As Schlesinger et al (2001, p 185) put it:

> Essentially the battles being fought in the Scottish Executive are about presentation. There is no fundamental point of ideological difference. The moderniser's reforms would clearly shift the culture of the civil service and of governance closer to the market than would the traditionalists' approach. But whichever approach wins, a new open Scotland is not in prospect.

Only weeks into the new Parliament the incestuous personal and professional blurring of PR, lobbying, politics and business was sorely exposed. Kevin Reid of public relations firm Beattie Media bragged to what he thought were US venture capitalists looking to invest in PFI schemes in Scotland about his access to the most senior Scottish Labour politicians in the Executive and at Westminster: "I know the Secretary of State very very well because he's my father" (Laurence, 1999). This came at the end of a long list of personal contacts within the 'special advisor policy team', known simply as the 'Specials' within the Civil Service:

> There's a special advisor policy team, policy unit, headed up by Brian Fitzpatrick who was a candidate for Labour in Glasgow. Three or four of those special advisors are close personal friends of mine, because I worked with them in the party. Chris Winslow in particular is a friend. He was at my wedding last month. We are personal friends. I worked for Jack [McConnell] and for Wendy [Alexander] and for Henry [McLeish] and for Donald [Dewar] on a one-to-one basis. (Laurence, 1999)

First Minister and former Secretary of the Scottish Labour Party, Jack McConnell, had also worked for Beattie Media's public affairs consultancy. Although the lobby industry asserts that it is staffed by professionals, Kevin Reid, 24-year-old son of senior Labour MP and UK Cabinet Minister, John Reid, failed to demonstrate before the Standards Committee any formal credentials that would qualify as professional. In such cases, social and personal contacts are of rather more importance than formal qualifications.

Ensuring that 'McCronyism' is eradicated by open systems of probity and accountability is made difficult by the Executive's obsessive appeal to 'commercial confidentiality'. With chunks of the welfare state being passed over to the private sector in the form of PFI/PPPs or placed under managerialist models floated in by business consultants and advisors it seems that the New Scotland begins to resemble the Old Britain. Interrelated individuals and groups have privileged access through their much-vaunted associational networks. Just as secrecy and cronyism infected the old bureaucratic welfare state behind appeals to technocratic expertise, New Labour's appeal now refers to the need for personal contacts and 'social capital' in the new entrepreneurial welfare state. What this all points to is that the close personal and professional networks around the Parliament work hard to court big business and, in turn, businesses and their front agencies are adept at taking full advantage of any opportunities they are presented with to pursue, what used to be called, their own sectional, rather than national, interests. As hostile outsiders turned favoured insiders, businesses do not need to 'capture' the Parliament and its social networks so much as to merely take up the invitation held out to them to become permanent tenants inside the lavishly furnished network.

Lobbying, public relations and 'spin' attempt to define the new reality of the devolved polity using business–friendly discourses. Yet, arguments for a "smart, successful Scotland" (Scottish Executive, 2001) remain confined to the networked few around the Parliament and have not permeated deeply into Scottish society, which remains broadly supportive of the political values represented by the redistributive welfare state. New Labour wants to occupy a centrist Third Way position. From its inception New Labour itself helped give shape to discourses about the free market, globalisation, wealth creation, competition, partnership, entrepreneurialism, the knowledge economy, and so on (Levitas, 1998; Fairclough, 2000). Such discourses are deeply inscribed in the habitual rhetoric of the Scottish Executive. A vision of reality is defined by the Executive that envisages dynamic worldwide flows, constant change, instability and uncertainty which only technological and knowledge leadership will be able to harness. Fear, danger, threat and risk are used as weapons in the discursive construction of the New Knowledge Economy to discipline workforces and citizens. Alternative definitions of reality are displaced or silenced as complacent, nostalgic or child–like utopias at best and potentially catastrophic at worst. As Mike Raco (2002, p 41) states of the discourses of economic governance in Scotland:

> If the business community is, as stated, the main player in delivering economic growth, then the new Parliament and Executive have had to find ways of mobilising businesses and transforming them into more productive, entrepreneurial agents. Developing a discourse of competitiveness and seeking to eradicate 'complacency' is one technique for achieving this end as is refocusing policy agendas towards networks, technological development and export clusters.

Such has been the power of ideological discourses of competitiveness within an entrepreneurial knowledge society that policy elites are compelled to embrace it or find themselves condemned as out-of-touch, old-fashioned, paternalists. Self-styled 'modernisers' in Scotland argue that the New Economy demands a new kind of consensus. For instance, influential policy insiders from the Scottish

Council for Development and Industry argue for a 'revolution' against the old rigidities of the welfare state:

> The new economic and policy climate demands new solutions. We have a very different and fast-changing economy. We have a new political class who are fast playing catch-up with the global realities of change. And we have more public agencies performing ever more demanding tasks as we ask and expect more of them. We believe the search for a new consensus and strategy has to break with some of the myths and misconceptions which have dominated Scottish policy debate for too long.... This would involve a revolution in attitudes from the old, inflexible public sector, from the NHS to Scottish Enterprise. (Duff and Hassan, 2000, p 12)

Hyperbole about Scotland being or becoming 'modern' and 'new' is not confined to New Labour, academics or policy officials. The modernising agenda to become 'new' is shared by Scottish nationalists. George Kerevan (1999, pp 62-3), for instance, an ultra-enthusiast for neoliberalism, claims that we are entering the post-ideological, anti-bureaucratic and pro-market age of the 'Y Generation':

> What does modernisation mean for the Y generation? Institutionally, it means the abolition of the quango state including Scottish Enterprise, the Arts Council and the rest. It means replacing it with a new, more fluid civil society and putting an end to Central Belt hegemony as towns such as Inverness and Perth rapidly grow. Politically, it means the wide-ranging development of democracy into every nook and cranny of our society – from judges to provosts to health boards – to bring in fresh thinking, youth, talent, openness. Culturally, for the Y generation modernisation means replacing the fixation with cynicism, workerism and parochialism born of the corporatist era with an internationalist, erotic, populist, confident cultural practice – in short, re-branding Scotland as modern not Braveheart. Economically, for the Ys are a generation of entrepreneurs, it means taking risks, being weaned off subsidies, concentrating on local entrepreneurship for world markets rather than foreign direct investment, growing customer-oriented service industries, making jobs rather than saving them, being Hong Kong to Europe's Asia. Already a large number of the cadres of the SNP are entrepreneurs, young bankers and high tech engineers – a far cry from Central Belt shop stewards or social workers.

Kerevan's vision of a progressive 'Y generation' of SNP cadres is not supported empirically by the attitudes that this exciting but admittedly vague group actually espouse. True, as the number of manual workers in Scotland declined the number of non-manual workers grew, both routine white-collar jobs and the New Middle

Class (or 'salariat'). However, much of this latter group of managers, professionals and administrators owe their very existence to the welfare and developmental state. When their vital interests and values seemed under threat from neoliberal Conservatism, sections of the New Middle Class in Scotland could indeed identify strongly with social democratic nationalism. Yet, as a class fraction the 'salariat' tend to be socially diverse and centrist in ideological persuasion. Indeed, far from being firmly wedded to left-wing social democracy or 'Y generation' (erotic!) Scottish nationalism, in the context of devolution the 'salariat' gravitated even more strongly to adopting right-wing ideological positions hostile to a redistributive welfare state. At the same time, support for left-wing political values grew among the working class (Paterson, 2002a, p 214).

This will not stop much of the network from getting on board for the runaway knowledge economy. Even usually less excitable groups like Universities Scotland seek to position themselves politically within this discourse. In their submission to the Scottish Higher Education Review (2002), for example, they place "higher education at the heart of this vision":

> We have reached a consensus in Scotland; we have to build our economy on knowledge because we cannot compete on low wages. In recent years this consensus has come to recognise that higher education has a central role in taking Scotland forward, and this has put higher education at the heart of economic development. That knowledge, ideas, innovation, understanding, adaptability and creativity are the foundation on which this economy will be built has been widely accepted. (Universities Scotland, 2002, p 1)

Scottish Enterprise (1999, p 3) map the future of the knowledge economy in terms where "economic value is found more in the intangibles, like new ideas, software, services and relationships", rather than physical products. It is not clear whether this was meant to be a parody of Tony Blair's former adviser Charles Leadbetter's (2000) much-derided book, *Living on thin air*, but it demonstrates the hegemony of discourses about 'knowledge capitalism' and 'immaterial labour'. Such hegemony even extends to the farthest edges of the anti-capitalism movement, as in Hardt and Negri's book, *Empire*, which defines 'immaterial labour' as that which produces "an immaterial good, such as service, a cultural product, knowledge or communication" (Hardt and Negri, 2001, p 290). Sure, a few knowledge-driven, symbol-manipulation start-ups will make a significant contribution to certain localities, as in the case of computer games designers clustering in Dundee. Yet few jobs are or will be occupied by workers creatively manipulating knowledge or signs. Of those that are, some will end up losing their on-the-job autonomy and face de-skilling and managerial surveillance (see Mackay, 2002, p 89). Much of the recent growth in the service economy in Scotland has been in call centre employment, where operators do manipulate information but in a technically managed, routine fashion (Taylor and Bain,

1998). Scotland has a relatively high number of call centres, in absolute terms the third highest in the UK, and the second highest in relative terms of the proportion of the population in call centre employment (Bishop, et al, 2003). Call centres clustered in Greater Glasgow, Edinburgh, West Lothian, Fife, Dundee and Falkirk are not exactly the knowledge-based networks supposedly the hallmark of a 'smart, successful Scotland'.

Networking the 'New' Scotland

Many commentators share an assumption that what might be called 'big states' are finished and that the future belongs to the much smaller geographical scale of 'micro-states', regions and localities. Only at such levels can the vicissitudes of those processes inadequately lumped together as 'globalisation' be negotiated successfully and social needs be met adequately (Held et al, 1999; Hirst and Thompson, 1996). Traditional nation-states like the UK are deemed to be too remote and ineffectual in the teeth of global processes but at the same time too overweening and centralised to be responsive to local or regional needs. Globalisation therefore provides nationalists in Scotland with an apparently compelling, non-democratic reason for devolving political and economic power. For some nationalists, a distinct Scottish state apparatus, whether within or wholly separate from the UK state, is exactly what the market appears to demand. As the nationalist George Kerevan (1999, p 64) put it:

> Small nations, like small companies, are the wave of the future because they mean shorter lines of communication and faster reaction times.

It has become something of a commonplace to note that welfare provision within the new globalised 'knowledge economy' depends on the development of loose, decentralised configurations of autonomous actors, institutions and technologies as self-ordering 'networks' (Amin and Thrift, 1995; Cooke and Morgan, 1998).

Old forms of state economic planning and regional development need to be discarded and a 'network paradigm' adopted which emphasises social relations and cultural embeddedness. In the new 'reflexive capitalism', interest groups, usually business-led, share cultural meanings and practices, technical knowledge and market advantages through evolving institutional networks, including those concerned with welfare provision, which begin to supplant market competition *within* regions the better to compete *between* them (Storper, 1997). Associational networks 'embed' global capital by maximising their specific cultural and political assets. The orthodoxies of the New Knowledge Economy shrug off the extensive, formal rules of administration in favour of more nebulous notions of trust, moral communities and social capital. As a set of conformist cultural apologetics they focus less on political analyses of welfare institutions and economic relations than on the morality inhering in the informal voluntary associations of civil society. For Fukuyama (1995, p 90), for instance, culture, tradition and moral community are the "key to the success of modern societies in a global economy". In civil society,

> [an] unwritten set of ethical rules or norms serve as the basis of social trust. Trust can dramatically reduce what economists call transaction costs – costs of negotiation, enforcement, and the like – and make possible efficient forms of economic organization that otherwise would be encumbered by extensive rules, litigation and bureaucracy. Moral communities as they are lived and experienced by their members, tend to be the product not of rational choice in the economists' sense of the term, but of nonrational habit.

Clearly, in demanding allegiance to an ethic of social capital and competitiveness the Scottish nation can be conceived as a non-rational 'moral community'. In Scotland, however, low levels of social trust tend to be exhibited by those who feel most intensely 'Scottish' while the small minority with more 'social capital' more strongly identify themselves as 'British' (Paterson, 2002b, p 23). As well as being distinguished by national identity, there is also a pronounced class cleavage, with higher majorities of those with low or no 'social capital' agreeing that MPs are out of touch, that the Scottish Parliament should take more powers for itself and that there is one law for the rich and another for the poor. Paterson identifies two broad class-based sets of attitudes, although the conception of class deployed is of the crude Weberian type. On one hand, a 'middle-class' type of liberal reformism or 'bourgeois constitutionalism' largely trusts the institutions of the British state. On the other hand, stand 'the socially excluded' for whom "the Scottish Parliament is a means of challenging the Union, challenging the civil society that has maintained Scotland's place in the Union, and, if not challenging the capitalist order, then wanting some fairly strong measures of social democratic reform" (Paterson, 2002b, p 30).

As is evident in the data for Scotland, the problem for generating 'non-rational habits' of 'trust' in traditional forms of corporate leadership in civil society is how to overcome popular memories of the state and capital's past examples of bad faith and sectional interests. Hence, much of the discussion of culture and associational networks smacks of the 'chicken and egg' ambiguity at the heart of New Labour's social cohesion and economic competitiveness programme. Here it is unclear if competitiveness is a necessary prerequisite to foster social cohesion or whether social cohesion is needed first in order to attain international levels of competitiveness. New Labour's framing of constitutional change in the UK was informed by the network paradigm as the most appropriate institutional form to let capital flourish (Lovering, 1999; Jones et al, 2004). This is the uncontested foundation for realising the entrepreneurial conception of social justice. In their public statements Scottish Enterprise and the Scottish Executive talk incessantly about knowledge, trust, cohesion, clusters, networks and innovation (see Scottish Executive, 2001).

Regional economic development is the crucial index by which devolution in the UK will be measured. Claims for the efficacy of associational networks, like those for the reality of globalisation or the knowledge economy, are more often asserted or prescribed than demonstrated. Associational models of networked regions forefront local cultures, trust and cooperation but tend to obscure the continuing power of global forces, regional rivalries and competition, and labour militancy to structure the fate of communities (Massey, 1984). Far from New Labour's tortured utilitarian chain of reasoning between social cohesion and competitiveness, economic and technological developments merely overlay the structured, unequal socioeconomic relations that produced 'social underdevelopment' in the first place.

Scotland already possessed an evolved institutional network and one that acquired an increasing emphasis on business needs, markets and entrepreneurial values. In line with the UK government's own Department for Education and Employment, the Scottish Executive merged the industrial policy functions of the Scottish Office with its responsibilities for education to form the Enterprise and Lifelong Learning Department (see Raco, 2003a, 2003b). It also transferred the LECs from the private sector to the public, making the Enterprise Network, including SEN and Highland and Islands Enterprise, more accountable but at the same time providing a renewed focus on entrepreneurial values and associational networking. Yet, as shown earlier in this chapter, the associational values of trust and cooperation supposedly essential to an effectively networked economy are not automatically present in Scotland. Repeated social, political and economic conflicts in Scotland around plant closures, the award of public contracts, the poll tax, motorway building, public–private 'partnerships', the closure of local services, and so on, have exposed the fissures between networked elites and the rest of the population.

Moreover, targets for economic development and social justice, however narrowly conceived, are not always compatible. As part of the 2004 review of the 'Smart, Successful Scotland' strategy, SEN campaigned to shed their 'social justice' remit for training marginal groups, such as former drug addicts, in the discipline of paid employment. Scottish Enterprise's Chief Executive Jack Perry, with the support of the Enterprise Minister, Jim Wallace, saw a need for Scottish Enterprise "to return to a sharper focus on economic development" and business targets rather than social policy objectives since "government has a duty to care for and support and, where possible, develop this latter group [the older, less skilled and illiterate] but I don't believe this should be the primary responsibility of an economic development agency" (Fraser, 2004). With such confusion at the heart of the entrepreneurial social justice agenda, it is perhaps not surprising that, since 1997, more people expect the Scottish Parliament to make little or no difference to the economy (Surridge, 2002). Although the lowering of public aspirations by politicians for some kind of democratic influence over the economy might be a factor here, the public are also deeply sceptical about the Parliament improving education, a devolved area unlike the economy.

Table 2.1: Expectations of impact of Scottish Parliament on the state of the economy

	1997	1999	2000
A lot better	18	6	4
A little better	46	37	32
Make no difference	24	37	45
A little worse	10	10	10
A lot worse	2	2	2
Sample size	657	1,482	1,663

Source: Surridge (2002, p 134, Table 6.6)

Even within the policy network itself, the prehistory of devolution created deep splits within and between business interests and their agents and the traditional network of trade union functionaries, policy officials, local government, and established public bodies. At the heart of this was the political economy of the welfare state. As the old social democratic consensus broke-up, ideological positioning became much less certain, especially around the proposals for the Scottish Parliament. Welfare nationalism contested the centralising authority of Westminster while business interests resisted devolution from its paranoiac fear of an enlarged welfare state funded by higher rates of taxation. As James Mitchell (1999, p 33) argues, business leaders that only recently, and vociferously, opposed devolution have been given a leading role in shaping the structure of post-devolution economic governance:

> Business leaders are feted by Labour and SNP leaders as Mandela-like saviours of the nation rather than business leaders seeking to reconcile themselves before the nation. A stranger to Scotland could be excused if she thought that business leaders had been at the vanguard of the home rule movement and that trade unions, unemployed and the poor had been its most vehement opponents.

Nor have business organisations become reborn egalitarians. As Mike Raco (2003a, pp 1869-70) reports in his research into post-devolution business organisations, even as they 'partner' the devolved government in Scotland they are sceptical about the Parliament's effectiveness and remain hostile to the potential for more regulatory measures and additional financial 'burdens'. While some sections of business positively embraced the opportunities presented by the devolved settlement, others claim to feel 'misunderstood' and neglected by MSPs, who seem more concerned with the 'short-term' political expediency of social welfare issues such as free health care for the elderly and teachers' pay than the long-term hard-wiring of economic competitiveness and productivity (Raco, 2003b). Nevertheless, in order to change what they see as the misguided welfare priorities of the Scottish Executive, business groups have been attempting to shed their knee-jerk Unionist image and redefine themselves less in terms of their sectional interests than in terms of their contribution to a distinctly Scottish national interest. In such ways, the organs of capital in Scotland push their own sectional interests as national-corporate ones, mobilising and deepening the pro-business spaces opened-up and promulgated by New Labour. One example where a pro-business agenda was furthered by devolution where it had been stalled pre-devolution came with the successful business lobby mobilisation to get the go ahead for a £250 million urban motorway project, the M74 in Glasgow (Raco, 2003b). For more than a decade, this motorway had been the subject of fierce local opposition, not least on the grounds of environmental health (see McNeish, 1999). Yet the Scottish Executive agreed to push it through on the basis of calculations of the benefit to the economic infrastructure whereas prior to devolution the political dangers made the M74 project too prohibitive for the Scottish Labour Party.

Conclusion

If a new welfare consensus could be established in post-devolution Scotland, it would not be around state intervention and public ownership. Instead, it emerged through market-oriented discourses of entrepreneurship, globalisation and the knowledge economy. A pro-business/low taxation agenda is now widely shared within the network. Those business interests that once opposed the creation of a Scottish Parliament continue to distrust those bodies that backed it. However, despite feeling misunderstood, pro-business assumptions are accepted at every level of the network. The contradictory result combines Scottish welfare nationalism with a parsimonious taxation regime at the UK and Scottish levels. The relationship between the Scottish Executive and Westminster has traded on the idea that the governing politicians are in partnership, helped by the fact that New Labour is the dominant power in both arenas.

However, this formula will be sorely tested by a downturn in the economy causing strains on the Exchequer's ability to satisfy the devolved public expenditure settlement. Unlike Wales and Northern Ireland, where allocations are higher per capita due to exceptional criteria, Scotland's fraction is calculated by the 'Barnett formula' of population share. In July 2004, Gordon Brown projected increases in public spending by 2007-08 in Scotland by almost 20%, not including retained costs for pensions and social security, optimistically premised on predictions of unstinting growth for the UK economy (*Financial Times*, 13 July 2004). On the other hand, Brown announced Civil Service job losses of 84,150 and a further 20,000 in the devolved assemblies. Even in the midst of relatively high levels of public sector funding, which in 2001 accounted for around 50% of GDP in Scotland compared to 39% for the UK overall, austerity is already felt to be a daily fact of life for much of state welfare sector, and its adjunct in the social economy sector where there exists an interminable struggle for repeat funding. Public sector trades unions in Scotland may be impelled to shift from the moderate 'partnership' arrangements that many have adopted with the Executive, local authorities and health boards, particularly since the less diverse Scottish economy may not readily absorb redundant public sector workers. While industrial relations have been strangely muted in the private sector in Scotland, in the public sector, particularly at the sharp end of welfare services, industrial militancy has begun to revive in such quarters as nursery workers whose strike in 2004 revealed the extent of low pay combined with a growth of on-the-job tasks and responsibilities (Mooney and McCafferty, 2005). Protection against the imposition on Scotland of a regime of deepening public sector austerity was, after all, the *raison d'etre* of the Scottish Parliament.

New Labour hoped that the Scottish Parliament would shore-up integral British welfare nationalism. Blair, Brown and David Blunkett were forthright in their efforts to strengthen British welfare nationalism. On the one hand, 'outsiders' such as asylum seekers and refugees are denied the most rudimentary human rights, while 'insiders', existing British citizens, are asked in return for their privileged access to the NHS and social security benefits to adopt the obligations and responsibilities of social cohesion and entrepreneurial action (Lister, 2001). Mann's 'zoo animals' remain as firmly imprisoned inside their national cages as ever, even if they are increasingly rubbing-up against its iron bars. Still, devolved welfare provision and the ideological effort to create entrepreneurial individualism inhibit any revival of integral British welfare nationalism as a source of social cohesion. In mediating the contradictions between neoliberal economy and social needs, or New Labour's bedfellows of competitiveness and social cohesion, Westminster cannot be seen to curtail the autonomy of the Scottish Parliament without risking the long predicted break-up of Britain. Scotland is becoming the focus of all future welfare demands. As such, struggles over welfare priorities will also critically test the notion of Scottish welfare nationalism itself as a source of social cohesion.

Further resources

Mooney, G. and Lavalette, M. (eds) (2000) *Class struggle and social welfare*, London: Routledge.

Newlands, D., Danson, M. and McCarthy, J. (eds) (2004) *Divided Scotland? The nature, causes and consequences of economic disparities within Scotland*, Aldershot: Ashgate.

Paterson, L., Bechhofer, F. and McCrone, D. (2004) *Living in Scotland: Social and economic change since 1980*, Edinburgh: Edinburgh University Press.

On the web ...

European Consortium for Political Research, 'The welfare state and territorial politics: an under-explored relationship'	www.essex.ac.uk/ECPR/events/ jointsessions/paperarchive/ edinburgh.asp?section=10
Scottish Centre for Research on Social Justice	www.scrsj.ac.uk
Scottish Executive	www.scotland.gov.uk

References

Amin, A. and Thrift, N. (1995) 'Institutional issues for European regions: from markets and plans to socioeconomics and powers of association', *Economy and Society*, vol 24, pp 41-66.

Billig, M. (1995) *Banal nationalism*, London: Sage Publications.

Bishop, P., Gripaios, P. and Bristow, G. (2003) 'Determinants of call centre location: evidence for UK urban areas', *Urban Studies*, vol 40, pp 2751-68.

Bond, R., McCrone, D. and Brown, A. (2003) '"National" identity and economic development: reiteration, recapture, reinterpretation and repudiation', *Nations and Nationalism*, vol 9, no 3, pp 371-91.

Bridgland, F. (2000) 'Travelling the domestic route', *The Scotsman Business*, 8 September, p 7.

Brown, G. (1989) *Where there is greed...: Margaret Thatcher and the betrayal of Britain's future*, Edinburgh: Mainstream.

Brown, M. (2000) 'A busload of bigotry', *Socialist Review*, July/August, p 15.

Cooke, P. and Morgan, K. (1998) *The associational economy*, Oxford: Oxford University Press.

Craig, C. (2003) *The Scots' crisis of confidence*, Edinburgh: Big Thinking.

CSJ (Commission on Social Justice) (1994) 'The UK in a changing world', in J. Franklin (ed) (1998) *Social policy and social justice: The IPPR reader*, Cambridge: Polity Press, pp 11-36.

Danson, M., Fairley, J., Lloyd, M.G. and Newlands, D. (1990) 'Scottish enterprise: an evolving approach to integrating economic development in Scotland', in A. Brown and R. Parry (eds) *Scottish government yearbook 1990*, Edinburgh: Unit for the Study of Government in Scotland.

Duff, I. and Hassan, G. (2000) 'The key steps to making Scotland a world-class economy', *The Scotsman*, 2 April, p 12.

Fairclough, N. (2000) *New Labour, new language?*, London: Routledge.

Ferguson, I., Lavalette, M. and Mooney, G. (2002) *Rethinking welfare: A critical perspective*, London: Sage Publications.

Forsyth, M. (1995) 'The governance of Scotland', in L. Paterson (ed) (1998 edn) *A diverse assembly: The debate on the Scottish Parliament*, Edinburgh: Edinburgh University Press.

Fraser, D. (2004) 'Wallace backs Perry on Scottish Enterprise's social targets', *Sunday Herald: Business*, 3 July, p 1.

Fukuyama, F. (1995) 'Social capital and global economy', *Foreign Affairs*, September-October.

Habermas, J. (1996) 'The European nation-state – its achievements and its limits: on the past and future of sovereignty', in G. Balakrishnan (ed) *Mapping the nation*, London: Verso, pp 281-94.

Hardt, M. and Negri, T. (2001) *Empire*, Cambridge, MA: Harvard University Press.

Harvie, C. (1994) *Fools gold: The story of North Sea oil*, London: Hamish Hamilton.

Held, D., McGrew, A., Goldblatt, D. and Perraton, J. (1999) *Global transformations*, Cambridge: Polity Press.

Hirst, P. and Thompson, G. (1996) *Globalisation in question*, Cambridge: Polity Press.

Hood, N. (1999) 'Scotland in the world', in J. Peat and S. Boyle (eds) *An illustrated guide to the Scottish economy*, London: Duckworth.

Jones, R., Goodwin, M., Jones, M. and Simpson, G. (2004) 'Devolution, state personnel, and the production of new territories of governance in the United Kingdom', *Environment and Planning A*, vol 36, pp 89-109.

Kellas, J.G. (1992) 'The Scottish Constitutional Convention', in L. Paterson (ed) (1998) *A diverse assembly: The debate on a Scottish Parliament*, Edinburgh: Edinburgh University Press, pp 216-21.

Kerevan, G. (1999) 'From "old" to "new" SNP', in G. Hassan and C. Warhurst (eds) *A different future: A modernisers' guide to Scotland*, Glasgow: Centre for Scottish Public Policy and *The Big Issue in Scotland*, pp 55-64.

Lang, I. (1994) 'Taking stock of Taking Stock', in L. Paterson (ed) *A diverse assembly: The debate on the Scottish Parliament*, Edinburgh: Edinburgh University Press, pp 232-8.

Laurence, B. (1999) 'What can I do for you ...', Interview Transcript Part 1, Balmoral House, *The Observer*, 31 August (www.newsunlimited.co.uk/scotland/story/0,2763,87017,00.html).

Law, A. (2004) 'Language and the press in Scotland', in J.M. Kirk and P. Ó. Baoill (eds) *Towards our goals in broadcasting: The press, the performing arts and the economy*, Belfast: Queen's University Belfast, pp 105-18.

Leadbetter, C. (2000) *Living on thin air*, London: Viking.

Lenman, B. (1977) *An economic history of modern Scotland, 1660-1976*, London: B.T. Batsford.

Levitas, R. (1998) *The inclusive society? Social exclusion and New Labour*, Basingstoke: Macmillan.

Lister, R. (2001) 'New labour: a study in ambiguity from a position of ambivalence', *Critical Social Policy*, vol 21, no 4, pp 425-47.

Lovering, J. (1999) 'Theory led by policy: the inadequacies of the new regionalism (illustrated from the case of Wales)', *International Journal of Urban and Regional Research*, vol 23, pp 379-95.

Mackay, H. (2002) *Investigating the information society*, London: Routledge.

McConnell, J. (2002) 'Delivering social justice', Speech to the Centre for Research on Social Justice, University of Glasgow, 1 July (www.scrsj.ac.uk/GlasgowLaunch/FMspeechtext.pdf).

McCrone, D. (1992) *Understanding Scotland: The sociology of a stateless nation*, London: Routledge.

McCrone, D. (2001) 'Who are we? Understanding Scottish identity', in C. Di Domenico, A. Law, J. Skinner, and M. Smith (eds) *Boundaries and identities: Nation, politics and culture in Scotland*, Dundee: University of Abertay Press.

McEwen, N. (2002) 'State welfare nationalism: the territorial impact of welfare state development in Scotland', *Regional and Federal Studies*, vol 12, pp 66-90.

McNeish, W. (1999) 'Resisting colonisation: the politics of anti-roads protesting', in P. Bagguley and J. Hearn (eds) *Transforming politics: Power and resistance*, London: Macmillan.

Mann, M. (1996) 'Nation-states in Europe and other continents: diversifying, developing, not dying', in G. Balakrishnan (ed) *Mapping the nation*, London: Verso, pp 295-316.

Marshall. T.H. (1950) *Citizenship and social class* (1987 edn), London: Pluto Press.

Massey, D. (1984) *Spatial divisions of labour*, London: Macmillan.

Miller, D. (2002) 'A question of privilege', *Scottish Left Review*, vol 13, p 8.

Mitchell, J. (1999) 'Consensus? Whose consensus?', in G. Hassan and C. Warhurst (eds) *A different future: A modernisers' guide to Scotland*, Glasgow: Centre for Scottish Public Policy and *The Big Issue in Scotland*, pp 28-33.

Mooney, G. and Johnstone, C. (2000) 'Scotland divided: poverty, inequality and the Scottish Parliament', *Critical Social Policy*, vol 63, pp 155-82.

Mooney, G. and McCafferty, T. (2005) '"Only looking after the weans"? The Scottish nursery nurses strike, 2004', *Critical Social Policy*, vol 25, no 2, pp 223-9.

Mooney, G. and Scott, J. (2003) 'The unhappy marriage of neoliberalism and social justice: the case of social inclusion in the devolved Scotland', Paper for *Policy & Politics* International Conference, 'Policy and Politics in a Globalised World', Bristol, 24-26 July.

Moore, C. and Booth, S. (1989) *Managing competition: Meso-corporatism, pluralism and the negotiated order in Scotland*, Oxford: Clarendon Press.

Nairn, T. (2000) *After Britain: New Labour and the return of Scotland*, London: Granta Books.

Naysmith, S. (2004) 'Curran backs tough love to beat yobs', *Sunday Herald*, 11 July, p 10.

Paterson, L. (1994) *The autonomy of modern Scotland*, Edinburgh: Edinburgh University Press.

Paterson, L. (1996) 'Liberation or control? What are the Scottish education traditions of the twentieth century?', in T.M. Devine and R.J. Finlay (eds) *Scotland in the twentieth century*, Edinburgh: Edinburgh University Press, pp 230-49.

Paterson, L. (ed) (1998) *A diverse assembly: The debate on a Scottish Parliament*, Edinburgh: Edinburgh University Press.

Paterson, L. (2002a) 'Governing from the centre: ideology and public policy', in J. Curtice, D. McCrone, A. Park and L. Paterson (eds) *New Scotland, new society*, Edinburgh: Polygon, pp 196-218.

Paterson, L. (2002b) 'Social capital and constitutional reform', in J. Curtice, D. McCrone, A. Park and L. Paterson (eds) *New Scotland, new society*, Edinburgh: Polygon, pp 5-32.

Peat, J. and Boyle, S. (1999a) 'Scottish business', in J. Peat and S. Boyle (eds) *An illustrated guide to the Scottish economy*, London: Duckworth.

Peat, J. and Boyle, S. (1999b) 'The regions', in J. Peat and S. Boyle (eds) *An illustrated guide to the Scottish economy*, London: Duckworth.

Raco, M. (2002) 'Risk, fear and control: deconstructing the discourses of New Labour's economic policy', *Space and Polity*, vol 6, pp 25-47.

Raco, M. (2003a) 'The social relations of business representation and devolved government in the United Kingdom', *Environment and Planning A*, vol 35, pp 1853-76.

Raco, M. (2003b) 'Governmentality, subject-building, and the discourses and practices of devolution in the UK', *Transactions of the Institute of British Geographers*, vol 28, pp 75-95.

Rosie, G. (2000) 'Whose got their snouts in the trough?', *Sunday Herald*, 12 March.

Schlesinger, P., Miller, D. and Dinan, W. (2001) *Open Scotland? Journalists, spin doctors and lobbyists*, Edinburgh: Polygon.

Scott, J. and Hughes, M. (1980) *The anatomy of Scottish capital*, London: Croom Helm.

Scottish Enterprise (1999) *The network strategy*, Glasgow: Scottish Enterprise Network.

Scottish Executive (2001) *Smart, successful Scotland: Ambitions for the network enterprises*, Edinburgh: Scottish Executive (www.scotland.gov.uk/library3/enterprise/sss.pdf).

Scottish Executive (2003) *A partnership for a better Scotland: Partnership agreement*, Edinburgh: Scottish Executive (www.scotland.gov.uk/library5/government/pfbs.pdf).

Stewart, A. (1987) 'The devolution maze', in L. Paterson (ed) (1998 edn) *A diverse assembly: The debate on a Scottish Parliament*, Edinburgh: Edinburgh University Press, pp 155-9.

Storper, M. (1997) *The regional world: Territorial development in a global economy*, New York, NY: Guilford.

Surridge, P. (2002) 'Society and democracy: the New Scotland', in J. Curtice, D. McCrone, A. Park and L. Paterson (eds) *New Scotland, new society*, Edinburgh: Polygon, pp 123-41.

Taylor, P. and Bain, P. (1998) 'An assembly line in the head: the call centre labour process', *Industrial Relations Journal*, vol 30, no 2, pp 101-17.

Universities Scotland (2002) *The knowledge society: A submission to the Scottish Higher Education Review*, Edinburgh: Universities Scotland.

THREE

Managing poverty in the devolved Scotland

Gill Scott, Gerry Mooney and Usha Brown

Governments both north and south of the border have made it clear that combating poverty and exclusion is a key task that requires policy makers to go beyond the cash transfers that are made within the social security system; the relief of poverty requires more than social security reform. As such, the Scottish Executive have a significant role to play in the development of services and interventions that can reduce the causes of poverty and inequality of opportunity as well as protect citizens from the impact of poverty. This chapter outlines the social and economic context in which policy has been developed and examines the impact this has had on a level of poverty that was one of the worst in Europe in 1999. The issues covered include:

- key principles underlying anti-poverty policies;
- the changing context for policy in Scotland;
- the main features of anti-poverty policy in the 'new' Scotland; and
- the problems that remain and the potential for Scottish policies to make an impact.

Introduction

Tackling poverty and social exclusion has been a major priority for the re-established Scottish Parliament in Edinburgh since its inception. There was a shared commitment by the relatively new Labour government in London and the new, Labour-dominated Executive in Scotland to address these issues through a clear anti-poverty strategy, albeit expressed as a social exclusion strategy. A consequence of devolution was that the Scottish Parliament had increased responsibility for key social policy areas that impact on the extent and experience of poverty.

Poverty was one of the major challenges facing national and devolved government in Scotland in the late 1990s. The policies they developed would have to deal with:

- a 15-year decline in public spending per head in areas such as housing, transport and health which had left those without market power with reductions in the resources they needed to maintain socially acceptable levels of autonomy and health (Scottish Executive, 2001a);

- a rise in relative poverty among children that had put Scotland and the UK near the bottom of the league in Europe. Between 1979 and 1997, the number of children living in households with incomes below 60% of the median increased from 1/10 to 1/3, in marked contrast to countries such as Denmark, Norway and Finland, where child poverty showed a marked decrease (UNICEF, 2000; Bradbury and Jantti, 2001; Kenway et al, 2002);
- a rise in the risks of poverty and exclusion for groups who had previously turned to the state for support, including lone parents, the elderly and the disabled. For example, the proportion of lone parents in the UK who were living in households below half average income increased from 19% in 1979 to 63% in 1996 (Brown et al, 1999);
- a decline in the industrial and manufacturing base and a volatile economy that had left areas of the country where heavy manufacturing had been the main economic activity, such as Glasgow, with a concentrated legacy of long-term unemployment and associated poverty, and a skills base that did not match newly developing areas of the economy (TUC, 2002);
- a rise in the risks and impact of poverty and exclusion for groups who had little power in the market but who had previously been able to turn to the state for financial support. A reduction of cash transfers to poor families during the 1980s and 1990s had led to market incomes having a greater significance for families' living standards (SASC, 2000);
- a growing divide between the most affluent and those with low incomes, and between those in secure, well-paid work and the unemployed or underemployed: a divide that not only affected household material resources but also the physical environment, health and aspirations of many (Brown et al, 1999; Shaw et al, 1999; Pantazis and Gordon, 2000; Brever et al, 2002; Scottish Executive, 2003a).

In short, the newly-devolved government in Scotland was faced with the challenge of how to understand and redress the increased rates of poverty of the previous 15 years, to ameliorate the impact of such poverty on life chances and aspirations, to stem the decline in the physical and social environment in which people lived and worked, and to reduce the growing polarisation in income between those in and out of work.

It was a challenge that the government was prepared to take up. A statement made by Scotland's first First Minister, Donald Dewar, noted:

> Too many Scots are excluded, by virtue of unemployment, low skills levels, poverty, bad health, poor housing or other factors from full participation in society. Those of us who benefit from the opportunities of life in modern Scotland have a duty to seek to extend similar opportunities too those who do not. Social Exclusion is unacceptable in human terms; it is also wasteful, costly and carries risks in the long

term for our social cohesion and well being. This Government is determined to take action to tackle exclusion, and to develop policies, which will promote a more inclusive, cohesive and ultimately sustainable society. (quoted in *Glasgow Herald*, 3 February 1998)

Important steps were taken to develop an anti-poverty strategy in Scotland after 1999, when statements of intent and policy, providing indications of how anti-poverty strategy began to be rolled out. These are particularly evident in three documents:

- *Social justice: A Scotland where everyone matters* (Scottish Executive, 1999);
- *A partnership for a better Scotland: Partnership Agreement between the Scottish Labour Party and the Scottish Liberal Democrats* (Scottish Executive, 2003a);
- *Closing the gap: Scottish budget for 2003-2006* (Scottish Executive, 2003b).

All were characterised by cross-party support and made specific the targets held to be central to delivery.

In this chapter, we look at what this has led to in terms of anti-poverty strategy and its effects. There are three sections to the chapter. Initially, we examine the key principles that have guided strategy and the economic, social and political context in which strategy has developed. This is followed by an analysis of two specific areas where policy has been developed and implemented – active labour market policies directed at reducing poverty and child poverty policies. These have been selected because they are ones in which relationships of, and tensions between, reserved and devolved governance are significant. Finally, the possible directions policy might take in the future are discussed and we consider whether the approach adopted since 1997 has limited itself by concentrating on reducing inequalities of opportunity.

Key principles underlying anti-poverty policies

There are different ways of thinking and talking about poverty, each of which carries ideas about causes and ways of dealing with the 'problem' (Howard et al, 2003). The underlying thinking that shaped the policy that emerged in Britain after 1997 included: a rejection of previous ideological approaches of the Left and Right for what was termed a 'pragmatic' approach; the promotion of new ways of working between departments; and the adoption of evidence-based policy development. We consider these three themes below.

A 'pragmatic' approach

Labour's strategy in relation to poverty has been one that stresses that the 'old certainties' about social protection and welfare do not hold the key to successful policy development. A pragmatic approach, focusing on policies and solutions (regardless of their place in the political spectrum) that would address the problems the country faced and improve people's lives was claimed to be the priority, the 'Third Way' (Blair, 1998; Giddens, 1998; Powell, 2002). The idea of the Third Way has been the subject of much debate and speculation. It is underpinned by the argument that both the 'tax and spend', nationalising and state interventionist policies of 'old' Labour, as well as the market-driven policies of the Conservatives, failed to fundamentally tackle poverty and disadvantage in Britain. Against these 'two failed pasts', New Labour sought to construct an approach that drew on new ideas and new ways of working and that was in line with recent economic and social developments, both in Britain and internationally. It was argued that what was needed was an approach that would take into account: changes in family structure and demographic profile in Britain; the 'new conditions' of 'globalisation'; and the need to transform Britain into a fit, healthy, knowledge-based economy, with a 'flexible', well-educated and highly-skilled workforce (see Chapter Two of this book) (Powell, 2002). There has been little identifiable difference between national and devolved government on this issue.

'Joined-up' policy and partnership working

The new governments (in Scotland and Westminster) stressed that poverty is a multi-faceted issue that demands joined-up solutions, solutions that cross departmental boundaries and require much greater cooperation between government departments. For example, improving education can be a means of enhancing the individual security and mobility that offers protection against poverty and social exclusion. Much of the onus for the development of anti-poverty policy in England has come through the activities of the Social Exclusion Unit (SEU) set up shortly after the General Election of 1997. In Scotland, the coordination of the anti-poverty strategy was largely carried out through the activities of the Minister for Social Justice. Both have pursued cross-departmental reviews and policies as a way of addressing poverty more effectively and developing new ways of addressing old problems (Scottish Executive, 2003b; SEU, 2004). The legacy of the Scottish Office – of a single government department with a wide range of substantive policy concerns – possibly explains the stronger capacity for cross-departmental integration of policy making and a cross-departmental commitment to the 2004 review of *Closing the gap* carried out across departments. Joining-up is viewed in large part as encouraging or requiring public service providers to work in partnership. However, partnership planning has also extended beyond the public sector agencies to include voluntary sector and private providers in joint planning and delivery of activity and services in the anti-poverty field.

Developing policy on the basis of evidence

Policy development and delivery was to be informed by robust evidence and evaluation: evidence-based policy became a mantra for policy thinking after

1997. The concept of 'evidence-based policy' had been gaining currency over the previous decade. It stresses the need to open up policy thinking to disciplined review and evaluation. 'Evidence' then becomes a key resource in arguing for policy development and change as well as in the development of management accountability. Interest in evidence-based policy has its origins partly in suspicions of established influences on policy, particularly within the civil service. In Scotland, concerns/distrust about local authorities' powers as well as those of a civil service influenced by the old Scottish Office was further fuelled by a desire for a new more open form of government that devolution promised. This led to greater consultation and evaluation at earlier and earlier stages of service delivery both in England and Scotland (Sanderson, 1998). The 1999 White Paper, *Modernising government*, indicates how New Labour adopted evidence-based policy and measurement of progress towards the eradication of poverty, particularly child poverty, as part of its philosophy. The setting and measurement of indicators has been a major feature of change. In its first session, 1999-2003, the Scottish Parliament consolidated its own social justice and anti-poverty agenda by choosing ten long-term objectives and 29 milestones that would monitor the progress in increasing opportunities across life stages and communities. The statistics that relate to the 29 'milestones' were published annually until 2003 in the *Social Justice Annual Report – Indicators of progress*. The format and conceptualisation of the different dimensions of poverty and social exclusion are similar to those of the Department for Work and Pensions' *Opportunities for all* (DWP, 2002).

Key ideas shaping anti-poverty policy

Three key values can also be seen to have shaped policy. These include the belief that social exclusion rather than simply income or material poverty should be addressed; a belief that anti-poverty strategy should be directed at those who were willing to help themselves; and finally a belief that there were anti-social values held by some families and communities that prevented anti-poverty strategies working effectively.

Social exclusion and social justice

The idea of change plays a crucial role in New Labour's project. Government – both north and south of the border since 1997 – share a similar discourse of a 'world that has changed'. Such changes are seen to include globalisation, the reshaping of employment and changes in household structure. Attempts to construct a new Third Way in general, and the goal of 'modernising' the welfare state in particular, helped to shape a changed approach to poverty. The government accepted the existence of income poverty, but felt that issues of disadvantage were wider, and it promoted the use of the concept 'social exclusion'. This is a term that has been adopted by the EU (Berghman, 1995). It represents a more dynamic and arguably more wide-ranging definition of the processes and relationships involved in poverty.

> Social exclusion draws attention to the multi-dimensional aspects of deprivation and helps us to understand the processes which lead to poverty. It may therefore be helpful in seeking new strategies for tackling poverty…. It is also helpful in that it focuses attention on who is deprived and why. (Long and Phillips, 2000)

There is an implicit promise in the notion of social exclusion to examine all of the processes contributing to poverty, including, for example, racism and sexism. However, as some critics point out, the term does beg such questions as, 'Who includes whom, on what terms? And in what are they included?' (Levitas, 1998). For example, the UK government and Scottish Executive have made it clear that their concerns are with social exclusion and poverty, not inequality. Policies have been aimed at increasing equality of opportunities, not equality of outcome. The aim was to create a system which would ensure 'work for those who can and security for those who cannot', and ensure that the long-term effects of poverty would not prevent new generations or areas becoming socially excluded. While this shows government accepted the existence of income poverty, and the role of work therein, it also indicates that issues of disadvantage were felt to be wider. The use of the concept 'social exclusion' has been promoted as a way of targeting policy towards work as the best route out of poverty, as well as directing policy towards families and communities rather than society. It is seen to represent the more dynamic and wide-ranging processes and relationships involved and it is in this specific policy space that the Scottish Executive largely functions, albeit that the term 'social inclusion' rather than 'exclusion' is used to define policy direction (Mooney and Johnstone, 2000).

In Scotland (as we saw in Chapter Two of this book), the concept of 'social justice' has added a further dimension to ideas about social exclusion and social inclusion. In November 1999, the Scottish Executive published *Social justice: A Scotland where everyone matters*, and defined social justice as:

> an investment in the people of Scotland and is the foundation of our prosperity. We are delivering social justice by improving public services for all, by tackling the social, educational and economic barriers that create inequality and by working to end poverty. We are investing to make every community a safe, attractive place to live, where everyone has the opportunity to make the most of their potential. (Scottish Executive, 1999, p 15)

In some ways, the term 'social justice' seems to frame the social inclusion agenda more explicitly. The use of the term was defined in opposition to social exclusion in Scotland. It emphasises having sufficient resources to be able to participate in society for all citizens. It has been central to the Scottish Executive's policies and programmes in assisting those most at risk of poverty and social disadvantage. As with social exclusion, it is based on the notion that poverty is multidimensional and extends beyond low income to poverty of opportunity and disadvantage in education, health, and housing. The addition which social justice brings, however, is the way in which anti-poverty agendas are complemented by equality strategies to a more explicit level than Westminster-based anti-poverty work. Scotland, like Wales, experiences considerable inequality in access to resources, wealth and services. In both devolved countries, this has been allied to a willingness to address the issues of inequality. In Scotland this tends to focus on ensuring equality of opportunity. In Wales, as was noted in Chapter One, there appears to be a greater willingness to discuss issues of how to create a more equal society (Davies, 2003).

Values and policy: from welfare to work

The concept of social exclusion rather than social inequality informs anti-poverty policy. It is a term that is largely, but not solely, understood as exclusion from work – defined as paid employment – and, in turn, social inclusion is principally dependent upon entering paid employment. This language has grown out of a different but related set of values to that espoused by previous administrations. The impact on policy was that the welfare state came to be seen increasingly as a tool through which the (at times forced) social inclusion of the poorest individuals and groups in society could be achieved (Levitas, 1998), a process defined largely in terms of paid employment. Debate about the future of welfare in Britain has also become increasingly focused on morality, behaviour and personal character (Mooney, 2004). In important respects, recent welfare 'reforms' have been as much about forging fundamental changes in the relationship between the individual and the state, as they have been about developing new ways of tackling poverty or social exclusion. The language of, and stress upon, 'responsibilities' and 'duties' has come to be a consistent feature of many social and welfare policies. In turn, this is linked to the idea of the 'greater good': that individuals have important duties to family, community and to society as a whole. For those who seek to side step their social responsibilities, an increasing range of penalties have developed as in, for example, the withdrawal of benefits for those neglecting to take up work.

The changing environment for policy in Scotland

Devolution

The introduction of devolution was a highly significant factor affecting anti-poverty policy in Scotland. It is hard to separate the effects of Westminster-based fiscal and employment policies from the impact of Scottish Executive-based and non-governmental initiatives on poverty and social inclusion in Scotland. Tax credits, taxation and benefits are Westminster-based policies and have a major impact on poverty, but there is much evidence for the view that social inclusion can improve with policies for which a devolved Scottish Parliament has responsibility. As we have seen in Chapter One of this book, there is a complex mix of reserved, devolved and concurrent powers that varies between Scotland and Wales. The key reserved and devolved areas pertinent to tackling poverty can be summarised as follows: education, health, housing, social work and economic development are devolved to Scotland and Wales. None of the devolved administrations have control over the reserved policy areas, such as the tax benefit system or employment legislation –two key policy areas that relate to poverty and social exclusion.

In terms of policies, there have been some high-profile divergences between the nations, such as free personal care for the elderly or the abolition of upfront tuition fees in Scotland (Chaney and Drakeford, 2004; Stewart, 2004). However, the picture is more subtly differentiated in relation to poverty not least because of its multidimensional nature and the array of policy instruments that need to be enlisted to reduce it. Nevertheless a recent review of approaches to child poverty among the four nations of the UK found that differences exist among the nations in the way that they have articulated an explicit poverty strategy. Policy measures are developing within the coordinates of established priorities and the political structures of each nation (Regan and Lohde, 2004).

Since 1999, the Scottish Executive has sought to present the attack on poverty as a central organising principle of the new Parliament. In some important respects this has involved a degree of divergence between Holyrood and Westminster. While it should not be overstated, nonetheless it is also significant that a different language is often mobilised in Scotland. Thus, there is a greater, if somewhat uneven, stress on social inclusion, as opposed to exclusion, on partnership, equality and, importantly, on social justice. There is now a Minister for Communities with responsibility for these issues. A cross-departmental approach is pursued to tackle poverty, and the Minister for Communities (formerly Social Justice), who is also responsible for equality issues, community regeneration, housing, the voluntary sector and digital inclusion, coordinates the joined-up efforts. All ministers are required to prioritise helping the most disadvantaged groups and areas in their mainstream programmes, and budget proposals are to reflect the ministers' contributions to the antipoverty agenda.

Economic change

An understanding of social policy requires an understanding of the economic, social and political context in which it occurs (Fergusson, 2004). The poverty and unrest that Britain's capitalist economy produced in the 19th century, for example, were part of the pressure for social policy reforms demanded and developed by the labour movement at the time. Such pressure is seldom explicit today but many would argue that economic success and social inclusion/cohesion are interdependent. As Scotland's First Minister expressed it in a speech to the Scottish Council for Development and Industry in 2002:

> The success of business is linked to the strength of our communities. Economic prosperity and social justice are mutually supportive, not mutually exclusive. (quoted in Turok, 2003, p 12)

You do not have to agree with this in order to recognise that economic and social policy are closely interrelated – changes in one resulting in changes in the other (see Chapter Two of this book). If government is intent on making policy decisions conditional on not undermining the pursuit of stable economic growth, then policies which stress supporting people into work as a route out of poverty are likely to be of high priority (Alcock, 2003). In Scotland, it has long been recognised that de-industrialisation, the decline of heavy industries in the 1980s and 1990s is strongly connected to poverty, but it is also increasingly clear that anti-poverty policy is often seen as a way to address both economic deprivation and social deprivation. The SEU's recent review of anti-poverty strategy in the UK concluded:

> Although significant inroads have been made into halting or reversing the worsening of a range of causes and effects of social exclusion there are important challenges for the future as some persistent problems and inequalities remain. Life chances for those born into poverty continue to be far worse than those from more privileged backgrounds, and high concentrations of worklessness remain in some areas. There is still a long way to go in tackling social exclusion. (SEU, 2004)

In a similar vein, Edward Glaeser's (2003) recent review of urban policy in Scotland commented that, like all erstwhile manufacturing cities, Glasgow and many of the neighbouring regions acquired concentrations of poverty and social distress: the great social problems of Scotland's urban corridor are in many ways the residue of the manufacturing exodus. His argument is that urban regeneration and economic and social policy need to be integrated in such a way that economic success can act as a key to the alleviation of poverty. The value of this approach, as Chapter Six explores further, is that it forces us to examine the nature of jobs, levels of pay, patterns of career progression, distribution of jobs and impact of economic policy on poverty and social exclusion.

Demographic change

Significant changes in the population of Scotland have recently been identified as affecting individual and social risks of poverty. Lone parent figures have grown and with them an increased vulnerability to poverty. Figures from the Office for National Statistics (ONS, 2004) also show that the population – already due to fall from 5.05 million to five million by 2010 – will stand at 4.77 million by 2030. This will see Scotland's population fall back to levels last seen in 1915 – with the working-age population supporting one of the highest proportion of pensioners in Western Europe. Chapter Five explores this in some detail but suffice it to say here that the population plunge, which has serious implications for the Scottish economy, is also a product of the country having the lowest life expectancy in Western Europe. Glasgow, for example, has the lowest life expectancy in the UK, an expectation very strongly related to poverty (Mitchell et al, 2000; MacIntyre, 2001; Blamey et al, 2002). A child born in the city is, according to official statistics, now likely to have a shorter life than one born in Iran or Puerto Rico (Joshi and Wright, 2003). Poverty is affecting the population needed to maintain a growing economy and the chance to address poverty itself.

The European Union

European Union policy is a significant factor in the development of anti-poverty policy in Scotland. While initially EU economic policy played little attention to the issue of social exclusion, the reform of Structural Funds in 1998 saw its permeation by social policy. The close links between unemployment, especially long-term unemployment, and social exclusion, led to social cohesion being made a priority objective of the EC alongside economic growth. Gradually, EU economic policy has targeted the problems associated with long-term unemployment, which are low levels of education, low levels of skills, early school leaving, school dropouts, inequality in the labour market, urban black spots, areas of rural disadvantage and membership of minority groups such as travellers and people with disabilities. Structural Funds are one of the EU's key mechanisms for reducing disparities between regions by promoting sustainable economic development in regions that are lagging behind or in decline.

Scotland has received Structural Funds for over 25 years. It has been associated with targeted intervention to regenerate communities, to strengthen their capacity to restructure and to re-skill local populations to take up jobs in new and growing industries, major policy interventions in the reduction of poverty. Between 2002 and 2006, Scotland was to receive over €150 million from Structural Funds. Some would argue that this large amount has distorted some thinking on economic development and anti-poverty strategies, others that it has provided the space to try new things out. Whatever the case, it would be wrong to ignore the impact of the funds on anti-poverty policy, and the impact of involvement in the National Action Plans that have developed from EU Anti-poverty Strategy (DWP, 2003).

Policy directions in Scotland

It is against this background of underlying assumptions, values and economic, social and political change that we need to examine the nature, range and impact of anti-poverty policy in Scotland. But first, let us consider the nature of poverty in the second term of devolution. Does it look very different than that which existed in 1997? Have there been major changes that have accompanied Scotland's relative level of independence in areas of social policy that have addressed the picture of poverty that we outlined at the beginning of this chapter? McCrone et al (2004) conclude that the nation is "a more affluent, comfortable and pleasant place" than it was in 1980. Change has occurred. However, they also say that "truly rosy spectacles" would be needed not to see that a significant minority had largely missed out on the rise in living standards, leaving Scotland a "seriously divided" country with a fifth of Scots still living in poverty, but "increasingly surrounded by affluence". A severe problem still exists.

The poor

The groups most at risk of poverty and exclusion remain very similar to those of the last 15 years:

- *Unemployed or economically inactive people, including 16- and 17-year-olds who have no job or no training place* (Brown et al, 2002). Exclusion from the labour market is most clearly identified empirically by the duration of people's level of participation in paid work. The 'distance' from secure employment that pays above-poverty wages is affected by confidence, motivation, employer perceptions, including discrimination, as well as access to new labour market opportunities and changes in the level of demand for labour.
- *Low-paid people.* Employment is no guarantee of escaping poverty. The New Policy Institute (Palmer et al, 2004) notes that, excluding pensioners, "almost half of both adults and children below the low-income threshold are in working households". Unskilled workers, women, ethnic minorities and young workers are all more likely than others to be low paid. The risk of living on a low income has recently increased in Scotland. There has been a rise in the 'working poor' – low-income households containing someone who is working; in 2001, 40% of households in poverty had at least one working adult. Employment appears to be particularly insecure; 45% of those making a claim for Jobseeker's Allowance in spring 2002 had previously claimed less than six months earlier (Palmer et al, 2004).
- *Rural households with low income and poor access to public services.* Information on rural poverty remains limited, but sudden closure of a large plant can have a devastating effect on a local area, and poor service provision plus the need to travel in order to access basic services may exacerbate poverty (SPICE, 2001).

- *People living in areas with high levels of economic inactivity, poorer housing and low levels of public amenity.* In comparison with the rest of the UK, Scotland is placed within the mid range of a number of indices. But there are areas of Scotland, particularly Glasgow, which are ranked among the poorest in the UK. The Scottish Household Survey (Scottish Executive, 2001b) reports that 'neighbourhood problems' are seen as most common in the 'four cities', followed by 'other urban areas' and then 'smaller accessible towns'.
- *Children in low-income households.* Their material and physical wellbeing is particularly at risk (Kemp, 2002; Adelman et al, 2003; McKendrick et al, 2003). The lives of children from low-income households has improved, but the advances in educational achievement and health seem to reach them more slowly than children in affluent households and inequalities of opportunity across generations remain a major problem. In an important study (Mitchell et al, 2000), researchers recently estimated the effects on life chances of eradicating child poverty. They found that some 1,400 lives would be saved per year among those aged under 15 if child poverty were eradicated (using the government's relative definition of child poverty). This represents 92% of all 'excess' child deaths in areas of higher than average mortality.
- *Disabled people or families with a disabled child.* Persons with a disability are over-represented in low-income groups. Working-age adults who are disabled or have a disabled partner make up around one third of households below the poverty threshold (Scottish Executive, 1999; Durie, 2001; Regan and Stanley, 2003).
- *Ethnic minorities* remain disproportionately represented in low-paid jobs and in areas with low amenity (Brown, 2001).
- *Female-headed households, particularly lone parents.* Lone parents are twice as likely to be poor as compared with couples with children. They are also more likely to experience persistent and severe poverty (Rosenblatt and Rake, 2003; Yeandle et al, 2003).
- *Pensioners dependent on state benefits or small occupational benefits.* Age Concern (2002) recently reported that around half of pensioners had incomes below the Family Budget Unit's 'Modest but Adequate' standard.

Many commentators now distinguish between 'old' poverty, caused by old age or illness – circumstances that can affect us all – and 'new' poverty, which is the particular experience of groups vulnerable to economic or social marginalisation. Marginalisation in the labour market – indicated by unemployment or low-paid insecure employment – is increasingly important for the experience of poverty from youth to old age: the increasing movement towards means-tested benefits and away from state pensions means working life affects income at all stages.

The policies

It is impossible in a relatively short chapter such as this to identify or cost all the policy directions and initiatives that have been adopted in relation to poverty and social exclusion in the last five years in Scotland. It is even harder to separate the benign effects of fuller employment from the impact of initiatives, or to separate the effects of Westminster-based fiscal and employment policies from the impact of Scottish Executive-based and non-governmental initiatives on the statistics listed earlier in this chapter. Nevertheless, it is important to start to examine the policies that have developed. A useful summary of the direction and content of the strategic approach that is developing across the UK in relation to poverty is the *UK's National Action Plan on Social Inclusion 2003-5* (DWP, 2003), developed as a result of the commonly agreed EU commitment to move towards eradicating poverty across Europe by 2010. Key features of the UK and devolved government's plan are attempts to reduce the risks of living in a jobless household through welfare to work policies, and to focus on reducing child poverty through a raft of income-focused and public services policy.

Reducing the risk of living in a workless household

Active labour market policies are crucial to New Labour's attempts in this area. In an approach that is consistent with the European agenda, a series of reforms have been implemented to take forward the welfare to work agenda including: reform of the tax and benefits system aimed at making work pay; the introduction of programmes such as the New Deal to tackle unemployment and obstacles to labour market participation; and a reformed welfare regime which emphasises in-work benefits, particularly for households with children. The Westminster government controls most as part of its reserved powers and concentrates on the 'supply-side' problems of the labour market. The Scottish Executive plays a role in this area in two ways: first, as a partner agency in delivering services to the most disadvantaged, and partly in its role in demand-side policies relating to job creation and training provision.

In addition to the operation of the New Deal and the newly-integrated employment and benefit services of Jobcentre Plus, several developments in Scotland contribute to the delivery of welfare to work. These include area-based initiatives but also services for particular groups such as those developed in response to the Beattie Committee review concerning vulnerable young people. These involve a 'key worker' service to "guide and support the young person through the network of other agencies" (Beattie Committee, 1999, p 49). A review of Careers Services in Scotland resulted in Careers Scotland being established within the Enterprise Networks with responsibility for ongoing development of the key worker service and a new All Age Guidance Service and a wide range of active labour market initiatives supported by European funding. These have generally involved attempts to understand and break down barriers to employment.

They have also included support for employment development in the not-for-profit sectors in similar ways to approaches across Europe involving social enterprises, intermediate labour market projects and social firms (Spear et al, 2001). Local authority economic development departments and local economic development agencies have also developed particular expertise in this area and have expanded their focus to those furthest from the labour market.

The 'third sector' also plays an increasingly important role in this area. Non-governmental agencies such as the Wise Group and One Plus in the west of Scotland are part of the landscape of agencies involved in shaping the 'welfare-to-work' agenda, particularly in the areas of highest poverty and unemployment. They provide a mix of training, personal development and paid work experience for the unemployed that prepares people for the job market and represent significant agency in the area – currently employing over 450 full-time workers between them and working with 3,000 'trainees' in 2002-03 (National Employment Panel, 2003; Wise Group, 2004; One Plus, 2004). The organisations generally operate with funding from, inter alia, European Social Fund, local authorities, regeneration agencies, the Department for Work and Pensions and Scottish Executive. Their involvement is mainly through the development of an Intermediate Labour Market (ILM), providing training and work experience for the long-term unemployed. In some ways, they are similar to the 'intermediary model' seen in the US, where specialist providers are funded by government to make welfare to work programmes effective. ILM projects hire participants for periods of six months to a year and provide individuals with work experience. The aim is to assist the long-term unemployed to re-enter the labour market and they aim to provide paid work together with training, personal development and active job seeking.

Three criticisms of the way in which active labour market policies have developed exist, which largely focus on failures to reduce inequalities and a noticeable increase in the control over the lives of the poor. First, the introduction of more restrictive controls over the unemployed has not necessarily reduced poverty for all those who experience poverty. While the percentage of families with children experiencing relative poverty appears to have seen improvements, as tax credits and the minimum wage take effect, the number of working age adults without children who were in income poverty remained constant between 1996/97 and 2001/02. Waged poverty has increased and for those without access to wage subsidy, the risk of poverty has increased. According to the Institute for Public Policy Research:

> Working-age adults without children constitute an 'unfavoured group', who have not benefited from government policy. In 1994 they constituted 25% of people in poverty [in the UK]. By 2002/03 this had increased to 31%. (Paxton and Dixon, 2004, p 18)

Between 1996/97 and 2001/02, there was a rise of 60,000 in the numbers of childless households in the deepest poverty; that is, households with less than 40% of median household income (Scottish Executive, 2003a).

Second, recent changes in social security illustrate the trend towards more state control over the poor first identified by Hillyard and Percy-Smith in 1988. Indeed, one of the more disappointing effects of recent 'employability' policy is its failure to moderate sharp social divisions and inequalities. Control may be in the interests of a service provider more than those in receipt of services and, as Piven and Cloward (1971) pointed out some 30 years ago, stricter forms of means testing may contribute more to the process of marginalising the poor than reducing their poverty.

And third, it appears that in those areas where Scottish Executive has most potential to reduce the barriers to work – transport, education, health, personal social services and community-based interventions – severe challenges face policy makers. A recent study of the challenges local agencies faced when supporting the economically inactive in Glasgow highlighted the lack of integrated approaches to individuals with low-level skills or work experience in situations where employment is changing. The evidence of *The Glasgow Challenge* report was:

> The organisations working with the non-JSA group are not as well engaged with their clients as we like to think. The high incidence of multiple barriers raises a number of key issues about the coordination between a city's welfare to work service providers. The funders of these services across the city need to come to a common view on the effectiveness of service integration and coordination. (Macdougall et al, 2003, p iii)

A focus on children and young people

Addressing child poverty has been the second major element of anti-poverty work in Scotland and the rest of the UK. In 1999, both the UK and Scottish government pledged to end child poverty within a generation. Such a pledge can be seen, as Williams (2003) argues, as an important element of the move towards a 'social investment state'. By this she means one in which the care and welfare of children is prioritised as an investment for the future. In a similar way to work being seen as a route out of poverty for adults and households as a whole, childcare and education become seen as an investment. For disadvantaged children, early years policies logically become an important focus for policy as a way to prevent future problems, not merely as a way to alleviate short-term effects of poverty. In a recent address to the Joseph Rowntree Foundation on the occasion Gordon Brown (2004) stated that:

> Our starting point is a profound belief in the equal worth of every human being and our duty to help each and everyone – all children and all adults – develop their potential to the full ... to help individuals bridge the gap between what they are and what they have it in themselves to become. (p 2)

Notice here that what are stressed are equal opportunities for children. Viewing government policy north and south of the border the overall approach has been one that involves attempts to tackle worklessness and low income, prevent disadvantage and improve communities. They include:

• attempts to ensure decent family incomes through the type of active labour market policies outlined above but with additional tax credit and family income support measures;
• support for parents in their parenting role; and
• increased attention to developing high-quality public services to break cycles of deprivation.

The vast majority of policy relating to the first of these aims have been delivered through policy changes such as changes in child benefit, the Working Families Tax Credit (WFTC) and its replacement Child Tax Credit, and changes in benefit rules for lone parents returning to work. They are largely the responsibility of the Treasury and the Department for Work and Pensions. Policy initiatives focusing solely on children and their families, on supporting parenting, childcare and education have generally been developed and delivered more through the Scottish Executive. It is interesting to note that, throughout Europe, family poverty is lowest where families are supported in gaining income from the state and from the labour market, and where the 'social wage' is high, especially in respect of childcare provision. Such a move may be becoming part of the basis for devolved and reserved government in this area. Regan and Lohde (2004, p 2) point out:

> The Child Poverty Review led by the Treasury in 2003 was set up to identify how the income-focused strategy can best be complemented through the improvement of public services related to education, health, housing. Most likely public services will have to become more important in the Government's plan to address child poverty and increase future life chances of disadvantaged children. There are challenges ahead. While income related poverty indicators are moving in the right direction the picture is less clear for health and educational attainment. Apart from the challenge to further mainstream the child poverty strategy across departments, the devolution of social policy areas is likely to complicate the formulation of a coherent and comprehensive strategy to eradicate child poverty by 2010 across the UK.

Does Scotland have any lessons in these areas that could be rolled out? Looking at the *Social Justice Annual Report* for the years 2000-2003 (Scottish Executive, 2001a, 2001b, 2003a, 2003b, 2003c, 2003d), the six indicators of child poverty adopted by the Executive to measure progress in policy impact from 1997 reflect this mixture of income-focused measures and public services:

- a 5% reduction of dependent children living in workless households;
- a 7% reduction in the proportion of children living in low-income households;
- a small change in the number of primary school pupils achieving minimum levels in reading, writing and mathematics;
- a significant increase in children attending a pre-school facility but no change in the percentage of mothers breastfeeding;
- no change in the percentage of low birth weight babies; and
- inconclusive evidence of a reduction of the numbers of children in temporary accommodation.

A number of the measures seen to have a role in reducing child poverty are affected solely by national policy, although as the recent review of child poverty in Wales (Williams, 2004) concludes, the devolved governments have a role to play in pushing for change. On the measures that might have had some impact on health and education, the Scottish Executive has more responsibility, and some achievements of the integrated and strategic approach called for by the recent Child Poverty Review published alongside the government's 2004 *Spending Review*. There is a growing body of shared expertise and policy evaluation in Scotland focusing on supporting parents across health, social work and education in initiatives supported by the Starting Well Fund, the Integrated Children's Service and the Working Families Fund (Cunningham-Burley et al, 2002; Scott et al, 2003b; Hayton and Myron, 2004). New approaches can also be seen as social policy has become more integrated with economic policy and local authority economic development and regeneration departments work with others through initiatives such as the Working Families Fund and the New Opportunities Fund.

Childcare is the area where there has been some of the greatest change. Its attraction lies in its potential to reduce barriers to employment for mothers and provide good quality services and a stimulating environment for children to 'prepare them for the future'. Historically, Scotland has developed quite significantly different models of childcare to England: the idea of universal public provision of pre-age five education was relatively further developed in Scotland prior to 1997 (Wincott, 2004). However the movement towards a more 'mixed economy of care' for working mothers with children of both pre-school and school age, fuelled by demand-side subsidies such as the childcare element of the WFTC, has brought Scotland closer to the experience of England. According to Wincott (2004), this has undercut some of the stronger local authority traditions of free pre-school care in Scotland:

> Policies using reserved powers designed in Westminster (apparently) with England in mind did not always suit Scottish circumstances, and may even have tended to undercut existing approaches and traditions in Scotland. Caught between traditionally powerful, but now somewhat weakened local government and the powers reserved for Westminster, it has taken some time for distinctive 'Scotland wide' policies for the early years to emerge ... yet the distinctive traditions and smaller scale of the 'central' government machinery in Scotland may make an important contribution. (p 7)

There is some evidence that this 'important contribution' is beginning to show. The longer time taken for Sure Start to bed down in Scotland in comparison to England (Cunningham-Burley et al, 2002) has not been matched in the same way by the uptake of the Lone Parents Childcare Grant (Ballantyne et al, 2003) or the development of Working Families Fund projects (Hayton and Myron, 2004). While each has had its problems, they constitute models of service development that has greater support than Sure Start and greater uptake than the childcare element of the WFTC. Nevertheless, focusing childcare in such a way as to assist economic and employment development for disadvantaged parents in areas of deprivation should be addressed with caution. There is, for example, evidence that combining childcare with regeneration can produce its own 'poverty trap' as local women are recruited to low-paid, insecure jobs in childcare (Scott et al, 2003). Caution must also be noted about focusing on work as the sole route out of poverty and on childcare as the main element of child poverty policy. If parents are to increase their disposable income and avoid their children's social exclusion then access to sustainable employment that makes work pay is important, but so also are access to affordable housing, to affordable loans and to services and finance that supports them at times of crisis and change.

Some critics have also argued that the means-tested income-focused policies and selective investment to reduce child poverty in areas of deprivation are hampering a faster reduction in child poverty. Child Tax Credit and its predecessor WFTC have both had problems of lower than expected take up and administrative difficulties that more universal policies that could have been done to ameliorate the effects of poverty for children (Phillips, 2002). There is consistent evidence that families experiencing transitions into and out of benefits or a change from two-parent to lone-parent household are strongly related to children experiencing both severe and persistent poverty (Adelman et al, 2003). Selective rather than universal benefits to support children can make such transitions harder.

The universal rather than selective debate was most obvious in Scotland when the Child Poverty Action Group (CPAG) supported a School Meals Bill campaign which would provide free school meals, and to which MSPs from five out of the six political parties gave their support when it was put to the Parliament in 2002 (Brown and Phillips, 2002). Food poverty is the result of complex reasons. They include lack of income, access (or lack of it) to decent food, higher cost of food for poor people, out-of-town supermarkets and fewer local shops, diminishing cooking skills, nutritional education, socialisation in families and information (Watson and Williams, 2003). It is no coincidence that Scotland has one of the highest rates of child poverty, the worst diet and the highest rates of diet-related illnesses in Europe. Campaigners argued that school meals have the potential to make a difference and would ensure a healthy diet for Scotland's children. Food is the largest component in the cost of a child with the exception of childcare costs (Oldfield and Yu, 2000). School meals are expensive. Only children who come from the poorest families – those who receive income support (or income-based jobseeker's allowance) – are entitled to a free school meal. Children whose families live in or on the margins of poverty but receive the minimum wage, WFTC, housing benefit, disability benefits or incapacity benefit have to pay for their children's school meal. Around 30% of children officially classified as living in poor households are not entitled to free school meals. Universal welfare services play a fundamental role in our wider welfare system. The NHS, state education and many local authority services are all major examples of welfare services provided universally free at the point of use and paid for through tax and National Insurance. The universalist argument for free school meals is that food poverty is a major problem in the UK, much of the work carried out to reduce food poverty aims to change individual behaviour rather than remove the structural barriers that prevent access to nutritional foods, policy is uncoordinated and school meals have a low take-up rate because they are stigmatising and fail to hit the target effectively. Universal free school meals would have a high take-up, would be easily coordinated, cost little to administer and represent a long-term investment for the nation's health. Supporting free school meals, moreover, offers the potential to increase disposable income even if benefits and taxes are reserved business. Such arguments, unfortunately, were not ones that MSPs as a whole supported, so that although the argument for universal services was won in relation to care for the elderly in this case, it failed to convince.

Conclusion

Many of the challenges that now face the Scottish Executive and the UK government as they address issues of poverty and social inclusion in Scotland are fundamentally linked to fiscal and social security issues of Westminster. However, they are issues that also need a local response, and one that engages fully with those at risk of poverty and exclusion. The last five years have provided invaluable experience of policy development and delivery at national level and within the new devolved Scotland. This is not to suggest that the understanding of poverty and the impact policy could and did make was not available in 1999 but the clearer targets for poverty reduction, the growing confidence of the devolved government and far more accurate, robust data at Scottish level provide a stronger, but by no means complete, base for evaluating policy and trends in poverty that are affected by the Scottish Executive. Nevertheless, much has still to be done to identify what levers policy can provide to reduce poverty and exclusion.

In summarising the results of current anti-poverty policy, this chapter has noted both achievements and deficits. The *achievements* include:

- a significant reduction in unemployment, particularly in the most disadvantaged areas;
- a reduction of both households and pensioners on low income; and
- a small but significant decrease in the numbers of children in poverty.

New ways of reducing barriers to employment, coupled with a range of locally based initiatives, are also noticeable insofar as they are beginning to open opportunities for the 'hard to reach' groups.

However, despite these achievements there remain a number of issues of concern. For example, economic inactivity – often described as 'hidden unemployment' – remains very high. Moreover, poverty in employment continues to grow: this is particularly true for those in households where workers are in part-time work. It is also noticeable that health has not improved at the same rate as the reduction in the numbers on low income (see Chapter Seven of this volume). Further, groups such as lone parents and people with disabilities at times of transition (from or to work) often experience increased poverty. Finally, reductions in poverty remain slow. Relative poverty has not disappeared and absolute poverty has not been eradicated: a significant minority of Scots live in poverty or on its margins.

It is clear that, while reductions in poverty have been achieved, a great deal more needs to be done. The current approach to poverty reduction is largely based on the view that exclusion from 'normal social activities', rather than inequality, should be the concern of government: a commitment to policies that stress work as the key route out of poverty; a belief in the value of joined-up policy; and the valuing of evidence and monitoring in providing future direction for policy. As we noted at the beginning of this chapter, the key assumptions underlying policy will always affect the direction and extent of the anti-poverty agenda. These approaches represent what some call a minimalist agenda in relation to poverty, largely premised on the idea of achieving equality of opportunity, not equality of outcome.

Hillyard and Percy-Smith (1998) go further and argue that the approach illustrates the contradictions in modern welfare systems. There is little to produce a level playing field if historic advantages enjoyed by 'contented majorities' mean they decide how need and opportunity are defined. While there is some evidence of policy directed at reducing the risk of poverty, there is little in current policy that would address the continuing growth of inequality in Scotland. Increased affluence has not been experienced by all. Family Expenditure Survey figures, for example, show that the 10% of households in the top income bracket spend nearly seven times as much as the 10% with the lowest incomes.

We would argue, moreover, that deepening inequality marginalises and excludes the poor, fosters the social isolationism of the rich and makes those in the middle increasingly insecure about their own position. One of the main factors in the growth of poverty in the 1980s and 1990s was the redistribution of resources from the least well off to the better off. Current anti-poverty policies do not appear to take account of these facts. Issues of power and privilege are avoided or obscured. Townsend argued in 1979 that:

> Characteristic of a policy worked out according to a principle such as social justice would be the de-stratification of society through economic, political and social reorganisation and the equal distribution and wider diffusion of all kinds of power and material resources. (pp 63–4)

A successful anti-poverty strategy must address the issues of inequality and the need for redistributive policies. However, how far the state should, at UK and Scottish level, step in to reduce the effects of a market-based society remains a question that divides both policy analysts and society. As a recent Joseph Rowntree Foundation (2004) report said:

> Whatever policy tools are chosen a powerful political case will have to be made that tackling social disadvantage is in the interests of all. (Timmins et al, 2004, p 19)

We must also recognise that such policy needs to be long term. The eradication of poverty is not a one-off venture. The causes of poverty are complex and have deep roots. In order to eradicate poverty we have both to end it and to ensure it does not re-surface. The eradication of poverty cannot depend only on the commitment of a particular government's policies. Governments come and go. Enduring institutions and mechanisms are required: adequate benefits, a decent minimum wage, access to work that pays and access to good quality public services. However, in addition, there needs to be a strong and continuing commitment from society as a whole. Without public commitment to a fairer and more just society, policies will not be effective or effected.

Further resources

Brown, U., Scott, G., Mooney, G. and Duncan, B. (eds) (2002) *Poverty in Scotland 2002: People, places and policies*, London: CPAG.

Howard, M., Garnham, A., Finister, G. and Veit Wilson, J. (2003) *Poverty: The facts* (4th edn), London: CPAG.

Levitas, R. (1998) *The inclusive society? Social exclusion and New Labour*, Basingstoke: Macmillan.

Percy-Smith, J. (ed) (2000) *Policy responses to social exclusion*, Buckingham; Open University Press.

Yeandle, S., Escott, K., Grant, L. and Batty, E. (2003) *Women and men talking about poverty*, Manchester: Equal Opportunities Commission.

On the web ...

Child Poverty Action Group in Scotland	www.cpag.org.uk/scotland/
HM Treasury Child Poverty Review (2004)	www.hm-treasury.gov.uk/ spending_review/spend_sr04/ a s s o c i a t e d _ d o c u m e n t s / spending_sr04_childpoverty.cfm
New Policy Institute: Monitoring poverty and social exclusion (including Scotland)	www.poverty.org.uk/
Poverty Alliance, The	www.povertyalliance.org/
Scottish Centre for Research on Social Justice	www.scrsj.ac.uk/
Social Justice Annual Report 2003	www.scotland.gov.uk/library5/ social/sjip03-00.asp
Scottish Poverty Information Unit	www.povertyinformation.org

References

Adelman, L., Middleton, S. and Ashworth, K. (2003) *Britain's poorest children: Severe and persistent poverty and social exclusion*, London: Save the Children.

Age Concern (2002) *Using budget standards to influence policy*, London: Age Concern and Family Budget Unit.

Alcock, P. (2003) *Social policy in Britain* (2nd edn), London: Palgrave Macmillan.

Ballantyne, F., Hendry, C. and Leishman, R. (2003) *Impact of childcare support for lone parent students*, Edinburgh: Scottish Executive Social Research.

Beattie Committee (1999) *Implementing inclusiveness: Realising potential,* Edinburgh: Scottish Executive.

Berghman, J. (1995) 'Social exclusion in Europe: policy context and analytic framework', in G. Room (ed) *Beyond the threshold: The measurement and analysis of social exclusion*, Bristol: The Policy Press, pp 10-28.

Blair, T. (1998) *The third way*, London: Fabian Society.

Blamey, A., Hanlon, P., Judge, K. and Muirie, J. (eds) (2002) *Health inequalities in the New Scotland*, Glasgow: Public Health Institute of Scotland.

Bradbury, B. and Jantti, M. (2001) 'Child poverty across the industrialised world', in K. Vleminck and T. Smeeding (eds) *Child well being, child poverty and child policy in modern nations*, Bristol: The Policy Press.

Brever, M., Clark, T. and Goodman, A. (2002) *The government's child poverty target: How much progress has been made?*, London: Institute of Fiscal Studies.

Brown, G. (2004) 'Our children are our future', Speech by the Chancellor of the Exchequer Gordon Brown at the Joseph Rowntree Centenary Lecture, London, accessed on 12 February 2005 (www.hm-treasury.gov.uk/newsroom_and_speeches/press/2004/press_65_04.cfm).

Brown, U. (2001) *Race, ethnicity and poverty*, Briefing, no 12, Glasgow: Scottish Poverty Information Unit.

Brown, U. and Phillips, D. (2002) *Even the tatties have batter*, Glasgow: CPAG.

Brown, U., Scott, G., Mooney, G., Duncan. B. (eds) (2002) *Poverty in Scotland 2002: People, places and policies*, London: CPAG.

Brown, U., Alvey, S., Sawers, C., Knops, A., Long, G. and Scott, G. (1999) *Poverty in Scotland 1999*, Glasgow: Scottish Poverty Information Unit, Glasgow Caledonian University.

Chaney, P. and Drakeford, M. (2004) 'The primacy of ideology: social policy and the first term of the National Assembly of Wales', in N. Ellison, L. Bauld and M. Powell (eds) *Social Policy Review 16: Analysis and debate in social policy, 2004*, Bristol: The Policy Press/Social Policy Association, pp 121-42.

Cunningham-Burley, S., Jamieson, L., Morton, S., Adam, R. and McFarlane, V. (2002) *Mapping Sure Start Scotland*, Edinburgh: Scottish Executive.

Davies, S. (2003) *Inside the laboratory: The new politics of public services in Wales*, London: Catalyst.

Durie, S. (2001) *Pathways to work: Towards an action agenda to create valuable and sustainable employment opportunities for people with mental health problems in Scotland*, Edinburgh: Scottish Development Centre for Mental Health.

DWP (Department for Work and Pensions) (2002) *Opportunity for all: Fourth annual report*, Cm 5598, London: The Stationery Office.

DWP (2003) *UK's National Action Plan on Social Inclusion 2003-5*, London: The Stationery Office.

Fergusson, R. (2004) 'Remaking the relations of work and welfare', in G. Mooney (ed) *Work: Personal lives and social policy*, Bristol: The Policy Press, pp 109-42.

Giddens, A. (1998) *The third way*, Cambridge: Polity Press.

Glaeser, E.L. (2003) *Four challenges for Scotland's cities: The Allander series*, Glasgow: University of Strathclyde.

Hayton, K. and Myron, M. (2003) *Working for families: Lessons from the pilot projects*, Edinburgh: Scottish Executive.

Hillyard, P. and Percy-Smith, J. (1988) *The coercive state: The decline of democracy in Britain*, London: Fontana.

Howard, M., Garnham, A., Finister, G. and Veit-Wilson, J. (2003) *Poverty: The facts* (4th edn), London: CPAG.

Joshi, H.E. and Wright, R.E. (2003) *Starting life in Scotland in the new millennium: Population replacement and the reproduction of disadvantage: The Allander series*, Glasgow: University of Strathclyde.

Kemp, P. (2002) *Child poverty in social inclusion areas*, Edinburgh: Scottish Executive Social Research.

Kenway, P. and Palmer, G. (2002) 'What do poverty numbers really show?', *Policy Analysis*, no 3, London: New Policy Institute.

Levitas, R. (1998) *The inclusive society? Social exclusion and New Labour*, Basingstoke: Macmillan.

Long, G. and Phillips, K. (2000) *Women's participation projects: A rights approach*, Glasgow: Active Learning Centre.

Macdougall, L., Glass, A., Higgins, K., Hirst, A., McGregor, A. and Sutherland, V. (2003) *The Glasgow challenge: Realising the potential of Glasgow's hidden unemployment*, Glasgow: Training and Employment Unit, University of Glasgow.

MacIntyre, S. (2001) 'Socio-economic inequalities in health in Scotland', in Scottish Executive, *Social justice ... A Scotland where everyone matters (Annual Report 2001)*, Edinburgh: Scottish Executive, pp 42-4.

McCrone, D., Paterson, L. and Bechhofer, F. (2004) *Living in Scotland: Social and economic change since 1980*, Edinburgh: Edinburgh University Press.

McKendrick, J., Cunningham Burley, S., Backett-Milburn, K. and Scott, G. (2003) *Life in low income families in Scotland: A review of the literature*, Edinburgh: Scottish Executive Social Research.

Mitchell, R., Shaw, M. and Dorling, D. (2000) *Inequalities in life and death: What if Britain were more equal?*, Bristol/York: The Policy Press/Joseph Rowntree Foundation.

Mooney, G. (ed) (2004) *Work: Personal lives and social policy*, Bristol: The Policy Press.

Mooney, G. and Johnstone, C. (2000) 'Scotland divided: poverty, inequality and the Scottish Parliament', *Critical Social Policy*, vol 20, no 2, pp 155-82.

National Employment Panel (2003) *Work works: Final report of the National Employment Panel's Steering Group on Lone Parents*, London: National Employment Panel.

Oldfield, N. and Yu, A. (2000) *Costs of a child: Living standards for the 1990s*, London: CPAG.

One Parent Families and OPFS (One Parent Families Scotland) (2003) *Education, training and lone parents: The role of education and training in the government's welfare to work policy*, Edinburgh: OPFS.

One Plus (2004) *Annual Report 2003*, Glasgow: One Plus.

ONS (Office for National Statistics) (2004) *Population trends: Spring 2004*, London: ONS.

Palmer, G., Carr, J. and Kenway, P. (2004) *Monitoring poverty and social exclusion in Scotland 2004*, York: New Policy Institute/Joseph Rowntree Foundation.

Pantazis, C. and Gordon, D. (eds) (2000) *Tackling inequalities: Where we are now and what can be done?*, Bristol: The Policy Press.

Paxton, W. and Dixon, M. (2004) *An audit of injustice in the UK*, London: IPPR.

Phillips, D. (2002) 'Child poverty in Scotland', in U. Brown, G. Scott, G. Mooney and B. Duncan (eds) *Poverty in Scotland 2002: People, places and policies*, London: CPAG, pp 97-102.

Piven, F. and Cloward, R. (1971) *Regulating the poor: The functions of public welfare*, New York, NY: Pantheon Books.

Powell, M. (ed) (2002) *Evaluating New Labour's welfare reforms*, Bristol: The Policy Press.

Regan, S. and Lohde, L. (2004) *Devolution in practice 11: Child poverty and devolution*, London: IPPR/ESRC.

Regan, S. and Stanley, K. (2003) 'Work for disabled people: the Achilles' heel of Labour's welfare-to-work agenda?', *New Economy*, vol 10, no 1, pp 56-61.

Rosenblatt, E. and Rake, K. (2003) *Gender and poverty*, London: Fawcett Society.

Sanderson, I. (1998) 'Beyond performance measurement. Assessing value in local government', *Local Government Studies*, vol 24, no 4, pp 1-25.

SASC (Scottish Affairs Select Committee) (2000) *Poverty in Scotland, Session 1999-2000*, London: House of Commons.

Scott, G., Brown, U. and Toner, V. (2002) *Enlarging justice for all: Next steps for black and community development project*, Glasgow: Scottish Poverty Information Unit, Glasgow Caledonian University.

Scott, G., Innes, S. and Gillespie, M. (2003b) *Breaking barriers: Poverty, childcare and mothers' transitions to work*, Glasgow: Rosemount Lifelong Learning and Scottish Poverty Information Unit.

Scott, G., Frondigoun, E., Gillespie, M. and White, A. (2003a) *Making ends meet: An exploration of parent student poverty*, London: CPAG.

Scottish Executive (1999) *Social justice: A Scotland where everyone matters*, Edinburgh: Scottish Executive.

Scottish Executive (2001a) *Scotland's people: Results from the 1999 Scottish Household Survey: Volume 1: Annual Review. Revised income tables*, Edinburgh: Scottish Executive.

Scottish Executive (2001b) *The Scottish Household Survey, Bulletin 6*, Edinburgh: Scottish Executive.

Scottish Executive (2003a) *Social justice report*, Edinburgh: Scottish Executive.

Scottish Executive (2003b) *A partnership for a better Scotland: Partnership Agreement between the Scottish Labour Party and the Scottish Liberal Democrats*, Edinburgh: Scottish Executive.

Scottish Executive (2003c) *Scottish economic statistics*, Edinburgh: Scottish Executive National Statistics Publication.

Scottish Executive (2003d) *Closing the gap: Scottish budget for 2003-2006*, Edinburgh: Scottish Executive.

SEU (Social Exclusion Unit) (2004) *Tackling social exclusion: Taking stock and looking to the future – Emerging findings*, London: SEU.

Shaw, M., Dorling, D., Gordon, D. and Davey-Smith, G. (1999) *The widening gap: Health inequalities and policy in Britain*, Bristol: The Policy Press.

Spear, R., Defourney, J., Favreau, L. and Laville, J. (2001) *Tackling social exclusion in Europe: The contribution of the social economy*, London: Ashgate.

SPICE (Scottish Parliament Information Centre) (2001) *Employment, housing and poverty in rural areas*, Research note prepared for the Rural Affairs Committee, Edinburgh: SPICE.

Stewart, J. (2004) 'Scottish solutions to Scottish problems? Social welfare in Scotland since devolution', in N. Ellison, L. Bauld, and M. Powell (eds) *Social Policy Review 16: Analysis and debate in social policy 2004*, Bristol: The Policy Press/Social Policy Association, pp 29-32.

Timmins, N., IPPR, Social Market Foundation, Policy Exchange, Scottish Council Foundation and Institute of Welsh Affairs (2004) *Overcoming disadvantage: An agenda for the next 20 years*, York: Joseph Rowntree Foundation.

Townsend, P. (1979) *Poverty in the United Kingdom: A survey of household resources and standards of living*, London: Penguin Books and Allen Lane.

TUC (Trades Union Congress) (2002) *Half the world away: Making regional development work*, London: TUC.

Turok, I. (2003) *Competitive places, divided spaces? Urban change in central Scotland*, Swindon: ESRC.

UNICEF (2000) *Innocenti Report Card No 1: 'A league table of child poverty in rich nations'*, Florence: UNICEF Innocenti Research Centre.

Watson, F. and Williams, V. (2003) *Review of existing UK work on food and low-income initiatives: A report for the Food Standards Agency*, Brighton: Food Matters.

Williams, C. (ed) (2004) *Report of the Child Poverty Task Group*, Cardiff: WAG.

Williams, F. (2003) 'Rethinking care in social policy', Paper presented to the Annual Conference of the Finnish Social Policy Association, Helsinki, July.

Wincott, D. (2004) 'Devolution, social democracy and policy diversity in Britain: the case of childcare and early years policies: devolution in Practice II, Public policy differences within the UK', Seminar paper presented to ESRC Devolution and the Comparative Territorial Analysis of the Welfare State seminar, London: ESRC.

Wise Group (2004) *Annual Report* 2003, Glasgow: Wise Group.

Yeandle, S., Escott, K., Grant, L. and Batty, E. (2003) *Women and men talking about poverty*, Manchester: Equal Opportunities Commission.

FOUR

Women, inequalities and social policy

Ailsa McKay and Morag Gillespie

Women have a particular role to play in the development and delivery of welfare in any society. Historically, they have also looked to welfare as a way to redress some of the social and economic inequalities that attach to gender. It was widely expected that women would have an unprecedented voice and place in the construction of social policy in Scotland after devolution. This chapter explores what has happened and examines the impact that devolved policy has had on women and inequality. The issues covered include:

- a growing commitment to mainstreaming equal opportunities in the Parliament and Executive;
- the equal opportunities models currently active in policy development;
- the difference that women have made to the political institutions of a 'new' Scotland;
- the impact of devolved government on some aspects of women's lives, including work and education; and
- a comparison of the impact of women on process and policy in Scottish politics.

Introduction

In writing this chapter, we began by trying to answer the simple question: Why, in a book focused on social policy developments in the 'new' Scotland, should there be a chapter dedicated specifically to examining issues concerning women, inequalities and social policy? For us, there are two main reasons. The first general point lies in the importance of bringing the position of women into analysis of social policy. Women are the main recipients of the services delivered within the remit of social policy, are the main workers in delivery of services and are the main providers of private forms of care (Pascall, 1997). Furthermore, welfare, work and care are "at once primary spheres of life and fundamentally defining of the quality of social life" (Daly and Rake, 2003, p 3). The second point specific to Scotland is that, although women are better represented within the new political institutions than in the past, evidence relating to patterns of employment, rates of pay, the division of labour within households, levels of poverty, incidences of domestic violence and the gender composition of senior positions in both the workplace and public decision-making bodies all indicate a pattern of women's relative disadvantage similar to the UK as a whole. Thus, five years into the new Scottish political and economic environment:

> Inequality between women and men is both a widespread and persistent feature of contemporary Scottish society. Although there have been many great advances for women over the last century and a higher profile for equal opportunities in Scotland since the establishment of the Scottish Parliament and Scottish Executive, in general women today still have less access than men to income and other material resources, less time that is their own, less political power and have a 1 in 5 chance of experiencing domestic abuse during their lives. (Strategic Group on Women, 2003, p 6)

The rationale for incorporating a chapter on women and inequalities in a book exploring social policy in the new Scotland, therefore, is obvious. For us, any attempt at evaluating the impact on women of social policy in the new Scotland involves identifying why such an apparently 'gender aware' political process has not yet led to policy interventions yielding more gender equitable outcomes. The new political institutions have adopted an apparently more open, transparent and participatory approach to governance, made an explicit commitment to mainstreaming equality concerns and have a focus on policies in which the role of women is central or pivotal. All of this implies a more favourable framework for advancing the social and economic position of women in Scotland. We argue that the equalities agenda of the new institutions has indeed led to *transparent positive developments* in terms of explicit commitments to a strategic mainstreaming approach. Such commitments imply a complete overhaul of the policy-making process across the Scottish Executive's responsibilities:

> Mainstreaming aims to change organisational cultures so that an equalities perspective becomes an integral part.... This means that the Executive must make sure that equality issues are considered in the formulation, design and delivery of policy/legislation/services. This approach will make sure that equality is considered in the development of policy from the start and is not a 'bolt-on' at the end of the process. (Scottish Executive, 2000, pp 14-17)

However, such commitments have not yet been translated into specific policy interventions that could similarly be described as *transparent positive developments*. That is, any gains made in terms of reducing existing gender inequalities have been limited in actual social policy terms. Thus, there appears to be a significant gap between rhetoric and practice. For us, the near exclusive emphasis on transforming the *process* in line with a mainstreaming strategy is, as yet, failing to deliver in terms of actual *policy* initiatives.

The distinction between policy and process is a key first step in assessing the impact devolution has had on social policy developments with specific reference to women and inequalities. The existing evidence indicates that the two remain separate and attempts to *transform* the policy-making process in the new Scotland, consistent with a commitment to mainstreaming, remain constrained by an approach that continues to treat gender concerns within a 'liberal model of equal opportunities'. That is, the focus is on 'acting' upon inequalities as they are identified or arise rather than 'transforming' the processes and structures that create and sustain such inequalities. Whether this is by accident or design is a matter for further research. The point being made here is that the significant potential for change facilitated by the devolution process has not yet been realised with respect to promoting gender equality. However, the potential remains and the purpose of this chapter is to seek evidence of progress made to date in working towards such an ambitious goal through exploring three questions:

• Where are women located in the political institutions of a 'new Scotland', and have they made a difference to how the new institutions evolve and operate?
• What difference has policy at devolved level made to their lives?
• Can a distinctive social policy agenda with reference to women be identified in the 'new Scotland'?

The next section explores answers to the first two questions, identifying how women across Scotland have engaged in a positive way through influencing the structure and processes of the new institutions, drawing mainly upon the work of the Scottish Women's Budget Group. The development of this group and their activities to date provide a valuable case study of how one women's group, representative of a wide range of interests and organisations, can successfully engage with a newly-emerging political and economic environment. Their efforts in promoting a more gender responsive approach to the process of resource allocation within the 'new' Scotland indicate how women can make a significant impact in informing the way in which the new institutions go about their business.

The subsequent section will go on to consider the difference that the Scottish Parliament has made to women's lives. We outline different models of equal opportunities to provide a framework for examining how the new institutions perceive and subsequently interpret the concept of equality mainstreaming in constructing and delivering policy. We explore some key areas of social policy that fall within the devolved powers of the Scottish Parliament to assess the impact of the apparently favourable political framework on the socioeconomic position of women in Scotland and examine whether a distinctive social policy agenda is developing with reference to women.

We conclude that the mainstreaming agenda adopted within the context of the Scottish public policy-making process is constrained by an approach which is informed by a 'liberal model of equal opportunities', an approach that is viewed primarily as a mechanism for 'adding-on' gender concerns. For us, this presents as the main reason for lack of progress in policy-related areas in that the 'process' is failing to embrace the concept of 'building-in' implied by a more progressive approach to mainstreaming. We argue that, although significant developments have taken place, there has been a distinct lack of progress in filling the void between commitment and practice. Also, progress may not be sustainable in the longer term unless there is a marriage between process and policy in relation to gender equality. The journey has indeed begun but gender equality in Scotland is a long way off:

> The new gender settlement in the Scottish Parliament stands as both a sign of how far we have come and reminder of how far we still have to go. (Mackay, 2002a, p 284)

Women and the political institutions of a 'new Scotland': exploring the difference they have made

Since the election of May 2003, 39.5% of MSPs are women, an improvement on the 37.2% achieved in the first Scottish Parliament. A more significant statistic with reference to gender divisions in political life refers to the number of those MSPs serving as convenors on parliamentary committees. At the time of writing, women convene seven out of a possible 16 of those committees. Given the powerful role of the committees in the Scottish public policy process, this indicates the potential for positive action in ensuring that issues relating to the position of women in Scottish society feature prominently in high-level political debate. Indeed, research exploring the impact of the increased presence of women in the new Parliament in the first two years of operation found that women MSPs felt that they had successfully influenced the political agenda and that many male MSPs were either more willing to raise women's issues themselves, or had at least recognised the significance of a 'different perspective' (Mackay, 2002b).

Some women, at least within a political institutional context, appear to be in an advantageous position with reference to promoting a gender equality agenda. It is worth noting, however, that such a position did not occur in a vacuum but rather is representative of the culmination of concerted effort involving a range of individual women, women's groups and some political groups across Scotland in the years leading up to the devolution settlement. The women's movement in Scotland recognised the potential opportunities offered by a devolved government to promote issues relating to gender equality and subsequently engaged positively with the pro-devolution campaigns. Many of these women were committed feminists who were also well placed because of their senior positions in public bodies, universities, trade unions, and other aspects of public life, to access senior politicians and decision-makers. Brown (2001, p 223) argues that:

> ... this coming together of women ... has helped strengthen the campaign for a more democratic and woman-friendly Scottish Parliament. They have also been mobilised by their belief that a Scottish

parliament where half the members are women will be 'different' and will deliver not only a more representative and democratic system of government but also one which encourages the participation of women and others in the community and which delivers the type of policies that people in Scotland want.

It would appear, then, that in addition to campaigning for equal representation, the activities of the women's movement proved to be instrumental in shaping the new institutions with specific respect to the Scottish public policy-making process. Key to this was their role in informing the Consultative Steering Group (CSG) established by the Secretary of State for Scotland in November 1997 to bring together a range of views and to develop proposals for the practical operation and working methods of the new Parliament. The report of the CSG, which served as the blueprint for the shaping of the new Parliament, recommended adopting a model of governance where the concepts of sharing power, accountability, access, participation and equal opportunities would be paramount (CSG on the Scottish Parliament, 1998). The priority given to the promotion of equal opportunities can be directly attributed to the influence of both individual women and organisations representing Scottish women working together to secure a gender sensitive political environment in the 'new' Scotland in which they contributed to recommendations of the CSG that:

> there should be a standing committee on Equal Opportunities, that a mainstreaming approach should be adopted and an Equality Unit established in the Scottish Executive and that Parliament should operate in a 'family friendly' manner. (McDonald et al, 2001, p 238)

Equal opportunities are therefore to be mainstreamed into the work of the Parliament and through the demands of and scrutiny by the Parliament into the work of the Executive.

The favourable policy framework implied by a commitment to mainstreaming, combined with the increased presence of women at such a high political level, indicates real potential for promoting gender equality throughout the policy process and across the range of public policy interventions. Indeed, the new political structures and processes have established transparent mechanisms to ensure women's voices across Scotland continue to be heard. The Women in Scotland Consultative Forum existed between 1998 and 2003 to "provide a mechanism for women's organisations in Scotland to communicate their views to the government, to meet with Ministers, to consider specific policy areas of interest and to suggest priorities" (Breitenbach, 2003b, p 1). More recently, the Scottish Women's Convention, funded by the Executive, was set up in 2003 to facilitate better engagement between the Executive and women's organisations across Scotland (Scottish Executive Equality Unit, 2003). Furthermore, the work of the Equality Unit of the Scottish Executive and the Parliament's Equal

Opportunities Committee serves to ensure that gender concerns remain a strategic priority of the new institutions. This leads Mackay (2002a, p 284) to the conclusion that:

> The presence of women MSPs – and the concerns of ordinary women – as a normal and unremarkable part of the polity presents a significant challenge to cultural stereotypes which still constrain and disadvantage, and to the traditional imbalance of power and influence.

Thus, women in the 'new' Scotland are more visible at an institutional level, have more influence, and have been very successful in engaging with both the structures and processes associated with the dynamics of a new and challenging political environment. However, if the concerns of 'ordinary women' are to be addressed and changes made to the traditional imbalance of power, the actual impact of such positive developments with reference to the differences such have made to women's lives in Scotland should be considered. In assessing the impact of women's engagement with the policy process, the work of the Scottish Women's Budget Group (SWBG) presents as an interesting case study. However, a brief synopsis of their activities to date will also demonstrate that, in terms of impact, questions remain as to whether the focus on process will serve to illustrate further how women can embrace the opportunity for initiating change but will question whether the emphasis on 'process' has in essence subsumed the policy agenda.

The Scottish Women's Budget Group: a question of policy versus process

In a briefing note prepared for the Strategic Group on Women[1], Esther Brietenbach acknowledges the work of the SWBG[2] with specific reference to the mainstreaming approach adopted by the Scottish Executive. She identifies the work of the group as a 'policy initiative' in advancing gender equality and argues that it "does not yet provide concrete examples of gender-sensitive budgeting in terms of shifts in policy priorities, though it offers insights into how concerns about gender inequalities can be advanced" (Breitenbach, 2003a, p 7). Examining how the SWBG has successfully worked with both the Executive and the Parliament in promoting gender responsive budgeting will highlight how the concept of mainstreaming equality, as applied within a Scottish policy context, may be failing to deliver the desired outcomes in terms of addressing gender inequalities. That is, we believe that the constraining nature of the adopted approach to mainstreaming is serving to limit the capacity of the new institutions to translate policy commitments into practice.

The SWBG, established in May 2000, has worked at various levels to ensure that gender responsive budgeting became a mainstream feature of the Scottish public policy process. In progressing this agenda, a number of significant achievements are worth noting.

- The Scottish Executive's Equality Strategy, launched in November 2000, contains a commitment to put in place a framework for assessing the Scottish Budget with reference to equality issues.
- The Scottish Executive established an advisory group (Equality Proofing Budgets and Policy Advisory Group), which acts to raise awareness and to develop understanding of equality proofing budgets both within the Executive and throughout the wider policy-making community in Scotland. The SWBG are formally represented on this group.
- The Equality Unit commissioned research into the Scottish budgetary process to map the first ever budget process of the new administration and to identify necessary steps in progressing with a gender budget initiative in the new Scotland. The research has informed various Parliamentary debates on the equality impact of proposed spending plans.
- Members of SWBG have met with ministers and MSPs to raise awareness at the highest political level and to ensure continued political support for gender responsive budgeting in Scotland.
- Scottish Women's Budget Group members have also given evidence at various Parliamentary committees; arranged and hosted a seminar for MSPs focusing on key developments; and addressed a cross party meeting of women MSPs, clarifying issues surrounding the processes involved in gender impact analysis.

All of this activity demonstrates how a group of women acted collectively and embraced the opportunity presented by the devolution settlement to engage with the new institutions in attempts to promote a more gender equal Scotland. Furthermore, their work has attracted significant attention from an international audience interested in exploring how women can make a difference to the public policy-making processes, particularly in the area of national budgeting practices (McKay et al, 2002).

However, in evidence presented to the Equal Opportunities Committee about the Scottish Executive's annual spending plans for 2005-06 (Scottish Executive, 2004c), the SWBG expressed frustration about the slow pace of change in the budget process and the distinct lack of gender specific targets (SWBG, 2004). We argue that, despite the apparent progress with reference to promoting gender budgeting, the work of SWBG has failed to secure any significant gains in terms of more gender equitable outcomes. One explanation for this may be that, although there is an apparent agreement that equal opportunities policies are necessary, there is at the same time competing and different models of equal opportunities policies at work.

Identifying competing models: liberal versus mainstreaming approaches to equality

Acknowledging the different models of equal opportunities policies that currently coexist in Scotland, and how such approaches are being applied in practice, assists in assessing the progress that has been made towards mainstreaming gender:

> If institutional discrimination is the problem which denies equality of life chances for the diversity of citizens, then equal opportunities policies are the means of overcoming that problem. (Edwards, 2004, p 37)

Edwards identifies four models of equal opportunities. Two of the models are described as add-on approaches that ameliorate the problem, described by Jewson and Mason (1986) as liberal and radical: the liberal model "largely underpins equal opportunities legislation in the UK (and) seeks to institute equal treatment or fair rules as a general principle of equal opportunity" (Edwards, 2004, p 37) and involves limited positive action measures; in contrast, the radical model seeks equality of outcomes and promotes positive discrimination to ameliorate discrimination or disadvantage. However, more complex issues are involved than in the tensions between liberal and radical perspectives of equal opportunities (Cockburn, 1989) and both of these models fail to address the root causes of discrimination (Edwards, 2004, p 37). By the end of the 1980s, equal opportunities was "widely seen as a tool of management that has sanitised and contained the struggle for equality" and people were "casting around" for alternative approaches to resolve the major contradictions of the radical approach (Cockburn, 1989, pp 213, 217).

The other two models that Edwards identified involve strategies that aim to eliminate the problem through building in equality considerations. The managing diversity model generally relates to human resources practice in which there is an individual rather than a group focus that emphasises the business case rather than the broader principles of social justice (Wilson and Iles, 1999). By comparison, mainstreaming equality has been described as:

> a social justice-led approach to policy making in which equal opportunities principles, strategies and practices are integrated into the every day work of government and other public bodies.... As a process it tackles the structures in society which contribute to, or sustain, discrimination and disadvantage.... The application of a mainstreaming approach can avoid the adoption of policies and programmes which replicate discrimination and exacerbate existing inequalities. (Mackay and Bilton, 2001, pp 1-2)

Rees (1998, p 197) argues that "equal treatment legislation needs to continue alongside further development of positive action measures while the mainstreaming approach is developed". She also notes (1998, p 190) that "there can be long and short agendas simultaneously at play" in relation to mainstreaming equality. At its shortest, the agenda may involve

> new measures to minimise bias in procedures.... At its longest, its most ambitious and most progressive, it has to be recognised as being a project of *transformation for organisations*. (Cockburn, 1989, p 218)

The Scottish Executive's Equality strategy sets out clear principles that should apply across all the work of the Executive in adopting a strategy of mainstreaming equality, but describes it as complementary to "the traditional approaches to promoting equality, such as legislation and positive action" (Scottish Executive, 2000, p 17). This raises questions about where equality mainstreaming sits in the 'hierarchy' of models of equal opportunities in Scotland. Is a process of transformation taking place or is equality mainstreaming being used as an add-on or tool to strengthen existing liberal approaches? What difference is the Scottish Executive's strategy for equality mainstreaming making to women's lives? These questions lead on to consideration of policy implications and outcomes for women – is social policy in Scotland taking a new form and transforming the position of women as an equality mainstreaming agenda would suggest, or is the short agenda of minimising bias limiting the gains for women?

What difference has the Scottish Parliament made to women's lives?

Key areas of social policy relevant to women's position in Scotland remain reserved functions, the most significant being social security, employment and equal opportunities. However, areas of devolved responsibility, crucial in determining the wellbeing of women in Scotland, include local government (housing, social work, education), health, economic development, justice, Further and Higher Education and transport. The Scottish Executive have also highlighted that, despite equal opportunities being a reserved matter,

> In respect of *legislation*, all Scottish Executive sponsored draft Bills have to be accompanied by a policy memorandum which states what the impact of the Bill is expected to be on equal opportunities. The Scottish Executive expects that each new draft Scottish Executive Bill should be examined to see whether equality clauses are necessary in the legislation. (Scottish Executive, 2004a, p 63; emphasis in original)

Legislation and equal opportunities for women in the 'new' Scotland

There are examples of legislative clauses that address equality concerns, including:

- The requirement on local authorities to encourage equal opportunities and the observance of the equal opportunities requirements in the arrangements it makes to secure Best Value (Scottish Executive Finance and Central Services Department, 2004) is one such example that has led to guidance on contracts being developed.
- The 2001 Housing (Scotland) Act requires Scottish Ministers, local authorities and social landlords to act in a manner that encourages equal opportunities and observes equal opportunities requirements in implementing the provisions of the Act.
- New guidance on homelessness that takes account of the 2001 Housing (Scotland) Act and the 2003 Homelessness etc (Scotland) Act provides a reminder of the terms of the legislation in relation to equal opportunities and stresses the importance of training for homelessness officers in a range of issues including anti-discrimination. In relation to women's needs, some references are made to links, liaison with and support for organisations such as Women's Aid refuges, but little other guidance is given on considering women's needs in relation to homelessness except to stress that:

> particular attention should be paid to ensuring that the different experiences of homelessness and service requirements of people of differing age, family background, race, disability, gender, sexual orientation and belief are recognised. (Scottish Executive, 2004b, p 27)

Relevant research is vital for providing the evidence that informs practice for those implementing such legislation. A literature review of research on gender inequality in Scotland found very little work on gendered issues in housing, no research on the gender implications of changing patterns of housing tenure in Scotland and little recent research on any general aspect of gender and housing, (Innes, 2002). This suggests there is a limited evidence base on which to measure progress in relation to women's housing needs and issues.

This is particularly worrying given the evidence of the link between domestic abuse and housing (Innes, 2002, para 183), and the focus the Executive has placed on the issue of domestic violence in Scotland. With reference to this focus, Scottish Women's Aid (2003, p 3) welcome the support but highlight that the statistics remain alarming:

> Every week in the UK at least two women are murdered by their male partner. 1 in 5 women will experience mental, physical and/or

sexual abuse at some time in their lives, with 90% of children in the same or next room while the abuse takes place.

The Executive's current approach to issues of domestic abuse, community safety and safety on public transport has been applauded by the Strategic Group on Women as excellent work. Furthermore, they consider that recognition of the gendered nature of the majority of domestic abuse "has been an important step in addressing the issue in Scotland" (Strategic Group on Women, 2003, p 53). However, they go on to highlight that further work is required to ensure that the needs of different groups of women are being met, including disabled women, older women, women from minority ethnic communities, women in rural areas and those in same sex relationships (Strategic Group on Women, 2003, p 54). We argue that the focus on domestic abuse, which fails to adequately take account of the whole range of policy areas this issue is relevant to, is one example of the 'short' agenda on equal opportunities. That is, the Executive appears to be addressing the disadvantaged position of women through *new measures*.

A review of Women and Transport by Reid Howie Associates (2000) highlighted a series of transport issues and needs for women and different groups of women. Addressing such issues through gender aware policy development and implementation would require a process of transformation and would be consistent with the Scottish Executive's position in relation to equality mainstreaming. The review recommended that the Scottish Executive provide a checklist for public transport providers that would serve in assessing the gender sensitivity of their specific services. A Women and Transport Guidance and Checklist was produced in 2002 as part of the Scottish Executive's commitment to promoting social inclusion in Scotland. A recent survey on bus passenger satisfaction reinforces concerns about public transport among women who have lower levels of satisfaction with bus services compared with men in general and particularly in relation to value for money (Colin Buchanan and Partners, 2004). In contrast, a review of transport provision for disabled people did not explore gender differences or specific issues relating to disabled women and transport (Reid Howie Associates, 2004). Most disappointing, however, is the recent White Paper on transport in Scotland (Scottish Executive, 2004d). Although there is an implicit recognition that public transport and related safety issues are more important to women, the White Paper does not go on to identify any specific initiatives or measures to address such concerns. Neither is there any evidence of attempts to put in place a formal mechanism for ensuring the implementation of the Guidance and Checklist.

The inclusion in legislation of equal opportunities clauses and the guidance and checklists on issues such as homelessness and women and transport are positive developments in terms of promoting gender equality within a Scottish public policy context. However, it is not clear whether, and to what extent, such measures are affecting access to, and delivery of, services that are sensitive to, and address the needs of, women and particular groups of women. The need for research and evaluation of the impact of policies remains important, not least for assessing whether approaches such as equal opportunities clauses, guidance and checklists make a difference or whether they need to be backed up by other measures and activities in order to effect *transformation*.

Work and women's poverty

Although key aspects of the welfare to work agenda in the UK are reserved to Westminster, the Scottish Parliament has reaffirmed the Labour government's commitment to eradicate child poverty in 20 years (Brown et al, 2002, p 158). There is a shared view that the best way to tackle poverty is through a combination of measures intended to assist individuals in their attempts at accessing the formal labour market (HM Treasury, 1998; Scottish Executive, 1999). The welfare-to-work agenda is therefore a key area of common purpose between the UK and Scottish parliaments. The unemployment and poverty traps have been recognised and addressed through the 'making work pay' approach (Dean and Shah, 2002; Scott, 2002; Gillespie and Scott, 2004), which at a UK level includes measures such as:

- the introduction of a modest national minimum wage;
- increased child benefits;
- expansion of New Deal programmes to assist people in (re)entering the labour market including a specific programme tailored for the needs of lone parents; and
- the introduction of tax credits – means-tested benefits for people in low-paid work that included financial support for certain childcare costs and the costs of disability.

At both a Scottish and UK level, there have been strategies on childcare and work/life balance employment initiatives that suggest issues highlighted by women have been recognised. In Scotland, there have also been a series of policies aimed specifically at addressing employment. These include job creation and training schemes, targeting both specific geographical areas and particular client groups (Scottish Executive, 2002), as well as measures intended to improve access to Further and Higher Education for disadvantaged groups including women returning to the labour market.

Despite these initiatives, significant barriers remain for women seeking to earn their way out of poverty, including the nature of the jobs women do, the wages they can expect and their caring roles. The gendered nature of poverty is well documented in the literature (see, for example, Glendinning and Millar, 1992). Women experience poverty in different ways from men, and throughout the life course they are at a greater risk of becoming poor than their male counterparts. This is attributed to a combination of social and economic factors, not least of which is their relative disadvantaged position in the labour market. In Scotland, women constitute 47% of the labour market (EOC, 2004). However, both horizontal and vertical segregation persist in employment patterns in Scotland and 'women's work' tends to be "lower-status and less well paid, reflecting the lower value placed on caring work" (Mackay, 2002a, p 279). Part-time work is particularly vulnerable to low pay and women continue to account for the vast majority of part-time workers in Scotland (EOC, 2004). Earnings for full-time women continue to lag behind those of men, with average hourly earnings 16% lower – and for women working part time, they are 37% lower than for men working full time (EOC, 2004).

In relation to women's wages, the Scottish Executive has recognised the gendered nature of work and earnings in Scotland and is involved in a range of initiatives that aim to improve the position of women. This has included measures to address the earnings gap such as the Close the Gap campaign that encourages employers to carry out pay reviews, using the EOC's equal pay review kits (Scottish Executive, 2004a, p 12). In terms of the Scottish Executive's own pay structures, an equal pay review found:

> no major discrimination. Although the review found gaps existed between men and women in each pay range, these gaps could be explained by combinations of different factors which are known to affect salary (for example, variations in performance appraisal markings and length of service). (Scottish Executive, 2004a, p 9)

In contrast to the Scottish equal pay review, the outcome of an equal pay review at the Welsh Assembly had a much more significant impact:

> the pay practices and structures of the legislature being reformed in a three year deal to address the gender pay gap that added a further 22.3% (£23 million) on to the Assembly's pay bill. Further associated measures were taken to ensure that the salaries of women workers taking maternity leave or staff taking career breaks do not fall behind. (Chaney, 2004, p 69)

There are targets set to increase the percentage of women in senior positions in the Scottish Executive's workforce by 2005. However, while the Annual Evaluation Report (Scottish Executive, 2004c, pp 90-1) indicates that progress is being made towards these targets, it is not clear whether issues such as the potential for discrimination relating to performance appraisal markings and factors affecting length of service are to be considered and addressed.

Not all women in paid work, nor even all women working in the public sector, have benefited from the greater focus on equalities concerns in relation to paid work. Nursery nurses are one example of a group of workers who do not yet share the benefits. Childcare has been an important factor in the government's welfare to work strategy, yet childcare work is often low paid and insecure, reflecting its low status (Scott et al, 2002; Fergusson, 2004; Mooney and McCafferty, 2005). Arising from their research among local authority nursery nurses who were on strike in 2004, Mooney and McCafferty argue that the National Childcare Strategy is notable "for completely failing" to address such matters as the pay and conditions of childcare workers. They describe the process as contradictory, at once seeking greater skills and qualifications but for less reward. They also identify that, while public sector provision is more regulated, there is a more "volatile and secondary labour market" with poorer pay and conditions of employment. In addition, Scott et al (2002, p 241) question the sustainability of the employment created by child care and "the extent to which current developments that are driven by economic considerations enhance or limit social regeneration at a local level". There are, then, few indications of a transformation taking place for childcare workers in that care work remains low paid and the sector continues to be dominated by women. Policy responses continue to treat care more as "a constraint on labour supply" (Daly and Rake, 2003, p 168) than act as measures to address gender inequality and, by creating low paid and insecure work, risk adding to rather than redressing existing gender inequalities in relation to employment.

Care work is one example of occupational segregation that contributes to the pay deficit for women. The Modern Apprenticeship (MA) scheme in Scotland is one area of devolved responsibility that has the potential to redress this by limiting occupational segregation and thus contributing to reducing the gender pay gap. Introduced in 1995, MAs place young people with an employer, enabling them to work towards a vocational qualification while being paid a wage (Thomson et al, 2004). MAs have shown some success in improving employment and skills levels among young people. A Scottish Executive study (SQW Ltd, 2001) showed that there were significant differences in participation in apprenticeships along traditional (mainly male) and non-traditional (mainly female) lines and that there were differences in the completion rates of apprenticeships with lower completion rates in non-traditional apprenticeships. Despite identifying these issues, however, "gender was not presented as an important issue by this review" (Thomson et al, 2004, p 15). The failure to draw out the gender implications in the review was identified at the time as a missed opportunity (Engender Women's Budget Group, 2002). This is particularly relevant when considering the increasing concern with regard to overall skills shortages in Scotland. By 'missing' the gender opportunity, the MA scheme is thus failing to realise its full potential in terms of both participants and the Scottish economy.

Thomson et al (2004) identify a range of factors that suggest there are sufficient differences in the operation of modern apprenticeships in Scotland compared to England and Wales. Among the factors identified is that more resources "continue to be put into the traditional frameworks that remain highly gender segregated and, in some occupations, exclusively male" (Thomson et al, 2004, p 27) and there is a lack of formal equal opportunities requirements in Scotland in contrast to the explicit equal opportunities remit in England and Wales that has existed since 1997. This suggested that equality considerations might be more entrenched in the activities of providers in England and Wales than in Scotland. However, further research on gender segregation in MAs found that the problems relating to gender segregation were almost identical (EOC Scotland, 2004).

Lone parents' access to education and training

Women as lone parents are particularly vulnerable to poverty. The lack of adequate and affordable childcare acts in creating a significant barrier for lone parents in their attempts to access the formal labour market. In recognition of the particular problems experienced by lone parents in making the transition from benefits to work, they have been targeted in welfare-to-work initiatives. At UK level, the New Deal for Lone Parents (NDLP) was introduced in 1998 and various measures have been initiated by the Scottish Executive to support access to education. However, paid work may be viewed as the main route out of poverty for lone parents, but it is no guarantee against being poor. For example, there is evidence that, in the NDLP, some lone parents go through the programme several times, moving in and out of work (Evans et al, 2003). As well as implying a lack of sustainable and financially worthwhile employment or training opportunities, this cycle in and out of work has been linked to the severe poverty experienced by children in some families (Adelman et al, 2003). Improving skills and qualifications are viewed as one way of reducing the chances of lone parents being caught up in this cycle of poverty. However, in accessing formal education, lone parents face the same barriers they come against when attempting to enter paid employment. That is, care responsibilities and the lack of fit between care needs and the availability and affordability of care remain central concerns for lone parents (Innes and Scott, 2002; Kasparova et al, 2003).

There is some evidence of the impact of measures in Scotland to help lone parents. Financial support has been made available for students from disadvantaged groups and help with childcare costs, particularly for lone parents, through waiving fees, access to free childcare for some further education students and a childcare grant for some higher education students (Scottish Executive, 2002, p 16). These measures acknowledge that the cost of childcare is a significant barrier for parents trying to access further or higher education as a route to improving skills and employability. An evaluation of the first two years of the Scottish Executive's childcare support measures found that access to free childcare in Further Education and the Lone Parent Childcare Grant of £1,000 for Higher Education students had helped some lone parents move into education. However, the cost of 'formal' childcare for an under-five for one academic year was estimated to be a minimum of £1,900. This meant that, for a lone parent student wishing to progress to a Higher Education course, the potential reduction in childcare support can be a major disincentive, compounded by the loss of benefits suffered on enrolling for full-time higher education study (Ballantyne et al, 2003, p 12). They also found that debt was a cause of stress and concern, consistent with other studies that show lone parent students risk building up debt and experiencing financial difficulties while studying and these financial difficulties largely derive from their responsibility for dependent children (Callender and Kemp, 2001; Callender, 2003; Scott et al, 2003). For a group of women in one study, "student loans, even with grants for childcare costs, were not a realistic prospect" (Gillespie et al, 2003, p 44). Although there are indications that more lone parents are accessing higher education (SPICE, 2001), the women participating in that study found barriers for them that went beyond childcare provision and grants:

> Part-time courses were an unhappy compromise that was financially driven because benefits are not paid during full-time higher education courses. Apart from the childcare measures, there was limited evidence identified of colleges taking steps, including flexibility in courses, to address other barriers to further education for women returners to the labour market. (Gillespie et al, 2003, pp 44)

It would appear from the evidence presented then that the devolution settlement brought with it a favourable setting for influencing a more gender aware and sensitive approach to the public policy process in the 'new' Scotland. However, an examination of select key areas of social policy has demonstrated that to date that 'favourable framework' is failing to translate into actual policy shifts that serve to have a positive impact in promoting a more gender equitable Scotland. In exploring the difference the Scottish Parliament has made to women's lives, we conclude that, at least in the short term, the explicit commitment to equality mainstreaming is not yet in practice securing the *transformation* implied by such a commitment. Rather, the evidence indicates that the impact of policy interventions in the 'new' Scotland, specifically aimed at promoting gender equality and improving the position of *all* women in Scotland, is limited. Some gains have been made in minimising bias and promoting a more gender sensitive approach to policy making, but the difference such has made to women's lives is much less apparent.

Conclusion: in the 'new' Scotland, is there a distinctive social policy agenda with reference to women?

This chapter began by looking at where women are located in the 'new Scotland' and discussed how women have made a difference to the way that the new institutions evolve and operate. The greater presence of women in the Parliament and as conveners of parliamentary committees, the incorporation of equal opportunities as a founding principle of the Parliament and the adoption of an equality mainstreaming strategy, all imply a favourable framework for promoting and progressing gender equality.

Women have embraced the opportunity for engaging with the new institutions to initiate change. The activities and achievements of the SWBG have been identified as prime examples of how women have made a difference in influencing the policy strategies of the new institutions. The Scottish Executive's Draft Budget 2004-05 (2004c) highlights equality considerations, and includes an equality statement in the introduction and each of the portfolio chapters. This represents progress towards equality proofing and is representative of positive progress in terms of processes and reinforcing the commitment to mainstreaming equality. However, such positive developments with reference to physical presence and the powers of engagement also need to make a difference to women's lives in Scotland.

By examining a number of policy areas we did not identify specific outcomes that demonstrated how the new approach to policy making, implied by the commitment to mainstreaming, was *transforming* the lives of women working and living in Scotland. That is, although the policy areas discussed were by no means comprehensive, those selected were identified as *key* in terms of impacting on the welfare of Scottish women. Little evidence was found of actual policy initiatives that could claim success with reference to improving the overall economic and social position of all women in Scotland. Furthermore, unacceptable gender inequalities remain an inherent feature of Scottish society, thus indicating that *transformation* remains a theoretical concept yet to be translated into practice.

In saying that, we also believe that all is not bleak. There are positive developments that can be cited such as consultation with women's organisations, some ground-breaking work on domestic abuse, and initiatives on childcare. In relation to the Scottish Executive's own staffing and pay structures, there is a positive action approach to increasing the proportion of women in senior positions, although there is less evidence of consideration being given to the wider range of factors that have implications for women's earnings in the organisation. The example discussed of support with childcare costs for lone parents in further and higher education indicates that there is a sense of equality in general and gender concerns in particular being addressed. In transport and housing, the specific clauses about fair or equal treatment and guidance and checklists highlight the extent to which many areas of policy remain gender blind in practice. Such initiatives serve as useful tools in promoting a more gender aware approach to the process from design through to implementation, evaluation and monitoring.

However, the case of the nursery nurses discussed above reinforces the view that improvements in working conditions are not universal for public sector workers. Those delivering care for children have been put under pressure by a policy focus on quality that has not been recognised in the remuneration of workers. It also acts as a reminder that policies intended to reduce the barriers and challenges for some can impact negatively on other groups. Furthermore in many key areas, the gender dimension of policy is not yet a serious consideration. Evidence in support of this claim was presented in discussing the work of the SWBG and highlighting the outcomes associated with the operation of the MA scheme. There remain a lack of gender-specific targets in spending plans and, in the case of modern apprenticeships, opportunities were missed that could take account of, and contributed to addressing, the occupational segregation that remains stubbornly resistant to change in Scotland.

We have argued that the specific policy initiatives examined can be accurately described as 'add-ons' that have responded to some specific concerns for women but have not yet significantly changed, far less transformed, key policy areas. Without pressure for change and indicators of progress, there is a risk that initiatives such as checklists and guidance notes, which are important to an equality mainstreaming approach, may remain the main outcome. The lack of follow-through in subsequent research and policy documents is a key concern that suggests women in Scotland have "the shopping list but not the groceries"[3]. There is a risk that, unless addressed differently, further consultation with women and women's groups may serve only to increase the size and content of the shopping list.

Is a distinctive social policy agenda with reference to women developing in Scotland? The commitment to mainstreaming equality, the increased participation of women both within the Parliament and Executive and the greater engagement of some groups of women with the Scottish policy process, all suggest that a distinctive approach is developing in Scotland. In fact, the Women and Equality Unit in the UK government (2003, p 68) view the strong commitment to mainstreaming in the devolved administrations as providing "a useful example for the UK Government to follow". However, they outline an approach of 'Policy Appraisal for Equal Treatment' guidelines on mainstreaming for all government departments, developed by the Women's Unit (Cabinet Office) in 1997, that has parallels with the guidance and checklists being developed in Scotland. This suggests that, in Scotland at least, the approach to implementation has not diverged significantly from that of the UK government.

In examining the approach to social policy developing in the 'new' Scotland, with specific reference to the promotion of gender equality, we are thus left with an overall impression that the implementation of policy remains grounded in a liberal model of equal opportunities. This is closely tied to the UK approach in which, arguably, while some groups of women have gained, many policies have impacted negatively on other groups of women. While the commitment to an equality mainstreaming agenda has been made explicit, the lack of tangible positive outcomes within an actual policy context follows from a continued practice of addressing gender issues as 'add-ons'. The more systematic and appropriate approach would involve a framework that acknowledges and acts on the impact of gender difference throughout all stages of the policy process. The implementation of an equality mainstreaming approach remains more of a policy ideal that is not yet well evidenced in policy implementation and transparency of outcomes for women in Scotland.

The reasons for the apparent failure to deliver may be attributable to the lack of political will to make difficult choices or it may be that it is simply too early to make such judgements given the short lifespan of the new institutions. These questions are worthy of further research. However, a chasm is emerging between process and policy in terms of promoting gender equality and there are dangers in such a separation continuing in the longer term. There are also structural concerns to be addressed. As the book's Introduction comments, Scotland continues to be divided by gender, but also by the interaction of gender with other dimensions such as class, race, age and disability. There is, however, little research that truly examines cross-cutting dimensions of inequality.

Lovenduski and Randall (1993) comment in their analysis of feminist politics that, "Where feminists have attempted entry on their own terms they have sometimes been able to affect the rules of the game" (p 174). The rules of engagement may indeed have shifted in the 'new' Scotland but it seems that, to date, women are not winning through. The emphasis on process has been at the expense of policy outcomes for women. While process and policy should not be viewed as distinct with reference to women, inequalities and social policy in the 'new' Scotland, the time has come to act on commitments. Women have made a difference in how the 'new' Scotland operates, but as yet the potential for the new Scotland to make a positive difference for women remains largely unfulfilled.

Notes

[1] This group was appointed by the Minister for Social Justice, Margaret Curran, in January 2003 to identify the issues faced by women in Scotland and to suggest an agenda for action for the next Scottish Executive. It was a 'short life' group, bringing together a number of women with experience in a range of sectors and interests, whose aim was to "recommend actions to improve the lives of women in Scotland and which promote and achieve equality between women and men" (Strategic Group on Women, 2003, p 17).

[2] The Scottish Women's Budget Group (SWBG), formally known as Engender Women's Budget Group was established in May 2000 with the overall aim of promoting gender responsive budgeting within a Scottish public policy context.

[3] Personal communication with John Veit-Wilson and one of the authors at the Annual Social Policy Association Conference, 2004. The quote is attributed to John Veit-Wilson and is reproduced with his kind permission.

On the web ...

The Equal Opportunities Commission (www.eoc.org.uk) has a range of publications and fact sheets that are relevant to gender mainstreaming and good links to other sites.

Oxfam GB has resources and publications on gender equality (www.oxfamgb.org/ukpp/resources/index.htm#gender).

> The National Development Plan (NDP) Gender Equality Unit in Ireland
> has a gender proofing handbook and other useful resources at
> www.ndpgenderequality.ie/publications/publications_01.html
> The Scottish Executive have a Mainstreaming Equality Toolkit
> (Researchers Guide) available at www.scotland.gov.uk/
> They also have links to a range of resources and sites:
> www.scotland.gov.uk/library5/social/lfel-00.asp.
> The Commonwealth Secretariat (www.thecommonwealth.org/gender) has
> a series of guides on gender mainstreaming.
> The Women and Equality Unit supports the Ministers for Women in the
> UK who are responsible for promoting and realising the benefits of diversity
> in the economy and more widely. They develop policies relating to gender
> equality and ensure that work on equality across government as a whole
> is coordinated. They have a range of publications;
> see www.womenandequalityunit.gov.uk/research/index.htm

References

Adelman, L., Middleton, S. and Ashworth, K. (2003) *Britain's poorest children: Severe and persistent poverty and social exclusion*, London: Save the Children.

Audit Scotland (2001) *A good start: Commissioning pre school education*, Edinburgh: Accounts Commission.

Ballantyne, F., Hendry, C. and Leishman, R. (2003) *Impact of childcare support for lone parent students*, Edinburgh: Scottish Executive.

Breitenbach, E. (2003a) *Summary and discussion of research reviews on women's and gender issues in Scotland*, Briefing Note for the Strategic Group on Women, Edinburgh: Scottish Executive, June.

Breitenbach, E. (2003b) *Women in Scotland Consultative Forum*, Briefing Note for the Strategic Group on Women, Edinburgh: Scottish Executive, June.

Brown, A. (2001) 'Deepening democracy: women and the Scottish Parliament', in E. Breitenbach and F. Mackay (eds) *Women and contemporary Scottish politics*, Edinburgh: Polygon.

Brown, U., Scott, G., Mooney, G. and Duncan, B. (eds) (2002) *Poverty in Scotland 2002: People, places and policies*, London: CPAG.

Callender, C. (2003) *Attitudes towards debt: School leavers and FE students' attitudes towards debt and their impact on participation in higher education*, London: Universities UK.

Callender, C. and Kemp, M. (2001) *Changing student finance: Income expenditure and the take-up of student loans among full and part-time Higher Education students in 1998/9*, Research report RRZ13, London: DfEE.

Chaney, P. (2004) 'The post-devolution equality agenda: the case of the Welsh Assembly's statutory duty to promote equality of opportunity', *Policy & Politics*, vol 32, no 1, pp 63-77.

Cockburn, C. (1989) 'Equal opportunities: the short and long agenda', *Industrial Relations Journal*, Autumn, pp 213-25.

Cohen, B., Moss, P., Petrie, P. and Wallace, J. (2004) A *new deal for children? Reforming education and care in England, Scotland and Sweden*, Bristol: The Policy Press.

Colin Buchanan and Partners (2004) *Bus Passenger Satisfaction Survey: Online*, Edinburgh: Scottish Executive Social Research (www.scotland.gov.uk/library5/transport/bpss.pdf).

Consultative Steering Group on the Scottish Parliament (1998) *Shaping Scotland's Parliament*, Edinburgh: Scottish Office.

Daly, M. and Rake, K. (2003) *Gender and the welfare state*, Cambridge: Polity Press.

Dean, H. and Shah, A. (2002) 'Insecure families and low-paying labour markets: comments on the British experience', *Journal of Social Policy*, vol 31, January, pp 61-80.

Edwards, J. (2004) 'Mainstreaming equality in Wales: the case of the national Assembly building', *Policy & Politics*, vol 32, no 1, pp 33-48.

EOC (Equal Opportunities Commission) (2004) *Facts about women and men in Scotland, 2004*, Glasgow: EOC.

EOC Scotland (2004) *Occupational segregation, gender equality and the Modern Apprenticeships scheme in Scotland* (Report of Phase 1 of the EOC's investigation into gender segregation and modern apprenticeships in Scotland), Glasgow: EOC.

Evans, M., Eyre, J., Millar, J. and Sarre, S. (2003) *New Deal for Lone Parents: Second synthesis report of the national evaluation*, Leeds: Corporate Document Services.

EWBG (Engender Women's Budget Group) (2002) *Accounting for gender: A response to Annual Expenditure Report Of The Scottish Executive: The Scottish Budget 2003-4*, Edinburgh: EWBG (now Scottish Women's Budget Group).

Fergusson, R. (2004) 'Remaking the relations of work and welfare', in G. Mooney (ed) *Work: Personal lives and social policy*, Bristol: The Policy Press, pp 110-44.

Gillespie, M. and Scott, G. (2004) *Advice services and transitions to work: A literature review*, Glasgow: Scottish Poverty Information Unit.

Gillespie, M., Scott, G. and Lindsay, C. (2003) *Women, poverty and transitions to work* (Research Report 2, Rosemount Lifelong Learning), Glasgow: Scottish Poverty Information Unit.

Glendinning, C. and Millar, J. (eds) (1992) *Women and poverty in Britain: The 1990s*, Hemel Hempstead: Harvester Wheatsheaf.

HM Treasury (1998) *The modernisation of Britain's tax and benefits system. Number three: The Working Families Tax Credit and work incentives*, London: HM Treasury.

Innes, S. (2002) *Literature review of research on gender inequality in Scotland*, Edinburgh: Centre for Research on Families and Relationships, University of Edinburgh.

Innes, S. and Scott, G. (2002) *Families, care and women's transition to paid work*, (Research Report 1, Rosemount Lifelong Learning), Glasgow: Scottish Poverty Information Unit.

Jewson, N. and Mason, D. (1986) 'The theory and practice of equal opportunities policies: liberal and radical approaches', *Sociological Review*, vol 34, no 2, pp 307-34.

Kasparova, D., Marsh, A., Vegeris, S. and Perry, J. (2003) *Families and children 2001: Work and childcare*, Research Report 191, Leeds: Corporate Document Services.

Lovenduski, J. and Randall, V. (1993) *Contemporary feminist politics: Women and power in Britain*, Oxford: Oxford University Press.

Mackay, F. (2002a) 'A slow revolution? Gender relations in contemporary Scotland', in G. Hassan and C. Warhurst (eds) *Anatomy of the new Scotland: Power, influence and change*, Edinburgh and London: Mainstream Publishing.

Mackay, F. (2002b) 'Women in the Scottish Parliament: making a difference?', *Towards Equality: Magazine of the Fawcett Society*, September.

Mackay, F. and Bilton, K. (2001) *Equality proofing procedures in drafting legislation: International comparisons*, Edinburgh: Governance of Scotland Forum.

McDonald, R. with Alexander, M. and Sutherland, L. (2001) 'Networking for equality and a Scottish Parliament: the Women's Co-ordination Group and Organisational Alliances', in E. Breitenbach and F. Mackay (eds) *Women and contemporary Scottish politics*, Edinburgh: Polygon, pp 231-40.

McKay, A., Fitzgerald, R., O'Hagan, A. and Gillespie, M. (2002) 'Scotland: using political change to advance gender concerns' in D. Budlender and G. Hewitt (eds) *Gender budgets make more cents: Country studies and good practice*, London: Commonwealth Secretariat, pp 133-51.

Mooney, G. and McCafferty, T. (2005) '"Only looking after the weans"? The Scottish nursery nurses strike, 2004', *Critical Social Policy*, vol 25, no 2, pp 223-39.

Pascall, G. (1997) *Social policy: A new feminist analysis*, Oxford: Oxford University Press.

Rees, T. (1998) *Mainstreaming equality in the European Union*, London: Routledge.

Reid Howie Associates (2000) *Women and transport: Moving forward*, Edinburgh: Scottish Executive (www.scotland.gov.uk/cru/kd01/blue/transport-00.htm).

Reid Howie Associates (2004) *Transport provision for disabled people in Scotland: Progress since 1998. Online*, Edinburgh: Scottish Executive (www.scotland.gov.uk/library5/transport/tptd.pdf).

Scott, G. (2002) 'Social policy and family poverty', in U. Brown, G. Scott, G. Mooney and B. Duncan (eds) *Poverty in Scotland: People, places and policy*, London: CPAG.

Scott, G., Brown, U. and Campbell, J. (2002) 'Child care, social inclusion and urban regeneration', *Critical Social Policy*, vol 22, no 2, pp 226-46.

Scott, G., Frondigoun, E., Gillespie, M. and White, A. (2003) *Making ends meet: An exploration of parent student poverty, family finances and institutional support*, Glasgow: Child Poverty Action Group in Scotland.

Scottish Executive (1999) *Social justice ... A Scotland where everyone matters*, Edinburgh: Scottish Executive.

Scottish Executive (2000) *Equality strategy:Working together for equality*, November, Edinburgh: Scottish Executive.

Scottish Executive (2002) *Closing the opportunity gap: Scottish Budget for 2003-2006*, Edinburgh: Scottish Executive.

Scottish Executive (2004a) *Strategic Group on Women – 'Improving the position of women in Scotland: An agenda for action': The Scottish Executive's response to the group's recommendations*, Edinburgh: Scottish Executive.

Scottish Executive (2004b) *Code of guidance on homelessness*, May, Edinburgh: Scottish Executive (www.scotland.gov.uk/library5/housing/cogh.pdf).

Scottish Executive (2004c) *Annual Evaluation Report 2005-2006*, Edinburgh: Scottish Executive.

Scottish Executive (2004d) *Scotland's transport future*,Transport White Paper, June, Edinburgh: Scottish Executive (www.scotland.gov.uk/library5/transport/stfwp1.pdf, www.scotland.gov.uk/library5/transport/stfwp2.pdf, www.scotland.gov.uk/library5/transport/stfwp3.pdf).

Scottish Executive Equality Unit (2003) 'Scottish Women's Convention: would you like to be involved?', Letter to Women's Organisations in Scotland,August.

Scottish Executive Finance and Central Services Department (2000) *The Local Government in Scotland Act 2000: Guidance on contracts SECTION 52* (Consultation), (www.scotland.gov.uk/consultations/finance/teicd.pdf).

Scottish Womens Aid (2003) *Annual Report for 2001/2002*, Edinburgh: Scottish Women's Aid.

Scottish Women's Budget Group (2004) *Response to Equal Opportunities Committee request for views on the Scottish Executive's Annual Evaluation Report 2005/06*, Edinburgh: Scottish Women's Budget Group.

SPICE (Scottish Parliament Information Centre) (2001) *Childcare support in Further and Higher Education*, Research Note For the Enterprise and Lifelong Learning Committee, RN 01/92, Edinburgh: SPICE.

SQW Ltd (2001) *Review of Modern Apprenticeships in Scotland*, Edinburgh: Scottish Executive Central Research Unit.

Strategic Group on Women (2003) *Improving the position of women in Scotland:An agenda for action*, Edinburgh: Scottish Executive.

Thomson, E., McKay, A. and Gillespie, M. (2004) *Modern Apprenticeships and gender-based occupational segregation in Scotland: A position paper*, Glasgow: EOC.

Wilson, E. and Iles, P. (1999) 'Managing diversity: an employment and service delivery challenge', *The International Journal of Public Sector Management*, vol 12, no 1, pp 27-48.

Women and Equality Unit (2003) *Delivering on gender equality: Supporting the PSA objective on gender equality 2003-2006*, London: DTI (www.womenandequalityunit.gov.uk/research/Delivering_on_Gender.pdf).

FIVE

An inclusive Scotland? The Scottish Executive and racial inequality

Philomena de Lima

This chapter considers how ethnicity, social inequalities and social exclusion are linked within the social structures of Scotland. The chapter also introduces the minority ethnic groups living in Scotland and outlines policies and mechanisms addressing racism, discrimination and racial inequality pre and post-devolution. The following issues are covered:

- *Scotland's minority ethnic groups:* demographic trends and policy implications, categorisation of ethnicity and changing identities.
- *Delivering racial equality in post-devolutionary Scotland:* structures, plans of the single Commission for Equality and Human Rights.
- *Social inclusion/exclusion:* policy discourses, change and continuity before and after devolution, participation in politics.
- *Immigration:* a reserved matter, population and migration trends, implications of an ageing and declining population in Scotland.

Introduction

There is widespread evidence which demonstrates that 'race', ethnicity and racism are significant factors in shaping the lives of minority ethnic groups in Scotland and the UK, making them more vulnerable to disproportionate levels of poverty, inequalities and racial harassment. The interaction of ethnicity with other forms of social divisions – class, age, gender, and faith – also results in complex cross-cutting divisions, identities and experiences. Hence, an understanding of the impact of racism on specific groups, and within specific social structures, is an essential element in any analysis of social divisions/social inequality, as well as an important prerequisite for devising appropriate social policy responses.

Concepts such as 'race', 'ethnicity' and 'racism', are highly contested, and although it is widely accepted that there is no scientific basis for 'race', the terms have continued to be perceived as an enduring dimension of social structures and cultural identity. The issue is not about whether 'race' exists or not, but rather that racialised frames of reference continue to exert influence on people's interactions and actions, with, at times, dire consequences. Increasingly, the employment of terms such as 'race' and 'racism' in policy and political discourses not only refer to the propagation of notions about biological race, but are also used interchangeably with 'ethnicity', emphasising cultural differences and expressions of inter-group conflicts/hostilities as well as ethnocentrism (Back and Solomos, 2003).

'Race', ethnicity and racism are dynamic concepts, difficult to pin down as they evolve and develop in response to changing political and policy discourses, impacting on groups and individuals in different ways. Consequently, it is critical that these concepts are analysed and located in specific historical, geographical, as well as socioeconomic, cultural and political contexts, taking into account the 'specificity of experience' – which for the purposes of this chapter is the Scottish devolutionary context – while also making appropriate links to the wider context, for example in this case England as well as the UK parliamentary context.

Given the highly-contested debates, the controversial nature of categorising and labelling groups as though they are homogenous has to be acknowledged (REAF, 2001). For the purposes of this chapter, the term 'minority ethnic' is adopted to refer to those people of African, Asian, Caribbean, Middle-Eastern and South American descent, people of mixed cultural or ethnic heritage and asylum seekers and refugees. While it is recognised that gypsy travellers and migrant workers are highly-discriminated groups, lack of space precludes the possibility of including them in this chapter. In addition, the prevalence of 'anti-English' sentiments does complicate the issue of racism in Scotland (and Wales), as does sectarianism. However, both these issues are beyond the scope of this chapter.

The issue of racism and discrimination is a wide and complex area. Having set the context, this chapter will provide an overview of Scotland's minority ethnic groups and some of the policy implications arising out of the 2001 Census. It will then move on to discuss three other policy issues:

- mechanisms established (and being proposed) for addressing racism and racial equality issues;
- the extent to which discourses and practices on social inclusion have addressed racism as an exclusionary factor; and
- the so-called 'demographic time bomb' and the need to recruit skilled labour in the context of Scotland.

This chapter will also attempt to highlight continuities and differences between pre and post-devolutionary Scotland as well as citing similarities and divergences in policy and practice in other parts of the UK, where appropriate. The chapter will conclude by identifying some of the recurrent themes that emerge and the implications for policy if racism is to be addressed, as well as highlighting the potential constraints in moving the policy agenda forward in Scotland.

———

The context

The growing prominence of immigration and racism in Scotland and the UK has been shaped by several developments and often contradictory discourses:

- the persistence of neoliberal policies (see Chapters One and Two of this book);
- the 2000 Race Relations (Amendment) Act;
- the emphasis on 'containment of the race relations problem', reflected in various restrictive immigration control policies since the 1960s (Law, 1996);
- the UK government's attempt to control the flow of asylum seekers and refugees;
- demographic trends which suggest an ageing and declining Scottish population and the need to recruit skilled labour to meet labour market shortages; and
- more recently, the debate on the need to do away with 'multiculturalism' while asserting a sense of 'Britishness'.

Research across Britain has consistently highlighted the vulnerability of minority ethnic groups to poverty, racial discrimination and harassment in a wide range of contexts (Hampton and Bain, 1995; Modood et al, 1997; Chahal and Julienne, 1999). At present, asylum seekers and refugees are undoubtedly the most 'demonised' group in public discourses, constantly being portrayed as "a drain on public welfare and other social resources and as posing a problem for social cohesion, they are portrayed as needing tight control on their freedom of movement ..." (Lewis, 2003, p 325). The relationship between state welfare and racism has been highlighted by a number of writers and is reflected in the various requirements and practices adopted in relation to minority ethnic groups to prove that they are 'deserving' (Law, 1996; Ahmed and Craig, 2003; Lewis, 2003).

Has devolved Scotland heralded changes with regard to policies, practices and discourses on 'race'? To what extent have 'race' and ethnicity been mainstreamed into policy discourses and practice? In contrast to England, where there have been some large-scale studies on minority ethnic groups (for example, Modood et al, 1997), an audit of research on minority ethnic groups in Scotland highlighted the lack of robust statistical information, a dearth of large scale studies and their limited geographical focus (Netto et al, 2001). In part, this neglect had been perpetuated through everyday discourse of 'Scotland being a nation of friendly, welcoming people' and racism portrayed as a predominantly 'English problem'. The origins of this discourse can be located in what McCrone (1996, pp 88-92) describes as the "powerful" and enduring "Scottish myth", reinforced by academics as well as "non-Scots", which portrays Scotland as a "more egalitarian society than England" and the Scots as inherently egalitarian.

Against this background, getting racism on the policy agenda has been problematic, as it undermines and challenges the egalitarian myth that underpins a great deal of Scottish political and policy discourses. Generally, policy responses have tended to either be dismissive that racism existed in Scotland, based on the assumption that the numbers were too small to have so called 'race problems', or assumed that the situation of Scottish minority ethnic groups were the same as in England and therefore did not warrant different policy responses. Miles and Dunlop (1986, p 119) attributed the neglect of racism in Scotland largely to the "absence of a racialization of the political process" in contrast to England and the dominance of the 'national question', where England continues to be the 'significant other'. However, they also recognised the potential for racism to come to the fore as support for Scottish nationalism waned in the late 1970s, Scotland faced a deep economic crisis and the British National Party (BNP) were beginning to develop a presence in cities, such as Glasgow and Dundee. So, who are Scotland's minority groups?

Scotland's minority ethnic groups

Minority ethnic groups: demographic trends

The 2001 Census is the first large-scale source of data available on minority ethnic groups in Scotland since the 1991 Census. The minority ethnic population comprised 7.9% of the total UK population, making up 2% of the population of both Scotland and Wales, 1% in Northern Ireland, as compared to 9% in England (ONS, 2003a, 2003b). Despite the variations in size and ethnic composition, the minority ethnic populations across the UK shared some similarities with regard, for example, to age distribution, patterns of ethnicity, settlement trends, economic activity rates, vulnerability to poverty and inequalities (for example in relation to access to services and employment). The Census data has also been important in highlighting that a simple 'black/white' divide is no longer meaningful in making sense of people's lives: ethnicity interacts with other factors, such as gender, age and social class, to shape experiences in a way that cannot be read off by focusing solely on ethnicity.

Drawing on an analysis of the 2001 Census undertaken by the Scottish Executive (2004a; see also GROS, 2003), the following are some of the main features of the Scottish minority ethnic population:

- While all local authority and Health Board areas in Scotland had recorded a presence of minority ethnic groups, 60% of minority ethnic people lived in Scotland's four largest cities, Glasgow, Edinburgh, Aberdeen and Dundee (Scottish Executive, 2004a, pp 24-7).
- The majority (70%) of the Scottish minority ethnic population were Asian. Pakistanis were the largest minority ethnic group, followed by the Chinese, Indians and those from 'Mixed Backgrounds' (Scottish Executive, 2004a, p 5).
- The age distribution among minority ethnic groups reveals a younger age profile than their 'White' counterparts. More than 20% of all minority ethnic groups, except the Caribbean group, were less than 16 years old, with the 'Mixed' group having the youngest age structure (Scottish Executive, 2004a, pp 6-7).

- At least 30% of Pakistani, Bangladeshis and African people were likely to live in overcrowded accommodation, in contrast to 12% of "White Scots" (Connections, 2004, p 5; Scottish Executive, 2004a, pp 20-3).
- Although African people, in general, were the most highly qualified and most likely to have degrees, there were variations in education qualifications across ethnic groups and age groups. In the 16-74 year age group, the Pakistanis were the least likely to have qualifications, followed by the Chinese and 'White' Scottish group (Scottish Executive, 2004a, pp 51-3).
- Minority ethnic groups were twice as likely to be unemployed than 'White' groups (Connections, 2004, p 5). However, Africans, Black Scottish and Other South Asians experienced the highest rates. There were also a much higher proportion of minority ethnic females of working age who had never worked. This was especially evident among the Asian groups, with Pakistani and Bangladeshi women more likely to be in this situation (Scottish Executive, 2004a, pp 37-8).
- While there were differences between minority ethnic groups in terms of sector of employment they tended to be concentrated in a fairly limited range of industries: Wholesale and Retail trade; Manufacturing; Health and Social Work; and Real Estate, Renting and Business Activities (Scottish Executive, 2004a, pp 42-3). The groups with the highest rate of self-employment were Pakistani, Chinese and Indian, with the lowest in the African group (2004a, p 38). In addition, approximately a quarter of the Indian, Pakistani and Chinese in employment worked 49+ hours per week, in contrast to 13% of "White Scots"(Connections, 2004, p 5)
- Home Office (2004, p 2) figures on asylum seekers and refugees reported a reduction of about 20% in the number of applications for asylum between January and April 2004 compared to the previous quarter. However, robust statistics on asylum seekers and refugees in Scotland are hard to come by. The Scottish Refugee Council (2003, cited in Charlaff et al, 2004, p 9) estimated that there were 10,000 refugees and asylum seekers living in Scotland, representing at least 50 different nationalities, the majority of whom were concentrated in Glasgow.

An audit of skills and aspirations revealed that, in general, refugees and asylum seekers were well qualified with a broad range of skills in 'trades and professions' and showing a high motivation to work and live in Scotland. However, those who were in paid work tended to be in jobs that "were not commensurate with their skills" (Charlaff et al, 2004, pp 6-7). While acknowledging good practice in working with asylum seekers and refugees at a local level, research has also highlighted the overwhelming negative images of these groups perpetuated by the media as well as discrimination and racism experienced by them on a daily basis (Netto et al, 2001; Barclay et al, 2003). Of course, asylum seekers are not the first groups in Scottish society to suffer from such negative representation, with both Irish and Italian immigrants in late 19th and 20th century Scotland suffering from racism, prejudice and negative stereotyping.

Policy implications rising from data

The Census data provides a useful basis for identifying relevant trends and patterns that are an important basis for policy making. For example, the youthfulness of the minority ethnic population does raise a series of policy questions for all agencies providing services for children and youth and which should be part of the debate on how these services evolve to adapt or mainstream the views of minority ethnic people as part of their core activities. However, there is also a need for further interrogation of the data and qualitative research to make it a more effective tool for policy making. For example, the Census showed a relatively high number of multiple Pakistani families living in the same household (Scottish Executive 2004a, pp 23, 33). To devise appropriate policy responses in this context, it is vital to have a more in-depth understanding of why this situation prevails (choice/lack of choice/other constraints) and what the preferences of the group itself are, before deciding on a strategy for housing this group.

While there are similarities in trends across minority ethnic groups (young age profile, settlement trends, and so on), the Census also highlights the importance of recognising the heterogeneity of minority ethnic groups in devising appropriate policy responses. For example, there are differences between groups in relation to issues such as educational qualifications and unemployment, as well as within groups, for example, gender differences in employment and age differences in qualifications. However, Scotland is no different from the rest of Britain and devolution has yet to make a real difference to policy formulation by 'mainstreaming' into the process the complex ways in which ethnicity interacts with other social factors.

Categorisation of ethnicity in the Census

One of the most contentious issues raised by the Census is the issue of ethnic categories, which has been characterised by highly polarised discourses in England as well as Scotland (Klug, 1999; REAF, 2001; Manwaring, 2002). Addressing the issue of ethnic categorisation is vital, not only for the development of disaggregated data on ethnicity for monitoring and evaluating the impact of policies, but also in developing appropriate policies to address the needs of specific groups and combating racism. In Scotland, the Race Equality Advisory Forum (REAF), provided the first opportunity for minority ethnic people to engage in a debate about the ethnic classifications adopted in the 2001 Census. For many people of African descent (and for groups such as gypsy travellers for whom no category existed) the inconsistent basis on which ethnic categories were defined meant a denial of their right to choose how they define themselves, thus reinforcing their exclusion and invisibility (see Gessesse, 2001, pp 13-14; REAF, 2001; Arshad, 2002, pp 12-13).

While the ethnic categories were not changed for the 2001 Census, it is difficult to envisage the engagement of minority ethnic people in such a debate before devolution. Following representations from the African and other communities, the General Register Office for Scotland (GROS) agreed to explore the possibility of presenting the Census outputs in a way that took into account the concerns expressed through REAF, while also agreeing that there was a need for further research (REAF, 2001; Scottish Executive, undated a). The concern with ethnic classifications is also mirrored at the UK level by the Office for National Statistics (ONS), which has highlighted the need to undertake further research to improve understanding of the issues involved in classifying ethnicity and to develop classifications that individuals feel they 'own' (ONS, 2001).

Changing identities

The discourses on ethnic classifications demonstrate the fluid and changing nature of identities and while there has been growing research which has sought to address identity and nationalism in a devolved context (for example, Jones, 2001; Bond and Rosie, 2002), minority ethnic group perspectives have largely been missing. Research on identity in England (Modood et al, 1997) and in Scotland reveals that minority ethnic people adopt multiple identities:

> Pakistanis find it easy to identify with Scotland – partly because their identities are primarily cultural rather than territorial. But in so far as there is a territorial dimension to Pakistani identities, it is Scottish rather than British. (Hussain and Miller, 2004, p 11)

However, the prevalence of racism in constraining and shaping minority ethnic identities has also to be recognised (see Qureshi, 2002; Rahman, 2002). While lack of space precludes an extended discussion of the subject, more recently the discourses on identity have been complicated further by the debate generated by the comments of Trevor Phillips, Chair of the Commission for Racial Equality (CRE), on the need to move away from multiculturalism, while striving towards asserting a "core of Britishness" (Asthana and Hinsliff, 2004; *Sunday Herald*, 2004). The statement not only seems to ignore the ongoing debates on identities within a devolved context but also the role of racism in shaping people's sense of who they are. Apart from the difficulties of arriving at a consensus on 'Britishness', the question of how the discourse generated will impact on the policy agenda and the funding of work on racism and racial equality issues remains to be seen.

Framework for delivering racial equality in post-devolutionary Scotland

Structures for delivering racial equality

In the devolved context, equality and immigration matters remain 'reserved powers', with two exceptions: the Scottish Parliament has the authority to encourage and ensure the observance of equal opportunities; and to "impose duties on Scottish public authorities and crossborder public authorities in relation to their Scottish functions" (Scottish Executive, 2000a, p 31). In Wales, similar provision was made in the 1998 Government of Wales Act for ensuring that appropriate arrangements were made for securing "equality opportunity for all people" in relation to Assembly business and its functions (CRE, undated b, p 12). The equality agenda for a devolved Scotland was anchored in two developments, prior to May 1999, which established the basic foundation for addressing racial equality issues in post-devolutionary Scotland (Arshad, 2000, 2002):

- the 1998 Scotland Act, in contrast to UK legislation, adopted a more inclusive definition of equal opportunities, including factors such as social origin, age and sexual orientation:

  > The prevention, elimination, or regulation of discrimination between persons of sex, marital status, on racial grounds, or on grounds of disability, age, sexual orientation, language or social origin, or of other personal attributes including beliefs or opinions, such as religious beliefs or political opinions. (1998 Scotland Act, cited in Scottish Executive, 2000a, p 4)

- The report of the Consultative Steering Group, a cross-party group established in 1997 by Donald Dewar, the Secretary of State for Scotland, recommended the adoption of four principles, which were endorsed in full by the incoming Scottish Parliament: power-sharing; accountability; access and participation; and equal opportunities for all (Arshad, 2000, pp 153-4).

Following the elections in May 1999, which returned an all 'white' Scottish Parliament, it engaged in a flurry of activity on the equal opportunities front, establishing a Parliamentary Equal Opportunities Committee and an Equality Unit within the Scottish Executive (see also Chapter Four of this book), both of which included racial equality within their remit. In addition, the CRE, together with the other equality bodies on gender and disability, operating through an office in Scotland has developed close links with the Scottish Parliament (CRE, undated a).

Following the establishment of structures within the Scottish Executive, two short-term ministerial groups were established in 2000 in response to the MacPherson Report (1999):

- a steering group to address issues within the criminal justice and police authorities;
- the Race Equality Advisory Forum to progress racial equality issues in a number of social policy areas.

Membership in both included a cross section of individuals and professionals drawn from a range of sectors. It was one of the first opportunities for many minority ethnic groups and individuals in Scotland to debate policy issues across a range of areas (for example, education, social services, and so on), culminating in the publication of a report, *Making it real*, with recommendations for addressing racism and promoting racial equality (REAF, 2001).

The Scottish Executive has convened other groups to meet specific needs (for example, the Scottish Refugee Integration Forum) and has helped to resource specific high profile initiatives (the National Resource Centre for Ethnic Minority Health and the Black Ethnic Minority Infrastructure in Scotland [BEMIS]). It has also taken some steps to embed race equality issues in legislation with regard to at least two devolved areas; for example, in the Standards in Scotland's Schools Bill and the Housing Bill (see CRE, undated a; Scottish Executive, undated a). Recognising that the achievement of equality depends as much on the Scottish public as the Scottish Parliament, a high profile media campaign, 'One Scotland, Many Nations', was launched in 2003, in order to improve race awareness, challenge racist attitudes and highlight the negative impact of racism.

In addition, the 2000 Race Relations (Amendment) Act has also provided an important impetus for public bodies and the Scottish Executive to take race equality issues seriously. However, it would seem that much of the investment in activity and resources has gone into preparing agencies for the act, with minimal investment into raising awareness of the implications of the Act among the communities themselves, which is vital if agencies are to be held to account. A report on a survey of public authorities undertaken by the CRE in 2003, to assess the activities they had undertaken to meet the duty and to establish a baseline to monitor future progress, painted an optimistic albeit cautious picture. It identified some areas of good practice, while also highlighting a patchy response and a possible lack of understanding on the part of some authorities of the scope of the duty (CRE, 2003, pp 41-2). It would seem that for many agencies, taking on a proactive role in promoting 'good race relations' is not an easy journey.

A new future? Commission for Equality and Human Rights (CEHR)

While it is important to acknowledge that Scottish devolution has facilitated a focus on racism and 'race' equality issues in ways that were previously absent, the capacity of UK organisations such as the CRE in representing the views of

Scotland's minority ethnic groups at the UK and Westminster levels has at times seemed limited. For example, this was demonstrated in the debate on ethnic categorisations used in the 2001 Census (see Arshad, 2002) as well as more recently in the lack of Scottish views being represented in Trevor Phillips' perspective on multiculturalism and 'Britishness' discussed earlier in this chapter. The ambivalent position of UK organisations with regard to representing and addressing discrimination and equality issues that are relevant to Scotland has led to an argument for a "Scottish Equality Commission [which] would adhere to a baseline requirement from the UK Equality Act but have sufficient autonomy for its identity and priorities to be shaped by Scottish people and Scottish issues" (Arshad, 2002, p 220), something which has not been taken up under the proposed new arrangements for establishing a Commission for Equality and Human Rights (CEHR).

The White Paper seeks to replace the current three commissions (Equal Opportunities Commission [EOC], CRE, and the Disability Rights Commission [DRC]) with a single commission. It could be argued that the two main drivers for change have been, first, changes in equality/discrimination legislation extended to cover previously excluded factors such as sexual orientation, religion and belief (2003) and age (legislation to be introduced in 2006) in areas such as employment and vocational training, and second, embedding "a culture of human rights" that focuses on a more inclusive approach (DTI, 2004, pp 12, 16).

Although, it is too early to assess all the responses to the DTI proposals, the little evidence that exists suggests that it is mixed. The inclusion of a human rights dimension in creating a single commission has raised anxieties about articulation between the Scottish Executive's commitment to human rights and establishing a Scottish Humans Rights Commission (SHRC) and the CEHR's role in promoting and monitoring human rights across the UK. Ongoing discussions and the proposals in the White Paper have suggested a Memorandum of Understanding as one way of ensuring clarity of roles and responsibilities, with SHRC being responsible for issues that fall within the devolved areas. The CRE's response (2004) in a recent press statement has been to "unequivocally reject" the proposals in the White Paper on the grounds that it had "little support from Black and ethnic minority communities", the volatility of communities, the persistence of discrimination and the high demands on the CRE as well as issues such as the lack of proposal for a single act.

What difference will establishing a CEHR make to addressing discrimination in general, and racism and race equality in particular for Scotland? On the one hand, it has been argued that bringing all equalities under one commission could potentially lead to a dilution of focus:

> [I]n Scotland, where policy development on equality issues such as race and disability is at an embryonic stage, integrating these issues into one commission may marginalise each equality area. This could create a functional mess. (Arshad, 2002, p 220)

This view reinforces the CRE view as expressed in the press statement discussed previously to some extent. On the other hand, it has been argued that a single commission might be in a better position to address 'crosscutting factors' (poverty/social exclusion), as well as issues of multiple discrimination within a framework that brings together equalities and human rights (DTI, 2004). Meanwhile, anxieties remain around two main issues: the extent to which the new Commission will be resourced to do its job effectively across the UK and the difficulties that may ensue from a lack of a single equality act which would underpin the new institution.

Apart from a formal commitment to establish Scottish and Welsh Committees and a requirement to report to the Scottish Parliament on its activities in Scotland, broadly, the governance structures proposed do not appear to be a major departure from the current commission structures (DTI, 2004). There also appears to be a lack of recognition of the different devolutionary arrangements in Wales and in Scotland, as defined in the 1998 Scotland Act, and the need, therefore, for different arrangements in Scotland. Furthermore, the appointment of one Commissioner, in contrast to three (one each for the EOC, CRE and DRC) at present could be interpreted as Scotland having less of a voice. Although the White Paper makes a commitment to ensure that the overall CEHR strategy will be informed by the priorities of the devolved countries, the extent to which the new arrangements will be effective in enabling Scotland to shape the equality agenda, and will reflect the views and address the priorities of those who live in Scotland, remains to be seen.

Social inclusion/exclusion

Policy discourses and context

Social inclusion/exclusion, as already been discussed in previous chapters, is one of the key policy areas of the Labour government, which in Scotland has been closely aligned with the Scottish Parliament's commitment to social justice (Scottish Executive, undated b). The definition of social inclusion adopted in Scotland is more or less modelled on that of the UK government:

> a term applied to the complex set of linked problems centred on the lack of opportunity and diminished life circumstances, including unemployment, poor skills, low incomes, poor housing, high crime environments, poor health and family break down. (Scottish Office, 1999, p 59)

Three priority areas with milestones and targets were identified: young people, communities and anti-poverty action, leading to spatial-based and group-focused initiatives (Scottish Executive, 2000b).

The vulnerability of minority ethnic groups to social exclusion on a range of dimensions (economic, social, political and so on) has been reported by a wide range of research (de Lima, 2003). Growing evidence demonstrates that some minority ethnic groups across Britain are more likely to experience poverty, unemployment, racial harassment, poor health and inadequate housing (Craig, 2001; Netto et al, 2001; Brown, et al, 2002; Netto and de Lima, 2002). To what extent have Scottish social inclusion policies addressed issues of ethnicity and racism as a factor that leads to social exclusion?

At a practical level, the approach has focused on funding specific projects through 'thematic' Social Inclusion Partnerships (SIPs) (see also Chapter Six that follows): one each in Fife and Glasgow, which have led to a range of initiatives (GARA, undated). However, as argued elsewhere:

> While the funding of thematic SIPs on 'race'/ethnicity in specific geographical areas may be a starting point, it does raise the question of whether this has the potential to lead to the ghettoisation of 'race'/ ethnicity. Given the emphasis on the multidimensional aspects of social exclusion in the Government documents, it is also unclear the extent to which the SIPs in general (other than those focusing on 'race') are addressing race equality issues within their work. (de Lima, 2003, p 658)

In general, Scottish Executive documents reporting progress on social justice include only very brief references to minority ethnic groups and their experience of discrimination (Scottish Executive, 2000b, 2002b). With the exception of two milestones in relation to employment and higher education (Scottish Executive, 2002b, p 1), and even in this context minority ethnic groups are treated as a homogenous group, there is no disaggregation by ethnicity across all areas, an issue also raised by Craig (2001) in his analysis of initiatives established to address social exclusion in England.

The privileging of integration in the labour market as the means to social inclusion and the tendency to use a "poverty model of social inclusion" (also discussed in Chapter Three of this book), rather than focusing on the multidimensionality of peoples' experiences has not been fully taken up in Scotland or England (Craig, 2001; de Lima, 2004). The tendency has been to focus on the characteristics of groups considered to be socially excluded, neglecting "the means by which the 'mainstream' of society generates social exclusion" (Burden and Hamm, 2000, p 193). The extent to which minority ethnic groups have been 'socially included' will be explored further by assessing their involvement in policy and political discourses in Scotland.

Continuity and change

As has been discussed earlier in this chapter, racism and race equality issues in Scotland before devolution were masked by what was happening in England.

There has been a lack of recognition of how the specific historical and contemporary economic, political and sociocultural context of living in Scotland has shaped the lives of minority ethnic groups. The attempt to involve a range of stakeholders from minority ethnic communities (for example, as discussed through REAF and so on) has meant that a devolved government has enabled 'outsiders' to have an involvement in Scottish policies in a way that was not previously possible with a Westminster government. While there have been criticisms from some sections of the minority ethnic communities about the nature of representation, there were also high expectations on the part of all those with a commitment to racial equality of the changes that were likely to ensue from such involvement and consultation (Netto et al, 2001).

The bringing together of key stakeholders from minority ethnic communities by the Scottish Executive has sparked off a range of activities. For example, there has been an increased focus on improving the information base of the communities in Scotland. A seminar on 'Researching Ethnic Minorities in Scotland' provided an opportunity for a range of stakeholders to identify issues that ought to be included in a programme of research (Reid Howie Associates, 2000). One of the first pieces of research to be commissioned was an audit of research on ethnic minorities in Scotland (Netto et al, 2001). An examination of the Scottish Executive Social Research website reveals an increase in commissioned research on minority ethnic communities (for example, see Scottish Executive, 2001).

In addition to an increase in commissioned research, consultations involving minority ethnic groups have increased and resources have been provided to support capacity building. The Scottish Executive has also made more of an effort to recruit a more diverse workforce and there are more minority ethnic individuals represented on non-governmental departmental bodies (Scottish Executive, undated a). However, we have yet to see a significant minority ethnic presence in senior executive positions across the public sector and the lack of a minority ethnic presence in the Scottish Parliament, discussed below, highlights the limits of social inclusion policies.

The gaps: lack of voice in politics

The Scottish Parliamentary elections in 2003 returned an all 'White' parliament yet again, and minority ethnic groups continue to be underrepresented in local authority councils. Hussain and Miller (2004) found that most of their participants while accepting the principle of devolution were "lukewarm about the practice" (p 11). The emphasis on symbols such as St Andrew (Scotland's patron saint; see McCrone, 1996, p 19, for further information), as well as the absence of minority ethnic groups in the Scottish Parliament, reinforced their social exclusion from the political process:

> almost half the Pakistanis feel the Scottish parliament was set up to
> satisfy nostalgia for a past they cannot share, rather than to improve

> the government in a future they can share. (Hussain and Miller, 2004,
> p 11)

Lack of political representation is a British-wide issue. O'Cinneide (2004, p 6) argues that minority ethnic people feel "let down" and alienated by the representative process, largely due to the failure of political parties to ensure that their candidates reflect the diversity of Britain and their "indifference to their needs and perspectives", most notably experienced through the role of Britain in the Iraq war. In Scotland, this triggered changes in party political support: for example, the majority of the Pakistani participants in the study undertaken by Hussain and Miller (2004) supported Scottish independence and were more likely to vote for the Scottish National Party (SNP), which opposed the Iraq war. O'Cinneide (2004) highlights a similar switch among Muslim voters in English local and by-elections to the Liberal Democrats.

Increasingly, traditional approaches to engagement in politics through 'community leaders' are being challenged. More demands are being made of parties to reflect the communities they seek to represent. Apart from the GARA 'Politician Shadowing Scheme', targeted at raising political awareness among youth (GARA undated), there is a dearth of initiatives to redress the deficit in political representation in Scotland. At times, the diversity and small numbers of minority ethnic groups (this applies to some areas and groups more than others) has militated against the development of strong social capital, which could potentially enable diverse groups to overcome some of their differences to ensure a stronger voice in Scottish politics. By contrast, in England, minority ethnic groups have established pressure groups, often however, emphasising religious identities (for example, Operation Hindu Vote, cited in O'Cinneide, 2004), which in reality are in danger of perpetuating 'inter-group' conflicts and reinforcing notions of homogeneity. In addition, the CRE and Operation Black Vote launched an MP Shadowing scheme in 1999 to increase minority ethnic representation in politics (Connections, 2003, p 6).

When it comes to making a real shift in the way in which power is exercised, it would appear that it is 'business as usual' in Scotland. Gessesse's (2001, pp 12-13) statement two years after the first elections continues to echo the sentiments of many minority ethnic individuals:

> while there seems to be willingness by politicians to listen to our experiences of marginalisation, nothing that could be seen as improving conditions for minority ethnic people has materialised. We remain excluded from all types of social and political platforms. We have an all white parliament, schools with all white head teachers.... Thus, in general terms minority ethnic communities are excluded from participation in decision making and from social policy issues at all levels.

Demographic trends and immigration

Population and migration trends

Asylum seekers, refugees, migrant workers and the enlargement of the EU, have all generated conflicting discourses and pejorative metaphors of 'British' life and culture being 'swamped', 'drowned', and so on (Geographical, 2004, p 38). On the one hand, the Labour government has been highlighting the need for migrant labour to plug the skills gaps, on the other hand, it wishes to appear 'tough' on immigration to appease the electorate and in response to the popular press who are only too willing to "depict Britain as a historically settled nation in urgent peril from foreign invaders who are, almost by definition, lazy and unscrupulous scroungers" (*Geographical*, 2004, p 38). It is important to acknowledge the 'racist' element in the discourses about immigration as Winder (2004, p 41) highlights "when most Britons speak about immigration they tend to mean coloured immigration. Many of the arguments are still, when it comes down to it, about race. But half of the immigration into Britain comes from within the EU". So, what are the population and migration trends that are the source of such emotive discourses?

As the debate on the best way to stem the decline in population has been unfolding in the Scottish press, the validity and robustness of statistics used to support claims and counter claims are often difficult to assess. The ONS (2004) estimated that the number of out-migrants and in-migrants in the UK in 2002 were the highest over the last decade, with more people migrating into the UK: 359,000 people left the UK and 513,000 arrived to live here for at least a year. However, evidence suggests that more and more people are leaving Britain to live elsewhere (Nicholson-Lord, 2004; Winder, 2004). Statistics on settlement patterns are difficult to obtain, however, Winder (2004, pp 40-1) suggests 50% settle in south-east England, 2.5% in Wales, 2.2% in northeast England and 0.7% in Northern Ireland, whereas in Scotland the "major issue is emigration".

GROS recorded a rise of 2,600 (since 2002) in population in June 2003 to 5,057,400. Deaths have outstripped births since 1997. People aged 25 years and under are decreasing while those aged 75+ are increasing. Migrants boosted the population by a net 9,000 and Scotland's population is projected to fall below five million in 2009, reaching 4.84 million in 2027 (GROS, 2004). At a UK level, the ONS (cited in Winder, 2004, p 40) estimated more than half a million vacancies in the British labour market. Organisations such as, for example, the Construction Industry Training Board, estimated that it would require 83,000 new workers each year for the next three years (cited in Winder, 2004, p 40).

Demographic 'time bomb' and immigration: Scottish responses

Against this background, the so-called 'time bomb', that is, Scotland's declining and ageing population, has given rise to wide-ranging debates in the Scottish media (Crichton, 2004; Denholm, 2004a).

However, it is the Scottish Executive's launch of the 'Fresh Talent Initiative' in February 2004 that has generated the most controversy. The initiative proposes to attract up to 8,000 people each year for the next five years by focusing on a range of strategies, including collaboration with Work Permits UK (WPUK) to promote Scotland among people applying for work permits in the UK and encouraging students at Scottish universities to stay in Scotland for two years after they have graduated (Scottish Executive, 2004b). Apart from the question of whether immigration is the appropriate strategy to address Scotland's demography, doubts have also been raised about Scotland's ability to compete with other nations in attracting immigrants (Crawford, 2004).

The proposal to increase immigration has opened a Pandora's box of reactions from welcoming to racist. Calls for the Scottish Parliament to be given more powers in relation to immigration issues, and for freeing up asylum seekers to work while their application for refugee status is being considered, have been rejected by the Home Secretary and dismissed as "unworkable" by the Scottish Executive (Dinwoodie, 2004). The proposed policy to attract immigrants to Scotland has also highlighted the persistence of racist attitudes, providing a platform for the BNP, which has fielded candidates for recent elections, reinforcing fears of 'foreigners' taking away jobs and housing from 'locals'.

Selling immigration to the electorate has not been easy, especially among groups where poverty persists and a wide range of people feel socially excluded. For example, a survey on attitudes to discrimination in Scotland, found that 26% of respondents with household incomes of £9,999 or below felt that minority ethnic "people take jobs" (Bromley and Curtice, 2003, p 31). More recently, a survey revealed divided opinions among the Scots on the Scottish Executive's proposal for immigration, expressing concerns about issues such as housing and costs of benefits. While 51% of those surveyed believed that immigrants should be welcomed, one in three did not believe they should be welcomed (MRUK, cited in Denholm, 2004b). Similar views were also expressed in an opinion poll that included Britain, leading to it being labelled "one of the most xenophobic countries in the world, surpassing France, Germany, Spain and Japan in its hostility to immigration" (Nelson, 2004)

Making a difference: the limits

It is difficult to envisage any fundamental departures in addressing immigration issues in Scotland due to it being a reserved power, but also because of the Labour Party's ambivalent track record on immigration legislation, which has been fundamentally racist in the way in which entry restrictions are applied selectively to some groups (Law, 1996). Scottish policies on 'race' and 'racial equality' do not operate in a vacuum even within a devolved context and have to be understood within the UK and European contexts that are crucial in setting the tone of the policies and discourses, and have the potential to limit what can realistically be achieved. Much of the debate on racism and racial equality continues to be underpinned by contradictory discourses and policies by those in government on issues of 'race' and 'immigration':

> The attempt to construct what has been termed 'consociationalism' (Lijphart, 1997, cited in Law as part of the quote used), where the liberal democratic state accommodates cultural pluralism, at the same time as attempts are being made to construct more ethnically exclusive criteria in the specification of citizenship in Britain and Europe, characterises not only the 'liberal settlement' of the 1960s, but the appeal of the 'management of ethnic diversity' in the 1990s' – and one might add early 21st century as well. (Law, 1996, p 198)

Conclusion

Given the ambivalence towards addressing racism and discrimination in pre-devolutionary Scotland discussed in this chapter, there has been a great deal of 'catching up' taking place since 1999, reflecting a similar situation in Wales (CRE, undated b). In Scotland and to a large extent in Wales, the small numbers of minority ethnic groups in relative terms has tended to shape policy and service providers' responses in a way that has implicitly perpetuated approaches to service delivery which have largely focused on the notion of 'economies of scale', while at the same time playing lip service to issues such as human rights. The key question is this: has Scottish devolution made a difference with regard to addressing issues of racism and discrimination?

In many respects, when it comes to issues of racism and discrimination, devolved Scotland is no different from the rest of Britain. Information emerging from research and the 2001 Census in Scotland as well as other parts of Britain reveals that the lives of minority ethnic groups are shaped by a range of factors – age, class, faith, gender and so on – resulting in complex cross-cutting identities which an exlusive focus on ethnicity ignores. Research across the UK has also consistently demonstrated that minority ethnic groups face similar challenges irrespective of devolution: they are vulnerable to discrimination and racial harassment in a range of contexts (employment, health, education and in the community), as well as to higher levels of unemployment and poverty. Asylum seekers and refugees continue to be at the receiving end of racism and largely negative reporting especially by the media in England and Scotland, providing a platform for right wing political parties such as the BNP. Furthermore, the situation in some communities, where asylum seekers and refugees have been settled, has been exacerbated by government policies on dispersal and their lack of consultation with local communities, as well as their concern to appear 'tough' on the issue by increasing restrictions.

The gap between policy statements and action continues, and is apparent in areas such as social exclusion, not just in Scotland but in England too – for example, the failure to take into account the multidimensional experiences of social exclusion and the lack of disaggregated data by ethnicity across all priority areas. The overwhelming emphasis on economic inclusion has led to a neglect of other dimensions of social exclusion, for example, the deficit in minority ethnic political representation. It is also fairly clear that the political parties and processes in Scotland, and in Britain generally, have a long way to go to ensure that they reflect the diversity of Scotland and close the gap between the rhetoric of 'One Scotland, Many Nations' and the lack of engagement of Scotland's minority ethnic groups in the 'real corridors of power'. The recent debate to ditch 'multiculturalism' and assert a sense of 'Britishness' seems disconnected from the discourses and debates on evolving definitions of identities in devolved Scotland as well as highlighting the limitations of UK organisations in representing the views of minority ethnic groups living in countries with devolved governments.

The issue of immigration in the context of Scotland's 'demographic time bomb' provides a useful illustration of how the discourses on ethnicity and racism are shaped by the specific needs of the different countries that make up Britain, while at the same time highlighting the constraints on the Scottish Parliament, given that immigration is a reserved matter. Some have argued that if Scotland had control over immigration policies, then hostility towards asylum seekers might be less (Henderson, 2004). It is difficult to see how, given Scotland's record so far, the negative attitudes of a small, albeit persistent, minority in Scotland toward minority ethnic groups and immigration issues; its poor record in coping with asylum seekers; and continued evidence of racial harassment and discrimination, Scotland is any different from the rest of Britain. Despite devolution, Scotland continues to operate within a neoliberalist framework and can make limited changes given its limited powers to redress the fundamentally racist nature of immigration and nationality legislation that has continued to shape race relations in the UK.

Despite the limitations, it is important to acknowledge that devolution has opened up new opportunities in Scotland to address racism and discrimination in ways that did not occur previously. It has led to a range of activities, for example, greater involvement of minority ethnic people in consultative activities; an increase in commissioned research to address the information deficit that has existed; targeted initiatives to address specific needs (for example, on health, social inclusion and capacity building); created possibilities of introducing legislative changes in devolved matters, such as education and housing; and provided opportunities for debate and discussion on issues of identity and belonging, based on a range of variables (for example, 'sub-national' regional and civic) in a way that has not hitherto been possible. What is now needed are more radical measures to address the deficit in areas such as political representation, for example, by building the capacity of the minority ethnic communities to engage in meaningful debate and participation at all levels and by ensuring that minority ethnic individuals are placed in winnable seats. It is also important to focus on developing policies that address cross-cutting/multiple discrimination issues such as poverty, sexuality, gender/age inequalities and disability with a view to moving beyond discourses and policies that perpetuate a simplistic 'White'/minority ethnic divide and finding a common ground to address inequalities and discrimination.

Further resources

de Lima, P. (2003) 'Beyond place: ethnicity/race in the debate on social exclusion/inclusion in Scotland', *Policy Futures in Education*, vol 1, no 4, pp 653-67.

Law, I. (1996) *Race, ethnicity and social policy*, Hertfordshire: Prentice Hall.

Netto, G., Arshad, R., de Lima, P., Almeida Diniz F., MacEwen, M., Patel, V. and Syed, R. (2001) *Audit of research on minority ethnic issues in Scotland from a 'race' perspective*, Edinburgh: Scottish Executive Central Research Unit.

On the web ...

Commission for Racial Equality	www.cre.gov.uk
National Statistics	www.statistics.gov.uk
Scottish Executive	www.scotland.gov.uk

References

Ahmed, W. and Craig, G. (2003) "'Race' and social welfare', in P. Alcock, A. Erskine and M. May (eds) *Social policy* (2nd edn), Oxford: Blackwells, pp 113-20.

Arshad, R. (2000) "'A man's a man for a' tha": equality for all in Scotland?', in G. Hassan and C. Warhurst (eds) *The new Scottish politics*, Norwich: The Stationery Office, pp 153-61.

Arshad, R. (2002) 'Daring to be different: a new vision of equality?', in G. Hassan and C. Warhurst (eds) *Tomorrow's Scotland*, London: Lawrence and Wishart, pp 207-21.

Asthana, A. and Hinsliff, G. (2004) 'Equality chief branded as "right wing"', *The Observer*, 4 April (www.observer.guardian.co.uk).

Back, L. and Solomos, J. (2003) 'Introduction: theorising race and racism', in L. Back and J. Solomos. (eds) *Race and racism: A reader*, London: Routledge, pp 1-28.

Barclay, A., Bowes, A., Ferguson, I., Sim, D. and Valenti, M. (2003) *Asylum seekers in Scotland*, Edinburgh: Scottish Executive Social Research.

Bond, R. and Rosie, M. (2002) 'National identities in post-devolution Scotland', *Scottish Affairs*, no 40, Summer, pp 34-53.

Bromley, C. and Curtice, J. (2003) *Attitudes to discrimination in Scotland*, Edinburgh: Scottish Executive Social Research.

Brown, U., Scott, G., Mooney, G. and Duncan B. (2002) *Poverty in Scotland 2002*, London: CPAG.

Burden, T. and Hamm. T. (2000) 'Responding to socially excluded groups', in J. Percy-Smith (ed) *Policy responses to social exclusion*, Buckingham: Open University Press, pp 184-200.

Chahal, K. and Julienne, L. (1999) *'We can't all be white!'*, York: Joseph Rowntree Foundation.

Charlaff, L., Ibrani, K., Lowe, M., Marsden, R. and Turney, L. (2004) *Refugees and asylum seekers in Scotland: A skills and aspirations audit*, Edinburgh: Scottish Executive Social Research.

Connections (2003) 'Who wants to be an MP?', *Connections* (CRE), Spring, p 6.

Connections (2004) 'Inequalities highlighted by Scottish census data', *Connections* (CRE), Spring, p 5.

Craig, G. (2001) '"Race" and welfare: Inaugural lecture as Professor of Social Justice', Hull: University of Hull.

Crawford, A. (2004) '"Fresh talent" won't come to Scotland. The executive's hope of attracting skilled workers to boost the economy faces a big hurdle: persuading potential immigrants', *Sunday Herald*, (3rd edn), 29 February, p 7.

CRE (Commission for Racial Equality) (2003) *Towards racial equality in Scotland*, London: CRE.

CRE (2004) *CRE Scotland: Statement on proposals for a Commission for Equalities and Human Rights*, 22 July, Edinburgh: CRE.

CRE (undated a) *CRE Scotland* (www.cre.gov.uk).

CRE (undated b) *Race equality in Wales*, CRE, Cardiff: Office in Wales (www.cre.gov.uk).

Crichton, T. (2004) 'Where have all the people gone?', *Sunday Herald*, 18 January, p 17.

Denholm, A. (2004a) 'Migrants help boost population figures in Scotland', *The Scotsman*, 1 May (news.scotsman.com).

Denholm, A. (2004b) 'Scots welcoming image suffers a blow', *The Scotsman*, 1 June (news.scotsman.com).

Dinwoodie, R. (2004) 'Blunkett controls could hinder Scots Fresh Talent scheme', *The Herald* (2nd edn), 8 May, p 8.

DTI (Department of Trade and Industry) (2004) *Fairness for all: A New Commission for Equality and Human Rights*, White Paper, Norwich: The Stationery Office.

GARA (Glasgow Anti-Racist Alliance) (undated) *Black perspectives*, Issue 8 (www.gara.org.uk).

Geographical (2004) *Geographical dossier: Immigration*, vol 76, no 7, pp 38-9, July.

Gessesse, T. (2001) 'A Scotland for all! A personal perspective', *Multicultural Teaching Journal*, vol 20, no 1, Autumn, pp 11-14.

GROS (General Register Office for Scotland) (2003) *Scotland's Census 2001* (www.gro-Scotland.gov.uk).

GROS (2004) *The Registrar General's Annual Review of Demographic Trends*, chs 1-2 (www.gro-Scotland.gov.uk).

Hampton, K. and Bain, J. (1995) *Poverty and ethnic minorities in Scotland*, Glasgow: Scottish Ethnic Minorities Research Unit, Caledonian University.

Henderson, D. (2004) 'Ageing Scotland needs an infusion of youth: call to immigrants', *The Herald* (2nd edn) 30 April, p 16.

Home Office (2004) *Asylum statistics – First quarter 2004*, p 2 (ind.homeoffice.gov.uk).

Hussain, A. and Miller, W. (2004) 'Multiculturalism and Scottish nationalism', *Connections* (CRE), Spring, pp 10-11.

Jones, W.R. (2001) 'On processes, events, and unintended consequences: national identity and the politics of Welsh devolution', *Scottish Affairs*, no 37, Autumn, pp 34-57.

Klug, B. (1999) 'Ticking the box marked "white"', *Connections* (CRE), Summer, pp 7-9.

Law, I. (1996) *Race, ethnicity and social policy*, Hertfordshire: Prentice Hall.

Lewis, G. (2003) 'Migrants', in P. Alcock, A. Erskine, A. and M. May (eds) *Social policy*, Oxford: Blackwells, ch 4.6.

MacPherson, W. Sir (1999) *The Stephen Lawrence Inquiry*, Cm 4262-I, London: The Stationery Office (www.archive.official-documents.co.uk/document/cm42/4262/4262.htm).

McCrone, D. (1996) *Understanding Scotland: The sociology of the stateless nation*, London: Routledge.

Manwaring, R. (2002) 'Tick box marked —?', *Connections* (CRE), Autumn, pp 14-15.

Miles, R. and Dunlop, A. (1986) 'The racialisation of politics in Britain: why Scotland is different', *Patterns of Prejudice*, vol 20, no 1, pp 23-32.

Modood, T., Berthoud, R., Lakey, J., Nazroo, J., Smith, P. Virdee, S. and Beishon, S. (1997) *Ethnic minorities in Britain: Diversity and disadvantage*, London: Policy Studies Institute.

Nelson, F. (2004) 'Poll shows Britons fear immigration has damaged Britain', *The Scotsman*, 27 May (news.scotsman.com).

Netto, G. and de Lima, P. (2002) 'Commentary: ethnic minorities and employment', in P. Kenway, S. Fuller, M. Rahman, C. Street and G. Palmer (eds) *Monitoring poverty and social exclusion in Scotland*, York: Joseph Rowntree Foundation.

Netto, G., Arshad, R., de Lima, P., Almeida Diniz F., MacEwen, M., Patel, V. and Syed, R. (2001) *Audit of research on minority ethnic issues in Scotland from a 'race' perspective*, Edinburgh: Scottish Executive Central Research Unit.

Nicholson-Lord, D. (2004) 'Exodus: the great British migration', *New Statesman*, 2 August, pp 16-18.

O'Cinneide, C. (2004) 'Democracy: which way now?', *Connections* (CRE), Spring, pp 6-7.

ONS (Office for National Statistics) (2001) *The classification of ethnic groups* (www.statistics.gov.uk) [Crown copyright material is reproduced with the permission of the Controller of HMSO].

ONS (2003a) *Ethnicity population size* (www.statistics.gov.uk) [Crown copyright material is reproduced with the permission of the Controller of HMSO].

ONS (2003b) *Ethnicity: Regional distribution* (www.statistics.gov.uk) [Crown copyright material is reproduced with the permission of the Controller of HMSO].

ONS (2004) *International migration: Record flows in 2002* (www.statistics.gov.uk) [Crown copyright material is reproduced with the permission of the Controller of HMSO].

Qureshi, R. (2002) in T. Devine and P. Logue (eds) *Being Scottish*, Edinburgh: Polygon, pp 217-19.

Rahman, S. (2002) in T. Devine and P. Logue (eds) *Being Scottish*, Edinburgh: Polygon, pp 220-1.

REAF (Race Equality Advisory Forum) (2001) *Making it real*, Edinburgh: Scottish Executive.

Reid Howie Associates (2000) *Researching ethnic minorities in Scotland: Social Justice Annual Report*, Edinburgh: Scottish Executive.

Scottish Executive (undated a) *A review of the Scottish Executive's response to the Race Equality Advisory Forum recommendations*, Edinburgh: Scottish Executive.

Scottish Executive (undated b) *Social justice ... A Scotland where everyone matters*, Edinburgh: Scottish Executive.

Scottish Executive (2000a) *Equality strategy*, Edinburgh: Scottish Executive.

Scottish Executive (2000b) *Social Justice Annual Report*, Edinburgh: Scottish Executive.

Scottish Executive (2001) *Ethnic Minority Research Bulletin No 1, October 2001*, Edinburgh: Scottish Executive.

Scottish Executive (2002a) *Committing to race equality*, Edinburgh: Scottish Executive.

Scottish Executive (2002b) *Social Justice Annual Report*, Edinburgh: Scottish Executive.

Scottish Executive (2004a) *Analysis of ethnicity in the 2001 Census – Summary report*, Edinburgh: Office of the Chief Statistician, Scottish Executive.

Scottish Executive (2004b) *Fresh Talent Initiative*, Edinburgh: Scottish Executive.

Scottish Office (1999) *Social inclusion: Opening the door to a better Scotland*, Edinburgh: Scottish Office.

Sunday Herald (2004) 'What they say about diversity in the UK', *Sunday Herald* (3rd edn), 4 April, p 12.

Winder, R. (2004) 'Labouring the point', *Geographical*, July, vol 76, no 7, pp 40-1.

SIX

Urban policy and the city in the 'new' Scotland

Charlie Johnstone and Chris McWilliams

This chapter is concerned with Scotland as a largely urbanised society. Outlining the severe social problems that Scotland's cities have to tackle, the chapter examines recent programmes and strategies around area regeneration. It also addresses the implications of main urban policy developments in Scotland and elsewhere in the UK, and discusses the Scottish Executive's recent reports on the issue. The following issues are considered here:

- New Labour's urban policy agenda;
- social and economic policies in post-devolutionary Scotland: competitiveness, economic growth and social cohesion;
- from the Conservative urban regeneration to New Labour's approach in a UK and a Scottish context: differences and similarities;
- Social Inclusion Partnerships: finances, power structures and community participation;
- the Scottish Executive's *Review of Scotland's cities* and community planning; and
- continuity and change in Scottish urban policy.

Introduction

> Our cities are central to Scotland's economic growth and dynamism, but they are not islands on their own. They are the fundamental building blocks of our country's future prosperity as well as our cultural and social well being. (First Minister Jack McConnell, Scottish Executive, 2003)

While this comment could be dismissed as mere rhetoric, it does at least emphasise the significance placed on cities to the health and wealth of Scotland by the Scottish Executive. It has long been recognised that cities are the engines of national economic growth and in this sense there is little that is new in the thinking of the Executive. However, it is also recognised that enhancing the contribution of Scotland's cities to the wider Scottish economy necessitates addressing the multiple problems that characterise much of the urban landscape of contemporary Scotland (Begg, 2002; Scottish Executive, 2003).

Scotland has six very heterogeneous cities. Glasgow (the largest city) and Edinburgh, (second largest and capital city of Scotland) have come overwhelmingly to dominate Scottish culture, politics (the new Scottish Parliament is located in Edinburgh) and are the predominant economic centres. The other four cities are Aberdeen, Dundee, and the recently designated cities of Inverness and Stirling, reflecting Scotland's position as one of the most urbanised population centres in Europe. However, while a largely urbanised society, several of Scotland's cities have an ongoing problem with population decline. Between 1961 and 1981, Glasgow lost a third of its population, while Edinburgh's population increased by 10% and Dundee saw a reduction of 8% (Scottish Executive 2003; also see Table 1 for recent figures). Part of the reason for population decline, particularly in the case of Glasgow, is due to local authority boundary changes in the 1980s and 1990s that saw parts of Glasgow moving to the authorities in East Dunbartonshire, East Renfrewshire and South Lanarkshire. Around one third of the population of Scotland live in Glasgow, Edinburgh, Dundee and Aberdeen and, along with their surrounding hinterlands, they account for 75% of Scotland's GDP. Each is faced with particular challenges and opportunities, although they share similar problems such as poverty and deprivation, albeit to varying degrees of intensity.

The cities of Scotland that once proudly boasted their contribution to the British Empire, especially Glasgow (Oakley, 1967; Checkland, 1981), are now contradictory centres of consumption and severe social problems. In the 'new' Scotland, poverty sits uncomfortably with wealth, never more noticeable than in its cities. One response to these changes to declining industrial centres has been the cultural planning approach to urban regeneration that involves upgrading the physical environment of the central parts of the city, the opening of new cultural arenas and events. Glasgow is often cited as a positive referent for this cultural planning approach (see, for instance, Bianchini and Bloomfield, 1996; Mooney, 2004). However, while this is an interesting area of study, it is not the focus of this chapter. Rather, this chapter will be concerned with a discussion and analysis of recent programmes and strategies around area/neighbourhood

Table 6.1: Population change in Scottish cities (1991 and 2001)

City	1991	2001
Aberdeen	182,133	184,788
Dundee	157,808	154,674
Edinburgh	400,632	430,082
Glasgow	658,379	629,501
Inverness	40,918	40,949
Stirling	29,768	32,673

Source: GROS (2003)

regeneration/renewal in 'deprived' communities. In other words, we focus on the social policy agendas of Scotland's cities.

As was discussed in Chapter Three of this book, poverty is a feature of the entire social and geographical landscape of contemporary Scotland. Without wishing to minimise or marginalise the major problems of rural poverty, in terms of extent and intensity, poverty in Scotland is primarily an urban phenomenon and it is the 'urban factor' that has pushed poverty to the fore as a key political issue facing the Scottish Executive, other statutory agencies and numerous and diverse third-sector organisations. Each of Scotland's main towns and cities has significant concentrations of poverty and disadvantage. However, political and policy-making attention has largely focused on the poverty 'problem' in West Central Scotland, centred on the Clydeside conurbation and the City of Glasgow in particular (see Danson and Mooney, 1998; Kenway et al, 2002; McWilliams, 2002; Turok and Bailey, 2003). Glasgow and its neighbouring areas have the highest levels of poverty not only in Scotland, but also in the whole of the UK. One-third of the working age population of the city is dependent on state benefits of various kinds, although this is much higher in some council estates and older inner urban areas (OECD, 2002, p 41).

Researchers at Sheffield Hallam University have consistently revealed that there is an extensive 'hidden unemployment' in many parts of Britain including Scotland's major cities and their hinterlands (Beatty et al, 1997, 2002). They have highlighted that a large number of unemployed people with health problems have been moved on to sickness-related benefits while others have been pushed into premature early retirement. Such men and women do not appear on the official unemployment register based on the claimant count. An example of the significance of this is that in Glasgow the official level of unemployment in 1997 stood at 11.8% while the real level of unemployment was 30.6%, equivalent figures for Dundee were 10.3% and 20.6%; for Edinburgh 7.1% as opposed to 13.8%; for Aberdeen the figures were 4.6% and 9.7% (Beatty et al, 1997). In short, the real level of unemployment in all Scottish cities was around double that of the official statistics. In a subsequent report in 2002, the Sheffield team concluded that little had changed and that the real level of unemployment in areas such as Glasgow, Dundee, North Lanarkshire and Inverclyde is between 16% and 23% (Beatty et al, 2002). A recent assessment of Indices of Deprivation in Scotland found that 16 of the 20 most deprived areas in Scotland were in Glasgow and more than half of the city's wards were in the poorest 10% for Scotland as a whole (Social Disadvantage Research Centre, 2003). A more detailed and nationwide study found that outside of the London local authority areas of Hackney and Tower Hamlets, Glasgow had the highest percentage of households living in poverty at 40.93% in 2001, up from 35.88% from 1991. The equivalent figures for Dundee saw an increase from 31.20% in 1991 to 34.08% in 2001, for Aberdeen up from 24.24 to 26.76% and Edinburgh up from 22.35 to 25.82% (Dorling and Thomas, 2004). Given these problems it is not too difficult to understand why Glasgow has dominated the postwar Scottish urban policy agenda.

However, more recently the Scottish Executive's (2003) *Review of Scotland's cities* has sought to widen the policy debate in the process encompassing all of Scotland's cities.

In this chapter, we address two main questions that arise from these policy developments. First, to what extent does urban policy in Scotland depart from the urban policy agenda being pursued elsewhere in the UK? Second, how far are the recent and developing urban policies of the Scottish Executive influenced by or diverged from the strategies pursued by previous Conservative and Labour administrations?

In the section that follows, we analyse urban policy changes nationally under New Labour before moving to focus on key aspects of contemporary urban social policy since the late 1990s in Scotland. From here, the discussion moves on to briefly discuss *New Life for Urban Scotland* (a Conservative-initiated urban policy, which was wound up by a Labour government in 1998), and to examine its successor in the form of New Labour's social inclusion policies, before concluding with a discussion of the Scottish Executive's *Review of Scotland's cities* and *Community planning* reports (2002a, 2003).

New Labour and the city

We do not have the space here to explore the connections between urban and area-based social policies with other aspects of the New Labour 'project' in detail or depth, suffice it to say that we would argue that New Labour's approach to disadvantaged communities and areas is – as in its other policy areas – based upon a celebration of the market and a commitment to a neoliberal social and economic programme (see Chapter Two of this book; also Ferguson et al, 2002; Imrie and Raco, 2003). It is also increasingly connected with other New Labour policy agendas.

One of the main criticisms that New Labour made of Conservative urban and area-based policies is that they concentrated overwhelmingly on the 'physical' aspects of regeneration, ignoring the 'social' dimensions in the process. For New Labour, there is a strong commitment to bringing the 'social back in' – to going beyond what has been termed a 'bricks and mortar' approach. This is reflected not only in urban social policies, but also in a myriad of other policy developments that affect 'marginalised' communities, such as the proposals for housing 'renewal'. Perhaps one of the clearest examples of this concern to re-centre the 'social' aspects in urban regeneration programmes is evidenced by the 1998 report from the Westminster-based Social Exclusion Unit (SEU, 1998) entitled *Bringing Britain together: A national strategy for neighbourhood renewal*. This report crystallises some of the key planks in New Labour's recent and current thinking about social excluded/disadvantaged/marginalised communities. This report and a host of others mark something of a return to neighbourhood and community in urban/ area-based social policy, with community now a key feature of New Labour social policy (although we would point out that 'community' and 'participation' in particular continued to figure as important mobilising and legitimising discourses in Scotland during the Conservative's *New Life for Urban Scotland* programme throughout the late 1980s and 1990s). We return to this issue later.

In this context, it is arguably the case that 'disadvantaged', 'poor' or 'socially excluded' communities play a crucial role in New Labour's symbolic register, although a number of academics are highly critical of the recent shift in emphasis by the Scottish Executive from a 'community empowerment' to a more vague 'community involvement' agenda (Bailey, 2002). New Labour deploys a particular spatialisation of social and economic problems, one that has historical echoes of the Community Development Programme (CDP) from the late 1960s and early 1970s and previous generations of area-based policies, together with a strong dose of area pathologisation (Alcock, 2004). However, there is an important shift in New Labour's approach to disadvantaged communities against those of previous governments: to see these as potential obstacles to economic growth and enhanced competitiveness. The economic costs of social exclusion are understood then in terms of the impact they have on Britain's capacity to compete globally. In relation to poor communities, it is their lack of 'connectedness' to processes of economic growth that is deemed to require urgent attention – not the impact of long-term structural inequalities. In the next section, we consider how these relate to other elements of New Labour's neoliberal agenda – and in particular how they relate to the emerging urban policy themes of *competitiveness* and *cohesion* (issues that were also discussed in Chapter Two of this book; see also Boddy and Parkinson, 2004).

Social and economic policies in post-devolutionary Scotland

For New Labour in both Scotland and England, social regeneration and the reactivation of community are part and parcel of the larger goal of creating a '21st-century welfare system', a welfare regime that is geared towards and tied to the goals of competitiveness and economic growth. However, there is an awareness of the potential problems this may create for what has been termed *social cohesion* and in terms of exacerbating problems of social exclusion. As Susan Fainstein has pointed out, the use of the term 'competitiveness' implies a commitment to market-driven growth while 'cohesion' implies social glue or bonds (Fainstein, 2001, p 884).

The dominant urban paradigm of the early 2000s is that competitiveness/ economic success and social cohesion can be integrated. Such a view characterises the developing urban policy agenda in Scotland as in the rest of the UK. This 'new liberal formulation', as Harloe (2001) has expressed it, marries, or attempts to marry, social justice and economic growth. As was argued in Chapter Two of this book, in the context of post-devolutionary Scotland, the pursuit of economic growth and the challenge of making Scotland more competitive and entrepreneurial, have been important goals of the Scottish Executive (see Raco, 2002, for a fuller exploration of this):

> international competitiveness is indispensable if Scottish enterprises and the Scottish economy as a whole are to survive ... prosper and expand. (Scottish Executive, 2001a, p 22)

The dominant economic development agenda in Scotland – as in the rest of Britain – is one that mobilises discourses of 'change' and 'modernisation', the need to 'gear-up' to compete in a more risky and uncertain world (see Chapter One of this book). While in Scotland such discourses are all too frequently couched in 'Scottish terms', by referring to perceived 'Scottish' 'needs' and 'interests', they share the same outlook: that social inclusion, social cohesion and opportunity are generated by economic growth. However, as Turok and Bailey (2003, p 17) point out, only 7-10% of sales by key firms in both Glasgow and Edinburgh are exports from the UK. In short, the external demand is mainly for a UK market and not a global or European one. More importantly, it will be interesting to see in the medium and long-term if the implementation of this 'new' urban agenda will have any real impact in reversing, never mind eradicating, the persistent and growing poverty and inequality that has been a long-term feature across urban Scotland (Dorling and Thomas, 2004).

The adoption of neoliberal social policy by New Labour is just as apparent in Scotland as it is elsewhere in Britain, even if it is couched in a different language at times (see Mooney and Poole, 2002) and despite the fact that the evidence suggests such a strategy has failed to tackle the deep-rooted poverty and inequality referred to earlier. For urban and area-based policy in Scotland, the agenda is clearly set. Speaking at the *Creating competitive and cohesive cities* conference in Glasgow in January 2003, the Scottish Social Justice Minister (responsible for the *Review of Scotland's cities*) spoke of the need to develop policies that promoted growth, opportunity and sustainability, arguing that economic growth and competitiveness were the key supports of social inclusion and social cohesion (Minister for Social Justice, 2003).

From New Life to New Labour

From the mid-1980s, when British urban policy still tended to be focused on the 'inner-city problem', attention in Scotland had shifted to the increasing problems of social and economic deprivation in the large peripheral housing estates located on the edges of the major cities. Alongside the New Towns, these council housing estates had been built during the early postwar years under an urban policy agenda that focused upon slum clearance and population decentralisation and dispersal. By the 1980s, it was recognised that these estates had deep-rooted social and economic problems in addition to physical and environmental decay (see Johnstone, 1992; Mooney and Danson, 1997). In 1988, the Conservative government selected four deprived council estates for a new urban regeneration initiative – *New Life for Urban Scotland* (Scottish Office, 1988; Bailey, 1995). The 10-year New Life programme was targeted at three major peripheral housing estates: Castlemilk in Glasgow; Whitfield in Dundee, Wester Hailes in Edinburgh, and the largely inter-war Ferguslie Park estate in Paisley, which had been the only area in Scotland chosen as one of the Britain-wide CDP programme areas in the late 1960s. It has to be remembered that Britain during this period was going through a phase of intense uneven development and that many towns and cities were faced with rapid economic decline and rising mass unemployment (see Friend and Metcalf, 1981; Rees and Lambert, 1985). Unemployment levels in cities like Glasgow in the mid-1980s exceeded 20%. At the outset of New Life, overall unemployment in Castlemilk, for example, was 22.8%. However, male unemployment on this estate stood at 30.9% compared with 23.1% for Glasgow City and 15.9% in Strathclyde Region. Significantly, the proportion of men unemployed for over a year was around 55%, and one in five men had been unemployed for five years or more. More compelling evidence could be provided that graphically depicts the problems facing the Castlemilk estate, but suffice it to say that Castlemilk's population suffered from acute and relentless forms of social exclusion (see Strathclyde Regional Council, 1989). Therefore, it is not surprising that such estates became the central focus of attention during this period. Nor should we be surprised that the then Secretary of State for Scotland, Malcolm Rifkind, commented that New Life:

> signalled a new and unique approach to the problems of urban regeneration with the bringing together in partnership of the private and public sectors and the communities themselves. (Scottish Office, 1990)

While each estate included in New Life was apparently chosen according to an analysis of standard indices of deprivation, there were estates, in Glasgow and other Scottish cities, which were arguably more deprived (see McWilliams, 2002, for a discussion of why Castlemilk in Glasgow was selected). New Life was regarded as "a landmark in the history of urban regeneration in Scotland" (Scottish Office, 1993). Not surprisingly, perhaps, the final evaluation of New Life speaks grandly of this urban 'experiment':

> As an experiment, it has been largely successful. As a programme of public expenditure, it has been value for money. There is a good chance that many of its achievements will be durable. New Life has created a platform which, with good continuation partnerships and fair economic weather, gives residents the chance of sustainable improvement in their quality of life. (Scottish Executive, 1999, p 183)

Given the fact that such views had tended to dominate a number of academic and policy agendas on urban regeneration strategies, it is of great interest to analyse and assess in what ways, if any, New Labour's approach to urban issues would differ from those put in place by a government that had spent many years building urban partnerships and regarding local authorities as little more than 'enablers'. The next section focuses on an empirical evaluation of these issues in a Scottish context. It utilises empirical findings from research conducted into the emergence of the Greater Pollok Social Inclusion Partnership (SIP) one of the most socially disadvantaged areas in Glasgow (see McWilliams, 2004). However, the discussion has relevance to SIPs in Scotland in general.

Social Inclusion Partnerships

Speaking in Glasgow's Easterhouse housing estate on Friday, 13 November 1998, the Prime Minister Tony Blair signalled New Labour's agenda for disadvantaged communities in Scotland. As with other government policies it was claimed that this 'new' approach to tackling exclusion and poverty placed more emphasis upon *prevention* rather than *cure*. In 1999, disadvantaged areas in Scotland were invited to bid for SIP funding through the then Scottish Office, now Scottish Executive (Scottish Office, 1998). The SIPs emerged from previous partnership initiatives that had existed in Scotland which were based on the partnership model at an area-based level. The role of SIPs was to continue and advance the work already in place with previous regeneration programmes but, crucially, to involve the community at the 'heart of the process' as part of a multiagency approach. This was to be achieved through funding of up to £60,000 per annum through the Empowering Communities Fund, which replaced the funding available under the previous Programme for Partnerships scheme (Scottish Executive, 2001b).

While there has been a great deal of publicity surrounding SIPs, very little in the way of new money has been made available to designated areas. For example, 48 SIPs (of which 34 were more traditional area-based initiatives and an additional 14 thematic initiatives on a range of subjects including 'routes out of prostitution' and 'health' with a strong focus on young people) established by 2000 had to share £53 million during the financial year 2000/01. More specifically in Greater Pollok (one of Glasgow's eight SIP areas), over the period 1999-2002, only £7 million was made available. It is claimed that SIP status is more important than the money directly allocated to each SIP (Greater Pollok SIP Strategy, 1999, p 1). The SIPs strategy envisaged that each of the main social inclusion partners would 'bend' existing mainstream budgets to the needs of each SIP area. In this sense, SIPs again display strong elements of continuity with the *New Life for Urban Scotland* programme (Scottish Office, 1988) and the Priority Partnership Areas (PPAs) initiative, which also relied upon existing agencies 'bending' their mainstream budgets. Further, while the rhetoric underpinning the SIPs strategy claimed that they were different from the 'urban policies' pursued by the

Conservatives when in power, in particular the PPAs and *New Life for Urban Scotland*, closer inspection reveals many aspects of *continuity* existed, particularly through the supposedly 'new' process of community planning (to which we return later in this chapter). For example, while the Scottish Office argued that "there is a need to involve communities in the decisions that affect them, and to support them to take on ever greater responsibility for taking those decisions themselves" (Scottish Office, 1999 p 6), this is not too dissimilar from New Life, which argued that "plans for the regeneration of problem areas must have the full understanding, involvement and commitment of the local community" (Scottish Office, 1988 p 9).

Moreover, while on the surface SIPs *appeared* to have been less ideologically driven than previous urban policy initiatives (for example, PPAs and New Life), they were both driven by an inward-looking perspective on the problems faced by these neighbourhoods and communities rather than acknowledging the wider structural factors which effect such places. Thus, while New Labour's approach recognised the importance of social criteria (hence the idea of social inclusion) when allocating resources, they had not dispensed with the practice of area competition and 'value for money' which was so pivotal in previous Conservative urban policies.

Thus, while the language of New Labour may be different from the Conservatives' attitude towards 'distressed' communities, it is altogether more questionable whether the policy mechanisms have altered to any great extent. Thus, New Labour may speak of 'community', 'participation', 'empowerment', 'inclusion' and 'partnership', all of which recognise the importance of the social in urban regeneration (see Ginsburg, 1999). However, the policies designed to tackle the problems of urban areas display a strong degree of continuity with the urban policies developed by previous Conservative governments in Scotland. For example, while New Labour's SIP policy stressed the need for *partnership* working, this is not too dissimilar to the Conservatives' *New Life for Urban Scotland* initiative, which also emphasised the need for partnership involving all levels of government, business and the community. In practical terms, SIPs were a continuation, albeit in another guise (especially in the language deployed by New Labour), of the Conservative's approach to urban policy. Behind the rhetoric of the social inclusion agenda there was a clear managerialist approach to solving urban problems. Further, SIPs were also partly influenced by notions of a burgeoning underclass, with the emphasis placed upon individuals and communities that are excluded from *mainstream* society. To borrow from Ruth Levitas's account of New Labour's understanding of social inclusion (Levitas, 1998), the SIPs agenda shares important elements of a 'moral underclass discourse', or MUD, with a strong emphasis upon crime and drug use, single parenthood and lifestyles (Byrne, 1999; Young, 1999). However, important aspects of another social exclusion discourse used by New Labour, the 'social integrationist approach' that seeks to emphasise that the route to inclusion is through paid work, is also evident.

New Labour's pursuit of holistic urban regeneration and 'joined-up' government is reflective of their recent emphasis on inclusion. In one sense, this is not entirely new. Throughout much of the 1980s, and especially the 1990s, the Conservative government sought greater coordination, collaboration and partnership in urban policy (Stewart, 1996). However, while the Conservatives viewed Labour local authorities with suspicion, New Labour have sought to 'reinclude' them as facilitators or 'key actors' of local partnerships where they are often seen as the key to achieving joined-up thinking.

Not only is it emphasised that the full range of 'stakeholders' are to find a place at New Labour's policy table, but the 'community' is also to be involved in policy decisions. New Labour's claim is that 'the community' is to be assigned a more pervasive and formalised role than ever before. In Scotland, social inclusion documents speak of building 'community capacity' (and more recently of enhancing 'social capital') to empower people in poor urban areas (Greater Pollok SIP Strategy, 1999). Again, there are clear links with previous Conservative government policies such as New Life, which also stressed community involvement in decision making. Social Inclusion Partnership guidelines required local partnerships to specifically and actively promote social inclusion, and to make provision for effective community 'involvement'.

New Labour's aspiration for inclusivity in urban regeneration is related in part to the need to weave together the disparate urban players that have emerged in recent years into networks of stakeholding 'partners' (Furbey, 1999, p 430). They all, it is claimed, have a role to play in the renewal of the urban environment. Furbey (1999) further argues that New Labour's urban discourse echoes the conservative applications of Social Darwinism a century ago together with the structural functionalism of Durkheimian social theory. Thus, New Labour's urban policy reflects the deepening problems of a 'dual society' (and the 'dual city'), with its focus on encouraging city competitiveness, and participation of the excluded (McWilliams, 2002).

While the language of New Labour's social inclusion policies speaks of 'partnership', in the case of the SIPs it is clearly not an equal partnership. Thus, despite the government's claims to establish a new context for urban regeneration, the application of the SIPs appeared to be characterised by the same limitations that characterised previous urban regeneration initiatives (Cambridge Economic Consultants, 1999). It is most noticeable that existing power structures and decision-making processes did not change (nor were they questioned). Power still emphatically lay with the Scottish Executive and policy officers, not the local community (see McWilliams, 2004). In addition, as Alcock (2004, p 94) points out, echoing criticisms of the CDP programme 30 years previously, in focusing on localised solutions, wider social problems and processes can all too often be marginalised and obscured:

> there is a danger that these broader economic and social commitments
> do not connect well with the rhetoric of social activation within the

area based social inclusion programmes, where the pressure is on to show what local people can do.... The (misplaced) belief that local problems require local solutions, may lead some national ... actors to assume that they do not have a role to play in these.

All of this is further evidence that, while the rhetoric of social inclusion policies claims to put 'the community' at the heart of decision making, the reality is that local people (especially in the most disadvantaged communities) are still largely excluded from key decisions which effect their lives. Moreover, it also highlights a contradiction in New Labour's thinking. Thus, while on the one hand New Labour stresses both decentralisation and the involvement of local communities in decision making, in reality they still want to retain central control, as existing research reveals that local people often feel excluded from strategic planning for their area (Anastacio et al, 2000). There appears little difference from previous partnership arrangements (for example, New Life and PPAs, both of which were very heavily centrally controlled) where devolution of power either to the partnerships themselves or to the local communities did not occur (Hastings, 1996).

Colenutt and Cutten (1994) argue that the growing importance attached to 'community' in urban policy in the 1980s (whereas we have argued there are strong connections with the strategy being pursued by the Scottish Executive in the early 2000s) has more to do with the political and financial objectives of government than it has for improving cities. They further argue that "by involving the community, government can legitimise its national policies, and by localising and internalising these problems firmly within the context of the community, it rids the government of responsibility for them" (Colenutt and Cutten, 1994, p 239). Others (for example, Duffy and Hutchison, 1997) are sceptical and pessimistic about what they call the *turn to community*. The fragmentation and disintegration of many communities under the impact of large-scale economic and social change, coupled with the rise in poverty and exclusion, make the task of involving the 'community' incredibly difficult. It is hard, therefore, not to disagree with Duffy and Hutchison (1997, p 359) when they say, "just as with earlier waves of urban policy, the experiment with 'community' is as likely to end in perceptions of failure".

Robinson and Shaw (1995) are more optimistic about involving community participation in the process of urban regeneration, claiming that the benefits can be enormous. They argue, "above all else community participation seems the only way to ensure that regeneration is relevant to meeting local needs" (Robinson and Shaw, 1995, p 71). While the potential benefits of community involvement may be enormous, it is also fraught with problems. The idea of community itself may be misleading. In reality, there are many 'communities of interest' with differing views and opinions. It is also important to ask who participates and why they participate. While there are always people who want to get involved, there are also many people who take little or no part in community affairs and politics. Robinson and Shaw (1995, p 71) point out how this creates problems, in that community participation often means "some groups are able to exert disproportionate influence while others (notably women, ethnic minorities, the unemployed) are almost ignored". All of this indicates that genuine community involvement, never mind empowerment, is not easy, which was perhaps part of the reason for the Scottish Executive to take a wider view of the problems faced by Scottish cities as outlined in the next section.

Review of Scotland's cities: developing a Scottish urban policy?

As has been argued in previous chapters of this book, following devolution successive First Ministers have committed the Scottish Parliament to the development of 'new' policies to address the multiple economic and social problems affecting Scotland's cities. The Scottish Executive's two-year long *Review of Scotland's cities* study was eventually published in January 2003. The remit of the project was to review the social, economic and environmental development of Scotland's six cities and to identify Executive policies that would improve the prospects of these cities, their surrounding hinterlands and, ultimately, the whole of Scotland (Scottish Executive, 2003). The key outcome of the review was the allocation of a £90 million 'growth fund' to Scotland's cities over a three-year period. Most noticeably, Glasgow (Scotland's largest city) will receive nearly half the total (£40 million), evidently a result of the fact that over half (56%) of Glasgow City's ward are in the most deprived 10% of wards in Scotland (Social Disadvantage Research Centre, 2003).

There has been a mixed response to the Review. On a positive note, it is regarded as the first time that a Scottish urban policy framework has been set-down. However, many see the review as a missed opportunity and misguided exercise that has promised very little and will deliver even less given the lack of serious money to back up the review (Adams et al, 2003). Viewed by some as, at best, a modest response to the problems and opportunities facing Scotland's cities, it fails to produce any real concrete proposals. More seriously, there is little foundation from which to construct a future, more comprehensive urban policy either by the Executive (in the form of a White Paper) or within each city-region (Turok, 2003). The city-region concept, while welcomed by some, is not without its challenges, particularly as the authorities in the main cities were required to work with nearby local authority partners to produce a 'City Vision' that would set out all the priorities for using the funding made available to the Scottish Executive. Also contained within the review was an indication that support would be given to the setting up of urban regeneration companies similar to those already operational in England. While allowing for a potentially more effective approach to city planning and development, a number of barriers to the successful application of such an idea exist (see Lloyd, 2003). Most notably, the abolition of Scottish Regional Councils in 1996 undermined the scope for effective city-region development and planning (Lloyd, 1996). In sum, the city-region idea should not be viewed as a panacea for the management of Scottish cities. In this context, Scotland is still in pursuit of a coherent and sustainable urban policy.

Further, it is unclear from the *Review of Scotland's cities* who will deliver effective city development strategies. While the review suggests the establishment of urban development corporations (UDCs), it is not clear exactly what powers and resources will be at their disposal, nor that these would be immune from the tensions that characterised UDC-council relations in England in the 1980s and 1990s. This raises the key issue of the role of local authorities in this brave new urban Scotland. Clearly, they are not *trusted* to deliver on the Scottish Executive's 'urban promises', as the suggestion that UDCs be introduced suggests. Such a perception is reinforced by the Executive's insistence that local government continues to work in partnership with other organisations.

As indicated earlier in this chapter, while the review acknowledges the importance of cities within their regional context, it says very little with regards to how to link this all together in a strategic manner that would be of benefit to all 'stakeholders'. In the case of central Scotland, which is the location for the two most important cities in Scotland (Glasgow and Edinburgh), this is potentially significant. A prosperous Scotland, according to dominant contemporary discourses, needs each of these cities to perform well, not just one. More recently, these two cities have worked in competition with each other when it would be preferable if they both developed a joint strategy that focused growth and development in the central belt corridor, which joins the two cities. It seems incredible that more serious attention has not been given to cooperation between the cities for mutual advantage. It is claimed that the potential benefits from such a joint venture could be enormous in terms of increased employment opportunities, improved infrastructural benefits (for example, road and rail links) and enhanced environmental quality (Turok, 2003). However, not only is the political leadership and will absent from both cities to follow such a path, but also equally it is not forthcoming from the Scottish Executive, at least as yet.

Finally, in undertaking this policy review there was an explicit attempt to build upon existing urban social policy programmes, notably the SIPs and on the Scottish Parliament's repeatedly stated commitment to the pursuit of a *social justice* strategy. Such a strategy is reflected in the various *social inclusion* strategies and programmes that have been developed since 1999 and these themes of social justice and social inclusion are central to the emerging urban social policy agenda in Scotland today, even if the SIPs programme has now come to an end. Further, as we discussed above and as has been argued in previous chapters of this book, a more dominant economic agenda prevails through, for example, the emphasis on competitiveness and on work as a route out of 'social exclusion', in Scotland as elsewhere in the UK.

Community Planning

> We, the Scottish Executive, are committed to building a Scotland where everyone has access to the opportunities and benefits of a fair and equal society. Our aim is to tackle the inequalities between communities by narrowing the gap between the disadvantaged and everyone else. We want a Scotland where every person can contribute to and benefit from, the community in which they live. (Scottish Executive, 2002b, p 7)

The outcome of the thinking inherent in this quotation led to the publication of *Closing the gap: Community regeneration statement* (Scottish Executive, 2002a). This was premised on an argument that 'targeted regeneration initiatives' were the way forward for urban policy in Scotland. The aspirations, as indicated in this extract, were obvious though the plans and strategies put forward to tackle the deep-rooted problems of Scotland's cities, were rather nebulous. Also, the Executive's proposals fail to recognise the significance of well-established grass-roots organisations in many of Scotland's most deprived neighbourhoods. As Hastings (2003, p 93) has argued, the Executive "fail to acknowledge the long tradition of local self-help as well as community and political activism and organisation which characterises many of Scotland's poor neighbourhoods".

Viewed as a potential solution to the increased institutional fragmentation within Scotland the rather vague idea of community planning is designed to improve local governance capacity and overall service delivery (Lloyd et al, 2001). The introduction of the 2003 Local Government in Scotland Act has given Scottish local authorities statutory responsibilities for introducing community planning. Local authorities are expected to lead the community planning process, yet they must also rely on other bodies, such as voluntary organisations, community groups and often the private sector, being able to be involved in an open and transparent manner. The important role accorded to the voluntary sector should not be underestimated here. In turn, this reflects the goal of reshaping the relationship between the role of the community, voluntary sector and the state in a new form of 'partnership'. This obviously raises serious issues of resource capacity and the need to reconcile institutional differences. For example, what scope is there for community planning to influence Scottish Executive policies and, crucially, funding? In sum, community planning is designed to promote 'joined-up' working between various public, private and voluntary and not-for-profit organisations. It is argued that community planning seeks to empower local communities and individuals by ensuring that the delivery of local services is more transparent and understandable and ultimately more responsive to local needs (Lloyd et al, 2001). In addition to this, a new aspect to thinking on regeneration strategy was introduced under the idea of 'building skills and confidence in disadvantaged communities'. While similar to some of the projects funded under SIPs, the newness in this document is focused on a community learning and development agenda:

> We will work with national and local partners to build a shared vision of community learning and development. We will also make sure that it is built into community planning so that local people can get involved in the process. At the same time, we want to increase the focus of those providing community learning and development on improving key service outcomes for deprived communities. (Scottish Executive, 2002b, p 11)

However, involving local communities, while desirable, can be somewhat problematic. Many lack the material capacity and resources to become adequately involved, while many local authorities have still to find an appropriate and effective means of involving local people (McWilliams, 2004). Further, many local organisations have little experience of working in genuine partnership and many institutional barriers still exist (not least the differing objectives of different sectors) which inhibit the pursuit of a partnership approach. A legitimate concern is that community planning partnerships, designed to bring partners to the table, will become mere 'talking shops' and that local communities could become disillusioned with the process and the effectiveness of their involvement, as has happened in past regeneration schemes such as the CDPs (Imrie and Raco, 2003, p 5). This has been acknowledged and recognised by the Scottish Executive (Scottish Executive, 2003). Clearly, the test for community planning is, will it succeed in producing improvements across the range in the quality of public services amidst financial constraints and the withdrawal of publicly-funded services in many areas?

Conclusion: continuity and change in Scottish urban policy

> Cities, towns and urban neighbourhoods need to develop clear economic identities which promote and foster clusters of specialist businesses that can work together and compete together within a global market place. (Urban Task Force, 1999, p 42)

New Labour's approach to an agenda for Britain's cities is again clearly evident in this quotation, underpinned as it is by a clear emphasis on the promotion of enterprise and entrepreneurialism. This fits neatly with the Scottish Executives agenda on 'social cohesion' and 'economic competitiveness'. However, the purpose of this section of the chapter is to consider the extent to which this is a 'new' urban policy agenda or whether it is a continuation and expansion of past policies which the Executive and academics have recognised as failing to solve the long-term social and economic problems of Scotland's cities. Is it continuity or change, or a mixture of both, that we are witnessing? At this stage, it is important to emphasise the obvious point that given the divergent histories and trajectories of Scotland's major cities, it is likely to be the case, despite attempts to promote 'joined-up' urban policy, that the future of these cities will be different from each other and that there will be vastly divergent experiences for the people who live and work in these cities. As in the past, they will be full of paradoxes and contradictions.

The continuity between New Labour and previous Conservative governments is remarkable. Both political parties have articulated a narrative that restricted 'urban problems' to discreet pockets of poverty in urban areas. Thus, the solution was to identify these areas then target the 'deviant' populations in the areas and modify their pathological behaviour. The causes of the problems were therefore deemed to originate within the areas concerned and thus do not require the consideration of wider societal forces. A clear advantage of this approach is that it is inexpensive. With more effective targeting of resources, little in the way of additional resources would be required to effectively address the problems of distressed communities.

New Labour's urban policy reflects the deepening problems of what some academics refer to as the 'dual society', with its focus on encouraging city competitiveness and participation of the excluded (Marcuse, 1989). The emerging dual structure within Scottish cities has resulted in the development of a 'dual urban policy' (Keating, 1988; McWilliams, 2002). In sum, this has resulted, on the one hand, in the development of robust entrepreneurial economic policies designed to support 'glamorous' city centre regeneration, and on the other hand, as an under-funded, fragmented social policy devised for 'problem' areas. Policies such as New Life and SIPs can be viewed as a residual, poorly-funded strand of urban policy, which has focused more on managing decline and social anomie, than creating any meaningful sustainable regeneration.

This chapter has sought to discuss the key issues concerning contemporary Scottish cities and recent government urban social policy initiatives. While there has been a great deal of fanfare (mainly from the Scottish Executive) surrounding the launch of social inclusion partnerships and the more recent *Review of Scotland's cities*, it is still appropriate to claim that Scotland still lacks a coherent and sustainable urban policy. It is interesting to note the striking contrast between the aspirational intentions of Lord Rogers Urban Task Force Report, *Towards an urban renaissance* (1999), produced for the Westminster government (and which strongly influenced the government's Urban White Paper) and the somewhat weaker Scottish Executive Cities Review document.

It is clear from the discussion in this chapter that New Labour's urban policy displays a large degree of continuity with previous Conservative policies. In this sense, the New Labour government and, more importantly, the Scottish Executive has accepted, adopted and re-imagined much of the Thatcherite discourse with regards to 'urban problems' and their solutions. Despite the establishment of a new Scottish Parliament, it has arguably still to make a distinctive mark by delivering 'Scottish policies' to address 'Scottish problems', not least in the field of urban policy. It could easily be argued that the people of Scotland deserve much better!

Further resources

Glendinning, C., Powell, M. and Rummery, K. (eds) (2002) *Partnerships, New Labour and the governance of welfare*, Bristol: The Policy Press.

Imrie, R. and Raco, M. (eds) (2003) *Urban renaissance? New Labour, community and urban policy*, Bristol: The Policy Press.

Lupton, R. (2003) *Poverty street: The dynamics of neighbourhood decline and renewal*, Bristol: The Policy Press.

Johnstone, C. and Whitehead, M. (2004) *New horizons in British urban policy: Perspectives on New Labour's urban renaissance*, Aldershot: Ashgate.

On the web ...

Each of Scotland's local authorities, including those for the six cities, have their own websites. In addition we recommend:

Communities Scotland   www.communitiesscotland.gov.uk

Scottish Executive   www.scotland.gov.uk

Scottish Urban Regeneration Forum   www.scotregen.co.uk

References

Adams, D., Allmendinger, P., Tiesdell, S., Watkins, C. and White, M. (2003) 'The Scottish cities review – a missed opportunity?', *Town and Country Planning*, vol 72, no 2, February, pp 40-1.

Alcock, P. (2004) 'Participation or pathology: contradictory tensions in area-based policy', *Social Policy and Society*, vol 3, no 2, pp 87-96.

Anastacio, J., Gidley, B., Hart, L., Keith, M., Mayo, M. and Kowarzik, U. (2000) *Reflecting realities: Participants' perspectives on integrated communities and sustainable development*, Bristol: The Policy Press.

Bailey, N. (1995) *Partnership agencies in British urban policy*, London: UCL Press.

Bailey, N. (ed) (2002) *Better communities in Scotland: Will the community regeneration statement close the gap?*, Conference Report, 31 July, Glasgow: University of Glasgow.

Beatty, C., Fothergill, S., Gore, T. and Green, A. (2002) *The real level of unemployment 2002*, Sheffield: Centre for Economic and Social Research, Sheffield Hallam University.

Beatty, C., Fothergill, S., Gore, T. and Herrington, A. (1997) *The real level of unemployment*, Sheffield: Centre for Economic and Social Research, Sheffield Hallam University.

Begg, I. (ed) (2002) *Urban competitiveness: Policies for dynamic cities*, Bristol: The Policy Press.

Bianchini, F. and Bloomfield, J. (1996) 'Urban cultural policies and the development of citizenship: reflections on contemporary European experience', *Culture and Policy*, vol 7, no 1, pp 85-113.

Boddy, M. and Parkinson, M. (eds) (2004) *City matters: Competitiveness, cohesion and urban governance*, Bristol: The Policy Press.

Byrne, D. (1999) *Social exclusion*, Buckingham: Open University Press.

Cambridge Economic Consultants (1999) *Summary paper of final evaluation of New Life for Urban Scotland programme*, Cambridge: Cambridge Economic Consultants.

Checkland, S. (1981) *The upas tree*, Glasgow: University of Glasgow Press.

Colenutt, B. and Cutten, A. (1994) 'Community empowerment in vogue or vain?', *Local Economy*, vol 9, no 3, pp 236-50.

Danson, M. and Mooney, G. (1998) 'Glasgow: a tale of two cities? Disadvantage and exclusion on the European periphery', in P. Lawless, R. Martin and S. Hardy (eds) *Unemployment and social exclusion*, London: Jessica Kingsley, pp 217-34.

Dorling, D. and Thomas, B. (2004) *People and places: A 2001 Census atlas of the UK*, Bristol: The Policy Press.

Duffy, K. and Hutchison, J. (1997) 'Urban policy and the turn to community', *Town Planning Review*, vol 68, no 3, pp 347-62.

Fainstein, S.S. (2001) 'Competitiveness, cohesion, and governance: their implications for social justice', *International Journal of Urban and Regional Research*, vol 25, no 4, pp 884-8.

Ferguson, I., Lavalette, M. and Mooney, G. (2002) *Rethinking welfare*, London, Sage Publications.

Friend, A. and Metcalf, A. (1981) *Slump city*, London: Pluto.

Furbey, R. (1999) 'Urban "regeneration": reflections on a metaphor', *Critical Social Policy*, vol 19, no 4, pp 419-45.

Ginsburg, N. (1999) 'Putting the social into urban regeneration policy', *Local Economy*, vol 14, no 1, pp 55-71.

Greater Pollok SIP (Social Inclusion Partnership) Strategy (1999) *Greater Pollok Social Inclusion Partnership Strategy*, Glasgow: Greater Pollok SIP Board.

Harloe, M. (2001) 'Social justice and the city: the new "liberal formulation"', *International Journal of Urban and Regional Research*, vol 25, no 4, pp 889-97.

Hastings, A. (1996) 'Unravelling the process of "partnership" in urban regeneration policy', *Urban Studies*, vol 33, no 2, pp 253-68.

Hastings, A. (2003) 'Strategic, multi-level neighbourhood regeneration: an outward-looking approach at last?', in R. Imrie, and M. Raco (eds) *Urban renaissance? New Labour, community and urban policy*, Bristol: The Policy Press, pp 85-100.

Imrie, R. and Raco, M. (eds) (2003) *Urban renaissance? New Labour, community and urban policy*, Bristol: The Policy Press.

Johnstone, C. (1992) 'The tenants' movement and housing struggles in Glasgow, 1945-1990', Unpublished PhD, Department of Sociology, University of Glasgow.

Keating, M. (1988) *The city that refused to die: Glasgow: The politics of urban regeneration*, Aberdeen: Aberdeen University Press.

Kenway, P., Mohibur, R. and Palmar, G. (2002) *Monitoring poverty and social exclusion in Scotland*, York: Joseph Rowntree Foundation.

Levitas, R. (1998) *The inclusive society: Social exclusion and New Labour*, London: MacMillan.

Lloyd, G. (2003) 'Scotland ties growth to its cities', *Regeneration and Renewal*, 24 January, p 14.

Lloyd, G., Illsley, B.M. and Graham, F. (2001) *Community planning in Scotland: A final report to the community planning task force project*, Dundee: Geddes Centre for Planning Research, University of Dundee.

Lloyd, M.G. (1996) 'Local government reorganisation and the strategic planning Lottery in Scotland', *Town Planning Review*, vol 67, no 3, pp v-viii.

McWilliams, C. (2002) *An analysis of the contemporary governance of Glasgow, 1975-2000*, Unpublished PhD, University of Glasgow, Department of Urban Studies.

McWilliams, C. (2004) 'Involving the local community in regeneration: the case of the Greater Pollok social inclusion partnership', *Local Economy*, vol 19, no 3, pp 264-75.

Marcuse, P. (1989) '"Dual city": a muddy metaphor for a quartered city', *International Journal of Urban and Regional Research*, vol 13, no 4, pp 697-708.

Minister for Social Justice (2003) Speech to the 'Creating Competitive and Cohesive Cities' Conference, Glasgow: Department of Urban Studies, University of Glasgow, 31 January.

Mooney, G. (2002) 'From New Lanark to New Labour: back to the future in welfare in Scotland?', The Robert Owen Commemoration Lecture, New Lanark, 19 April.

Mooney, G. (2004) 'Cultural policy as urban transformation? Critical reflections on Glasgow, European City of Culture, 1990', *Local Economy*, vol 19, no 4, pp 327-40.

Mooney, G. and Danson, M. (1997) 'Beyond "culture city": Glasgow as a "dual city"', in N. Jewson and S. MacGregor (eds) *Transforming cities*, London: Routledge, pp 73-86.

Mooney, G. and Poole, L. (2002) 'Is Scotland different? Lessons from New Labour and privatisation in Glasgow', Social Policy Annual Conference 'Localities, Regeneration and Welfare', Middlesbrough, 16-18 July.

Oakley, C. (1967) *The second city*, London: Blackie.

OECD (Organisation for Economic Co-operation and Development) (2002) *Glasgow: Lessons for innovation and implementation*, Paris: OECD.

Raco, M. (2002) 'Risk, fear and control: deconstructing the discourses of New Labour's economic policy', *Space and Polity*, vol 6, no 1, pp 25-47.

Rees, G. and Lambert, J. (1985) *Cities in crisis*, London: Hodder Arnold.

Robinson, F. and Shaw, K. (1995) 'Urban regeneration and community involvement', *Local Economy*, vol 6, no 1, May, pp 61-73.

Scottish Executive (1999) *An evaluation of the New Life for Urban Scotland initiative in Castlemilk, Ferguslie Park, Wester Hailes and Whitfield*, Edinburgh: Scottish Executive Central Research Unit.

Scottish Executive (2001a) *Created in Scotland: The way forward for Scottish manufacturing in the twenty first century*, Edinburgh: Scottish Executive.

Scottish Executive (2001b) *Empowering communities. Package of support for community representatives: Terms and conditions of funding*, Edinburgh: Scottish Executive (www.communitiesscotland.gov.uk).

Scottish Executive (2002a) *Closing the gap: Community regeneration statement*, Edinburgh: Scottish Executive.

Scottish Executive (2002b) *Social justice: A Scotland where everyone matters: Annual report 2002*, Edinburgh: Scottish Executive.

Scottish Executive (2003) *Review of Scotland's cities: The analysis*, Edinburgh: Scottish Executive.

Scottish Office (1988) *New Life for Urban Scotland*, Edinburgh: Scottish Office.

Scottish Office (1990) *Urban Scotland into the 90s: New life two years on*, Edinburgh: Scottish Office.

Scottish Office (1993) *Progress in partnership*, Edinburgh: Scottish Office.

Scottish Office (1998) *Social inclusion partnerships: Invitation to submit expressions of interest*, Edinburgh: Scottish Office.

Scottish Office (1999) *Social inclusion strategy: Opening the door to a better Scotland*, Edinburgh: Scottish Office.

SEU (Social Exclusion Unit) (1998) *Bringing Britain together: A national strategy for neighbourhood renewal*, London: SEU.

Social Disadvantage Research Centre (2003) *Scottish indices of deprivation 2003*, Oxford: Department of Social Policy and Social Work, University of Oxford.

Stewart, M. (1996) 'Competition and competitiveness in urban policy', *Public Management*, July-September, pp 21-6.

Strathclyde Regional Council (1989) *Strathclyde economic trends, No 23: Unemployment by community area*, Glasgow: Strathclyde Regional Council.

Turok, I. (2003) 'Will the Scottish Cities Review be the start of a new beginning?', *New Urban Futures*, p 7.

Turok, I. and Bailey, N. et al (2003) *Twin track cities? Linking prosperity and cohesion in Glasgow and Edinburgh*, Glasgow: Department of Urban Studies, University of Glasgow.

Urban Task Force (1999) *Towards an urban renaissance. Final Report of the Urban Task Force*, London: Spon.

Young, J. (1999) *The exclusive society*, London: Sage Publications.

SEVEN

Criminal justice in the devolved Scotland

Hazel Croall

This chapter examines the major changes taking place in Scottish criminal justice policy. It introduces the main actors involved in the criminal justice process in Scotland and explores the most distinctive characteristics of the system. The areas included are:

- links between crime and social exclusion;
- the criminal justice process;
- Scottish criminal justice agencies;
- strategies, trends and policies in the process;
- distinctive Scottish developments: the Children's Hearing System, social work, rehabilitation, youth justice: fast-track hearings and youth courts;
- imprisonment: throughcare, women in prison;
- plans for a single criminal justice agency; and
- Community Safety and the Antisocial Behaviour Bill.

Introduction

It has generally been argued that the Scottish approach to criminal justice shows a greater commitment to welfare than the rest of the UK. In the last few years, however, all elements of criminal justice have faced what ministers in Scotland have described as profound changes accompanied by a more punitive discourse. The courts have been 'modernised', provisions have been made for victims and vulnerable witnesses and a Sentencing Commission and a Risk Management Authority for sexual and violent offenders have been set up. Reviews of the Children's Hearings and the organisation of prisons and Criminal Justice Social Work (CJSW) are currently under way. The passing of the 2004 Antisocial Behaviour (Scotland) Bill aroused considerable controversy. Many of these developments parallel England and Wales and many fear that Scotland's welfarist tradition is under threat.

Despite its distinctiveness, there is little about Scotland in British texts on criminal justice, which normally focus on England and Wales. This chapter will introduce the main agencies involved in Scottish criminal justice. It will then outline major shifts in criminal justice policy that provide the context for exploring the Scottish approach. As no one chapter could hope to cover all criminal justice issues, selected areas will be explored in more depth, chosen for their relevance to social policy and because they represent what have been identified as the most distinctive features of the Scottish system (Young, 1997; McAra, 1999), namely youth justice, criminal justice social work, aspects of imprisonment, and community safety.

Crime and social exclusion

The close relationship between criminal justice policy, social policy and social exclusion can be illustrated by a brief outline of key characteristics of crime. While the recent politicisation of crime suggests rising crime rates, it is widely acknowledged that levels of recorded crime in Scotland, as elsewhere, have fallen. In 2003, recorded crime is reported to have decreased by 5% from 2002 (Scottish Executive, 2004). It is also well established that the majority of convicted offenders are male, that a large proportion are young and drawn overwhelmingly from among the most deprived. This is not to argue that these groups have a greater propensity to offend as recorded crime rates exclude some crimes. White-collar crime, for example, is less visible, less easy to detect, less likely to be reported and less likely to be prosecuted than, for example, the crimes of young people which are more likely to be 'street' rather than 'suite' crime (Croall, 2001). The criminal justice system, therefore, deals disproportionately with some kinds of crime and some groups of offenders.

While it lies beyond the scope of this chapter to look at the 'causes of crime', it is generally acknowledged that crime is associated with characteristics of individual offenders and their wider social and economic environment. Individual 'risk factors' include adverse family circumstances, the 'quality' of parenting, such as whether parents know where their children are, poor achievement at school, poor employment prospects, housing and health problems. Many young offenders in prison have been in residential care, have few educational qualifications, are unemployed and have experienced abuse in the home (SCCCJ, 2000), characteristics also shared by those coming before Children's Hearings who are 'victims' as well as 'villains' (Waterhouse et al, 2004). These individual factors are affected by the wider social and economic environment – low incomes, casual employment and unemployment, for example, can reduce parents' ability to care for their children (SCCCJ, 2000). In addition, the combination of concentrated poverty in some areas and affluence in others means that young people are confronted with the attractions of a global consumerist culture in which they cannot participate, leading to relative deprivation which may provide the motivation for drug-taking and the theft of highly-desirable consumer goods (Croall, 1998; Downes, 2004).

Imprisonment is strongly related to indices of deprivation. Using postcode data, a recent report for the Scottish Prison Service indicates that 28% of the prisoner population came from the poorest housing estates, compared to 10% of the general population. So strong is this association that imprisonment is seen to be a correlate of social deprivation as the report estimates that about one in nine of young men from deprived communities will have spent time in prison by the time that they are 23 years old (Houchin, 2004).

The victims of crime are also drawn disproportionately from similar backgrounds. In 2000, for example, around 40% of crime in Scotland was suffered by 4% of all victims. Thus, a minority of victims, typically those living on low incomes, living in poor housing and high crime areas suffer from a large proportion of crimes (SCCCJ, 2000).

The criminal justice process

Criminal justice involves detecting, prosecuting and dealing with those suspected, and found guilty, of committing a crime. Its goals are seen as being to protect the public by deterrence or by imposing sentences that reduce crime, either by incapacitating or rehabilitating offenders. At the same time, it must deal with suspects and offenders according to principles of justice, due process and human rights and carry out its functions efficiently. These goals may conflict – protecting the public can lead to calls for punitive policing, prosecution and sentencing policies that might undermine rights to a 'fair trial' or a proportionate sentence. They may also suggest long periods of incarceration, which may impede rehabilitative strategies. All criminal justice systems face conflicting pressures and, in practice, criminal justice policy incorporates a combination of approaches with a shifting balance between different priorities.

Criminal justice is often described as a system. However, the range of decisions and agencies involved mean that it is more accurately described as a 'process' (Young, 1997; Davies et al, 2004). Crimes and offences pass through different stages of arrest, prosecution, trial, conviction and sentencing. Many exit the process at different stages, either because there is not enough evidence to proceed or by being diverted to, for example, social work or psychiatric services. Many different agencies are involved in this process.

Scottish criminal justice agencies

The main responsibility for criminal justice lies with the Justice Department, created after devolution. The Education Department is responsible for the Children's Hearing system, Local Authorities for Criminal Justice Social Work, and the Communities Ministry for Community Safety Partnerships and arrangements for administering Antisocial Behaviour Orders. In addition:

• Eight **police** forces in Scotland deal with detecting crime, crime prevention and public order and also have a wider role in liaising with agencies involved in community safety, dealing with victims and witnesses and diverting offenders.

- The **Crown Office and Procurator Fiscal Service** (COPFS) is the public prosecution service for Scotland. It has high amounts of discretion to prosecute offenders or to divert them by means of a Fiscal warning, a fiscal fine or a conditional offer, and it may also refer offenders to psychiatric, psychological or reparation and mediation services (SCCCJ, 2000). It also encompasses a new Victim Information and Advice Service, which supplies information to victims and next of kin about the progress of cases.
- The **Scottish Courts Service** (SCS) is an Executive Agency of the Justice Department and encompasses the Supreme Courts and the 49 Sheriff Courts. District Courts deal with minor summary offences.
- The **Scottish Prison Service** (SPS) was granted agency status in 1993. It is responsible for holding prisoners securely and in humane conditions and administers a number of rehabilitative programmes. There are also private prisons run by security companies.
- The provision of **social work** services, which involves work with those diverted from the courts, preparing reports to the court and supervising offenders given community sentences, is the responsibility of Local Authority **Criminal Justice Social Work** (CJSW) services. These services receive 100% of their funding from the Scottish Executive.
- The vast majority of children under 16 who offend are referred to the Children's Reporter who refers some of these to a Children's Hearing, a system administered by the **Scottish Children's Reporter Administration** (SCRA).
- All local authority areas have **Community Safety Partnerships,** which deal with a range of issues concerning community safety.

A number of voluntary organisations also play a major role in providing services for offenders and in participating in consultations about criminal justice policy. These include Safeguarding Communities – Reducing Offending (SACRO), the Howard League for Penal Reform in Scotland, APEX Scotland and the children's charity, NCH. Victim Support Scotland (VSS) is a voluntary organisation that provides practical and emotional support to the victims of and witnesses to crime, and administers services in court. The Scottish Consortium on Crime and Criminal Justice (SCCCJ, www.scccj.org.uk) brings together these organisations, responds to consultations and prepares reports seeking to "promote open dialogue" about key issues in criminal justice.

Issues in criminal justice policy

Discussion of criminal justice policy in any jurisdiction must take account of global as well as local trends (Garland, 1999) and Scotland has adapted and applied ideas and policies from other jurisdictions (Duff and Hutton, 1999). A brief account of major issues in criminal justice policy is therefore necessary to contextualise Scottish policy.

For much of the 20th century, criminal justice and penal policy were affected by the 'criminological project', which attempted to relate criminal justice policy to the 'causes' of crime. These were seen to lie in psychological, psychiatric or environmental 'pathologies' on the part of individual offenders that could be addressed by rehabilitative strategies. Social work and psychiatric services developed in prison and in the community through Probation Orders. This approach was particularly relevant for young offenders who, it was argued, could be saved from a criminal career and most jurisdictions developed separate arrangements for juvenile delinquents. Rehabilitative approaches, however, were criticised as being 'too soft', as not protecting the public sufficiently and as ineffective. Towards the latter part of the 20th century, there was considerable 'disillusionment' with rehabilitation as research evidence seemed to indicate that 'nothing works'. The growth of the welfare state and increasing affluence were accompanied by increasing crime rates that challenged links between crime and poverty (Young, 1994).

There have been many theoretical accounts of the so-called penal transformations which followed (Garland, 1996; McAra, 1999). To Feeley and Simon (1994), a 'new penology' based on actuarialism, involving a culture of performance indicators, risk management and an emphasis on organisational goals replaced a concern with welfare and rehabilitation, and offenders were increasingly seen as a group to be managed according to a series of 'risk assessments'. To Garland (1996), governments faced the problem of rising crime rates which the criminal justice system seemed incapable of reducing, along with the 'fiscal' crisis created by increasing costs. This led to a strategy of 'responsibilisation' (placing the responsibility for crime on individuals and families and away from wider issues of social inequalities and deprivation) and to developing measurable indicators of success, thus managing rather than attempting to transform the social divisions which contributed to higher levels of crime. This was accompanied by a rise in 'popular punitivism' (Bottoms, 1994), whereby governments sought to be seen to be 'tough' on offenders.

These trends could be seen in England and Wales where crime and criminal justice, hitherto not seen as major political issues, became politicised, particularly during and after the General Election of 1979, with the victorious Conservative Party promising strong action against crime and arguing that it could not be 'explained away' by social conditions. To them, crime was seen as the responsibility of individual offenders and their families. Attention turned from looking at offenders' motivations to the situations in which crime took place – offenders, it was argued, 'rationally' choose to commit crime but can be prevented if crime is made more difficult by physical measures such as security devices, greater surveillance and the installation of CCTV. Crime prevention also focused on 'social' and 'community' crime prevention – looking at measures to target groups all thought to be 'at risk' of committing crime.

Governments also adopted 'twin track' or bifurcatory policies, reserving tough punishment for so-called 'dangerous' or 'high risk' offenders and attempting to divert less serious offenders to community alternatives. A punitive turn was signalled during the 1990s following the then Home secretary Michael Howard's famous argument that 'prison works', which led to higher rates of imprisonment. Community sentences became cast as 'punishment in the community', and the association of the Probation Service with social work was severed by the abandonment of social work training for officers and a strong emphasis on public protection.

This popular punitivism was considered to be an electoral advantage and the Labour Party, often characterised as 'soft' on crime, developed the approach indicated in Tony Blair's famous slogan, first contained in a 1993 *New Statesman* article, entitled, 'Crime is a socialist issue', "tough on crime, tough on the causes of crime", with the causes seen to be lying in families and communities (Young and Matthews, 2003). In government, New Labour's approach to criminal justice policy has been described as 'populist' and as 'punitive managerialism' (Cavadino and Dignan, 2002). Most agencies now have performance indicators, centralised crime reduction targets and a strong emphasis on 'risk management'. A moralising tone has accompanied the introduction of tougher measures against offenders such as Antisocial Behaviour Orders (ASBOs), parenting orders, curfews and electronic tagging. The Probation Service has recently been placed in a new National Offender Management Service (NOMS) along with the Prison service.

Criminal justice in Scotland

Shortly before devolution, a number of commentators argued that Scottish criminal justice had resisted many of these influences and retained a welfarist approach (Young, 1997; McAra, 1999; Duff and Hutton, 1999). It had its own legal system and its own set of institutional arrangements. Scottish criminal procedure, pre-trial and prosecution arrangements displayed elements of both Anglo-American and European systems (Young, 1997). The Scottish public prosecutor, the Procurator Fiscal, has a high amount of prosecutorial discretion and there was more judicial discretion in sentencing which had not been strongly influenced by just deserts or populist punitivism (Hutton, 1999). These writers argued that while managerialism and an emphasis on public protection were evident, they had not undermined a commitment to welfare.

The Children's Hearings system is universally described as 'unique', and while its development, following the Kilbrandon Report of 1964, echoed similar reforms elsewhere, it took the radical path of decriminalising children under 16 who offend by removing them from the criminal courts. Children's Hearings are not courts deciding guilt or innocence, and their decisions are guided solely by the needs of the individual child. Under the Kilbrandon philosophy, children who offend are seen as little different to other children who require care. While widely supported, this approach was criticised as 'soft' and the Children (Scotland) Act of 1995 allowed welfare considerations to be overruled where the protection of the public from serious harm was an issue (Asquith and Docherty, 1999). Nonetheless, welfarism remained the dominant principle (McAra, 1999).

The arrangements for social work are also distinct. The Probation Service was abolished in 1968 and criminal justice social workers became part of a generic social work service. National Standards, introduced in 1991, retained a greater commitment to non-custodialism than their English counterpart and community sentences were not faced with the rhetoric of 'punishment in the community' (McIvor and Williams, 1999). The introduction of managerialism did not supplant welfarism, therefore, but rather, argues McAra (1999), sharpened the focus of effective social work intervention. While there was some emphasis on the role of physically demanding work in community service, suggestions to provide offenders on community service with clearly marked clothing were withdrawn (McIvor and Williams, 1999).

Prisons also showed a commitment to rehabilitation and had developed "some of the most progressive prison regimes to be found anywhere" (Young, 1997, p 116). The 'penal crisis' was less severe in Scotland and while there were periods of prison unrest, the SPS document *Opportunities and responsibility* stressed the notion of the responsible prisoner and the need for 'positive' regimes; thus managerialism was accompanied by a strong commitment to rehabilitative programmes (McAra, 1999).

A stronger commitment to welfare therefore permeated the system. In part, this could be explained by Scotland's different legal system and its geographic distance from the rest of the UK (Young, 1997). This enabled the development of a distinctive criminal justice culture and policy network consisting of senior civil servants in the Crown Office, Directors of Social Work and the Judiciary who were not part of the UK government, producing a situation in which policies could be tailored to the distinctive conditions in Scotland. In addition, McAra (1997) suggests that if government legitimacy is low, as it was during the 1990s, the influence of this policy network can increase. Moreover, she argues, the commitment to welfare reflects the civic culture in Scotland, a stronger commitment to Labour policies, and to social welfare in general.

After devolution, this culture faced a government in Edinburgh which while devolved was dominated by a Labour party influenced by the New Labour policies that had had an impact south of the border. Rapid change has ensued accompanied by a 'sudden and dramatic politicisation' of criminal justice in Scotland (McNeill and Batchelor, 2004). Strong elements of popular punitivism were evident in the 2003 General Election during which the First Minister, Jack McConnell, famously attacked the 'ned culture' and 'antisocial behaviour'. The welfarist approach, therefore, is seen to be under threat, as illustrated in the following outline of selected areas.

Youth justice in Scotland

The Children's Hearings system

The Children's Hearings system has attracted international attention but has recently been subject to considerable criticism and re-evaluation. The Children's Charity, NCH, recently conducted a wide-ranging review, *Where's Kilbrandon now?* (NCH, 2004), taking evidence from experts and from children themselves. A major question it addressed was whether the system itself was wrong or whether its problems lay in the way it was run and resourced (Mellon, 2003). It identifies a number of problems, chief among which is under-resourcing, which leads to delays and difficulties in implementing Children's Panels' recommendations. A recent Audit Scotland (2003) report found, for example, that around half of the children referred for supervision were only seeing social workers once a month. In some areas, there were no care or action plans, in part attributable to a shortage of qualified social workers. Both Audit Scotland and the NCH inquiry found that social work and police services were not meeting nationally agreed time standards for referrals and reports. Other problems included difficulties of recruiting and retaining panel members, their lack of social diversity and the lack of any systematic evaluation and review.

Overall, the *Where's Kilbrandon now?* inquiry, having looked critically at evidence about the more punitive system in England and Wales, supports the current system, which, it argues, involves multi-agency working and information-sharing and is economic and effective. Its deficiencies lie in a lack of resources and shortcomings in other systems. It needs strengthening and more information about the system should be made public to enhance public confidence. The Executive is currently undertaking a major review due to be completed sometime in 2005, said to be necessary as the system is faced with a changed society and has not been thoroughly reviewed since its inception. It also cites difficulties of dealing with persistent offenders, issues concerning children in care and local variations in delivery (www.childrens-hearings.co.uk/review.asp accessed 15 May 2004). There are fears that the attitude of ministers could lead to the hearing system being reserved for non-offenders and that offending children will be referred increasingly to the courts. The development of Fast Track Hearings and Youth Courts could be taken to signal such a move.

Fast track hearings and Youth Courts

There have been recurrent concerns that the hearings have insufficient powers of disposal for persistent young offenders (Tombs, 2000), who constitute around a tenth of children referred to panels and are responsible for around a third of offences. It is difficult to identify this group, currently defined as "young people who have been referred to a Children's Hearing on offence grounds in respect of at least five offending episodes in the last six months" (McNeill and Batchelor,

2004, p 11). Research indicates that they suffer more severely than other offenders from a range of family, housing and educational problems and come from more deprived backgrounds (Tombs, 2000).

Delays in the hearings system enable persistent offenders to continue offending before effective intervention can be made, a problem addressed in a pilot system of 'fast track' hearings. An initial report found that, on the whole, the initiative was supported, that speedier referrals had resulted and the extra resources were welcomed (Scottish Executive, 2003a). There was, however, an initial 'overload' caused by a backlog of cases, some doubted that there would be adequate funding in the long term, and there were concerns that a focus on fast track cases should not be at the expense of other elements of the system. There were also concerns that children already in care have been targeted by the new system and that some children have been referred for persistent but non-serious offences. One example cited is a youth charged with 'kicking council trees' (Naysmith, 2004).

Another problematic group are young people aged 16-18 who are normally dealt with in criminal courts, producing a situation in which they may be faced with a punishment as opposed to a welfare approach, sometimes overnight (McNeill and Batchelor, 2004). Youth Courts were recently piloted for this age group and were presented as a tough option to tackle serious and persistent offending. Nonetheless, argue McNeill and Batchelor (2004), the second objective of these courts is to promote "the social inclusion, citizenship and personal responsibility of young offenders while maximising their potential" (Scottish Executive, 2003b, cited in McNeill and Batchelor, 2004, p 9).

The youth justice system, therefore, faces major changes, and continues to display the tension between punishment, public protection and welfare (Asquith and Docherty, 1999). There are signs of greater convergence with England and Wales, and perceived threats to the primarily welfarist approach – also threatened, argue some, by the changes introduced by the 2004 Antisocial Behaviour (Scotland) Bill.

Criminal justice social work in Scotland

As outlined earlier in this chapter, the generic arrangements for criminal justice social work also set Scotland apart from England and Wales and the National standards stressed a non-custodial approach. The generic approach, however, may have dispersed the specialist skills of a dedicated Probation service (Young, 1997); there were concerns about the viability of probation and after-care services within generic social work departments (Robinson and McNeill, 2004) and the apparent 'laxness' and lack of effectiveness of supervision attracted criticism (McAra, 1999). Some of these issues were addressed by the National Standards and by the allocation of 100% central funding. There was, however, considerable diversity of provision and smaller local authorities were less able to meet their requirements. In 2002, the Scottish Executive publication, *The tough option*, indicated a toughening attitude by stating that the paramount aim of probation was public safety, an attitude reiterated in the 2001 *National priorities* for criminal justice social work (Robinson and McNeill, 2004).

Robinson and McNeill (2004) point to other contrasts between approaches north and south of the border where the Probation Service has become more of 'law enforcement' than a social work agency. While the primary aim of both systems is the protection of the public, the second of the Scottish *National priorities* is 'to reduce unnecessary custody by providing effective community disposals'. Indeed, a recent Justice Committee review of alternatives to custody explored how courts might be encouraged to make greater use of community sentences (McIvor, 2004). There is no equivalent aspiration in England and Wales where the second priority is 'reducing offending'. The third of the *National priorities*, to promote the social inclusion of offenders, has no counterpart in England and Wales, where punishment and enforcement are seen as legitimate objectives but are not present in the Scottish priorities document.

These differences can enable variations in interpretation and implementation. While both governments share a commitment to evidence-based policy, and to a 'what works' approach, developed in response to the 'nothing works' pessimism, this has tended, in England and Wales, to have been dominated by a 'medical model' emphasising cognitive behaviour therapy which focuses on personal 'defects' and thinking and social skills. This can neglect offenders' social circumstances and the Scottish approach has been more personalised and holistic, incorporating offenders' employment and other problems (McIvor, 2004).

This may also involve a 'desistance' approach, which looks not only at 'what works', but at "when, how and why change occurs" (McNeill, 2002, p 1). Research suggests that age and gender, maturity, developing social bonds and life transitions, such as marriage and employment, are all important factors affecting desistance along with the 'narratives' which offenders use to interpret their offending behaviour and motivation to stop (McIvor et al, 2000). Social work intervention, that aims to support offenders in these key aspects of their lives, may therefore have a greater impact as can supervision that offers someone who 'believes in' the offender. This, argues McNeill (2002, 2004), challenges the correctionalist approach of assessing offenders as 'risks', of managing groups rather than focusing on individuals and approaches that seek to exclude offenders and see them as 'other', 'bad' or beyond redemption.

A personal, holistic approach has also been found to have a more positive impact in relation to Community Service, which, argues McIvor (2002), has considerable reintegrative potential. In one survey, lower rates of recidivism were found in those placements which offenders found most rewarding and involved a 'degree of reciprocity or exchange'. Contact with beneficiaries gave offenders an insight into themselves and others and they felt that acquiring skills had given them greater confidence and self-esteem.

These kinds of approaches are more possible within the Scottish framework in which social work interventions can be justified as better protecting the public (McNeill, 2004) and McIvor (2004, p 324) argues that there are still "reasons to be optimistic that policy and practice will resist being driven by the narrow empiricist agenda that has typified recent developments in England and Wales". Nonetheless, there are signs of convergence as well as divergence. In addition to the priority accorded to public protection, the Scottish Executive has indicated that it is considering the creation of a single agency for dealing with offenders, which will be discussed later in this chapter.

Imprisonment

Young (1997, p 116) argues that Scotland has a reputation for "penal harshness and for penal innovation", imprisoning proportionately more of its population than most other European countries but having introduced particularly progressive prison regimes. The harshness continues, with the SPS having recorded its highest-ever prison population of 6,723 in May 2002, and in 2003 it had the fourth highest rate of imprisonment in the EU, at 129 people per 100,000 of population (although this remains lower than England and Wales). Conditions within prisons remain harsh, with as many as 1,200 inmates still having to slop out, now rare in England and Wales (BBC News, 2004). This practice has been held to breach a prisoner's human rights and, while the Scottish Executive is to appeal this decision, it could face claims for compensation. Recurrent reports of the Scottish Prison Inspectorate stress poor conditions. It was recently reported that 22% of inmates in Edinburgh Prison had to slop out and lived in cells with no electricity other than lighting (BBC News, 2004). Scotland also imprisons high numbers of fine defaulters, a particularly acute problem for women (Tombs, 2004a).

At the same time, it can be argued that Scotland has a tradition of progressive regimes having pioneered the special unit at Barlinnie Prison for serious offenders. As seen earlier in this chapter, *Opportunities and responsibility* stressed rehabilitation and the need for 'positive' regimes although the primary task of prison is seen as custodial (McManus, 1999). Prisons also face difficulties in implementing a rehabilitative agenda: they have to receive all prisoners whom the courts send to them making planning difficult, and as many prisoners are there for very short sentences there is no time for rehabilitation (McManus, 1999). In addition, poor conditions and the requirements of security may also impede rehabilitative efforts.

The current 'vision' of SPS, developed in 2000, continues to show a mixture of managerialism and rehabilitation. Its stated aim is to pursue a 'Correctional Agenda', which 'helps to reduce recidivism' and it discusses 'sentence management' and 'risk assessment'. In the 2000 document, *Intervention and integration for a safer society*, it acknowledges the special challenges posed by groups drawn from the most disadvantaged and it is committed to 'Making a Difference' to prisoners' lives and to 'reducing offending and enhancing inclusion'. It has an Inclusion Branch which aims to improve life and work skills, and a 'what works' unit offering accredited offending behaviour programmes dealing with cognitive skills and the Sex Offender Treatment Programme (STOP).

Throughcare

Throughcare programmes address the issue that prisoners' problems most often lie outside the prison. These programmes aim to tackle problems from the point of sentence, working closely with social workers and other agencies who will be dealing with offenders and their families after release, thus distinguishing them from 'after care' or 'prisoner re-entry' schemes (Tombs, 2004a). The first throughcare centre, involving APEX, was set up in Edinburgh Prison and provides a 'one-stop shop' for prisoners to receive help with employment issues, such as preparing a CV and accommodation and other problems. Partnerships between different agencies, information sharing and planning are all crucial to the success of these programmes (Tombs, 2004b), and an evaluation found that the scheme was popular with prisoners who felt that they had been assisted. While initial results should be treated with caution and were based on a short-term follow up, it was found that up to 88% did not return to custody, comparing well with an average 22% return to custody rate across Scotland. There were some problems with developing full partnership working, the lack of a shared information system to track individual prisoners, and resource constraints which meant that officers had limited time to make reports and work with partners (Tombs, 2004c). Prisoners were on occasion also taken out of the centre for security reasons.

Women and imprisonment

The numbers of women in prison have increased in Scotland as they have elsewhere (McIvor, 2004) and it has long been recognised that women face particular problems in prison and that poverty is a major underlying factor (Carlen, 1983). Recurrent suicides of women in Cornton Vale prison in Central Scotland have also occasioned concern, with a spate of seven suicides in 30 months, linked to a history of drug abuse (McIvor, 2004). An influential report, *Women offenders: A safer way* (Social Work Services and Prisons Inspectorates for Scotland, 1998), concluded that the "background of women in prison is characterised by the experience of abuse, drug misuse, poor educational attainment, poverty, psychological distress and self harm" (p 52). It found that women tend to commit minor, mainly property, offences and stressed the link between women's offending and poverty. It recommended a 'twin track' strategy involving more services for women on bail and a reduction in imprisonment for fine default along with limitations on prison places to achieve a reduction in the population at Cornton Vale from 170+ to 100 or less by 2000, including plans to end the use of prison for women aged under 18. Since that report, however, the numbers of women in prison have increased disproportionately to men and by 2002, the average daily population at Cornton Vale was 213. There had been more suicides and 15 year olds were still being incarcerated (McIvor, 2004; Tombs, 2004a). The population in 2004 has been consistently well over 300.

Tombs (2004a) analyses the reasons for the failure to achieve a reduction.

While the government accepted many of the recommendations of *A safer way*, endorsing the provision of more community options and setting up an interagency forum in Glasgow, it shifted the responsibility for reducing prison places to the courts and the judiciary. In addition, argues Tombs, it decontextualised the report's emphasis on poverty as a root of women's offending. A 2000 Annual Report of the Inter-Agency Forum on Women's Offending (IAF) attributed women's offending to 'addiction, abuse and anxiety', or other forms of psychological distress. It did not address the target of reducing the numbers of women in prison. Tombs argues that its recommendations stress processes, such as monitoring the possibility of a daily court for women, building on existing diversions and considering the value of Arrest Referral Schemes, rather than outcomes such as a reduction of women in prison.

A ministerial group on Women Offenders in 2000 issued *A better way*, which also stressed 'addiction, abuse and anxiety' rather than material circumstances, and did not refer to specific decarceration targets. It did consider how a reduction of the numbers of women in prison could be achieved estimating that if the courts restricted imprisonment to women convicted of violent and drugs offences, made better use of community options and targeted measures on young women the average daily population of Cornton Vale could be reduced by 27 – still more, comments Tombs, than the average number in prison at the time of *A safer way*. There is space, she argues, given Scotland's apparent commitment to welfare strategies and an explicit policy arguing for reduction in the numbers of women in prison, for a decarcerative policy, which must see a reduction in the number of prison places and should consider the morality of sending women to prison for minor property offences, fine default and problematic drug use.

Re:duce, Re:habilitate, Re:form

The high costs and relative ineffectiveness of prison in reducing offending is acknowledged by the Executive who launched a major consultation, 'Re:duce, Re:habilitate, Re:form' in 2004, in which they spell out the reasons why change is essential. These include high reconviction rates: around 30,000 (67%) individuals convicted in 2002 had at least one previous conviction between 1993 and 2002. In addition, 60% of offenders released from prison in 1999 were reconvicted of another offence within two years. They are considering the creation of a single agency combining the SPS and CJSW, in which they aim to achieve a "coordinated service which manages offenders throughout their sentence to re-entry into a law abiding lifestyle". They argue that the different agencies dealing with offenders are not well coordinated, use different risk and need assessment tools and that there is a lack of consistency in the design, quality and delivery of programmes, which makes it difficult to evaluate their impact. Reference is made to single agencies in other societies, such as the Nordic countries.

These proposals have encountered strong opposition. At the time of writing, the consultation has finished with the majority of over 100 submissions opposing the idea of a single agency while supporting the emphasis on reducing the numbers of short prison sentences (Adams, 2004). A response from the SCCCJ (2004), for example, points to the strength of community-based provision for offenders, which is better enabled within community planning structures encompassing health, community care, community safety, antisocial behaviour and children's services. It would therefore be more appropriate, they argue, to develop community prisons rather than a centralised agency, which would divorce criminal justice from communities and from other community interventions. They, along with others, fear that prisons would become the dominant partner in any single agency. This can be counter-productive. In a report on New Zealand, Andrew Coyle from the Centre for International Prison Studies, points out that the creation of a Department of Corrections in 1995 to manage custodial and non-custodial services has been associated with a dramatic rise in rates of imprisonment from 129 per 100,000 to 161 per 100,000 in 2004 (cited in Adams, 2004). So strong was this oppposition that it was announced in December 2004 that plans for a single agency had been abandoned.

This discussion of imprisonment echoes earlier discussions in that it shows elements of convergence with England and Wales, where the single-agency approach can be interpreted as a shift towards the 'new penology' in that it seeks to manage offenders and aims at punishment and reducing offending which to McNeill (2004, p 6) affirms the expressive, instrumental and correctionalist aspects of new penology. 'Re:duce, Re:habilitate, Re:form' clearly stresses the need for efficiency and public protection, although in its strong statements about reducing numbers in custody and its emphasis on rehabilitation it retains some of the emphases seen as more typical of the Scottish approach.

Community safety and the Antisocial Behaviour Bill

A major shift in policies concerned with crime reduction has been the growth of strategies of crime prevention and community safety. In England and Wales, the 1998 Crime and Disorder Act required all local authorities to set up Crime and Disorder Partnerships, who must carry out audits of crime and disorder and develop five-year targets for the reduction of vehicle crime, burglary and robbery under the government's Crime Reduction Programme (Newburn, 2003). Some fear that these centralised performance targets will impede partnerships' ability to focus on local issues and priorities and others are critical of the way in which community safety – a term capable of encompassing a broad range of issues – has been dominated by an emphasis on 'crime and disorder'. In what is described as the 'criminalisation of social policy', critics argue that community safety can be associated with the marginalisation of fundamental public issues except insofar as they are related to their criminogenic qualities (Hughes, 2002). Community safety is also related to the growing concern about antisocial behaviour, a term difficult to define, but which has assumed the status of a 'moral panic' and been largely associated with social housing tenants and young people (Brown, 2004).

Antisocial Behaviour Orders (ASBOs) are civil orders, but breaches can lead to criminal convictions.

In Scotland, community safety is broadly defined. In the 1998 document published by the Scottish Executive, *Safer communities through partnerships – A strategy for action*, it is defined as "protecting people's right to live in confidence and without fear for their own safety or the safety of other people". Crime prevention, it argues, must form an important part of community safety but it also covers road and fire safety, the provision of play areas and the prevention of minor anti-social behaviour. Unlike England and Wales, partnerships are not mandatory and were initially slow to conduct proper audits or joint plans (Audit Scotland, 2000). In 2002, the Community Safety Award programme was launched to provide funding for partnerships based on the size of the population and crimes per head of population, with a variable award for which local authorities must apply. Applications are assessed according to a points system in which evidence must be given that partnerships are in place at a strategic level, that there has been a community safety audit carried out and statistical evidence to support the strategy and action plan (www.scotland.gov.uk/pages/news/2004/02/p_SEJD414.aspx).

While broadly conceived, community safety partnerships would appear, as in England and Wales, to be dominated by concerns about crime. One study of the Glasgow CSP found that it tended to be dominated by the police and, while broader safety issues were part of its remit, crime featured highly in its definition of key problems (Helms, 2003). In local forums, what were essentially maintenance issues became defined as safety issues along with 'street people', such as beggars and prostitutes – signalling elements of the criminalisation of social policy. Also indicative of this is the dominance, in the last year, of discussions of community safety by debates about the Antisocial Behaviour (Scotland) Bill, passed in June 2004, and the introduction of antisocial behaviour units and the provision of community wardens.

This bill introduces a number of measures:

- councils and chief constables will publish plans to deal with antisocial behaviour in their area;
- ASBOs for those aged 12-16;
- the police will be able to designate 'dispersal zones' and disperse groups. A refusal to disperse can lead to a fine or period of imprisonment;
- parenting orders: councils and children's panels will be able to issue orders against the parents of badly-behaved children, which will be enforceable by a fine;
- electronic tagging will be extended to under 16s; and
- children's hearings will be given power to restrict children's movement and tag them as an alternative to secure accommodation.

This bill was preceded by a consultation paper in 2003, *Putting our communities first – A strategy for tackling antisocial behaviour.* A report on responses (Flint et al, 2003), found opinions to be deeply divided. While many did see antisocial behaviour as a serious problem, and welcomed some parts of the proposals, there were serious and fundamental objections. Young people doubted the effectiveness of proposals and expressed resentment that they were being targeted and stigmatised. Some feared that the measures would increase tensions between them and the police – a point also made by the police (*The Scotsman*, 7 January 2004). Some argued that electronic tagging could become a 'badge of honour' (Naysmith, 2003). Others found the proposals to be over-punitive and neglected the root causes of antisocial behaviour, arguing for a more holistic approach taking account of wider issues of social inclusion, health, education and regeneration. Some, such as the housing charity, Shelter Scotland, saw the proposals as socially divisive by targeting young people, social housing tenants and residents in deprived communities and others feared that resources to make strategies effective would not be forthcoming.

Particularly contentious were proposals to extend ASBOs and electronic monitoring to under 16s. Parenting orders were seen to encourage a 'blaming culture', which did not take account of the full circumstances and powers to disperse groups of young people were seen as unnecessary, draconian and unlikely to be used. The Children's Commissioner warned that tagging children under 16 could be in breach of the UN Convention on the Rights of the Child, which prohibits 'degrading treatment or punishment' (Fraser, 2004). The Executive argued strongly that they were responding to people's concerns in communities and rejected the arguments of so-called 'experts'. In a widely-reported response, First Minister Jack McConnell commented that critics were commenting from the 'trendy heights' and were 'out of touch' (Denholm, 2004a). Introducing the bill, the Communities Minister, Margaret Curran, argued that sometimes politicians had to disagree with professionals to respond to the concerns of ordinary Scots, many of whom, she said were plagued by group disorder:

> we owe it to those communities who have been pleading for these powers, even in the light of scorn from those who think otherwise, to give them the respite it will afford. (quoted in *The Scotsman*, 18 June 2004, p 12)

Also controversial have been the use of Community Wardens, who will be employed by all councils, although some fear that they may amount to 'policing on the cheap' (Denholm, 2004b) and that the money would be better spent on more police officers. Antisocial Behaviour Units have also been set up.

These initiatives, and the discourse used in their introduction, arguably provide a good example of 'penal populism' in which the Executive has firmly rejected the opinions of key groups and proceeded with proposals by appealing to popular opinion and fears of antisocial behaviour. It also illustrates further signs of convergence between New Labour policies north and south of the border. While few dispute that there is a 'problem' of antisocial behaviour, it is a socially constructed term, and the use of ASBOs can criminalise young people and social housing tenants, as well as being exclusive. They signal the criminalisation of social policy and also, argues Brown (2004), blur the boundaries between criminal and other forms of social control.

Conclusion

This outline of criminal justice in Scotland well illustrates the tensions and shifts characteristic of contemporary criminal justice policy. Before devolution, there was a clearly distinct set of policies in Scotland, with a criminal justice culture showing a greater commitment to welfare as opposed to punishment, to inclusionary rather than exclusionary penal strategies, and which had resisted some of the excesses brought about by popular punitivism. Since devolution, criminal justice policy has been politicised and there are clear signs of penal populism, seen most clearly in the Executive's seeming determination to forge ahead with unpopular proposals such as the single agency and antisocial behaviour legislation in the face of strongly voiced concerns from practitioners and other experts. Whereas until recently, informed commentators were optimistic that the welfare tradition would survive, some now fear that the effects of punitive policies may undermine key elements of the system. The Kilbrandon Philosophy of the Children's Hearings for example could be threatened by the more punitive policies and tone of electronic monitoring, ASBOs, fast-track hearings and youth courts and a correctionalist turn in relation to criminal justice social work could threaten holistic forms of social work intervention (McNeill and Batchelor, 2004).

Nonetheless, it has also been seen that most criminal justice systems oscillate between different approaches and some doubt the all pervasiveness and inevitability of the broad trends of 'responsibilisation' and popular punitivism. These were initially resisted in Scotland and policy still arguably shows a greater commitment to social inclusion and anti-custodialism than other parts of the UK. The strong criminal justice culture in Scotland will not vanish overnight and there are many suggested alternatives. In England and Wales, taken by many to exemplify a punitive approach, not all elements of welfare have disappeared. Some see a return to rehabilitative policies with the emphasis on 'what works', and others see the youth justice system, particularly with its emphasis on restorative justice, as not entirely given over to punitive strategies.

In Scotland, much will depend on what changes are made and how they will be implemented. For example, it has been seen that, so far, fast-track hearings and Youth Courts have retained some of the principles of the hearings system, although there are fears about the potentially divisive way in which they have been implemented. Many options remain. Proposals for the single agency could take a more community-based approach as suggested by SCCCJ, rather than creating a centralised agency dominated by the Prison service. Much more could be done within the hearings system to promote restorative justice and, along with the provision of social work, to provide more programmes which, while focused on desistance and reducing offending, are not punitively oriented but take account of offenders' social and economic circumstances. The focus of community safety could be widened and much will depend on how ASBOs, and the other powers recently introduced, are actually implemented.

Acknowledgement

I would like to thank the many authors who provided material and helpful comments during the preparation of this article, in particular Professor Jackie Tombs.

Further resources

For excellent sources of information about the situation pre-devolution see Duff and Hutton (1999) and Young (1996). There is no comprehensive account of the situation post-devolution; good accounts of specific elements can be found in NCH (2004) and Robinson and McNeill (2004).

On the web ...

An invaluable website for Scottish Criminal Justice is www.cjscotland.org.uk, which contains links to all the major agencies and government departments along with an archive of press releases and reports.

References

Adams, L. (2004) 'Ministers push single agency for offenders', *The Herald*, 8 June (www.theherald.com).

Asquith, S. and Docherty, M. (1999) 'Preventing offending by children and young people in Scotland', in P. Duff and N. Hutton (eds) *Criminal justice in Scotland*, Aldershot: Ashgate/Dartmouth, pp 243-61.

Audit Scotland (2000) *Safe and sound: A study of community safety partnerships in Scotland*, Edinburgh: Audit Scotland, May.

Audit Scotland (2003) *Dealing with offending by young people: A follow up report*, Audit Scotland, November.

BBC News (2004) 'Report critical of Edinburgh jail' (newsvote.bbc.co.uk/go/pr/fr/-/1/hi/scotland/3793003.stm).

Bottoms, A. (1994) 'The philosophy and politics of punishment and sentencing', in C. Clarkson and R. Morgan (eds) *The politics of sentencing reform*, Oxford: Oxford University Press, pp 17-49.

Brown, A. (2004) 'Anti-social behaviour, crime control and social control', *Howard Journal of Criminal Justice*, vol 43, no 2, pp 203-11.

Carlen, P. (1983) *Women's imprisonment*, London: Routledge and Kegan Paul.

Cavadino, M. and Dignan, J. (2002) *The penal system: An introduction* (3rd edn), London: Sage Publications.

Croall, H. (1998) *Crime and society in Britain*, Harlow: Addison Wesley Longman.

Croall, H. (2001) *Understanding white collar crime*, Buckingham: Open University Press.

Davies, M., Croall, H. and Tyrer, J. (2004) *Criminal justice in England and Wales* (3rd edn), Harlow: Addison Wesley Longman.

Denholm, A. (2004a) 'McConnell claims bill critics "out of touch"', *The Scotsman*, 4 February (www.scotsman.com).

Denholm, A. (2004b) 'Critics say wardens plan is policing on the cheap', *The Scotsman*, 19 February (www.scotsman.com).

Downes, D. (2004) 'New Labour and the lost causes of crime', *Criminal Justice Matters*, no 55, Spring, pp 4-5.

Duff, P. and Hutton, N. (1999) 'Introduction', in P. Duff and N. Hutton (eds) *Criminal justice in Scotland*, Aldershot: Ashgate/Dartmouth, pp 1-13.

Feeley, M. and Simon, J. (1994) 'Actuarial justice: the emerging New Criminal Law', in D. Nelken (ed) *The futures of criminology*, London: Sage Publications, pp 173-201.

Flint, J., Atkinson, R. and Scott, S. (2003) *A report on the consultation responses to Putting Our Communities First: A strategy for tackling anti-social behaviour*, Edinburgh: Scottish Executive (www.scotland.gov.uk/library5/social/stabmr-OO.asp).

Fraser, D. (2004) 'Behaviour bill "threat to children's rights"', *Sunday Herald*, 7 March (www.sundayherald.com).

Garland, D. (1996) 'The limits of the sovereign state: strategies of crime control in contemporary society', *British Journal of Criminology*, vol 36, pp 445-71.

Garland, D. (1999) 'Preface', to P. Duff and N. Hutton (eds) *Criminal justice in Scotland*, Aldershot: Ashgate/Dartmouth, pp xiii-xvi.

Helms, G. (2003) 'Towards safe city centres? Remaking the spaces of an old-industrial city', Unpublished PhD, Department of Geography and Geomatics, University of Glasgow, August.

Houchin, R. (2004) 'Social exclusion and imprisonment in Scotland', Unpublished draft report for Scottish Prison Service.

Hughes, G. (2002) 'Crime and Disorder Reduction Partnerships: the future of community safety?', in G. Hughes, E. McLaughlin and J. Muncie (eds) *Crime prevention and community safety: New directions*, London: Sage Publications, pp 123-41.

Hutton, N. (1999) 'Sentencing in Scotland', in P. Duff and N. Hutton (eds) *Criminal justice in Scotland*, Aldershot: Ashgate/Dartmouth, pp 166-81.

McAra, L. (1999) 'The politics of penality: an overview of the development of penal policy in Scotland', in P. Duff and N. Hutton (eds) *Criminal justice in Scotland*, Aldershot: Ashgate/Dartmouth, pp 355-80.

McIvor, G. (2002) *What works in community service?*, CJSW Briefing Paper 6, Edinburgh: CJSW Development Centre (www.cjsw.ac.uk/documents/CJSWBriefing_2002_08_1.pdf).

McIvor, G. (2004) 'Getting personal: developments in policy and practice in Scotland', in G. Mair (ed) *What matters in probation*, Cullompton: Willan Publishing, pp 305-26.

McIvor, G., Jamieson, J. and Murray, C. (2000) 'Study examines gender differences in desistance from crime', *Offenders Programs Report*, vol 4, no 1, p 509.

McIvor, G. and Williams, B. (1999) 'Community based disposals', in P. Duff and N. Hutton (eds) *Criminal justice in Scotland*, Aldershot: Ashgate/Dartmouth, pp 198-227.

McManus, J. (1999) 'Imprisonment and other custodial sentences', in P. Duff and N. Hutton (eds) *Criminal justice in Scotland*, Aldershot: Ashgate/Dartmouth, pp 228-42.

McNeill, F. (2002) *Beyond what works: How and why do people stop offending?*, CJSW Briefing Paper 5, August, Edinburgh: CJSW Development Centre (www.cjsw.ac.uk/documents/CJSWBriefing_2002_08_1.pdf).

McNeill, F. (2004) 'Desistance, rehabilitation and correctionalism: developments and prospects in Scotland', *Howard Journal*, vol 43, no 4, pp 420-36, September.

McNeill, F. and Batchelor, S. (2004) 'Persistent offending by young people: developing practice', *Issues in Community and Criminal Justice* (Monograph no 3), London: National Association of Probation Officers.

Mellon, M. (2003) 'Where's Kilbrandon now?' Reviewing child justice in Scotland', *Criminal Justice Matters*, no 54, Winter, pp 18-19.

Naysmith, S. (2003) 'Youths tell Jack: stop stereotyping us as criminals and troublemakers', *Sunday Herald*, 26 October (www.sundayherald.com).

Naysmith, S. (2004) 'Fast track panels "biased" against children in care', *Sunday Herald*, 11 January.

NCH (2004) *Where's Kilbrandon now? Report and recommendations from the inquiry*, Glasgow: NCH (www.nch.org.uk/kilbrandonnow).

Newburn, T. (2003) *Crime and criminal justice policy*, (2nd edn), London: Longman.

Robinson, G. and McNeill, F. (2004) 'Purposes matter: examining the "ends" of probation', in G. Mair (ed) *What matters in probation*, Cullompton: Willan Publishing, pp 277-304.

SCCCJ (Scottish Consortium on Crime and Criminal Justice) (2000) *Rethinking Criminal Justice in Scotland*, Edinburgh: SCCCJ.

SCCCJ (2004) *Response to Scottish Executive Justice Department Consultation: 'Re:duce, re:habilitate, re:form'*, Edinburgh: SCCJ (www.sccj.org.uk).

Scottish Executive (2003a) *Fast track hearings research: Interim report*, Edinburgh: Scottish Executive.

Scottish Executive (2003b) *The report of the Feasibility Group on youth crime pilots*, Edinburgh: Scottish Executive.

Scottish Executive (2004) Press Release (www.scotland.gov.uk/pages/news/2004/06/SEjdrecc.aspx), June.

Social Work Services and Prisons Inspectorates for Scotland (1998) *Women offenders – A safer way*, Edinburgh: The Stationery Office.

Tombs, J. (2000) *Youth, crime and Justice*, Edinburgh: SCCCJ.

Tombs, J. (2004a) 'From "A safer to a better way": transformations in penal policy for women', in G. McIvor (ed) *Women offenders*, London: Jessica Kingsley, pp 66-81.

Tombs, J. (2004b) *Throughcare: A process of change*, CJSW Briefing Paper 7, February, Edinburgh: CJSW Development Centre (www.cjsw.ac.uk/documents).

Tombs, J. (2004c) *The chance for change: A study of the Throughcare Centre Edinburgh Prison*, Edinburgh: SPS Occasional Papers Series.

Waterhouse, L., McGhee, J. and Loucks, N. (2004) 'Disentangling offenders and non offenders in the Scottish Children's Hearings: a clear divide?', *Howard Journal of Criminal Justice*, May, pp 164-79.

Young, J. (1994) 'Incessant chatter: recent paradigms within criminology', in M. Maguire, R. Morgan and R. Reiner (eds) *The Oxford handbook of criminology* (2nd edn), Oxford: Clarendon Press, pp 69-124.

Young, J. and Matthews, R. (2003) 'New Labour, crime control and social exclusion', in R. Matthews and J. Young (eds) *The new politics of crime and punishment*, Cullompton: Willan Publishing.

Young, P. (1997) *Crime and criminal justice in Scotland*, Edinburgh: The Stationery Office.

EIGHT

Health and health policy

Carol Tannahill

Two of the most defining features of Scotland's health are the lower life expectancy of its population and the persistent gap in health experience between the most affluent and deprived communities. This chapter examines the major changes taking place in Scottish health policy that might address these issues. The areas included are:

- Scotland's changing pattern of health and health inequalities;
- the meanings attached to healthy public policy and the contribution that health services and socioeconomic factors make to health improvement; and
- the influences on Scottish health policy post devolution and the distinctiveness of debate and policy in comparison to health policy in England.

Introduction

People living in Scotland tend to have poorer health and lower life expectancy than people in the rest of the UK. Scotland's health is also poorer than that of virtually all other Western European nations, with our nearest neighbours in the health 'league table' of European nations being Slovenia and Portugal (Hanlon et al, 2001). These facts have been stated so often now that they have almost become an integral – and sometimes even accepted – part of our culture, with the image of Scotland inexorably linked with the tag 'unhealthy'. It is to the challenge of turning around these statistics, and the 'sick country' image of Scotland, that health policy in the new Scotland must rise.

Scotland's health

There is no simple summary to be made of health in Scotland, but the following issues represent key aspects of the picture. (For more detailed information, see, for example, Hanlon et al, 2001; Scottish Executive, 2003a, 2004.)

Life expectancy at birth in Scotland has improved steadily over the last century: for men, from 50.1 years in 1910 to 72.8 years in 2000; for women, from 53.2 years in 1910 to 78.2 years in 2000. Increases in life expectancy are found consistently across Europe, and reflect many factors, including general improvements in standards of living, nutrition and hygiene, the decline in infectious diseases, and improvements in health and social care. The comparisons with other Western European countries highlight a startling fact, however; most of the other countries have had a steeper rate of improvement. Scotland's position in this European health league table has deteriorated. In 1950, our life expectancy was in the middle of the European pack for both men and women, but by 1995 males in Scotland had the second lowest life expectancy at birth in Western Europe. Females in Scotland had the lowest (Leon et al, 2003).

Life expectancy counts all years of expected life the same, regardless of whether they are enjoyed in good health. In contrast, the measure of 'healthy life expectancy' represents the number of years that an individual can expect to live in good health. It is therefore a much better measure of the health of a population – and indeed of the success of policies that aim to prevent the onset or progression of disease and illness, or to boost well-being and quality of life. Clark et al (2004) have produced the first healthy life expectancy estimates for Scotland. They found that only approximately 73% of life years from birth are expected to be free from limiting long-term illness. Since 1980, healthy life expectancy at birth has increased slightly, but it has not kept pace with increases in life expectancy. In other words, the extra years of life gained are not likely to be enjoyed in good health.

Every year, cancer, coronary heart disease (CHD) and stroke account for about 65% of all deaths in Scotland. Health outcomes for these conditions have improved consistently since the NHS was established. The Scottish Executive set a target of reducing the age standardised mortality rate from CHD for people aged under 75 by 50% between 1995 and 2010. This target is likely to be achieved if present trends continue. Reductions in cancer mortality have been more modest, and the number of people diagnosed with cancer is rising, but five-year survival rates have increased overall and for the four most common cancers (Audit Scotland, 2004).

Health-related behaviours, including the risk factors for these major killers, are the most visible expression of the health of a population. Behaviours such as cigarette smoking, alcohol consumption, physical activity and diet (and their expression through smoke-filled rooms, drunkenness, obesity, and so on) form part of the ethos of a society. They are symbols of what is normal or acceptable, they influence people's perceptions of a society, and therefore they form part of the definitions given to populations and places. In Scotland, just under one third of adults smoke (figures for men and women are now almost identical). The steep drop in adult smoking levelled out in the early 1990s and reductions have been more modest since. Compared with England, a greater proportion of Scottish adult males and females report that they are current smokers and fewer report that they have quit smoking. Scottish smokers also tend to report heavier daily smoking rates. Hospital admission rates related or attributed to alcohol have risen by 45% over the last ten years in Scotland. Levels of adult obesity also appear to be rising: one in five adults are now obese, and hospital admission rates for diabetes (for which obesity is a major risk factor) have risen by 111% over the last ten years. Mental health problems are also very common. Scotland spends 40% more per head of population on anti-depressant drugs than does England. Scotland's suicide rate is much higher than the rate for the UK as a whole, and the rate of increase over recent decades is among the highest in Europe. Suicide is now the leading cause of death in young men in Scotland (Leon, 2003; NHS Health Scotland, 2004).

Perhaps the most striking feature of Scotland's health, however, is the persistent gap in health experience (on a wide range of dimensions) between the most affluent and deprived communities. Scotland has higher rates of premature mortality than England for each social class. This is particularly pronounced, however, for social class V and gives rise to greater inequalities between the most affluent and most deprived communities in Scotland than in England. In its overview of the performance of the NHS in Scotland (which considered the range of NHS responsibilities, including efficiency, waiting times, access, outcomes, joint working, and health improvement), Audit Scotland concluded that "reducing this gap may be the biggest challenge for NHSScotland" (Audit Scotland, 2004).

Analysis of progress in reducing health inequalities in Scotland over recent decades yields a mixed picture. Comparisons of parliamentary constituencies show that the gap in life expectancy between the 'best' and the 'worst' has increased from 7.8 years in 1991 to 13.7 years in 2001 (NHS Health Scotland, 2004). Looking at specific aspects of health, most show no significant change in health inequality ratios (examples here are dental caries in children, breastfeeding, suicides among young people, teenage pregnancies, adult smoking, obesity and mental health – GHQ12 scores[1] – and mortality rates in older people). A few indicators show a widening of health inequalities (most notably relating to mortality rates among adult males) and there has been a significant narrowing of inequalities in relation to mothers smoking during pregnancy (Measuring Inequalities in Health Working Group, 2003). At a local level, encouraging data from the Greater Glasgow Health and Well-being Survey (2002) suggest that in some aspects of health the inequality gap between Social Inclusion Partnership (SIP) and non-SIP areas may be narrowing (NHS Greater Glasgow, 2004). However, these data only relate to comparisons between 1999 and 2002, using separate cross-sectional samples. Further time series data will be needed to build confidence that the gap is truly narrowing.

There is much more to be said about Scotland's health, but even from this brief summary some key points can be highlighted:

- Scotland's health is not uniformly bad. Parts of the country experience health comparable to the best in the UK, and most 'unhealthy' behaviours are carried out by a minority.
- While Scotland as a whole now sits at the bottom of the Western European health league table, it has not always done so. Therefore, there is nothing inevitable about our current position. If Scotland is to move up the league table, however, our health will need to improve more quickly than the

improvements taking place in other European countries (including the rest of the UK).
- While some trends are going in the right direction, many (for example obesity, alcohol-related admissions, sexual health, mental health) are extremely worrying and show no sign of abating.
- Inequalities in health in Scotland are more striking than in England, and on most dimensions of health have shown no reduction in recent decades.

Faced with this picture, what should be the policy response? The next sections consider how health might be created in a country such as Scotland, what Healthy Public Policy might look like, and the relationship between NHS spend and outcomes.

Healthy public policy

Since the 1970s (Fuchs, 1974), a key issue for health policy makers has been securing the 'right' balance between a focus on medical care and a focus on the wider environmental factors that influence health.

Many studies have been undertaken on aspects of the conundrum, and great strides have been taken in the development of theoretical and conceptual frameworks describing the roles and relationships between the many factors that determine the health of populations. While much has become clearer, there remains a lack of convincing evidence about attribution, about the relative cost effectiveness of different policy interventions, and about the relative independent effects of the many health determinants that interact across sectors. In short, there is not evidence of the precise relationships beloved by policy makers to inform resource allocation decisions with the aim of improving health outcomes (Kindig et al, 2003).

Public policy to improve population health needs to recognise the many factors that determine health (economic factors, aspects of the physical environment, the social environment, the accessibility and effectiveness of services, the role of individual behaviour and physiological reactions, and so on) and it needs to recognise that these interact; but it needs to accept that the relative effects of the different factors are to a large degree unknown, that the precise relationships between them are unpredictable, and that there is a relative dearth of evidence on the effectiveness of interventions to improve population health and reduce inequalities.

The contribution to be made by health care in this context is of particular interest, given the scale of resource allocated to it and the public perception of health services as the 'givers' or 'creators' of health in society. Bunker et al (1994) have estimated the contribution of medical care in improving life expectancy, concluding that medical care can be credited with three of the approximately seven years of increased life expectancy experienced in the US and Britain since 1950. Their calculations also indicate that if effective clinical services were provided more widely, they have the potential of extending life expectancy by an additional one and a half to two years. Bunker (1994) argues for an emphasis on the role of medical care not to be lost, and while acknowledging the importance of other factors such as unhealthy lifestyles, he states that "their modification has yet to be shown to have had a favourable impact on the population's life expectancy" and that "the potential beneficial effect on life expectancy of behavioural modification … is no greater than, and possibly less than, the benefits that could accrue from wider access to clinical services that have been shown to be effective" (p 1657).

Bunker's analyses form an interesting counter current to the bulk of evidence on the determinants of health in populations. They remind us of the contribution to be made by health care and of the evidence of effective health care interventions, but most commentators emphasise the strength of influences that lie outside the health services. Within the US, estimates of the relative contributions made by different factors to premature mortality suggested that socioeconomic factors accounted for 80%, behaviour/lifestyle accounted for 50%, environmental exposure 20%, and health care 10% (Lee and Paxman, 1997). The basis for the specific figures can be questioned, as can their direct transferability to the Scottish or UK context, but the relative ranking of these different types of influence on health has general support. Emphasising the importance of socioeconomic factors in an editorial for the *British Medical Journal*, Ken Judge (1994) stated:

> We have been indoctrinated into accepting the superiority of biomedical and disease oriented explanations of the determinants of health to the detriment of socioeconomic ones. For example, probably the dominant lay view in modern industrial societies is that the main causes of premature death are cancer and heart disease. The almost inaudible counterview is that the principal killers are the 'lack of social support, poor education, and stagnant economies' (Lomas and Contandriopoulos, in Evans et al, 1994). (Judge, 1994, p 1454)

In the same editorial, Judge argued for "a radical change of direction away from tinkering with the organisation of health care towards developing new approaches to health policy".

Recognition of the importance of socioeconomic factors raises the question of the health benefit to be accrued through wider social policies. There has been a strong emphasis on the policy implications of the links between socioeconomic disadvantage and ill health in the UK throughout the 20th century, exemplified by the Black (Black et al, 1980) and Acheson (1998) reports, the Whitehall studies (Marmot et al, 1978), and more recently the Department of Health's cross-cutting review on tackling health inequalities (DH, 2002). Looking at how the health gap between the healthiest and least healthy constituencies could be narrowed through the implementation of key government social policies, Mitchell et al (2000) examined the potential impact on premature mortality of three policies: a modest redistribution of wealth, achieving full employment, and eradicating child poverty. The research suggests that annually, across Britain:

- some 7,500 deaths (age<65) could be prevented if inequalities in wealth returned to 1983 levels, the majority of the lives saved being in the poorer areas of Britain;
- some 2,500 deaths (age<65) could be prevented were full employment to be achieved, two thirds of these in areas with higher than average levels of premature mortality; and
- some 1,500 lives could be saved among those aged under 15 if child poverty were eradicated (representing 92% of 'excess' child deaths in areas of higher than average mortality).

A third current (in addition to the role of health services, and the role of socioeconomic factors in the broadest sense) that flows into health policy is that of individual behaviours, and the linked notion of individual responsibility for health. Estimates exist of the numbers of premature deaths in Scotland caused by specific behaviours. For example, it has been estimated that 2,500 people in Scotland die prematurely each year due to physical inactivity (Physical Activity Task Force, 2002) and 13,000 from tobacco use (heavily weighted towards those in poorer socioeconomic circumstances) (Callum, 1998). These are undoubtedly very large numbers, and must make a major impact on policy makers. Moreover, for some behaviours (such as cigarette smoking), there is a reasonable and growing evidence base of effective interventions.

In summary, the development of healthy public policy must take into account the range of factors that determine health in the population, and place the contribution of health and social care services within that wider context. Health is created in everyday life, as a consequence of the circumstances in which people live and their responses (behavioural and biological) to those circumstances. The primary focus of policy makers on the delivery of services misses that point, although it reflects the focus of financial investment.

> To date the economics of health has been relatively neglected in favour of the economics of health care.... The production function for health has not been adequately described, although there is considerable literature on health determinants. (Elliott et al, 2003, p 6)

Spending on the NHS in Scotland

Around one third of the total funding available to the Scottish Executive is spent on the NHS in Scotland. In 2002/03 this amounted to around £7 billion spent on providing healthcare services (Audit Scotland, 2004), equating to around £1,400 per person (set to rise to approx £1,700 in 2005/06). The current level of spending is more than in the rest of the UK and is around the European average. Scotland is already delivering on the Prime Minister's aspiration and Labour Party Manifesto commitment to "bring UK health spending up to the EU average" (Labour Party, 2001, p 12).

The relatively high levels of spend on the NHS in Scotland predate devolution. Post-devolution, the Scottish Executive has maintained the historically high investment in the NHS and spending is due to increase further. Much of the increase is likely to be absorbed by cost pressures, however, such as improving healthcare buildings and facilities, and pay modernisation. Scotland has more doctors and nurses per head of population than elsewhere in the UK, and so 'Agenda for Change' (the new pay system which applies to all directly employed NHS staff except for very senior managers and those covered by the doctors and dentists pay review body), recent changes to doctors' contracts, and European working time directives will consequently have a commensurately higher relative impact in Scotland.

The question is often asked as to the relationship between Scotland's poor health statistics and its relatively high levels of spend on the NHS. As Elliott et al (2003) state:

> the Scottish [standardised mortality] rates are dramatically higher than the EU15 despite comparable levels of health spending [and] markedly inferior to those in England and Wales, where spending is lower. (p 3)

If the question to be answered by policy makers is, 'How can this be so?', the answers are relatively easy to find. First, spending on the NHS will, as already discussed, make only a relatively small contribution to the health of a society. Second, there is a high level of need for a well-resourced health service in Scotland because there is a high level of health need in Scotland. Given that we already have a sicker population, we have a greater need for treatment services. A greater focus on prevention, on working up stream, should reduce the need for health care in the future but does not deal significantly with extant levels of disease and illness. Third, the particular geographical and demographic characteristics of Scotland have implications for the ways in which services are delivered. It is more expensive to deliver services in remote communities, for example.

The level of investment being made in NHS Scotland, therefore, is partly historical, partly a response to high levels of health need, and partly a reflection of demography and geography. All of that is objectively true. It is probably not the complete picture, however, and avoids the question of how the NHS in Scotland compares with south of the border in delivering value for money. Following a comparison of health policy in Scotland and in England, a further look will be taken at the influences on, and direction of, Scottish health policy post-devolution.

Post-devolution health policy in Scotland

It is interesting to look back and see the predictions made prior to devolution about its likely effect on health policy. Excellent summaries of the political influences on the NHS in Scotland and the management structures pre-devolution are provided by Woods (2003) and Stewart (2004).

Writing just before the establishment of the Scottish Parliament in May 1999, Leys (1999) drew comparisons with the experiences in Canada (federal budgeting) and in Europe (Spain, Finland, Sweden). In the federal system, he argued, the extent of central government funding results in a high degree of uniformity across provinces, despite health being a provincial responsibility.

> Where powers are merely devolved ... the freedom of regional authorities to deviate from patterns laid down by central government is narrower still. The scope for significant local variation is really determined by the possibility that local public opinion will be mobilised on some issue that threatens to test the central–local division of powers. (Leys, 1999, p 1155)

The different dynamics and experiences of decentralised health policy making in Europe illustrate, according to Leys, that, "The prospects for change ... depend on distinctive national culture and expectations". One such distinctive trait in Scotland that is highlighted by Leys is the critical mass of professional expertise, strongly linked to and involved with public life. Convergence of this professional opinion with public opinion would therefore be one route for securing change.

Looking particularly at the issues of resource allocation and party policies in relation to inequalities in health, Pollock (1999) emphasised the difficulties in predicting whether or how devolved powers would be used to enhance the public's health and increase equity:

> Much will depend on the wisdom, imagination, and vision of their leaders and whether there is the will to redress the legacy of policies that have widened the gap between rich and poor and those living in sickness and health. (p 1197)

What path, then, has Scottish health policy taken post-devolution? A stated aim of the Scottish Executive is to improve the health and quality of life of the people of Scotland and deliver integrated health and community care services, making sure there is support and protection for those members of society who are in greatest need. To achieve this, it has recently set four objectives for the NHS in Scotland (Scottish Executive, 2003b):

- to work towards a step change in life expectancy for Scots, particularly disadvantaged members of the community including children and older people;

- to ensure swift and appropriate access to integrated health care, covering primary, community and acute care;
- to improve patients' experience of services provided by the NHS; and
- to improve services for older people, at home and in care settings.

Each of these objectives is supported by a small number of SMART targets, amounting to 14 in total. There are also 12 national priorities for NHS Scotland:

1. Service redesign
2. Health improvement
3. Delayed discharges
4. 48-hour access to a member of the primary care team
5. Cancer
6. Coronary heart disease and stroke
7. Mental health
8. Waiting times
9. Public involvement
10. Workforce development and staff governance
11. Healthcare acquired infection and hygiene
12. Financial break-even.

The first major statement of post-devolution health policy was *Our national health – A plan for action, a plan for change* (Scottish Executive, 2000a), known as 'The Scottish Health Plan' to emphasise its distinction from *The NHS plan* (DH, 2000) produced six months earlier. Woods (2003, p 22) highlights that Scottish Ministers had no need to "follow suit … they could have produced something completely different", but they "chose an approach closer to … a Scottish version of the English proposals". The plan was produced after a significant consultation and participation process with the people of Scotland, and its relative continuity with what had gone before perhaps reflects public and professional familiarity with the structures in place, following the turbulence of the introduction of the NHS Market during the 1990s, as well as the well-recognised default position of incremental rather than radical change.

The focus of *Our national health* was "a shift from the development of policy to the delivery of change" (Scottish Executive, 2000a, p 5). It emphasised the need to build a national effort to improve health and reduce inequalities, and it heralded future change programmes to:

- rebuild a truly *national* health service;
- increase public and patient involvement in the NHS; and
- change and modernise services.

Health Boards and NHS Trusts were to be brought together to form unified boards of governance in each health board area, responsible for a single Local

Health Plan for their area. Primary Care Trusts and Acute Trusts were to be retained as separate legal entities, formally accountable in their own right to Ministers and Parliament, and responsible for implementing the strategic plans of the NHS Board by organising and providing healthcare services, under the direction of Trust Management Teams. Membership of the unified NHS Boards was to be enlarged considerably from that of Health Boards, to include elected members from local authorities, as well as stronger professional and staff representation. Another significant theme within *Our national health* was the emphasis it placed on partnership – with staff, with patients, with local authorities, voluntary bodies and others – giving a sense of building a national movement and shared responsibility for improving Scotland's health.

The changes in governance arrangements initiated in *Our national health* were developed in *Rebuilding our National Health Service* (Scottish Executive, 2001) and implemented thereafter. The direction of change was taken further in *Partnership for care: Scotland's health White Paper* (Scottish Executive, 2003c), with the dissolution of Trusts and the move towards 'single-system working'. Like *Our national health*, *Partnership for care* starts with an emphasis on improving Scotland's health:

> This Health White Paper is about the promotion of health in the broadest sense and the creation of a health service that is fit for the 21st century. (Scottish Executive, 2003c, p 7)

The need to reduce health inequalities is reiterated alongside the four pillars of the post-devolution Health Improvement Challenge (Scottish Executive, 2003d): early years, teenage transition, healthy working lives, and communities.

In launching *Partnership for health*, Malcolm Chisholm, Minister for Health and Community Care, stated:

> One of the key themes of this White Paper is decentralisation of decision making and an end to traditional command and control approaches to reforming the health service. (Scottish Executive Press Release, 27 February 2003)

To deliver this, NHS Boards were to bring forward plans to dissolve NHS Trusts and to put in place new operational units including Community Health Partnerships (CHPs) to be established from April 2005 to enable a wider range of services to be delivered locally in communities. Follow-up guidance (Scottish Executive, 2003e) expanded on the key principles for single-system working including: schemes of delegation to operating divisions, the repositioning of NHSScotland management (for example, all chief executives to have cross-system, regional or national leadership roles), and changes to membership of NHS Boards.

Alongside these landmark policies have been a wealth of other health policy developments in post-devolution Scotland. Key among these have been *Fair shares for all* (Scottish Executive, 2000b), which established a new formula for redistributing funds to NHS Boards that more fully recognises the influence of deprivation and remote and rural areas on Scotland's health and health care needs[2]; policies to support the development of the NHS workforce; strategies for individual clinical conditions; and a raft of issue-specific strategies on children's health, improving mental health and well-being, oral health, tobacco control, and so on. Amid all of this, two policies stand out as demonstrating the Scottish Executive's ability to take a different legislative stance to that south of the border on specific issues:

- the 2001 decision not to charge elderly people in Scotland for personal and social care;
- the 2004 decision to ban smoking in all enclosed public places.

Linked to all of this policy development is a degree of public, media and political debate on health issues of a completely different scale to that which existed prior to devolution. In the first 18 months alone of the Scottish Parliament, there were around 50 debates on health and community care matters (Scottish Executive, 2000a). Post-devolution health policy has also been characterised by a recognition of the connections between health and wider social policy agendas – and in particular the Scottish Executive's flagship commitments to Social Justice (Scottish Executive, 1999) and Social Inclusion (Scottish Executive, 2000c).

Health policy in England

Over the same time period, developments in the NHS in England have been driven by *The NHS plan: A plan for investment, a plan for reform* (DH, 2000). Its purpose and vision was "to give the people of Britain (sic) a health service fit for the 21st century: a health service designed around the patient", and the proposals were championed as "the most fundamental and far reaching reforms the NHS has seen since 1948" (2000, p 9). A prime concern was to improve standards of care and to redesign the NHS around the needs of patients, through processes of modernisation "from top to toe" (2000, p 9). As well as significant financial investment in facilities and staff, new mechanisms for achieving the desired changes included a proposed move away from centralisation to a system of earned autonomy, devolving greater power to local health services as they demonstrate their ability to meet standards and improve performance. In other words, local organisations that performed well would 'earn' more freedom to run their own affairs. The Department of Health would set national standards, and an independent inspectorate (the Commission for Health Improvement) would carry out regular inspections of the extent to which local health systems were meeting these standards. The NHS Plan also introduced, for the first time, a concordat with private providers of healthcare. This was to enable the NHS to make better use of private healthcare facilities – thereby helping to relieve waiting times. Attention to population health improvement came towards the end of the NHS Plan (by contrast, it forms the first chapter of the Scottish post-devolution health policies), highlighting among other things the intention to increase and improve primary care in deprived areas and to create, for the first time, a national health inequalities target.

The NHS Plan's move away from centralisation was further developed in the following year in *Shifting the balance of power within the NHS – Securing delivery* (DH, 2001), which sought to operationalise a shift towards frontline staff "who understand patients' needs and concerns" and towards local communities "so that they reconnect with their services and have real influence over their development" (2001, p 5). The changes attached responsibilities to the different parts of the NHS in England as follows:

- Primary Care Trusts (PCTs) were to become the lead NHS organisation in assessing need, planning and securing all health services, and improving health. Partnership with local communities and joint work with local government were important additional responsibilities.
- National Health Service Trusts were to continue to provide services, working within delivery agreements with PCTs, and with greater responsibility devolved to clinical teams. High performing trusts would earn greater freedoms and autonomy.
- About 30 Strategic Health Authorities would replace 96 Health Authorities and lead the strategic development of the local health service. They would have responsibility for performance management of PCTs and NHS Trusts.
- The Department of Health would "change the way it relates to the NHS, focusing on supporting the delivery of the NHS Plan" (2001, p 6).
- Patient Advocacy and Liaison Services and Patients' Forums would be established in every NHS Trust and PCT.

Recently, *The NHS improvement plan: Putting people at the heart of public services* (DH, 2004) supports the commitment to a ten-year process of reform made in the NHS Plan, and sets out priorities for the NHS to the year 2008. A key theme is that of choice, ensuring

> that a drive for responsive, convenient and personalised services takes root across the whole of the NHS and for all patients.... This means that there will be a lot more choice for patients. (DH, 2004, p 1)

From the end of 2005, patients are to have the right to choose from four to five different healthcare providers. PCTs will also be able to commission care from a wider range of providers, and the target for year 2008 is that the independent sector will provide up to 15% of procedures. The Improvement Plan also commits to establishing Foundation Trusts, to making a real difference to the quality of life of people living with chronic illnesses, and to placing much stronger emphasis on prevention. "Financial incentives and performance management will drive delivery of the new commitments" (2004, p 4), with resources flowing "to those hospitals and healthcare providers that are able to provide patients with the high-quality and responsive services they expect" (2004, p 5). All in all, there is a move away from what might be called a single system with a single funding formula to a much more mixed system, with fewer national targets and the ability for local services to set their own targets – albeit with a strong emphasis on national standards and regulation. Walshe (2002) has commented on the increase in regulation in the NHS in England, arguing that the regulatory paradigm is moving more towards deterrence (this paradigm assuming that organisations have to be forced to behave well, and therefore require demanding standards and enforcement) rather than compliance (which assumes that organisations generally do the right thing when they can, and should be given support and advice from regulators). At the time he was writing, five new national agencies had been created to regulate the NHS: the National Institute for Clinical Excellence, Commission for Health Improvement, Modernisation Agency, National Patient Safety Agency, and National Clinical Assessment Authority. He also commented (2002) that the rise in regulation seems to represent a "strengthening of central government's control of managerial and clinical practice" (p 970), as the regulators are government agencies, headed by ministerial appointments and centrally funded.

Health policy in Scotland and England: similarities and differences

It is clear from what has been discussed that, although concerns with health and health policy have been at the heart of devolution and the subject of a heightened level of public, political and professional debate, to a considerable extent health policy in Scotland has remained consistent with that in England, since the establishment of the Scottish Parliament. Woods (2003) states that it is the continuity (from a single NHS) that remains dominant, and cites forces such as inherited policy and party allegiance, the UK identity of the NHS, and the Barnett formula as important determinants of that continuity. Stewart (2004), similarly, highlights the ongoing "close familial relationship" (p 131) between NHS Scotland and the other UK health services.

Of course, even with a strong appetite for transformation it will take more than five years to effect significant change in an organisation as large and complex as the NHS, or to turn around Scotland's long-playing record of ill health. And there are some early shoots indicating issues on which Scottish policy may be branching off in a rather different direction to England.

1. *Public health:* a stronger emphasis is placed on improving health and reducing health inequalities in Scottish policy than it is in England. The Scottish Executive has shown a great deal of policy commitment to these issues, and not only through the health department. Recognition has been given to the importance

of social justice and social inclusion as routes to reducing health inequalities; a wide definition of health has been adopted consistently; a duty to promote well-being has been placed on Local Authorities; and the priorities of improving health and reducing health inequalities have been emphasised at the top of all major policy developments for the NHS in Scotland. One of the most courageous decisions made by the Executive has also been in the area of public health. Its decision on 10 November 2004 to ban smoking in all enclosed public spaces in Scotland was a much bolder decision than that taken in Westminster the following week.

> An outright ban was the right and courageous thing to do. Let us hope in time ministers [at Westminster] appreciate their timidity and do the right thing. (Dickson, 2004)

Admiration for the Scottish Executive's stance has come from many quarters – although not (yet?) from the licensed trade – and has been taken to show a determination, where the evidence exists, to tackle causes of ill health and to turn around Scottish culture. Scottish ministers have also indicated an appetite for more of the same, but time will tell.

2. *Long-term care:* the Scottish Executive's decision that personal and social care for the elderly would be provided free of charge, formed the first major policy inconsistency with Westminster, formalised in the 2002 Community Care and Health (Scotland) Act. (John Stewart, 2004, has provided a full analysis of this area of policy divergence.) The UK government rejected recommendations that general taxation means should be used to fund personal care, and therefore Scotland must find the money internally (or use its tax raising powers). In this example of divergence, there is not only a different policy decision, but the impact of Treasury policies "is proving to be a general obstacle to the policy of making personal care free at the point of delivery" (Pollock, 2001, p 312).

3. *Regulation and accountability:* the Department of Health's approach to regulation of the NHS in England has been described earlier in this chapter, as has the emphasis on incentives and 'earned autonomy'. The most visible output of the inspection processes is the Star Rating System. Ratings (0–3 stars) are published by the Healthcare Commission, to provide "an overview of how good the Trust's service is to its patients – how well it is run and whether it is performing well on important factors like reducing treatment waiting times" (www.nhs.uk/england/aboutTheNHS/starRatings/). The final rating provides a single summary of a Trust's performance against a range of targets and indicators and (from 2004) incorporates a clinical governance review assessment. In Scotland NHS performance is assessed using the Performance Assessment Framework (PAF) – a largely self-completed document supplemented by data on performance on a range of quantitative health outcomes. It comprises over 100 qualitative and quantitative indicators, covering seven assessment areas. The PAF is completed for each NHS Board area, and (unlike in England) no

single summary measure is compiled. The PAF findings significantly inform each Board's annual accountability review. Its data are made publicly available (on the Information and Statistics Division website), as is the accountability review outcome letter (in the Boards' annual reports). There is not the same level of public debate about Boards' performance in Scotland (as measured by PAF) as the star ratings provoke in England. Nor is there the same direct link to performance incentives at a system or organisational level. In their review of experiences and perceptions of PAF, Farrar et al (2004) found that the PAF was generally welcomed by managers in NHSScotland, and they highlight a number of issues for further attention and development. The publication of high profile summary measures and the concepts of organisational rewards and 'earned autonomy' are not among them. Indeed, they state (2004):

> The Scottish PAF differs from other performance assessment systems (in particular the English 'Star' system) in two main ways. It does not have strong financial or non-financial incentives attached to performance and it does not publish the data in the form of league tables. These two characteristics are important in securing high commitment ... and may be instrumental to the system's success. (p 35)

4. *NHS Trusts and their responsibilities:* while 1990s forces such as GP fundholding did not take hold as much north of the border as they did in England, health policy in Scotland post-devolution has sought to move away from the internal market in the NHS and to re-establish a single national service. PCTs in Scotland were not given the same responsibilities as those in England for commissioning secondary and tertiary care services for their patient populations; and, as described earlier in this chapter, the current move back to unitary NHS organisations and 'single-system working' (Scottish Executive, 2003e) reinforces the responsibility of a single Board in each NHS area for strategic planning, governance and performance management and emphasises regional and national planning. While in Scotland, the NHS Trusts are evolving into Divisions of unitary NHS organisations, in England the policy direction is for NHS Trusts to be given increased responsibility and autonomy (the concept of 'earned autonomy' as a result of good performance) and the ability to evolve into Foundation Trusts with a greater degree of financial and decision-making freedom. Both the Scottish and the English policies state a commitment towards devolved decision making and greater patient involvement, but the structures, incentives and accountabilities being put in place to establish this end are strikingly different.

5. *Patient choice and the role of non-NHS providers:* on this set of issues, Scotland has remained more closely wedded to the 'traditional' conception of the NHS – in other words, to a health service provided almost exclusively by the NHS in NHS-run facilities – than has England. 'Modernisation' of health services is a

strongly espoused aspect of Scotland's health policy, but its attainment has been fraught with difficulty. Attempts to alter the pattern of health service provision both for reasons of financial viability and to ensure compliance with standards of clinical safety have time and again met with resistance. Public petitions and 'save our local hospital' campaigns have become a regular feature of attempts to modernise the Scottish NHS. Such campaigns have been taken up enthusiastically by newspapers and have formed the 'single-ticket' basis for the election of an MSP[3]. The public concern generally focuses on a desire to preserve NHS services within a local area. There is no similarly loud public cry in Scotland for greater choice or diversity, and hence the health policy direction in Scotland (unlike that in England) has not emphasised these concepts. Patient choice in Scotland is largely limited to choice of NHS providers (for example, this clinic in this hospital or a similar clinic in the neighbouring hospital), is rarely made explicit and is not often exercised. The mixed economy being advocated by the Department of Health and developed in England is not matched in Scotland.

In spite of the strong evidence of post-devolution consistency in health policy between Scotland and England, these five areas represent ways in which the policy direction in the two countries seems to be diverging. Some, such as the decision on free personal care for the elderly, represent clear, specific policy differences. Others, such as the Scottish emphasis on 'single-system working' are differences of degree. In the concluding section of this chapter, the factors influencing the direction of health policy in Scotland will be considered.

Influences on health policy in the new Scotland

The starting point for this chapter was an analysis of Scotland's health. That analysis seems, reassuringly, to be a driving force behind the direction being taken by health policy in Scotland. Health services are not the sole focus of the health policy agenda: there is a broad understanding of health and its determinants, strongly located within the context of social justice. Some have argued that this should be taken further (Stewart, 1999). Others, applauding the fact that health inequalities are high on the political agenda in Scotland and that there have been determined attempts to promote social justice, have noted mixed progress towards the social justice milestones and the need for more attention to be paid to the distributional aspects of these milestones (Blamey et al, 2002). Scotland's health challenge remains enormous, but the commitment to this aspect of health policy is to be commended. The Scottish Executive places considerable weight on the need to develop understanding about how to achieve a step-change in Scotland's position in the health league table, and in particular how to improve the health of those with greatest health need. The recognition that current approaches are unlikely to be enough led to the partnership agreement commitment to establish a new Glasgow Centre for Population Health in 2004 (see the Partnership

Agreement between the Scottish Labour Party and the Scottish Liberal Democrats, *A partnership for a better Scotland*, www.scotland.gov.uk/library5/government/pfbs-00.asp).

A second influence on health policy in the new Scotland is our ability to use evidence to inform policy. Describing some of the distinctively Scottish dimensions to the public health research environment, Wimbush et al (2004) remind us that,

> Whatever our commitment to applying evidence and to learning from evaluations, we should remember that in complex post-industrial societies, it is unlikely that there will be any single, simple solutions. Progress is likely to be made through the synergy of multiple interventions. (p 20)

The application of an evidence base is easier in the more enclosed setting of clinical practice with defined patient groups than at a whole population level in community settings. In addition, those policies that require amendment to enable evidence-based clinical practice are more readily within the devolved powers of the Scottish Parliament. While some aspects of public health policy are devolved (as the smoking ban decision exemplifies), others are not. For instance, a good example would be the Scottish Executive seeking to apply to Scotland the learning from the Gary, Indiana study which examined the impact on child health of reducing income inequality (Kehrer and Wolin, 1979). In this study, a negative income tax programme increased the incomes of eligible families with resulting birth weight increases (thought primarily to be due to maternal nutrition) in the income-supplemented group. Would the powers of the Scottish Executive enable the introduction of such a programme in Scotland?

A third type of influence on Scotland's health policy comes from the public. As described earlier in this chapter, the people of Scotland have been strong and vocal advocates for the types of health services they want (they have been much less vocal on a national scale on public health issues). The mobilisation of communities, mass media and politicians in support of health issues has been a prominent feature of post-devolution Scotland, evident throughout the length and breadth of the country. Concerns about proposed changes are quickly politicised, with the policy arguments for change rapidly being hard to hear amid the public clamour to protect established services. One consequence of this is that, despite the policy aspiration for local decision making, issues are frequently brought back up to the national arena through processes of public petitioning and advocacy. The relatively small size of Scotland and the linked fact that politicians, professionals and public are all readily accessible to each other, facilitate a high degree of public influence on policy making.

The prevailing culture in Scotland also has a bearing on the direction of the public influence on policy making. Scottish culture is characterised as having a strong emphasis on social cohesion and cooperation (Craig, 2003). Collectivity is regarded as being more important than the individual. There is a strong sense of Scottish identity, and of civil society. Those behaving differently from the norm of acceptable behaviour are criticised and censured. Compared to the English (who are described as being more tolerant, open-minded and pragmatic), Craig (2003) highlights the Scots' pronounced sense of right and wrong, tenacity and commitment to principles. If this analysis is an accurate description of Scottish culture, is it reflected in Scotland's health policy? Arguably, yes. As noted earlier in this chapter, health policy in Scotland is striving to remain true to the original ideal and traditions of the NHS. The Scottish people are proving resistant to NHS 'modernisation'. There is also a strong policy emphasis on equity in health, and on collaboration and cooperation across structures. From Craig's analysis, these are all traits that might be predicted. However, the other implication of her analysis is that those who 'put their head above the parapet' and argue for something different will be criticised.

A final influence on health policy in the new Scotland is, of course, the influence of politics, specifically party politics. The high degree of congruence of health policy between Scotland and England reflects the current dominance of the Labour party in both countries. There are different versions of the political philosophy of Labour (to a considerable extent reflecting, and reinforcing, the cultural differences described here), however, and these variations around a shared core philosophy are beginning to be demonstrated in some divergence of policy, as set out earlier in this chapter. Furthermore, the effect of the coalition with the Scottish Liberal Democrats has led to the inclusion of some policies in Scotland that are not evident in England. The success at the last Scottish Parliamentary election of a number of smaller political parties might suggest the advent of a more politically diverse Scotland, where a wider range of views on health are heard in the processes of political debate and decision making. Where this will lead us in the Scotland of the future cannot be predicted, but we must hope that the recognition to date of the need to keep a balance between the medical and non-medical determinants of health remains. It is in relation to population health and health inequalities that Scottish solutions tailored to our Scottish problems are most needed.

Notes

[1] GHQ12 is the 12-item version of the General Health Questionnaire. The questionnaire is used to detect the presence of non-psychotic psychiatric morbidity in community settings.

[2] This approach differs significantly from that of England, where the role of financial incentives for good performance is increasingly being emphasised (as discussed later in this chapter).

[3] For example, Jean Turner was elected in 2002 to save Stobhill Hospital.

Further resources

Davey Smith, G., Dorling, D. and Shaw, M. (eds) (2001) *Poverty, inequality and health in Britain 1900-2000: A reader*, Bristol: The Policy Press.

Evans, R.G., Barer, M.L. and Marmor, T.R. (eds) (1994) *Why are some people healthy and others not? The determinants of health of populations*, New York, NY: Aldine de Gruyter.

Woods, K. and Carter, D. (eds) *Scotland's health and health services*, London: The Nuffield Trust.

On the web ...

Glasgow Centre for Population Health	www.gcph.co.uk
Public Health Institute of Scotland	www.phis.org.uk
Scottish Council Foundation	www.scottishcouncilfoundation.org
Scottish Executive on Health	www.scotland.gov.uk/Topics/Health
Scottish Health Statistics	www.isdscotland.org

References

Acheson, D. (1998) *Independent inquiry into inequalities in health report*, London: The Stationery Office.

Audit Scotland (2004) *An overview of the performance of the NHS in Scotland*, Edinburgh: Audit Scotland.

Black, D., Morris, J., Smith, C. and Townsend, P. (1980) *Inequalities in health: Report of a research working group*, London: DHSS.

Blamey, A., Hanlon, P., Judge, K. and Muirie, J. (eds) (2002) *Health inequalities in the new Scotland*, Glasgow: Public Health Institute of Scotland.

Bunker, J.P., Fraizier, H. and Mosteller, F. (1994) 'Improving health: measuring the effects of medical care', *Milbank Memorial Fund Quarterly*, vol 72, pp 225-59.

Bunker, J.P. (1994) 'Medicine's core values', *British Medical Journal*, vol 309, p 1657.

Callum, C. (1998) *The UK smoking epidemic: Deaths in 1995*, London: Health Education Authority.

Clark, D., McKeon, A., Sutton, M. and Wood, R. (2004) *Healthy life expectancy in Scotland*, Edinburgh: Information and Statistics Division.

Craig, C. (2003) *The Scots' crisis of confidence*, Glasgow: Big Thinking.

DH (Department of Health) (2000) *The NHS Plan – A plan for action, a plan for reform*, London: DH.

DH (2002) *Cross-cutting review of health inequalities*, London: DH.

DH (2001) *Shifting the balance of power within the NHS – Securing delivery*, London: DH.

DH (2004) *The NHS Improvement Plan: Putting people at the heart of public services*, London: DH.

Dickson, N. (2004) 'Let's do the right thing', *The Guardian*, 17 November.

Elliott, R.F., Cairns, J., Ludbrook, A., Scott, A., Ryan, M. and Munro, A. (2003) *Future research in health economics in Scotland: Research priorities in light of the Wanless Report*, Stirling: University of Stirling, Scottish Economic Policy Network (scotecon).

Farrar, S., Harris, F., Scott, T. and McKee, L. (2004) *The Performance Assessment Framework: Experiences and perceptions of NHS Scotland. A report to the Analytical Service Division, Directorate of Performance Management and Finance, Scottish Executive Health Department*, Edinburgh: Scottish Executive.

Fuchs, V.R. (1974) *Who shall live? Health, economics and social choice*, New York, NY: Basic.

Hanlon, P., Walsh, D., Buchanan, D., Redpath, A., Bain, M., Brewster, D., Chalmers, J., Muir, R., Smalls, M., Willis, J. and Wood, R. (2001) *Chasing the Scottish effect – Why Scotland needs a step-change in health if it is to catch up with the rest of Europe*, Glasgow: Public Health Institute of Scotland.

Judge, K. (1994) 'Beyond health care', *British Medical Journal*, vol 309, pp 1454-5.

Kehrer, B.H. and Wolin, C.M. (1979) 'Impact of income maintenance on low birth weight: evidence from the Gary experiment', *Journal of Human Resources*, vol 14, no 4, pp 434-62.

Kindig, D., Day, P., Fox, D.M., Knickman, J., Lomas, J. and Stoddart, G. (2003) 'What new knowledge would help policymakers better balance investments for optimal health outcomes? Policy implications', *Health Services Research*, vol 38, no 6, part II, pp 1923-378.

Labour Party, The (2001) *Ambitions for Britain: Labour's manifesto 2001*, London: The Labour Party.

Lee, P. and Paxman, D. (1997) 'Reinventing public health', *Annual Review of Public Health*, vol 18, pp 1-35.

Leon, D.A., Morton, S., Cannegieter, S. and McKee, M. (2003) *Understanding the health of Scotland's population in an international context: A review of current approaches, knowledge and recommendations for new research directions*, London: London School of Hygiene and Tropical Medicine.

Leys, C. (1999) 'The NHS after devolution', *British Medical Journal*, vol 318, pp 1155-6.

Marmot, M., Rose, G., Shipley, M.J. and Hamilton, P.H.S. (1978) ' Employment grade and coronary heart disease in British civil servants', *Journal of Epidemiology and Community Health*, vol 32, pp 244-9.

Measuring Inequalities in Health Working Group (2003) *Inequalities in health: Report of the measuring inequalities in health working group*, Edinburgh: Information and Statistics Division.

Mitchell, R., Shaw, M. and Dorling, D. (2000) *Inequalities in life and death: What if Britain were more equal?*, Bristol/York: The Policy Press/Joseph Rowntree Foundation.

NHS Greater Glasgow (2004) *Health and well-being of the Greater Glasgow population: Survey 2002*, Glasgow: NHS Greater Glasgow.

NHS Health Scotland (2004) 'A report card: Trends in life circumstances, behaviour, disease and inequalities', Prepared for the Faculty of Public Health Scottish Conference 2004, Glasgow: NHS Health Scotland.

Physical Activity Task Force (2002) *A strategy for physical activity – A consultation*, Edinburgh: The Scottish Executive.

Pollock, A.M. (1999) 'Devolution and health: challenges for Scotland and Wales', *British Medical Journal*, vol 318, pp 1195-8.

Pollock, A.M. (2001) 'Social policy and devolution: Scotland's decision on long term care challenges a centralised NHS and treasury', *British Medical Journal*, vol 322, pp 311-2.

Scottish Executive (1999) *A Scotland where everyone matters: Our visions for social justice*, Edinburgh: Scottish Executive.

Scottish Executive (2000a) *Our National Health – A plan for action, a plan for change*, Edinburgh: Scottish Executive.

Scottish Executive (2000b) *Fair shares for all: The report of the national review of resource allocation for the NHS in Scotland*, Edinburgh: Scottish Executive.

Scottish Executive (2000c) *Social inclusion: Opening the door to a better Scotland*, Edinburgh: Scottish Executive.

Scottish Executive (2001) *Rebuilding our National Health Service. Guidance to NHS Chairs and Chief Executives for implementing 'Our National Health' – A plan for action, a plan for change*, Edinburgh: Scottish Executive.

Scottish Executive (2003a) *Health in Scotland 2002*, Edinburgh: Scottish Executive.

Scottish Executive (2003b) *Scottish Executive draft budget 2004-05*, Edinburgh: Scottish Executive.

Scottish Executive (2003c) *Partnership for Care: Scotland's health White Paper*, Edinburgh: Scottish Executive.

Scottish Executive (2003d) *Improving health in Scotland: The challenge*, Edinburgh: Scottish Executive.

Scottish Executive (2003e) 'A framework for reform: devolved decision making moving towards single-system working', Health Department letter 2003(11), Edinburgh: Scottish Executive.

Scottish Executive (2004) *Health in Scotland 2003*, Edinburgh: Scottish Executive.

Stewart, J. (2004) *Taking stock: Scottish social welfare after devolution*, Bristol: The Policy Press.

Stewart, S. (ed) (1999) *The possible Scot: Making healthy public policy*, Edinburgh: Scottish Council Foundation.

Walshe, K. (2002) 'The rise of regulation in the NHS', *British Medical Journal*, vol 324, pp 967-70.

Wimbush, E., Tannahill, C. and Hanlon, P. (2004) 'Health promotion research and the public health function on Scotland: prospects for the future', *Health Education Journal*, vol 63, no 1, pp 15-21.

Woods, K. (2003) 'Scotland's changing health system', in K. Woods and D. Carter (eds) *Scotland's health and health services*, London: The Nuffield Trust.

NINE

Social work and social care in the 'new' Scotland

Iain Ferguson

This chapter is written against a background of far-reaching and significant changes in social work in Scotland. New policies have been developed, new regulatory structures implemented and social work training and education has been restructured. In addition, however, social work is increasingly faced with problems of staff recruitment and retention in part a consequence, it is argued here, of the increasing dominance of market-based and neoliberal social policies that have impacted on social work in different ways. Such problems contribute to the sense of social work as a profession in 'crisis'.

This chapter considers developments in three key areas of social work policy and practice in contemporary Scotland:

- community care
- children and families, and
- criminal justice social work.

Introduction

Social work and social care services in Scotland in the first decade of the 21st century present a complex, sometimes contradictory picture. Since devolution in 1999, there has been a continuous stream of policy initiatives in almost every area, often leading to new legislation and major organisational change. These have included the introduction of free personal care for older people, major policy and/or legislative developments in areas such as homelessness, drugs, and mental health, as well as the extension to Scotland of UK-wide schemes such as Sure Start (offering support to families with young children in deprived areas) and Supporting People (supported accommodation for vulnerable adults). Within social work, new regulatory bodies (the Scottish Social Service Council and the Scottish Commission for Social Care) have been established, a new educational body (the Scottish Institute for Social Work Excellence) has been created to coordinate and develop social work education, and a new four-year honours degree has replaced the Diploma in Social Work as the main professional qualification. Senior figures present a positive view of the state of social work, based on what appears to be substantial investment by the Scottish Executive and underpinned by advertising campaigns promoting social work as a career. As the Chief Social Work Inspector noted in his Third Annual Report, "Social work services across Scotland continue to be at the forefront of major changes in public services" (Scottish Executive, 2003). That a lot has been 'going on' is indisputable. What *is* disputed, however, is the direction of this programme of reform, the ideological assumptions which underpin it, and the extent to which it can be seen as representing a specifically *Scottish* social care and social work agenda. Many of the innovations described here – in social work education, for example – have already been introduced in some form in the rest of the UK. Similarly, Best Value, which has been the key framework for the development of a commercial ethos and business practices within social work in England and Wales and which rests on the assumption that competition is the best guarantor of high quality public services, (Harris, 2003), has also been central to the development of services in Scotland and is now incorporated into the 2003 Local Government in Scotland Act. Prima facie, therefore, there seems limited evidence to suggest that the neoliberal agenda which underpins New Labour's approach to public services, including social care and social work south of the border (Jones and Novak, 1999; Lymbery, 2001; Ferguson et al, 2002; Harris, 2003), is any less influential in Scotland. Whether or not the harsh social and moral authoritarianism which some have identified as the other central element of New Labour's approach to social policy (Lavalette and Mooney, 1999; Butler and Drakeford, 2001) is also reflected in the policies of the Executive or whether, in areas such as criminal justice, there is, as some have argued, greater evidence of a commitment to social inclusion and social justice (McIvor, 2004) is something which this chapter will explore.

The chapter will focus on developments in the three main areas of social work and social care provision – community care, children and families, and criminal justice social work (the latter has been addressed more fully in Chapter Seven of this book). Given the sheer volume of new policy coming out of Holyrood, it will not be possible to do justice to all aspects of policy in these three areas and inevitably, important areas of policy, such as drugs policy or homelessness policy, have had to be omitted. Before looking at these policy developments, however, it is necessary to locate social care and social work in Scotland in their recent historical context.

Old Labour and social work: the 1968 Social Work (Scotland) Act

The 1968 Social Work (Scotland) Act has been the basis of social work and social care in Scotland for more than three decades. Like the parallel legislation south of the border of one year later, this act created unified social work departments and the development of what Howe (1994), Parton (1994) and others have referred to as 'modern' social work, in the sense of a profession underpinned by a shared knowledge base. While there were important differences between the Scottish and English legislation, which I shall discuss later in this chapter, it is important also to recognise that many of the problems which the Kilbrandon Committee in Scotland and the Seebohm Committee south of the border were addressing were identical (such as the fragmentation of services, poor coordination, and geographical unevenness of services), and that the solutions they produced were often also very similar. Nor was it the case that Kilbrandon was always more 'progressive' than Seebohm: Seebohm, for example, argued strongly for citizen involvement in social work in a way which predated the current emphasis on service-user involvement.

That said, in three important respects, the Scottish legislation *was* different, in ways which have an important bearing on current developments within social work (Hartnoll, 1998). First, there was the children's hearing system. The aim of this new system, in the words of a member of the Kilbrandon Committee:

> was to remove children under 16 years of age from adult criminal procedures, with the exception of extremely severe offences ... and to bring all cases in need of 'compulsory measures of care' before a lay panel of three members, the Children's Hearing. This, it was judged, would provide the necessary conditions for satisfactory assessment and appropriate disposal: namely, an informal, relaxed setting, with reasonably skilled interviewers provided with reliable background information, with adequate time to promote effective communication between all concerned, and especially, an atmosphere conducive to the child's participation. (Stone, cited in NCH Scotland, 1995, p 3)

Crucially, the hearing's system was based on a welfare philosophy which rejected the distinction between children who offend and children in need of care and protection, with the committee finding that the distinction was of 'little practical significance' when the underlying needs and circumstances of the children were examined (cited in McGhee, 2003, p 87). In most cases, these circumstances involved poverty, poor housing and family breakdown. (A major study by Waterhouse et al, 2000, into the circumstances of 1,155 children appearing before hearings in 1995 found that these circumstances had not changed.)

Second, in contrast to the situation in England and Wales where there is a separate Probation service to work with offenders, work with offenders would be part of the role of the generic social worker.

Finally, and underpinning the whole act, section 12 of the Act placed a duty on local authorities 'to promote social welfare', suggesting a proactive, preventative approach, as opposed to a reactive, targeted approach.

The act was a reflection of two things. First, like the Seebohm Report for England and Wales, it reflected the optimism of that period that problems like poverty were largely residual and, given the will, could be solved, as well as the belief that social change and social justice should be at the heart of social work. Second, again like Seebohm, it was underpinned by the belief (now seen as 'Old

Labour' but in fact largely shared by both major parties in the 1960s) that the State, in this case, the local authority, in which the new social work departments were located, was the best vehicle for effecting this change. With justification, Langan (1993) describes this period of the late 1960s and early 1970s as "the high tide of social work". Sadly, the confidence and optimism which characterised this period were soon dented, first by the media reaction to the death of Maria Colwell in 1973, the first of what was to be a long string of child abuse tragedies which undermined public confidence in social work and then, much more severely, by the massive spending cuts implemented by the Wilson/Callaghan Labour government in 1976 (Clarke, 1993).

From 1979 until 1997, Conservative governments were in office, with the third Thatcher/Major administration in particular (1987-92) committed to the introduction of market principles into every area of life, including health and social care (Timmins, 1996). It was this period that saw the emergence of 'the social work business', in the sense of the application of market principles to social work and social care, initiated by the Conservatives but continued and developed under New Labour governments committed to Third Way approaches (Harris, 2003). To what extent have the principles of that act underpinned the policies of the Scottish Executive in the area of community care?

Community care

The 1990 NHS and Community Care Act marks a key turning-point in the provision of social care and social work in Britain. Under the banner of such motherhood and apple-pie concepts as 'choice', 'user empowerment', and 'needs-led assessment', the act's main achievement was the creation of a 'quasi-market' through the introduction of a purchaser/provider split which restricted the role of local authorities to the commissioning and purchasing of services on the one hand, while explicitly fostering an 'independent' sector of not-for-profit and private providers on the other. Driving this process forward was a managerialist ideology that saw the old welfare regimes as wasteful and inefficient and saw managers as the key individuals who would transform these services into modern and dynamic organisations. As Harris (2003, p 47) has noted, the attraction of managerialism was that it "promised that state goals could be attained with the use of fewer resources".

While the 1990 act applies throughout the UK, there *were* some differences in the way in which the process it initiated unfolded north and south of the border. As Mooney and Poole (2004, p 464) have noted, a history of greater statutory provision and a higher level of institutional care meant that the development of community care in general and of the private sector in care in particular proceeded more slowly in Scotland than in England and Wales. In addition, the requirement that 85% of earmarked funds be spent in the private sector did not apply in Scotland. In other respects, however, it is the twin processes of *marketisation* (the application of business principles, including competition, to social care) and *managerialism* (which locates problems and solutions in the more effective use of existing resources, rather than in increased resources) that have underpinned the development of services in Scotland, as in the rest of the UK. The overriding emphasis on the 'integration of services', for example, which is at the heart of the Executive's core strategy in the area of community care, the Joint Future Agenda, can be seen as reflecting this managerialist approach. Central to Joint Future is the notion of Single Shared Assessment (SSA), one aim of which is to end the practice of multiple assessments by a range of different professionals, such as social workers, occupational therapists and district nurses. Initially applying only to older people, the Executive's intention is to extend this to all community care service user groups from 2004. The 2002 Community Care and Health (Scotland) Act also includes provisions which extend this notion of partnership further (for more details, see Petch, 2003).

At a common sense level, reducing the number of assessments to which service users are subjected makes obvious sense. If, in addition, this encourages closer working between different groups of health and social care professionals, whose relationships in the past have often been characterised by suspicion and boundary disputes, then that too is to be welcomed. That SSA will significantly benefit service users, however, is less clear. First, as is widely recognised, assessment under the 1990 NHS and Community Care Act (which continues to underpin policy and practice in this area) has never been simply concerned with identifying people's needs but is also (or, more accurately, primarily) a basis for the rationing of scarce resources. Whether or not service users will benefit from SSA will depend in large part therefore on the extent to which adequate and appropriate services are made available. Second, while greater integration of services and partnership working may reduce bureaucracy and lead to better relationships among service providers, it is far from clear that this in itself will empower service users. Despite the rhetoric of empowerment which surrounded the introduction of the 1990 Act, for example, it is clear that the main people who were empowered were often not the user/customers but rather care managers, purchasers and providers of services (Smale et al, 1993). Third, SSA is likely to highlight and exacerbate the power and status differentials that already exist between different professions, with the likely winners being those linked to medicine and the likely losers being social work and the voluntary sector. Finally, the Joint Future Agenda, from which SSA is derived, assumes the continued existence of the market in social care, introduced by the 1990 Act, a process usually justified in terms of 'increasing choice'. 'Choice' is of course a very powerful discourse that both major political parties have stated will be central to their next General Election campaigns. Yet, as one health worker wrote in *The Guardian* (20 July 2004) shortly after a major speech by Tony Blair on this issue, in terms which apply no less to social care:

> Choice sounds like a good thing, but there can be no meaningful
> choice between two things unless one is better than the other. One

wonders who would choose the dirty hospital and the long waiting list and the insensitive doctor with the bad shoes. Those for whom choice is theoretical: the people without resources to get to, or live near, the good hospital, perhaps.... The introduction of the choice agenda and the hiving-off of NHS services to various private sector "care" providers represents the most fundamental change the service has endured. And we might notice that, in among all the talk, we will have no say in the real decision: we are not to be given a choice about choice.

Overall, there is little evidence in the area of community care of much divergence between the policies of Scottish Executive and the policies of UK government, in terms of the overall content and direction of policy. In two specific areas, however, the care of older people and services for people with mental health problems, the Executive's policies do seem both more generous and less stigmatising than those in England and Wales, as well as relying more heavily on the views of service users. To what extent does policy in these areas suggest a distinctively Scottish agenda?

Free personal care

In a report published in 1999, the Royal Commission on Long-Term Care (the Sutherland Commission) made a key recommendation that personal care for older people (which includes things like bathing and hair washing, assistance with eating or with medication, and help with getting up and going to bed) should be free, both at home and in residential settings. One consequence of the recommendation, if implemented, would have been that older people would be under less pressure to sell off their homes in order to pay for their care. In fact, the recommendation was rejected as too costly by both the UK government and also initially by the Scottish Executive. However, at the 11th hour, in order to avoid a damaging parliamentary defeat which would have split the Labour Party from their Liberal Democrat coalition partners and could have ended coalition government in Scotland, the Executive did a U-turn and agreed to accept the commission's recommendation (with a nationwide campaign for free personal care involving many older people's organisations having added to the pressure on the political parties) (Shaw, 2003). The result is that from 1 July 2002, for people aged 65+ in Scotland, all personal care charges for those cared for in their own homes have been abolished; those needing nursing care, at home or in a care home, will receive it free of charge; those in residential accommodation who pay toward the cost of their care will receive a 'free personal care' weekly payment; and those in a nursing home will receive a 'free personal and nursing care' weekly payment. In political terms, it means that there is now a divergence between the policies of the UK government and the Scottish Executive, with older people in Scotland entitled to free personal and nursing care, now enacted in the 2002 Community Care and Health (Scotland) Act. In that sense, it might be claimed as an example of Scottish difference and has certainly been seen as such. That said, as this account makes clear, the process by which the decision was arrived at can hardly be claimed as evidence of a different, more social democratic, political culture north of the border. In addition, while the measure has been widely welcomed, as bodies such as Age Concern have pointed out, without increased funding and increased investment in resources, the likelihood is that private homes will simply increase their costs to cover loss of revenue, leaving many poor older people with no money and little increase in choice.

The 2003 Mental Health (Care and Treatment) (Scotland) Act

In the area of mental health, the Mental Health (Care and Treatment) (Scotland) Act 2003 will come into force in April 2005 and will replace the 1984 Mental Health (Scotland) Act. The act is much less punitive in its tone and provisions than the parallel English proposals (which have currently been taken back for discussion) and most of its provisions and underpinning principles, including non-discrimination, respect for diversity, and participation, have the support of mental health organisations, including user and carer organisations, in Scotland. Perhaps reflecting what appears to have been a genuine consultation process (Rosengard and Laing, 2001), the act also goes quite far in seeking to meet the wishes of the service users' movement. Thus, it allows for the drawing up of (non-mandatory) Advance Statements which will permit mental health service users to state how they would like to be treated in the event of their becoming unwell; requires local authorities to provide for the establishment of advocacy services; and creates a system of (less formal) mental health tribunals to replace Sheriff Courts in considering applications for compulsory detention. Insofar as these measures redress to some extent the huge power imbalance between mental health professionals on the one hand and users and carers on the other, they have been widely welcomed. That said, the act also contains other, less progressive features. A key provision, for example, allows for the compulsory treatment of people within the community, a measure which the Conservative governments of the 1990s failed to get onto the statute book and which was opposed by more than 50 mental health organisations in Scotland in a campaign led by the Scottish Association for Mental Health (Ferguson, 2003). More generally, the act has little to say about the *prevention* of mental ill-health and there is no requirement on local authorities or health boards to set up the kind of *preventative* services, such as crisis services, which would obviate the need for compulsory treatment in the first place. In the absence of these, and with no means of enforcing the principle of 'reciprocity' that underpins the Act, it is difficult to see how the legalistic focus on compulsory treatment which characterised the earlier legislation can be avoided, despite the progressive content and intentions of much of the Act.

Children and families

The starting-point for any discussion of social care and social work with children and families in Scotland has to be the country's exceptionally high levels of child poverty, which spiralled under the Conservatives but remained high well into the second term of a New Labour government. While reducing child poverty is a stated aim of New Labour in Westminster, in fact a study of poverty in Scotland carried out for the Joseph Rowntree Foundation at the end of 2002 found that the number of children living in low income households – roughly a third of all children – had not changed since 1997, in contrast to the rest of Britain where it has declined (Kenway et al, 2002). Despite this, the same managerial and market-based prescriptions which have guided policy in the area of community care, rather than the more redistributive approaches which this level of poverty might have suggested (even within the limits imposed by the devolution settlement) have also shaped policy responses in this area. Thus, the Executive's main response to the report *For Scotland's children* (Scottish Executive, 2001), which described children's services as 'chaotic' and 'close to crisis', has been to emphasise the need for greater integration of children's services. Where the development of services has taken place, as the authors of the 2001 report noted, it has usually involved the diversion of spending into short-term initiatives, rather than into improving mainline services (although that report failed to recognise the ways in which the acceptance of a competitive market in social care encourages such short-term funding).

While greater integration of services in this area as in community care has been generally welcomed by workers and service users, as have such measures as the extension of the Sure Start programme to Scotland and the creation of a Children's Commissioner, given the extent of child poverty referred to earlier in this chapter, the impact of these measures is clearly limited. Moreover, while the new-found emphasis on prevention in programmes such as Sure Start is also welcome, this is a particularly narrow form of prevention which fits well with a New Labour moral worldview which sees the roots of problems as lying with 'failing parents' rather than the effects of poverty and failing services. In general, the Executive has eschewed more macro-responses to the problem of child poverty. Thus, it failed, for example, to give support to a proposal in 2003 to provide free school meals to all Scottish children in state education, despite strong support for the proposal by the Child Poverty Action Group and the Scottish Trades Union Congress and despite substantial evidence that this measure would have had a real impact on children's health. Moreover, against the commitment to pre-school care and education which programmes like Sure Start suggest, must be set the Executive's failure to intervene in support of several thousand poorly paid nursery nurses (whose professionalism and commitment will be central to the success of any pre-five strategy) in their long and bitter battle for a professional salary with (mainly Labour-controlled) local authority employers in 2004.

Children and families' social work

Child poverty impacts on every aspect of social work practice with children and their families. A study by Waterhouse et al (2000), for example, found that out of 1,155 children referred to children's hearings in 1995, 55% came from families dependent on state benefit, 46% from lone-parent families and 72% lived in local authority housing – all key indicators of deprivation, and figures well above the national average. However, it has been the narrow issue of child protection, rather than a wider concern to address the social, physical and emotional needs of these children that has tended to dominate social work policy and practice in this area since 1999. Here too, the response to the deaths of children where there has been social work involvement has often reflected a managerialist emphasis on improved standards, tougher inspection regimes and revised procedures, rather than a primary concern with the social and material context of the abuse or the pressures on front line social workers. In response to the recommendations of a major review of child protection, for example, which followed the death of a child in the Scottish Borders (Scottish Executive, 2002), the Executive outlined a programme of action whose main points were:

- a three-year programme of sustained activity to reform child protection services by establishing clear practice standards, developing the role and responsibilities of Child Protection Committees, and building capacity to deliver;
- a team of experts from relevant agencies, with top-level backing from the Executive, to work directly with local agencies to implement the reform programme and tackle poor performance;
- a tough new system of inspection to monitor progress over the next three years to ensure that reform is delivered;
- a Children's Charter, to be drawn up in conjunction with professionals and children, to set out the support that children have the right to expect;
- extra support to be given to helplines that provide counselling and support for children – Childline and Parentline – including £500,000 to allow Childline Scotland to open up a new call centre and increase by up to 60% the number of children they are able to help (www.scotland.gov.uk).

Other than the provision for some additional funding for helplines, the overall thrust of this response appears to be driven by a managerial agenda of standards, regulation and inspection. The wider perception that 'social work is failing' and in need of 'reform' has been reinforced by subsequent tragedies, most notably the death of 11-week-old Caleb Ness in Edinburgh in 2001 at the hands of his father. Once again, the resulting enquiry was highly critical of social work at all levels and led to the resignation of Edinburgh's Director of Social Work (unusually, since it is normally front-line workers who are forced to resign). No less significant in terms of social work's long-term future was Edinburgh City Council's response to the enquiry. In a move that may be followed by other authorities, it closed down its social work department and replaced it with a new Department of Children and Families and a new Department of Health and Social Care.

Whatever mistakes individual social workers may have made in particular cases, the pressures faced by staff in children and families' social work do not always seem to be fully acknowledged in wider discussions of child protection reform, despite the finding, for example, in *It's everyone's job to make sure I'm alright* (Scottish Executive, 2002), that some teams were up to 50% understaffed. Yet, as one Edinburgh social worker told a journalist following the Caleb Ness enquiry:

> The very last place people want to come and work now is with children and families. The risk of getting a judgement even slightly wrong is so dangerous, and the levels of responsibility are not commensurate with the pay. (*Sunday Herald*, 9 May 2004)

Young people who offend

One area in which the moral authoritarianism of the UK New Labour government has been most evident has been in its treatment of young people who offend. As noted earlier in this chapter, the basis of the children's hearing system, which has now been in operation for more than 30 years, is a rejection of the distinction between young people in need and young people in trouble, with young people's criminal behaviour seen as only one aspect of their life experience. While that system has come under considerable pressures in recent years, in part because of this welfare-based approach, in part because it is increasingly seen by social workers among others as the only means of accessing services for young people, its basic strengths have been re-affirmed by recent research reports (Waterhouse et al, 2000; NCH Scotland, 2004; Whyte, 2004). Despite that, the pressure to be seen to be responding to the 'problem' of youth crime has led to a hardening of approach to children involved with crime within the children's hearing system. At the time of writing (June 2004), two alternatives to the traditional children's hearing system are being piloted: youth courts and 'fast-track hearings'. The former have been set up to target young offenders in the 16- to 17-year-old age group, with the 'flexibility' to deal with 15-year-olds in certain circumstances. The latter are being piloted in six sites, with their key element being that any young person with five offending episodes in six months is deemed a 'persistent offender' and brought into the fast track system. The case is then processed more quickly, with a full assessment of risk of future offending being undertaken and the young person guaranteed a place on whatever service they need. While workers and others have tended to be fairly positive about these schemes (not surprisingly, since they provide access to far more resources than would normally be available), a number of specific downsides have been identified in initial research evaluation, such as young people being referred for petty offences and quickly being labelled 'persistent offenders', as well as a disproportionately high number of young people who came into the system coming from residential care (*Sunday Herald*, 11 January 2004). More generally, they clearly undermine the principles on which the hearing system was based and there is concern that a review of the hearing system, announced in 2003 and currently ongoing, will undermine these principles even further.

More evidence of the Executive's willingness to adopt a punitive approach towards young people is provided by the 2004 Antisocial Behaviour, etc (Scotland) Act, which was the 'flagship' bill of the Executive's second term. While the behaviour of some children and young people undoubtedly causes misery to their neighbours and others, especially in the poorest areas, there is no evidence that stigmatising young people as 'neds' (as several leading ministers did in the discussion around the bill), criminalising the behaviour of children aged 12+, introducing electronic tagging, giving the police powers to break up groups of two or more young people, and imposing parenting orders on their parents will make a substantial difference to their behaviour. (For a discussion of the ineffectiveness of Antisocial Behaviour Orders [ASBOs] south of the border, see Foot, 2004.) It smacks more of electoral populism than the kind of 'joined-up thinking' that recognises the link between young people's behaviour and the despair, boredom and lack of hope which so many young people in poorer areas experience (Davies, 1998), rooted in the appalling poverty so clearly outlined in the reports like *For Scotland's children*. Nor can the bill be portrayed as a response to a sudden increase in the kinds of behaviours the bill seeks to address. As Whyte (2004, p 406) has noted, the number of young people referred to the children's hearing system for offending in 2000/01 is no more than it was in 1974 when the system was set up, while the Executive's own figures show that recorded crime in general fell in 2004 to its lowest level in almost a quarter of a century (www.scotland.gov.uk). It is perhaps not surprising, then, that the act has been condemned by, among others, Scotland's first Children's Commissioner, who argued that "ministers seem to have succumbed to the temptation to go for the short, sharp shock rather than the long-term solution and I don't think that it is going to work" (*Sunday Herald*, 20 June 2004).

The children of asylum seekers

Finally, no discussion of childcare policy and practice in Scotland in recent years could fail to mention the experience of the children of asylum seekers. While much good work has been carried out with these children and with unaccompanied minors by teachers and social workers, particularly in Glasgow, the detention of school-age children for periods of more than a year in Dungavel Detention Centre has been described as a national scandal. Article 37b of the UN Convention on the Rights of the Child states that:

> No child shall be deprived of his or her liberty unlawfully or arbitrarily. The arrest, detention or imprisonment of a child shall be in conformity

with the law and shall be used only as a measure of last resort and for
the shortest appropriate period of time.

Despite a national campaign which united the churches, the quality press in
Scotland, as well as campaigning organisations, particularly over the experience
of the Ay family who were detained in Dungavel for more than a year, the
Executive maintained a stony silence, on the grounds that immigration and asylum
were matters reserved to the Westminster Parliament on which they could not
comment. The fact that the Executive has shown willingness to debate other
non-devolved matters, including, for example, the war in Iraq, makes this
explanation less than convincing.

Criminal justice social work

Social workers no longer 'advise, assist and befriend'; they 'advise,
assist and guide'. With this shift of emphasis has come an apparent
alteration in the role of the social worker. The social worker is now to
be less concerned with meeting welfare needs than with addressing
offending behaviour. Dealing with 'criminogenic' need is a means to
an end in dealing with agenda of reducing crime in society. The
social worker is responsible for getting offenders to take responsibility
for their actions. (McKay, 2003, p 107)

As criminal justice policy in Scotland is addressed elsewhere in this book, this
section will focus briefly on the role of criminal justice social work. This quotation
from McKay points to the shift that has taken place in the content of social work
in this area, a shift which Howe (1996, p 88) has conceptualised in terms of a
distinction between 'depth' and 'surface' social work practice, with the latter
concerning situations where "social workers become more inclined to respond
to the *act* than treat the *actor*. Thus, a concern with *behaviour* replaces an interest
in *action*".

As noted earlier in this chapter, social work with offenders in Scotland has
differed historically in remaining within generic social work departments as
opposed to being part of a separate probation service, as it is in England and
Wales. However, since the introduction of the *National objectives and standards for
social workers in the criminal justice system* in 1991, involving protocols of practice,
ring-fenced funding and dedicated social workers, social work practice in this
area has diverged considerably not only from practice in the areas of children
and families and also community care but also from more traditional conceptions
of the social work role.

At the UK level, two main factors have driven policy and practice in this area.
On the one hand, there was the growing recognition through most of the 1980s
(often based on research from within the Home Office itself) that prison simply
does *not* work, leading to a greater willingness to explore community-based

alternatives. On the other hand, there has been the desire on the part of leading politicians of both major parties, driven primarily by electoral considerations, to appease right-wing populist sentiment by being seen to be 'tough on crime' (a strategy that came to a head following the death of the toddler James Bulger in 1993 at the hands of two other children) (Ferguson, 1994). While there has been some divergence in the way in which these tensions have been managed north and south of the border, there have also been considerable similarities in developments within the two criminal justice systems. In both cases, there is a formal emphasis on the need for work with offenders to be 'evidence-based', to draw on research that identifies 'what works' (McGuire, 1995). At the same time, that apparently rationalist, evidence-based approach is frequently offset by lurches into punitive approaches which are far from evidence-based and seem much more concerned with appeasing public opinion, particularly in the area of youth offending. The now abandoned curfews on children is one example, the anti-social behaviour legislation another. Perhaps, the greatest irony, however, for governments which profess to base their criminal justice policy on a 'what-works' approach is that in both Scotland and in the UK as a whole, prison populations are currently higher than they have ever been, despite the manifest evidence that prison does not work, with Scotland having more people in custody than any other country in Europe

Against this context of huge prison populations, it is understandable that the alternative strategy of community treatments based on a 'what works' approach is much more attractive to many practitioners. That strategy too, has its limits, however.

First, there is the question of what counts as 'evidence'. In practice, it has tended to mean structured approaches that are more amenable to measurement, in particular cognitive-behavioural approaches. Not only does this mean that more fuzzy, qualitative issues such as quality of the worker/client relationship or the experience of service users may not be counted but also, as I have argued elsewhere, that this approach:

> ... presents social and personal change as essentially a technical matter – issues of values or ideology are excised. We are concerned with what works in achieving a specific end – such as reducing crime – rather than looking at the wider causes of that behaviour. (Ferguson, 2004, p 6)

In similar vein, McIvor (2004, p 308), while arguing that the approach to criminal justice policy in Scotland has been more inclusive and less 'top-down' than south of the border, nevertheless suggests that:

> Whatever the merits of cognitive-behavioural interventions, it could be argued that the emphasis placed upon them has had the effect of narrowing the focus of offender supervision in an unhelpful way, by

diverting attention from the social and economic context in which offending occurs. Cognitive-behavioural approaches with offenders are rarely conducive to the development of practice that is aimed at empowerment, enhancing social justice and promoting inclusion within society.

Discussion over the future of criminal justice social work in Scotland in recent years has been dominated on the one hand by the debate on youth crime (considered in the previous section of this chapter) and also by the proposal that criminal justice social work be merged with the Prison Service into a new Corrections Agency. There can be no doubt that, had the latter proposal gone ahead, the Scottish Prison Service would have been the more powerful voice within in the new agency, with social work (and the values it represents) very much the junior partner. Opposition from a range of bodies, including the Convention of Scottish Local Authorities (COSLA), the Association of Directors of Social Work in Scotland and also Unison, appears to have persuaded the Scottish Executive not to proceed with the proposal. It is clear, however, that the overall strategy of encouraging more 'integrated working' in this area as elsewhere will continue, with criminal justice social workers encouraged to pursue an agenda which, in Tony Blair's celebrated phrase, may indeed be 'tough on crime' but shows less and less interest in addressing 'the causes of crime'.

Conclusion: addressing the crisis of social work?

The establishment by the Scottish Executive of an independent enquiry into '21st Century Social Work' in July 2004, following yet another abuse case in the Scottish Borders, this time involving a woman with learning disabilities, involves a recognition that social work in Scotland (as in much of the rest of the UK) is in crisis. One aspect of that crisis concerns staffing. A COSLA review carried out in 2003 showed that social work vacancies in Scotland were currently running at between 350 and 400 (cited in Wilson et al, 2003). Some of the ways in which Executive has responded to this staffing crisis, including advertising campaigns and a new four-year degree, were discussed in the introduction to this chapter. There is a sense, however, that most of these responses are essentially cosmetic. A national pay-regrading scheme, for example, similar to that enjoyed by Scottish teachers as a result of the recommendations of the McCrone Commission, appears to have been ruled out. Instead, there is a bidding war between Scottish local authorities to attract staff through measures such as 'golden hellos' of up to £5,000, paying off of student loans, relocation schemes and other measures which may meet short-term needs but in the longer term simply move the problem around and increase resentment on the part of existing staff who do not benefit from these measures.

Low wages compared to other professional staff, however, is only one aspect of the current crisis. The other is low morale. In part, this is due to a perceived lack of resources to do the job properly. In part, however, it is due to the changed nature of the job itself. In this respect, the findings of Wilson et al's (2003) study of career pathways in Scottish Social Services closely mirror those of Jones' (2000) study of the experience of front-line local authority workers in England. In the Scottish study, the main reason given for becoming a social worker was the wish to work directly with people and help make a difference in their lives, individually or collectively. While a majority (60%) felt that social work had met their expectations in this respect, many did not. As Wilson et al (2003) comment:

> there is a mismatch between the motivation and values of social work staff and the current nature of a social worker's job…. In common with other public services, social work is now run in accordance with a managerial rather than professional ethos, so that service development is guided by considerations of cost effectiveness and organisational efficiency. On the positive side, this is intended to improve standards. However, it can also reduce the scope for professional discretion and result in services being provided on the basis of organisational expectations and procedures, rather than working out with an individual client what would be most helpful in a specific situation.

Similarly, in their interviews with social workers in children and families' teams, the authors of the child protection audit and review *'It's everyone's job to make sure I'm alright'* (Scottish Executive, 2002, p 98) found that:

> In their day-to-day work it was the lack of opportunities to directly work with children and their families that frequently frustrated them. Many saw the voluntary sector as attractive because it focused on the needs of children and enabled staff to use their core skills of working with children and families.

What this suggests is that the managerial and market-based approaches which have dominated social work throughout the UK for more than a decade have created an increasingly dissatisfied workforce who feel that they are being denied the opportunity to utilise the values and skills which brought them into social work and social care in the first place. Yet, as Jones et al have argued in the web-based *Social work and social justice: A manifesto for a new engaged practice* (www.liverpool.ac.uk/sspsw/manifesto), it is precisely the voices of these workers which have been silenced for over a decade in which the voices of social work employers have dominated. If social work in Scotland and the rest of the UK is to have a future, then the starting-point must involve listening to the voices both of the people who use services and of the front-line staff who provide them. In practice, making that voice heard will require much stronger self-organisation of users and front-line workers than exists at present.

Further resources

Baillie, D., Cameron, K., Cull, L.-A., Roche, J. and West, J. (2003) *Social work and the law in Scotland*, Basingstoke: Palgrave Macmillan.

Harris, J. (2003) *The social work business*, London: Routledge.

Jones, C. and Novak, T. (1999) *Poverty, welfare and the disciplinary state*, London: Routledge.

On the web ...

Age Concern Scotland	www.ageconcernscotland.org.uk
The City of Edinburgh Council	www.edinburgh.gov.uk
Positive Action in Housing	www.paih.org
Scottish Association for Mental Health	www.samh.org.uk
Scottish Executive	www.scotland.gov.uk

References

Butler, I. and Drakeford, M. (2001) 'Which Blair project? Communitarianism, social authoritarianism and social work', *Journal of Social Work*, vol 1, no 1, pp 7-19.

Clarke, J. (ed) (1993) *A crisis in care?*, London: Sage Publications.

Davies, N. (1998) *Dark heart*, London: Vintage.

Devine, T. (1999) *The Scottish nation 1700-2000*, London: Penguin.

Ferguson, I. (1994) 'Containing the Crisis: crime and the Tories', *International Socialism*, vol 62, pp 51-70.

Ferguson, I. (2003) 'Mental health and social work', in D. Baillie, K. Cameron, L.-A. Cull, J. Roche and J. West (eds) *Social work and the law in Scotland*, Basingstoke: Palgrave Macmillan/Open University, pp 65-76.

Ferguson, I. (2004) 'Neoliberalism, the Third Way and social work: the UK experience', *Social Work and Society*, vol 2, no 1, pp 1-9.

Ferguson, I., Lavalette, M. and Mooney, G. (2002) *Rethinking welfare: A critical perspective*, London: Sage Publications.

Foot, M. (2004) 'Leave our kids alone', *Socialist Review*, October 4, pp 6-7.

Harris, J. (2003) *The social work business*, London: Routledge.

Hartnoll, M. (1998) 'A struggle around an ideal: Kilbrandon or the Kilkenny Cats?', in M. Barry and C. Hallett (eds) *Social exclusion and social work: Issues of theory, policy and practice*, Lyme Regis: Russell House Publishing, pp 39-49.

Howe, D. (1994) 'Modernity, postmodernity and social work', *British Journal of Social Work*, vol 24, no 5, pp 513-32.

Howe, D. (1996) 'Surface and depth in social work practice', in N. Parton (ed) *Social theory, social change and social work*, London: Routledge.

Jones, C. (2000) 'Voices from the front-line: state social workers and New Labour', *British Journal of Social Work*, vol 31, no 4, pp 547-62.

Jones, C. and Novak, T. (1999) *Poverty, welfare and the disciplinary state*, London: Routledge.

Kenway, P., Fuller, S., Rahman, M., Street, C. and Palmer, G. (2002) *Monitoring poverty and social exclusion in Scotland*, York: Joseph Rowntree Foundation.

Langan, M. (1993) 'The rise and fall of social work', in J. Clarke (ed) *A crisis in care? Challenges to social work*, London: Sage Publications/Open University.

Lavalette, M. and Mooney, G. (1999) 'New Labour, new moralism: the welfare politics and ideology of New Labour under Blair', *International Socialism*, vol 85, pp 27-47.

Lymbery, M. (2001) 'Social work at the crossroads', *British Journal of Social Work*, vol 31, pp 369-84.

McGhee, J. (2003) 'The social work role in the Children's Hearing System', in D. Baillie, K. Cameron, L.-A. Cull, J. Roche and J. West (eds) *Social work and the law in Scotland*, Basingstoke: Palgrave Macmillan/Open University, pp 87-102.

McGuire, J. (ed) (1995) *What works: Reducing reoffending. Guidelines from research and practice*, Chichester: Wiley.

McIvor, G. (2004) 'Getting personal: developments in policy, practice and research in Scotland', in G. Mair (ed) *What matters in probation*, Cullompton: Willan Publishing.

McKay, R. (2003) 'Social work practice in the criminal justice system', in D. Baillie, K. Cameron, L.-A. Cull, J. Roche and J. West (eds) *Social work and the law in Scotland*, Basingstoke: Palgrave Macmillan/Open University, pp 103-14.

Mooney, G. and Poole, L. (2004) '"A land of milk and honey?" Social policy in Scotland after devolution', *Critical Social Policy*, vol 24, no 4, pp 458-83.

NCH Scotland (2004) *Where's Kilbrandon Now? Report and Recommendations from the inquiry*, Glasgow: NCH Scotland.

Parton, N. (1994) 'The nature of social work under conditions of (post) modernity', *British Journal of Social Work*, vol 24, no 1, pp 9-32.

Petch, A. (2003) 'Care in the community', in D. Baillie, K. Cameron, L.-A. Cull, J. Roche and J. West (eds) *Social work and the law in Scotland*, Basingstoke: Palgrave Macmillan/Open University.

Rosengard, A. and Laing, I. (2001) *User consultation on the Millan Report*, Edinburgh: Scottish Executive.

Royal Commission on Long-Term Care, The (1999) *With respect to old age: Long-term care – Rights and responsibilities* (Sutherland Report), Cm 4192-I, London: The Stationery Office.

Scottish Executive (2001) *For Scotland's children*, Edinburgh: Scottish Executive.

Scottish Executive (2002) *'It's everyone's job to make sure I'm alright'*, Edinburgh: Scottish Executive.

Scottish Executive (2003) *Progress with complexity: The 2003 National Overview Report*, Edinburgh: Scottish Executive.

Shaw, E. (2003) 'Devolution and Scottish Labour: the case of long-term care for the elderly', Paper presented to the Annual Conference of the Political Studies Association, Leicester.

Smale, G. and Tuson, G., with Biehal, N. and Marsh, P. (1993) *Empowerment, assessment, care management and the skilled worker*, London: HMSO.

Stone, F. (1995) 'Foreword', *The Kilbrandon Report*, Edinburgh: Scottish Office.

Timmins, N. (1996) *The five giants: A biography of the welfare state*, London: Fontana Press.

Waterhouse, L., McGhee, J., Whyte, W., Loucks, N., Kay, H. and Stewart, R. (2000) *The evaluation of Children's Hearings in Scotland*, Edinburgh: Scottish Executive Central Research Unit.

Whyte, B. (2004) 'Responding to youth crime in Scotland', *British Journal of Social Work*, vol 34, pp 395–411.

Wilson, M., Walker, M. and Stalker, K. (2003) *Career pathways in Scottish Social Services: A pilot study*, Stirling: Social Work Research Centre, University of Stirling.

TEN

Devolution, territorial politics and the politics of education

Margaret Arnott

Scotland's educational system has always been distinct from that in England. The most high profile example of this since devolution must be the decision that Scottish university students studying in Scotland would not have to pay tuition fees while studying, but instead would make a contribution after they start earning. The difference, then, is not one of whether students would pay, but when. Another lower profile but arguably more significant difference, however, can be traced in approaches to secondary education, and it is this that forms the central focus of this chapter. Policy directions in the education system both pre and post-devolution Scotland are explored with particular emphasis on secondary schooling. The chapter then goes on to analyse the distinctiveness of Scottish educational policies in comparison with those in the rest of the UK. The following issues are considered:

- the way to devolution, and expectations of the Scottish Parliament;
- the 'Scottish myth' – values, attitudes and the role of education;
- New Labour's 'modernising' agenda in education – responses in England and in Scotland;
- the distinctiveness of the Scottish policy agenda – privatisation, diversity and performance management;
- convergence and divergence between Scottish and English education policy – social actors, school structure and social inclusion.

Introduction

This chapter considers some of the implications of the new constitutional arrangements for social policy in Scotland, with particular reference to education at secondary school level. While differences of view remain about the exact extent to which social policy pursued in Scotland was distinct from that in the rest of the UK prior to 1999, it would be accepted that 'territorial management' in the British state did allow for policy differentiation (Keating, 2002). This was certainly the case in education at school level. The analysis of education policy gives insight into the 'new' post-devolution Scotland and, more generally, helps towards an understanding of the changing nature, and increased importance, of territorial politics for social policy in Scotland since 1999. By focusing on secondary education policy it is possible to explore pressures for convergence and pressures for divergence in social policy between Scotland and England.

The establishment in 1999 of a Scottish Parliament three centuries after the original subsumption into the structures of the British state gave rise to talk of a 'new Scotland' (see the Introduction to this volume). Territorial distinctiveness within the British state which had evolved earlier in the 20th century in the form of administrative devolution (Bulpitt, 1983; Mitchell, 1996) had not occasioned similar consideration of a 'new Scotland', but still had had considerable implications for policy development.

In the advent of the Scottish Parliament expectations ran high that a distinctive policy agenda would follow in Scotland post-devolution (Brown et al, 1999). It was widely, if loosely, assumed that the new devolution framework and more generally, territorial politics would not prevent a Scottish Parliament from pursuing distinctive policies. The term 'loosely assumed' may be justified by the fact that there was very little debate about the direction or content of policies on devolved areas during the run up to the establishment of the Scottish Parliament. Little public debate was evident about the implications for the policy process for those areas 'retained' by Westminster. Generally there was a vague expectation that there would be a 'Scottish solution to Scottish problems'. There was little in the way of serious debate, notably on the part of the political parties, about what a devolved assembly might be expected to achieve. Indeed since the setting up of the new parliament there have been strong pressures, at least initially, for continuity with the past. One explanation for this may be the lack of debate pre-1999 about what a new parliament might do in policy terms.

Continuity is also reflected in people's perceptions that little has changed since the setting up of the Parliament. Drawing on survey data collected since the 1997 Referendum, Curtice and Seyd (2001, p 229) noted:

> It does confirm the impression that many people in Scotland now appear to be wondering whether their new parliament will improve the way they are governed at all.

They found that initial high expectations of the Scottish Parliament had fallen away. After a year of legislative devolution, 44% of Scots felt that the creation of the Scottish Parliament had made little difference. Education was one of the policy areas in which the Scottish Parliament was expected to make a positive impact. In 1997 a majority of Scots (71%) thought a Scottish Parliament would increase standards of education in Scotland. By 2000 this was a minority view (36%) (Curtice and Seyd, 2001). While the new Parliament may be perceived as not making as much as an impact as expected, this has not translated into a questioning of its continued existence. It appears that increasing numbers of Scots agree that the Scottish Parliament should be given more powers, and that, although they may believe that the new Parliament may not have created a 'new

Scotland', there is little sign that they believe it has made Scotland worse (Surridge, 2002). The changing expectations of the Scottish Parliament have not affected public support for devolution in Scotland.

This chapter will explore developments since 1999 in relation to secondary education policy and offer insights into the extent to which legislative devolution has created a 'new Scotland'. The discussion of policy below is not exhaustive. It is intended to allow reflection on the following key issues: Has policy distinctiveness between Scotland and England in secondary education policy become more pronounced since 1999? What have been the key themes of policy and to what extent have such policies been seen as contributing to wider aims of the Scottish Parliament and the Scottish Executive to create a 'new' Scotland? What role does secondary education policy play in attempts to promote 'social inclusion'?

Traditional approaches to territorial management were challenged by the Thatcher governments in the late 1980s (Arnott, 1992; Mitchell, 1996). Education was one of the key areas in which such challenges occurred. To understand the current policy environment, especially in terms of secondary education policy, it is essential to recognise the legacy of this Thatcherite experiment. One of the main motivations for legislative devolution in the 1980s and 1990s grew out of concern about the democratic legitimacy of how Scotland was being governed. Questions of democratic legitimacy before 1997 were part of debates about the 'Anglicisation' of social policy in Scotland. Education policy, especially the secondary sector, featured prominently in such debates. Policies introduced in the late 1980s – national testing, opting out and school boards – were intrinsic to debates about the Scottish Office adopting a Thatcherite agenda which applied across the UK (Arnott, 2000). The legitimacy of the Conservative government was called into question by educational professionals in local authorities and schools and also by parents. This was seen in the campaign in the early 1990s against national testing in primary schools which involved education authorities, parents and teaching unions. Subsequent legislation in Scotland differed significantly from the equivalent legislation in England. Teachers were given much more professional autonomy in implementing the tests and there was no central collection of test data which could be used to produce league tables.

The analysis of secondary education policy helps towards understanding the impact of devolution, more generally the changing nature and increased importance of territorial politics on social policy in Scotland and the extent to which a 'new Scotland' has developed. One might expect that looking at education since 1999 one would see the emergence of an increasingly distinct picture. The myths and traditions of Scottish education have had a continuing influence on the development of policy over the 20th century and also on wider debates about the need for constitutional reforms (McPherson and Raab, 1988; Paterson, 2000). There is a received wisdom that there was, and continues to be in Scotland, a specific outlook, informed by the 'Scottish myth' or more specifically the 'democratic tradition', on the purpose of education. The popular belief in the

'Scottish myth' has been maintained in three respects. Firstly, many features of contemporary education can be traced back to the 19th and early 20th centuries (Anderson, 1983). For instance, the four-year degree course in Scottish universities has been interpreted as part of the 'generalist tradition' that still exists in Scottish education. Secondly, the Scottish educational tradition was and continues to be an important component of Scottish national identity. The 'Scottish myth' reflects the values and attitudes that allegedly pervade Scottish society. It has been used to maintain a sense of Scottish nationhood. For instance, the 'Scottish myth' has been used as evidence that Scottish society is more egalitarian than English society. David McCrone, referring to the Scottish education system, claims that myths and traditions continue to have contemporary significance:

> Like traditions, myths connect with past realities. They do, however, draw selectively from the past, a process which involves selective exclusion as well as inclusion. In doing so, myth becomes a contemporary and active force providing, in most instances, a reservoir of legitimation for belief and action. (McCrone, 1992, p 90)

The third way in which the 'Scottish myth' has been maintained is through the language and arguments that have been articulated in debates about education policy in Scotland. There is a tendency to set such arguments in the context of the 'Scottish myth'. From their study of the post-war education policy in Scotland McPherson and Raab developed the concept of the 'Scottish education community'. Central to that community was a shared culture that drew on the myths and traditions that inform the Scottish education system:

> Communities have their own moral systems of value and belief, their own procedures for recognising or excluding members, and their own internal relationship of trust and deference ... the 'Scottish myth', traditional and popular view that has been taken of the egalitarian nature of Scottish society and of its realisation through the school system. This view was linked to issues of national identity, and it provided an ontological basis for a community of values and beliefs. (McPherson and Raab, 1988, p 409)

On the other hand, there are pressures for convergence. New Labour has attached particular importance to education and regards it as crucial to a wide range of policy areas, especially economic policy and attempts to promote the 'knowledge economy' (Jones, 2003). How wider forces such as 'globalisation' are translated by differing national policies is also important (Jones, 2003). The long-standing myths and traditions which continue to influence the 'Scottish education community' and the more recent wider economic context have each had implications in recent years for the New Labour policy agenda and specifically education policy. The wider policy environment, in particular the interdependency between economic and educational policy goals, could act as a force for policy convergence.

Education, New Labour and the 'modernising' agenda in Scotland and England: convergence and divergence

Two stereotypical views of policy development post-1999 in Scotland have emerged. In one view, legislative devolution has increased Scottish control of direction and content of policy. A related argument is that changes in policy-making processes increased accountability to rectify the 'democratic deficit' associated with Conservative governments of the 1980s and 1990s. The opposing view highlights the interventionist agenda of central government, the extent to which common UK-wide policies are evident, and the influence of the New Labour 'modernising' agenda especially in relation to the public sector. The Blair government, in this view, seeks policy coordination to ensure that policy delivery is achieved. There was a marked changed in government priorities in 1999 following Blair's 'forces of conservatism' speech about the public sector to the British Venture Capitalist Association (Richards and Smith, 2004). While still arguing that 'joined-up' government was important, the real energies of Blair and the 'centre' switched to improving delivery of public services.

Jack McConnell as First Minister has highlighted the importance of policy delivery and the importance of 'doing less better'. The *Partnership Agreement* drawn up after the 2003 Scottish Parliament Elections includes improving public services, particularly in schools and hospitals, as one of its key commitments (Scottish Executive, 2003a). The commitments set out in the Agreement for education are part of a common UK 'modernising' agenda. Claims to 'modernise' schooling, a commitment to a school building programme, extending ministerial powers to intervene in 'failing' schools, the setting out of national standards, all feature in equivalent policy documents south of the border. However, there are signs that in Scotland 'modernisation' of schooling is influenced by a different political environment.

In contrast to practice in England, the Scottish Executive frames its policies from the starting point of the continuation of the 'comprehensive schooling' system in which professionals at both school and local authority levels, rather than parents or volunteers, play a key strategic role. For instance, increased devolved decision making in schools in Scotland is promised to the head teacher and not to the school board as one might have expected. There is also a commitment to 'promote improved assessment of individual schools' progress as a better measure than national league tables' (Scottish Executive, 2003b). South of the border school governors and also the private sector have been given increasing roles in the running of schools and improving standards at school level. In Scotland 'underperforming' schools are to be subject to ministerial intervention as 'a last resort' but Her Majesty's Inspectorate of Education in Scotland (HMIE) and local authorities have been given key roles in 'maximising schools' performance'.

It could be argued that the Scottish Executive has taken a UK 'modernising' agenda and adapted it to distinctive Scottish circumstances.

In two respects the Scottish Executive has mirrored the New Labour approach south of the border. Firstly, the use of targets, monitoring progress of these targets and disseminating this information to the public is part of a wider effort to improve 'policy delivery' and regain the 'trust' of the electorate. In 2002 the Scottish Executive published a progress report on the two *Programme for government* documents published since 1999. These two documents contained 327 commitments. By publishing information on the progress made on these commitments the Scottish Executive argued:

> [this] ... has helped the Scottish Parliament and the public to see for themselves how the Scottish Executive was setting its objectives and performing against them.... The targets set out in the two documents have provided a clear focus for the Executive's work, and encouraged a new emphasis on delivery and accountability. (Scottish Executive, 2002, p 5)

The 2002 *Recording our achievements* report listed progress on 35 targets relating to education and young people (Scottish Executive, 2002). Many of the targets in the first *Programme for government* document related to early education and primary schools that chimed with priorities set by the first Blair government. Key targets related to teachers' pay and conditions and to improving standards in Scottish schools. A commitment was also made that 61 New Community School Projects would be running by 2001. The intention was that New Community Schools (now renamed Integrated Community Schools) would improve educational attainment and also promote social inclusion.

The second similarity with the New Labour approach south of the border is that there is considerable overlap in terms of the priority areas of the Scottish Executive, in education policy, with those of the Blair government. Nursery education, teachers' pay and conditions, school improvement and school building programmes all feature. Nevertheless, the approach to tackling these issues need not be uniform. As we shall see below in relation to teachers' work and school improvement, the Scottish Executive has arguably pursued distinctive approaches that have set the New Labour 'modernising' agenda in a Scottish context. However, tensions exist and it is a balancing act.

Legitimacy and control of policy making were key questions in devolution debates in Scotland in the 1980s and 1990s. Demands of pro-devolutionists in Scotland for constitutional change grew out of the reaction to Thatcherism and desires to move away from the 'Westminster style' of politics. For Blairites, on the other hand, devolution is just one part of attempts to modernise the UK constitution and the British state (Richards and Smith, 2002). These two views have different starting points and different emphases. The differences arguably created tensions between the UK Labour government and the Labour Party in

Scotland, especially during the period of Henry McLeish's leadership as First Minister.

The balancing act between Scottish and British agendas is important to territorial politics for the Labour Party throughout Britain (Brown et al, 1998). This was the case before 1999. It remains so after the establishment of the Scottish Parliament, given the translation of New Labour's 'modernising' agenda to those areas such as education where Scotland had significant policy distinctiveness before 1999. In Scotland, the Labour Party has to deal with a much more influential left wing opposition that includes the Scottish National Party and the Scottish Socialist Party. Party competition in Scotland has become increasingly distinct from south of the border, especially after 1999.

Tensions between London and Edinburgh did spill out into the open, principally concerning McLeish's desire to push ahead with the policy of free personal care for older people. However, since McConnell has assumed the post of First Minister the desire "to mend fences with London" has been evident (Macwhirter, 2002, p 32). Has such fence mending had significant implications for the direction of education policy in Scotland? We might expect, given arguments about the extent of 'autonomy' before 1999 and the assumptions that legislative devolution would give the new Parliament policy making powers, that the 'core executive', including Downing Street, would not expect to pursue uniform schooling policies in Scotland and England. However, education policy in Scotland and England has been and continues to be crucial to the programme of 'modernising' reforms, and as noted above, has become increasingly interdependent with economic policy goals. Macro-economic policy is a retained area. Public service delivery as a particular concern of a McConnell-led administration is not inconsistent with New Labour reforms of public sector south of the border (Mitchell, 2003). To understand the significance of the potential pressures for convergence it is necessary to explore the elements of 'New Labour' education policy in more detail.

McCaig (2000) argues that New Labour wants its education policy to be appealing to the electorate, especially to the aspiring voter or parent, but at the same time its policies must be relevant to the traditions and ideology of the Labour Party. The aspiring voter is taken to be 'middle class'. Blair has identified delivering public sector reform as crucial to the attraction of such voters. If Labour is to deliver on its promises in terms of social equality and social inclusion, the argument runs, it must retain middle-class support. The 'modernising' agenda in the public sector is an attempt to prevent the middle classes 'opting out' of the public sector and buying private social services especially in education and health. At the same time schooling is part of the 'knowledge economy' and "compulsory education needs to offer the kinds of specialism which will produce differentiated and flexible workforce" (McCaig, 2000, p 189). Schooling policy has become part of economic and industrial policy making and not solely confined to social policy (Stedward, 2003).

A distinctive aspect of New Labour's education policy has been the promotion of both 'equality' and 'economic development' (Naidoo and Muschamp, 2002). These elements are evident in secondary education policies in both Scotland and England. In Scotland the 'social democratic' legacy is still an important aspect of political debate and the wider political context (Curtice and Seyd, 2001; Paterson, 2002). Especially in terms of education there is a perceived stronger commitment in Scotland to social equality and public provision (Bromley et al, 2003). As noted earlier, the Labour Party in Scotland is operating arguably in a more left wing environment and does not face electoral pressures identical to those of the Party south of the border. In Scotland the middle classes have a greater commitment to the public sector including comprehensive schools. One electoral motivation underlying the 'modernising' agenda in England is arguably less relevant north of the border.

In their analysis of education policy in England since 1997 Brehony and Deem (2003, p 180) argue that New Labour have set aside the "social democratic legacy" of the party "in favour of the concept of social exclusion". This shift has led the Party to pursue a vast array of education policies which are aimed at promoting economic efficiency. David Blunkett, former Secretary of State for Education, argued "the work of the DfEE fits with a new economic imperative of supply side investment for national prosperity" (cited in Jones, 2003, p 144).

Given the importance of educational reforms to 'economic development', it is perhaps not surprising that the Treasury has become more interventionist in social policy, seeking to influence the policy agenda but also to control policy outcomes. To understand the direction of education policy in England it is necessary to look to the role of the Treasury. In their comparison of policies on teachers' work in Scotland and England since 1997, Menter et al (2004, p 203) argue that in Scotland under the McCrone settlement teachers were trusted with a pay reward before the changes were introduced to their conditions whereas in England teachers' pay was a "Treasury driven policy [which] meant that teachers were only given 'something for something'". This is different in Scotland. The influence of the Treasury is still evident but, as before 1999, the nature of relations differs because of territorial management. The importance of education to 'New Labour' reforms has not just resulted in the Treasury becoming increasingly engaged in social policy; we have also seen the influence of Blair and the Downing Street Policy Unit in education, especially schools policy. Tomlinson (2001, p 90) has pointed to relationships, sometimes confrontational, which developed between the Department for Education and Employment and the Downing Street Policy Unit over the direction of policy.

In England reforms since 1997 have attempted to 'modernise' the comprehensive system and move towards a more diverse system of schooling (DfEE, 2001). Comprehensive schooling in Scotland remains relatively homogenous compared to developments south of the border. Moves towards 'faith-based' schools and also 'specialist' schools have been much more extensive in England. Attempts to improve standards and reduce inequalities are premised on extending diversity in the schooling system. The discourse of the market also continues to influence the policy agenda. That the 'third way' in relation to secondary education should be operating differently north and south of the border is not surprising. One of the features of governing before 1999 was the 'autonomy' which was afforded to the Scottish Office and the public sector in Scotland in translating public policies, especially in education, to Scottish circumstances. Paterson (1997) has described such distinctiveness as developing from 'negotiated autonomy'. Whitehall departments allowed the Scottish Office some flexibility in interpreting how policy areas under its competence should be implemented.

To explore whether the Scottish Executive has moved towards a more distinctive policy agenda in secondary education compared to England, the following broad, interrelated themes are considered:

- 'privatisation'
- diversity
- performance management.

These themes are far from exhaustive, but exploring each will help to shed light on the broad analytical question of the impact of legislative devolution on education policy and on some of the implications for social equality. There are pressures for policy convergence, especially in terms of 'privatisation' and 'performance management', but these pressures are set within the context of an arguably increasingly distinctive policy environment. Moreover, one could argue that attempts to translate the 'modernising' agenda in secondary schooling to Scottish circumstances are part of an older pre-legislative devolution tradition of territorial politics.

'Privatisation'

The private sector has become more involved in education in both Scotland and England in the past five years or so. The independent sector in both countries has grown although in Scotland this remains at a very small scale (with the possible exception of Edinburgh) (Denholm and Macleod, 2002). Most controversial has been the use of the private firms in the state sector. Private Finance Initiatives (PFIs) have been used to fund school building programmes throughout Britain. PFIs were first introduced in 1992 and cover a range of contractual arrangements extending approximately 25 years. Labour renamed this initiative Public Private Partnerships (PPPs).

In Scotland, the use of PPPs may have been unavoidable given the financial borrowing constraints placed on the Scottish Parliament and the Scottish Executive by the UK government (Keating, 2003). In 1999 the Scottish Executive also inherited a substantial commitment to PFI in Scotland in a range of public services. For the Executive, PPPs are part of the 'modernisation' agenda and play an essential role in improving the delivery of public services. It is in education that the Scottish Executive has been its most enthusiastic in promoting PPPs "as the only game in town". The school building programme has been the Executive's most extensive use of PPPs, with nearly £3 billion worth of contracts (Crawford and Paul, 2004). In 2002 the Accounts Commission questioned the nature of PFI contracts in school building (Accounts Commission, 2002). Indeed it was implied that local authorities should not automatically assume that their options were limited to the use of PFIs. The Accounts Commissions was also critical of the PFI contract charges. In October 2003 East Lothian Council ran into major difficulties with its PPP project because the main contractor went into administration; the project could not be relaunched until April 2004 after an alternative contractor had been found (Fallis, 2004). Nevertheless, since 2002 the use of PFI contracts has been 'rolled out' further. The Scottish Executive aims to replace or substantially refurbish 300 schools by 2009 (Fallis, 2004).

In this policy initiative the nature of private sector engagement is largely limited to construction rather than having a direct role in schooling (Jones, 2003). It is here that we see the clearest evidence of policy divergences between Scotland and England. For instance, the Department for Education and Skills' intervention in schooling extended to giving private companies contracts to run failing comprehensive schools. In March 2000 the Blair government announced the creation of city academies to replace existing 'failing' schools. These schools could be run by businesses, churches or voluntary bodies and were independent of local authorities. Early interest from the private sector came from firms such as Boots the chemist and Reg Vardy the car dealer (Pring, 2001). In May 2003 head teachers in Essex bypassed their local education authority and negotiated their own private sector support package (Stewart, 2003). Menter et al (2004) in their research on changes to teachers' work have argued that in England there is extensive involvement of the private sector in schools, not just in delivering policies such as 'Threshold Assessment' but also significantly in policy making. This, they conclude, is in sharp contrast to the situation in Scotland. However, there have been signs that the Scottish Executive is moving towards accepting the involvement of private sector funding. There have been reports in the media that Jack McConnell had met with a small number of entrepreneurs to discuss funding a new model of school in the most deprived areas. A Scottish Executive source was quoted as confirming that such meetings had taken place and that Scotland would follow a distinctive policy agenda:

> We don't think city academies are the right approach for Scotland, but we are already working with a number of Scottish entrepreneurs on a different model that will meet the aspirations and ambitions from some of our most deprived communities. (quoted in MacLeod, 2004)

In August 2004, in a speech to Labour activists in Edinburgh, Jack McConnell raised the prospect of private funding for a new type of secondary school, but in contrast to policy developments in England, ruled out the private sector running such schools (McConnell, 2004).

The increasing involvement of the private sector in English schooling led in March 2004 to the Schools Minister, David Miliband, having to deny that in Labour's next UK general election manifesto, the government would include the privatisation of secondary schools to allow private companies to run schools for profit, along the lines of US Charter schools. Differences in the extent and role of the private sector in secondary schooling highlight the extent to which national contexts do impact on the New Labour agenda in Scotland and England, including policies designed to reduce social inequalities.

Attempts within secondary education policy to tackle social inequalities have also followed distinctive lines north and south of the border. Education Action Zones (EAZs) in England were part of the first Blair government's flagship 'Excellence in Cities' programme designed to deal with poor performance of inner-city pupils. Initially launched in six urban areas in 1999 the programme was extended in 2001 to cover 58 areas, and by August 2001 there were 81 EAZs in total (Naidoo and Muschamp, 2002). Each EAZ included about 20 schools and while the government provided some funding, additional funds had to be found from the private sector. The government was also eager that the private sector should run as many zones as possible (Gewirtz, 2002). In Scotland, the private sector was not involved in attempts to tackle issues of social exclusion through the schooling system. The Scottish Executive followed a different path, choosing to work through local authorities rather than creating 'zones' outside direct local authority control. However, following the 2003 Scottish Parliament elections, there have been signs that the Scottish Executive is willing to consider reforms which would change the relationship between local authorities and secondary schools (Fraser, 2004). For instance, in the summer of 2004 McConnell announced that the Schools Minister, Peter Peacock, would engage the private sector as well as educational professionals and parents in "the most comprehensive programme in Scotland's secondary schools for a generation" (McConnell, 2004).

The New Community School policy was introduced in 1998 by the then Secretary of State for Scotland, Donald Dewar, and was continued by the Scottish Executive after 1999. The policy was developed from an initiative in Washington and then related to Scottish circumstances as a 'flagship policy', first by the Scottish Office and after 1999 by the Scottish Executive (Nixon et al, 2002). Unlike initiatives south of the border such as EAZs and specialist schools, the Scottish Office, while setting out 'essential characteristics' for the New Community School, allowed education authorities local flexibility in applying such characteristics to local circumstances (Nixon et al, 2001). The final evaluation report of the pilot programme which ran from 1999-2002 found that nearly two thirds of secondary schools involved believed that the initiative had had a 'considerable' impact on pupil attitudes, but fewer, just over half the secondary schools, reported that impact on attainment had been more 'limited' (*Times Education Supplement Scotland*, 2003).

The approach in Scotland to social inclusion "directly link[s] social exclusion and poverty" (Ozga, 2003b, p 12). According to this approach the government should ensure that opportunities exist rather than constructing the problem where individuals have failed due to individual underachievement. As Ozga has argued, the Blair government has attempted to advance the business model in schooling policies, especially those related to 'underachievement', in an attempt to 'encourage the enterprising self' (Ozga, 2003b). The approach in Scotland, as demonstrated in the policy of New Community Schools, has been somewhat different, continuing to draw on more social democratic traditions stressing redistributive politics.

Diversity

The structure of the secondary schooling sector has long been an area of distinctiveness between Scotland and England (Green, 1990). However, over the past 20 years we have seen increasing diversity develop. Structural or administrative distinctiveness does not necessarily imply that common UK policies have not been pursued. In the late 1980s, for instance, the Conservative government attempted to pursue common themes, especially the promotion of 'market forces', through an array of policy initiatives. Scotland, Wales and Northern Ireland experienced to varying degrees market-based policies and managerialism, especially with respect to secondary schooling. In England market reforms, competition and engagement with the private sector went much further, but variants of such policies could be found in the rest of the UK.

The Labour government inherited in 1997 a secondary schooling system which in England had become increasingly diverse and fragmented over the 17 years of Conservative government. Seventeen per cent of all secondary schools in England had opted out of local authority control (Jones, 2003, p 166). Specialist schools had been introduced under the Major government. This differentiation of the schooling system has been extended significantly since 1997 in England. Although the 1998 Schools Standards and Framework Act removed the grant-maintained sector, among the three main types of secondary schools created by this legislation were 'foundation' schools, which had similarities with the Conservative grant-maintained schools. More recently 'city academies' were also to be independent of local authorities. The first White Paper published by the Blair government on education made it clear that 'standards not structures' would be the focus of new policies (DfEE, 1997). Such arguments meant that central government rejected policies which were premised on social democratic views of redistributive politics. The 'modernising' agenda of the Blair government's education policies would seek to promote further diversity in attempts to raise standards and encourage individuals to develop skills necessary to move them out of poverty.

Other types of schools introduced in England include beacon schools and specialist schools. Beacon schools were introduced in the first Blair government. On the basis of Ofsted data these schools would be the 'top performers' and in return for sharing experiences would receive additional funding (Jones, 2003). The range and number of 'specialist schools' have been expanded (DfEE, 2001). First introduced by the Major government in 1993, there were approximately 200 specialist schools by the 1997 General Election. In recent years these schools have become increasingly important to the 'New Labour' agenda in education. After the 2001 UK General Election, the government announced the target of 1,500 specialist schools by 2005 and by May 2004 had exceeded this target with nearly 1,700 schools becoming 'specialist' schools, accounting for over 50% of secondary schools in England (Shaw, 2004).

Reforms to the structure of secondary schooling mark one area where the Conservative reforms have been continued and intensified. As Newman (2001) has argued, the managerialist agenda of the Blair government has led to the continuation and often intensification of neo-liberal Conservative reforms. Extending the diversity of secondary schooling ran alongside the regulatory regime of targets, audits and performance management. However, the Blair governments would stress that such reforms were part of a wider 'social exclusion' agenda. Policy developments that have brought further diversity have led some to become suspicious about the implications for any attempts to reduce social inequalities (Hill, 2003). Edwards and Tomlinson (2002) have argued that since 1997 the Blair governments have presided over the extension of selection by ability especially in the grammar school sector and 'specialist schools'. Such policies, they argue, have led to 'covert social selection' that accentuates social inequalities. Again, the Scottish Executive has not followed this English model of diversity and specialisation. In contrast to England, the Scottish Executive has chosen to stress 'choice' by students within comprehensive schools rather than 'choice' of different types of schools. McConnell's speech in August 2004 stressed that there should be more choice available to students within secondary schools in terms of curriculum and teaching methods. Whether policies designed to promote choice for students within secondary schools would lead to more diversity in school types and perhaps selection is unclear.

Compared to England it remains true that the secondary schooling system is much more homogenous, and as responses to the Scottish Executive's National Debate revealed, levels of support and confidence in comprehensive schools remain high (Scottish Executive, 2003b). The Scottish Executive decided against the introduction of 'specialist schools' similar to those in England. Rather than introduce an array of policies designed to promote diversity and specialisation, the Scottish Executive has sought to work within the current comprehensive structure. It has advocated more flexibility within comprehensive provision especially curricular rather than stressing the need for selection and differentiation.

Performance management

In England concerns about the implications of 'performance management' approach and about teachers' workload have become increasingly evident since

1999. Policy developments by the Department for Education and Employment and now the Department for Education and Skills support the view that teachers are an obstacle to change rather than 'partners' in the social democratic use of the term. The regulatory framework, established and subsequently developed through a wide range of policies starting from the 1998 Schools Standards and Framework Act, places teachers as "operationally central but strategically marginal" (Jones, 2003, p 162). Tomlinson (2001, p 93) has argued that in England "teachers were to be even more heavily policed, with management of their performance based on private sector models".

It was not inevitable that Scotland would fail to follow the 'English model' of 'performance management'. Indeed, after Labour was elected in 1997 the policy documents published by the then Minister of Education, Brian Wilson, suggested that elements of target setting might be developed in Scotland (Scottish Office, 1998). This approach was continued by his successor Helen Liddell, and subsequently by the first Minister for Education in the Scottish Parliament, Sam Galbraith (Scottish Executive, 1999) . Arguably, it was with McConnell's appointment to the schools portfolio in 2001 under Henry McLeish as First Minister that policy in Scotland reverted to the style and approach associated with the 'Scottish education community'. Education professionals, McConnell claimed, should run the education system free from central interference (Paterson, 2002a). Attempts to settle ongoing disputes with teachers led to the Scottish Executive accepting the recommendations of the McCrone Report (Scottish Executive, 2001a). Teachers secured a pay rise of 21.5% over three years and a 35-hour working week in return for more flexible working practices. Although there have been difficulties in implementing the McCrone proposals, especially in terms of funding, acceptance of the proposals did suggest that teachers' status would continue to be given particular importance in the development of policy post-devolution. Support for 'professional autonomy' in the day-to-day running of schools in Scotland appeared to be strong (Paterson, 2002a). A consensus that the professionals should have such 'autonomy' informed the policy-making environment in Scotland. However, there were some signs that teachers and also education authorities would be subject to new forms of regulation. For instance, the General Teaching Council was given powers to judge the competency of registered teachers. The 2000 Standards in Scotland's Schools etc Act also required that education authorities should be subject to inspection (Scottish Executive, 2000).

What is common to both Scotland and England is that the modernising agenda includes strategies for centralised regulation that are linked to concerns about public sector delivery and specifically standards and performance. In England governing bodies have been identified by central government as a key instrument of 'steering' and regulation. Governing bodies have been used as a key strategic lever of control. The educational agenda of raising standards and improving schools requires governors to set standards, assess head teacher performance and hold schools to account. In Scotland, central direction is evident via the 'National

Priorities' published by the Scottish Executive. Under the 2000 Standards in Scotland's Schools etc Act, schools boards were given statutory responsibility for school improvement. However, in reality it was the educational professionals at school and local authority level who were regarded as the key policy participants in the implementation of reforms rather than school board members.

The Scottish Parliament approved five national priorities in December 2000 which were to shape educational policy making, namely: achievement and attainment; framework for learning; inclusion and equality; values and citizenship; and learning for life (Scottish Executive, 2001b). However, as Ozga (2003a) has argued, educational professionals at school and authority level have been given more scope to judge the 'progress' of these priorities and 'school performance' using both qualitative and quantitative indicators of 'quality'. At school level, performance includes an element of self-evaluation by the professionals, centring on the HMIE document *How good is our school?* (HMIE, 2002). Local authorities in Scotland are expected to assess their own performance and to have improvement plans. These national priorities place added importance on the need for 'performance management' and, as Croxford has argued, local authorities and schools now have a requirement to monitor inequalities in performance (Croxford, 2003). Moreover, the "Scottish education system currently does not have a system that measures inequality in pupils' attainment" and this could be partly due to suspicions that such data could be used in a "judgemental rather than an enabling manner by government" (Croxford, 2003, p 2).

In March 2002 the then Minister for Education and Young People, Cathy Jamieson, launched a national debate on the future of education policy. Concurrently the Education, Culture and Sports Committee of the Scottish Parliament launched a review on the purposes of Scottish Education. It could be argued that the launch of these reviews was a sign of a desire to extend consultation beyond the traditional participants of the 'Scottish education community'. Humes (2003, p 81) has argued that post-devolution the position of one of the key categories of participants in the 'education community', namely the educational professionals, has been strengthened, as the Scottish Executive has to consult on an array of policy initiatives. Moreover, he argues that experiences of the first significant piece of education legislation introduced by the Scottish Executive in 1999 does not support arguments that devolution would lead to a more consultative and participative style of policy making. The educational professionals continue to hold a key role in the policy process in Scotland even after reforms to the HMIE that followed the Scottish Qualifications Authority (SQA) crisis. Reviewing the post-McCrone period, Menter at al (2004, p 201) argue:

> Scottish developments appear to be based on a continuation of a public service ethic, trust in teachers, and an absence of performativity.

This brief examination of key New Labour themes reveals the continuing significance of inherited policies in Scotland. In secondary education policy some of the 'modernising' rhetoric may be similar to that in England but the means of achieving desired policy goals, such as reducing social inequalities, appear to be becoming increasingly distinct. The role of the private sector, the involvement of local authorities and teachers, a continuing commitment to non-selective comprehensive schooling, are areas where the Scottish Executive and the Whitehall departments appear to be diverging.

Convergence and divergence in education policy between Scotland and England

One reason for policy divergence in secondary education policy has been the distinctive administrative and institutional structure of the schooling systems north and south of the border. Another reason, as clearly evidenced with regard to secondary education policy, is the "legacy of policy styles, networks and practices" before 1999 (Keating, 2003, p 432). In secondary education it is also necessary to acknowledge the role which 'crisis' and 'policy disasters' played in shaping the direction of policy, notably industrial disputes with teachers and the SQA crisis during the first term of the Scottish Parliament.

Three areas of policy divergence or distinctiveness seem apparent. The first relates to use of social actors in the delivery and regulation of policies and particularly to performance management. In Scotland, responsibility for delivery and regulation primarily lies with the educational professionals in both local authorities and schools although central agencies are brought into play. Schools and education authorities have responsibility for implementing the five national priorities set out by the Scottish Executive. In England attempts to increase and also change the nature of participation by parents and governors were designed in part as attempts to hold educational professionals to account, but also to ensure delivery of policies. Teachers could not themselves be trusted to deliver changes and improve standards. School governor engagement has become part of wider attempts to improve standards and extend diversity in the schooling system. As Peters (2003, p 49) argues, by enhancing participation "uniformity is no longer as important for good public service as conventional wisdom has made it". The paradox is that by trying to 'regulate' and 'steer' policy through the engagement with governors (who are volunteers) central government may find it harder to coordinate policy:

> At the same time that involvement brings many disadvantaged people into the political process, this process has also made programmes more difficult to control, and has presented consequent problems of accountability. (Peters, 2003, p 49)

The second area of distinctiveness concerns the structure of the secondary schooling system. Here the key difference lies with the role of local government in schooling and the involvement of the private sector. Seventeen years of market-based reforms before 1997, followed by reforms which have sought to engage the private sector and also school governing bodies in secondary schooling provision, have undermined local government provision in England. In Scotland, in contrast, flagship policies, such as New Community Schools, continue to be implemented by local government.

The third area of policy divergence relates broadly to policies aimed at 'social inclusion'. Here there are two areas of distinctiveness. Secondary education policies in both Scotland and England have aimed to enhance participation. Whereas in England participation has centred on governing bodies, policy initiatives in Scotland have focused much more on engagement with students and children. Perceptions of teachers as obstacles to change have shaped the policy agenda south of the border and led to attempts to use governors to 'regulate' teachers. The second area of distinctiveness, in terms of 'social inclusion' policies, relates to the continued influence of the myths and traditions associated with the social democratic consensus and redistributive politics in Scotland. The policy environment continues to be shaped by the view that social inequalities can be tackled via collective action rather than on an individual basis. For instance, the Scottish Parliament's Education, Culture and Sports Committee, in its report on the *Inquiry into the purposes of Scottish education*, argued:

> It is agreed that Scotland's non selective system of schooling ... has been successful in raising aspirations and levels of achievement.... Education should seek a balance between cohesion and diversity, but the general view was that promoting social cohesion should be the more important priority. There was no support for specialist models as seen in other parts of the UK. (Scottish Parliament, 2003)

Divergence in these three areas suggests that political and professional discourse surrounding education policies and, more generally, welfare policies in Scotland, continues to be informed by 'social democratic' perspectives of welfare provision. External influences from globalisation and the 'knowledge economy' do present pressure for policy convergence, but this has been transmitted through what remains a largely social democratic discourse in Scotland. However, tensions are apparent between social democratic and managerialist discourses advanced in the 'modernising' agenda.

It seems that Scotland is unlikely to experience the extension of the private sector in school governance or the development of specialist schools, although the direction of policy, especially under a McConnell administration, is likely to feature elements of the 'modernising' agenda, especially in relation to public service delivery. Examples are the PPPs in school building programmes and the development of regulation and audit as seen in local authority inspections.

Conclusion

Policy making is much more complex now than three decades ago. Responding to such complexity is an issue that faces both the Scottish Executive and the Blair government. Part of the 'new style' of politics in Scotland was to extend consultation. Consultation could make the policy-making environment in Scotland more complex. This may be why the Scottish Executive has adopted a more conservative approach compared to policy development south of the border. It may be that it is the continued importance of 'consensus', in particular support both for non-selective comprehensive schools and for the 'professional autonomy' of teachers, which mainly accounts for perceptions of a rather more conservative approach in Scotland. Much of the difference between Scotland and England since 1999 can be accounted for by the different starting points for policy development. In particular in England the legacy of the Conservative governments is arguably more lasting and this in turn has shaped the direction of policy development. One might expect divergences in secondary education policy given the stronger commitments to comprehensive schooling and 'professional autonomy' north of the border. Added to this reason for divergence is the role of the Treasury in social policy south of the border. The use of policy instruments such as Public Service Agreements has led to departments, including the Department for Education and Employment and latterly the Department for Education and Skills, to be bound to targets and standards which have given added edge to public service delivery, especially 'performance management'.

Questions about the success of legislative devolution are highly contentious especially in terms of the impact on the lives of those who live in Scotland. Mitchell has argued that a key function of devolution is related to democratic legitimacy and it is in this respect that perhaps the success of the Scottish Parliament is best judged. In Mitchell's words:

> No significant section of Scottish society today questions the democratic foundations of the constitutional order. (Mitchell, 2003, p 137)

Paterson (2002b, p 59) argues that one of the important contributions of the Scottish Parliament is that it has "begun to establish a public forum, a space in which social policy in Scotland is truly being debated beyond the still secretive (and still firmly British) ranks of the Scottish civil service". The committees of the Scottish Parliament provide space for pressure groups to be consulted. While the Scottish Parliament provides additional public space for consultation and participation in the policy process this does not necessarily mean that there will be a change in the direction of policy. It remains an open question whether this extension of consultation has been absorbed by the 'Scottish education community'. This could be a force for continuity on the grounds that engagement with actors who belong to the 'education policy community' has enabled them to gain more space in consultative processes rather than extending the range of interests engaged or giving such interests more influence in the policy process. A feature of 'Scottish education community' demonstrated in the work of McPherson and Raab (1988) was that participants were bound by a culture that was informed by myths and traditions. Features of such a culture included views that the schooling system in Scotland was more democratic and of a high quality. As Paterson (1997, p 143) has argued, this culture was built on a "fairly homogenous Scottishness". The continued influence of such myths, admittedly somewhat dented by the SQA crisis, would potentially act as a force for 'conservatism' and may also hide cultural diversity in Scotland. For instance in their review of the distinctiveness of Scottish education Humes and Bryce (2003, p 113) point to prevailing myths having led to a "standardised and idealised model of Scottish life" which hides considerable cultural diversity in contemporary Scottish society.

That the policy process has become more complex and fragmented is undeniable. However, it is a clear 'core' of actors of the Scottish education community (especially in secondary education) who continue to play a significant role in policy making and also implementation of policy, especially when comparisons are drawn with experiences of policy process south of the border.

The consideration of secondary schooling policy has revealed that differences existed before 1999 between Scotland and England, and that, following the creation of the Scottish Parliament, the Scottish Executive has chosen to pursue a largely conservative agenda which is shaped by the myths and traditions associated with the social democratic consensus. Failure to adapt the more radical aspects of the 'modernising' agenda to such a consensus would mean that Labour had not learnt one of the most important lessons of the Thatcherite approach to the government of Scotland. Failing to accommodate policies to Scottish myths in education centring around notions of a more democratic and socially inclusive schooling system is likely to produce 'implementation gaps'. For a Party which has become increasingly preoccupied with policy delivery since 1997 throughout the UK, and which in Scotland came to support devolution as a reaction to the Thatcherite approach to territorial politics, the adoption of more 'radical' policies pursued south of the border would potentially be both politically and electorally disastrous.

Further reading

For a comprehensive account of policy developments in Scottish education since 1999 see Bryce, T.G.K. and Humes, W.M. (eds) (2003) *Scottish education: Post devolution*, Edinburgh: Edinburgh University Press. For a good overview of developments in the Scottish education system across the 20th century, see Paterson, L. (2003) *Scottish education in the twentieth century*, Edinburgh: Edinburgh University Press.

<table>
<tr><td colspan="2">On the web ...</td></tr>
<tr><td>Scottish Executive</td><td>www.scotland.gov.uk/</td></tr>
<tr><td>Her Majesty's Inspectorate of
Education in Scotland</td><td>www.hmie.gov.uk/</td></tr>
<tr><td>*Times Education Supplement Scotland*</td><td>www.tes.co.uk/scotland/news/</td></tr>
</table>

References

Accounts Commission (2002) *Taking the initiative using PFI contracts to renew council schools*, Edinburgh: Accounts Commission.

Anderson, R.D. (1983) *Education and opportunity in Victorian Scotland*, Edinburgh: Edinburgh University Press.

Arnott, M.A. (1992) 'Thatcherism in Scotland: an exploration of education policy in the secondary sector', PhD thesis, University of Strathclyde.

Arnott, M.A. (2000) 'Restructuring the governance of schools: the impact of "managerialism" on schools in Scotland and England', in M.A. Arnott and C.D. Raab (eds) *The governance of schooling: Comparative studies of devolved management*, London: Routledge/Falmer, pp 52-76.

Brehony, K. and Deem, R. (2003) 'Education policy', in N. Ellison and C. Pierson (eds) *Developments in British social policy 2*, Baskingstoke: Palgrave Macmillan, pp 177-93.

Bromley, C., Curtice, J., Hinds, K. and Park, A. (2003) *Devolution: Scottish answers to Scottish questions? The Third Scottish Social Attitudes Report*, Edinburgh: Edinburgh University Press.

Brown, A., McCrone, D. and Paterson, L. (1998) *Politics and society in Scotland*, Baskingstoke: Macmillan.

Brown, A., McCrone, D., Paterson, L. and Surridge, P. (1999) *The Scottish electorate*, Basingstoke: Macmillan.

Bulpitt, J. (1983) *Territory and power in the United Kingdom*, Manchester: Manchester University Press.

Crawford, A. and Paul, A. (2004) 'Revealed: how Scotland's new PPP "gamble" could cost the nation £25bn', *Sunday Herald*, 13 June.

Croxford, L. (2003) *Measuring performance: Tackling inequalities*, Briefings No 26, Edinburgh: Centre for Educational Sociology, University of Edinburgh.

Curtice, J. and Seyd B. (2001) 'Is devolution strengthening or weakening the UK?', in A. Park et al (eds) *British Social Attitudes 18th Report*, London: Sage Publications, pp 228-43.

Denholm, J. and Macleod, D. (2002) 'Educating the Scots: the renewal of the democratic intellect', in G. Hassan and C. Warhurst (eds) *Anatomy of the new Scotland: Power, influence and change*, Edinburgh: Mainstream Publishing.

DfEE (Department for Education and Employment) (1997) *Excellence in schools*, London: The Stationery Office.

DfEE (2001) *Schools building on success: Raising standards, promoting diversity, achieving results*, London: The Stationery Office.

DfES (Department for Education and Skills) (2001) *Schools achieving success*, London: The Stationery Office.

Edwards, T and Tomlinson, S. (2002) *Selection isn't working: Diversity, standards and inequality in secondary education*, Catalyst Working Paper, London: Catalyst Forum.

Fallis, R. (2004) 'Scottish schools' funding plan unveiled', *Times Education Supplement Scotland*, 1 June.

Fraser, D. (2004) 'Labour vision of schools that select their pupils', *The Herald*, 31 August.

Gerwitz, S. (2002) *The managerial school: Post-welfarism and social justice in education*, London: Routledge.

Green, A. (1990) *Education and state formation*, London: Macmillan.

Hill, M. (2003) *Understanding social policy*, Oxford: Blackwell Publishing.

HMIE (Her Majesty's Inspectorate of Education) (2002) *How good is our school? Self-evaluation using qualitative indicators*, Edinburgh: HMIE

Humes, W.M. (2003) 'Policy-making in Scottish education', in T.G.K. Bryce and W.M. Humes (eds) *Scottish education: Post devolution*, Edinburgh: Edinburgh University Press, pp 62-73.

Humes, W.M. and Bryce, T.G.K. (2003) 'The distinctiveness of Scottish education', in T.G.K. Bryce and W.M. Humes (eds) *Scottish education: Post devolution*, Edinburgh: Edinburgh University Press, pp 108-20.

Jones, K. (2003) *Education in Britain: 1944 to the present*, Oxford: Polity Press.

Keating, M. (2002) 'Devolution and public policy in the United Kingdom: divergence or convergence', in J. Adams and P. Robinson (eds) *Devolution in practice: Public policy differences within the UK*, London: IPPR, pp 3-19.

Keating, M. (2003) 'Social inclusion, devolution and policy divergence', *Political Quarterly*, pp 429-38.

MacLeod, C. (2004) 'Tycoons talk to McConnell over private cash for state schools', *The Herald*, 9 July

Macwhirter, I. (2002) 'The new Scottish political class', in G. Hassan and C. Warhurst (eds) *Anatomy of the new Scotland: Power, influence and change*, Edinburgh: Mainstream Publishing.

McCaig, C. (2000) 'New Labour and education, education, education', in S. Ludlam and M.J. Smith (eds) *New Labour in government*, Baskingstoke: Macmillan, pp 184-201.

McConnell, J. (2004) 'One Scotland: ambition and opportunities', Speech to Labour activists, Edinburgh, 30 August (www.scottishlabour.org.uk/onescotland/).

McCrone, D. (1992) *Understanding Scotland: A sociology of a stateless nation*, London: Routledge.

McPherson, A. and Raab, C.D. (1988) *Governing education: A policy sociology of education in Scotland*, Edinburgh: Edinburgh University Press.

Menter, I., Mahoney, P. and Hextall, I. (2004) 'Ne're the twain shall meet? Modernising the teaching profession in Scotland and England', *Journal of Education Policy*, vol 19, no 2, pp 195-214.

Mitchell, J. (1996) 'Scotland in the Union 1945-95', in T.M. Devine and R. Findlay (eds) *Scotland in the twentieth century*, Edinburgh: Edinburgh University Press.

Mitchell, J. (2003) 'Third year, third First Minister', in R. Hazell (ed) *The state of the nations 2003: The third year of devolution in the United Kingdom*, Exeter: Imprint Press, pp 119-37.

Naidoo, R. and Muschamp, Y. (2002) 'A decent education for all?', in M. Powell (ed) *Evaluating New Labour's welfare reforms*, Bristol: The Policy Press, pp 101-22.

Newman, J. (2001) *Modernising governance: New Labour, policy and society*, London: Sage Publications.

Nixon, J., Allan, J. and Mannion, G. (2001) 'Educational renewal as democratic practice: "New Community Schooling in Scotland"', *International Journal of Inclusive Education*, vol 5, no 4, pp 329-52.

Nixon, J., Walker, M. and Baron, S. (2002) 'From Washington Heights to the Raploch: evidence, mediation and the genealogy of policy', *Social Policy and Society*, vol 1, no 3, pp 237-46.

Ozga, J. (2003a) *Measuring and managing performance in education*, Briefing Paper No 27, Edinburgh: Centre of Educational Sociology, University of Edinburgh.

Ozga, J. (2003b) 'Two nations? Education policy and social inclusion/exclusion in Scotland and England', Paper Presented to the British Educational Research Association Conference, Edinburgh, September.

Peters, B.G. (2003) 'Governance and the welfare state', in N. Ellison and C. Pierson (eds) *Developments in British social policy 2*, Baskingstoke: Palgrave Macmillan, pp 41-55.

Paterson, L. (1997) 'Policy-making in Scottish education: a case of pragmatic nationalism', in M. Clarke and P. Munn (eds) *Education in Scotland: Policy and practice from pre-school to secondary*, London: Routledge, pp 138-55.

Paterson, L. (2000) *Education and the Scottish Parliament*, Edinburgh: Dunedin Academic Press.

Paterson, L. (2002a) 'Ideology and public policy', in J. Curtice et al (eds) *New Scotland, new society*, Edinburgh: Edinburgh University Press, pp 196-218.

Paterson, L. (2002b) 'Civic democracy', in G. Hassan and C. Warhurst (eds) *Anatomy of the New Scotland: Power, influence and change*, Edinburgh: Mainstream Publishing.

Pring, R. (2001) 'Privatisation and schooling', in C. Chitty and B. Simon (eds) *Promoting comprehensive education in the 21st century*, Stoke on Trent: Trentham Books.

Richards, D. and Smith, M.J. (2002) *Governance and public policy in the United Kingdom*, Oxford: Oxford University Press.

Richards, D. and Smith, M.J. (2004) 'The "hybrid state": Labour's response to the challenge of governance', in S. Ludlam and M.J. Smith (eds) *Governing as New Labour*, Baskingstoke: Palgrave Macmillan, pp 106-19.

Scottish Executive (1999) *Improving our schools: Consultation on the Improvement in Scottish Education Bill*, Edinburgh: Scottish Executive.

Scottish Executive (2000) *Standards in Scotland's Schools etc Act 2000*, Edinburgh: Scottish Executive.

Scottish Executive (2001a) *A teaching profession for the 21st century: Agreement reached following recommendations made in McCrone Report*, Edinburgh: Scottish Executive.

Scottish Executive (2001b) *National priorities in school education*, Edinburgh: Scottish Executive (www.scotland.gov.uk/education).

Scottish Executive (2002) *Recording our achievements: Main report*, Edinburgh: Scottish Executive.

Scottish Executive (2003a) *A partnership for a better Scotland: Partnership agreement*, Edinburgh: Scottish Executive.

Scottish Executive (2003b) *Educating for excellence: Choice and opportunity: The Executive's response to the national debate*, Edinburgh: Scottish Executive.

Scottish Office (1998) *Setting targets: Raising standards in schools: A strategy for improvement by schools*, Edinburgh: Scottish Office Education and Industry Department.

Scottish Parliament (2003) *Inquiry into the purposes of Scottish education Volume 1 Report*, Edinburgh: Scottish Parliament.

Shaw, M. (2004) 'Not so specialist as schools lose status', *Times Education Supplement*, 21 May.

Stedward, G. (2003) 'Education as industrial policy: New Labour's marriage of the social and the economic', *Policy & Politics*, vol 31, no 2, pp 139-52.

Stewart, W. (2003) 'Essex heads ditch LEA support and go private', *Times Education Supplement*, 30 May.

Surridge, P. (2002) 'Society and democracy: the New Scotland', in J. Curtice et al (eds) *New Scotland, new society*, Edinburgh: Edinburgh University Press, pp 123-41.

Times Education Supplement Scotland (2003) 'Evaluation report finds community schools need more time', 5 September.

Tomlinson, S. (2001) *Education in a post welfare society*, Buckingham: Open University Press.

Social policy in Scotland: imagining a different future?

Gill Scott and Gerry Mooney

It's the economy, stupid!

> Any study of Scotland today must start from where people are, the realities of day-to-day living, extremes of wealth and poverty, unequal opportunities at work, in housing, health, education and community living generally. The gross inequalities which disfigure Scottish social life (and British society as a whole) have been obscured by a debate which merely poses the choice between separatism and unionism. For there are rich Scots, very rich Scots – and very poor Scots. (Brown, 1975, p 9)

Does this also apply to Scotland in 2004? Well (and here's a typical social science response), yes and no. Yes, in that Scotland continues to be a highly unequal and polarised society, one in which rich and very rich Scots have seen their material position reinforced and consolidated to a degree that few, Gordon Brown included, could have foreseen in 1975. Against the claims made by Paterson et al (2004, p 149), in this respect Scotland of the early years of the 21st century is *only too recognisable* as the same place of the early 1980s. However, alongside these important continuities there have been significant changes in the period since Brown's *The Red Paper on Scotland* (or indeed the follow-up, *Scotland: The real divide* [1983]) was published. No longer is the debate simply one between separatism and unionism, although this continues to be a very important feature of Scottish politics post-devolution, but between a market-driven social and economic agenda on the one hand, and those who are committed to a different kind of project in which tackling those very inequalities highlighted by Brown come to occupy centre stage.

The contributors to this book share a range of political outlooks and theoretical approaches. However, they are motivated by a belief that, through a critical analysis of social policy in contemporary Scotland, a new vision for the future development of Scottish social policy can begin to be constructed. It would be churlish of us to ignore the fact, as we note in this book's Introduction, that the Scottish

Parliament has been 'very active' in the sphere of social policy. Building on the not inconsiderable autonomy that the Scottish Office had exercised in this field since the late 19th century, much of the policy work of the Scottish Executive has continued to revolve around social and welfare 'concerns'. However, to talk of the Holyrood Parliament as a 'social policy Parliament for Scotland', to borrow Chaney and Drakeford's representation of the Welsh Assembly (2004, p 124), would perhaps lead to an underestimation of the scope for policy making that the Scottish Parliament enjoys in other areas, in addition to its tax-raising powers. Nonetheless, a strong argument can be made that it is social policy, widely conceived, that is a key 'driver' of the Scottish Parliament. Understandably, such a claim might be seen as highly contentious on two main accounts, especially given the arguments that have come to the fore throughout this book. First, that while there is some policy divergence between Scotland and the rest of the UK, there are also marked signs of policy convergence. As many of the contributors to this collection have highlighted, the existence of reserved powers under the devolution settlement works to severely limit the autonomy of the Edinburgh-based Executive. As we have seen, in relation to key areas of social policy, such as employment and social security legislation, industrial relations and immigration policy to name but a few, it is Westminster that calls the tune. Second, to suggest that it is social policy that drives both the Scottish Executive and Scottish Parliament only makes sense if we locate that social policy ('modernisation' and 'reform') within New Labour's overriding goal of increasing economic competitiveness. In a speech to the Trade Union Congress in 1997, Blair laid out the two key elements of Labour's modernisation agenda:

> The first is to create an economy fully attuned to a new global market; one that combines enterprise and flexibility with harnessing the creative potential of all our people. The second is to fashion a modern welfare state, where we maintain high levels of social inclusion based on values of community and social justice, but where the role of government changes so it is not necessary to provide all social provision, and fund all social provision but to organise and regulate it most efficiently and fairly. (Blair, 1997)

Importantly, this doctrine applies across the UK state.

Throughout this book, the 'wider' context of New Labour's political project has been an ever-present aspect of the analysis offered and this is no accident. Chapters One and Two in particular highlighted different key elements of this project, setting the stage for the exploration of key social policy areas. However, when we refer to this wider context, we are also recognising that social-divisions and social inequalities have a highly-significant bearing on policy development and on welfare and social policy 'outcomes'. Therefore, each of the contributors has, in different ways and to varying degrees, located the discussion of Scottish social policy post-devolution in the context of an unequal and divided Scottish society, divided by class, gender, race and ethnicity and by place. What we are all collectively arguing for here is a study of social policy in the devolutionary context that connects (or, to borrow the language of New Labour, 'joins-up') the analysis of welfare policy developments, the institutions and of the processes through which welfare is delivered, with the wider social and economic context.

This also means, importantly, extending the scope of social policy analysis. As has been remarked by many writers, social policy (as with much of academic social science) has tended to look 'down' the social ladder, focusing on 'social problems' *as well as those defined or constructed as 'a problem'*. This is not to suggest for a minute that we should not be analysing the effects of poverty or low wages or ill health on 'marginalised' groups in society. However, it does mean that we need to take account of the social relations that generate poverty, ill health and other 'social problems'. By adopting such an approach, a more structural approach, we can begin to understand the relationship between poverty and wealth, between the reproduction of disadvantage and the drive to increasing profitability (Jones and Novak, 1999). Increasingly, New Labour social policies across the UK are targeted at smaller and smaller sections of the population. Thus, for instance, in relation to poverty policy, reductions in the levels of poverty have been restricted to children and pensioners while poverty levels among childless couples, a group largely neglected by the government, has increased between 1994/95 and 2002/03 (Paxton and Dixon, 2004, p 18). The key driver to reducing poverty has been seen as the economy, but protection from the vagaries of the market has been limited to the young and old. While the poor have long been constructed as a minority residualised group, the existence of another minority, a highly-privileged and powerful minority – the rich, passes with relatively little comment by comparison (see Westergaard, 1995). 'Joined-up' thinking does not stretch as far as seeing that there is a relationship between poverty and wealth, it would seem.

In all the talk in recent years of 'joined-up' policy/social policy, it is often astonishing to note how little effort has been expended on examining the multiple and diverse ways in which New Labour – *in Scotland as much as in other parts of the UK* – has been concerned to link social policy and economic policy (see Stedward, 2003); in other words, how it has endeavoured to tie social policy increasingly to the pursuit of economic competitiveness, labour market flexibility and to the marketisation of important areas of what we used to refer to as the welfare state. Some would argue that a strong, successful economy is the only way in which welfare can be afforded, but here, as always, questions of power occupy centre stage. Economic development is seldom neutral: the role that business and the market now play in the shape and delivery of social policy is unprecedented (see Ferguson et al, 2002; Clarke, 2004). In such a climate, the private sector enjoys unparalleled access to policy making, in part through New Labour's fondness for 'partnerships' of different forms. As we have seen, increasingly, welfare services and social policies are being redirected towards the perceived needs of 'the economy', ensuring a better 'fit' between business and social policy outcomes. The result is deregulation, marketisation and the increasing penetration of 'heartland' areas of welfare and public service delivery all too evident across the length and breadth of Scotland; in the Public Private Partnership (PPP) programmes that now shape the restructuring of school provision in many council areas or in the growing number of Private Finance Initiative (PFI)-built hospital schemes, to highlight just two examples. That such a 'fit' has been pursued in Scotland as much as elsewhere in the UK, and with, it would seem, considerable success, is evidenced in a major report, *Wealth creation in Scotland*, published by the Royal Bank of Scotland (RBS, 2004). The authors of the report highlight that the majority of Scotland's largest firms are the product of privatisation:

> The Scottish corporate sector has been heavily influenced by the dynamics of privatisation and deregulation. The background of 14 of the top 20 Scottish firms is linked to this process. (RBS, 2004, p 6)

That such a 'fit' enhances welfare is much more questionable. The benefits to business are on previous evidence likely to be much more tangible.

The Scottish Parliament and social policy: a five-year report card

Many of the chapters in the book have noted the tensions that exist around a central element of the devolution settlement: the existence of reserved as well as devolved powers. Across the welfare spectrum, albeit in different, uneven and partial ways, there is a range of factors that are pushing towards increasing divergence and continued convergence at one and the same time. Taken together, these tensions have worked to rule out any radical departures in policy post-devolution, with instead gradual and the most modest of incremental changes being the order of the day. However, they do not operate in this way alone. There is also the question of political will, and thus far there have been few signs that there is much of a drive towards radical policy development among the New Labour–Liberal Democrat coalition Executive. Lest we be accused otherwise, we acknowledge here that Scottish devolution is still in its infancy. In answering the question, 'Has devolution made a difference?', John Stewart (2004, p 139) comments:

> The Scottish Parliament has only been in existence for a short time and operates under particular constraints. There has been a perceived need to rebuild the public services after a long period of neglect, a neglect that should not be underestimated. The social problems from which Scotland suffers were, moreover, unlikely to evaporate overnight. Given all this, the Executive has done reasonably well since 1999 and its strategy can be deemed a qualified success.

That the Scottish Parliament has been re-convened for only five years should not prevent a critical interrogation of the policies that it has generated, nor should we ignore the considerable evidence that suggests that post-devolution there is a growing disillusionment with both devolution itself and with the overall political process. And the experience of the past few years, and the commitment to entrepreneurial-led governance, tells us much about the future direction and shape of social policy in Scotland. One of the great claims made prior to devolution was that it would increase accountability, openness and access. However, one 2003 study found that the proportion of those who thought that 'ordinary' people were having more of a say in how Scotland is governed declined from 64% in 1999 to 38% in 2001 (Curtice, 2003, p 269). There is an argument that perhaps this was to be expected, once the limits of devolution had become more widely understood. And as Hassan and Rawcliffe (2003, pp 82-3) further note, instead of a break with the past there has been considerable continuity in policy and culture. In an important sense, there has been a dumbing down of expectations in the years since devolution. Here we are reminded again of Adams and Robinson's (2002) claim of a 'race to the bottom'. However, to suggest that this dumbing down results from the limitations of devolution alone, as many have done, is mistaken. 'More devolution' is not the answer to the structural inequalities that characterise contemporary Scottish society, and in making this claim we are once more cognisant of the wider social context, a UK context in which a UK government is pursuing a market-driven agenda that is shaping the future direction of welfare and social policy across the whole of the UK.

Throughout this book, we have noted that, despite claims to Scotland's "stronger emphasis on collectivist values, a stronger social democratic tradition", to quote Hassan and Rawcliffe (2003, p 81), 'Scotland' has not been immune from this neoliberal agenda. Arguably, the devolution Settlement and the furore around the costs of the Scottish Parliament building at Holyrood has distracted attention from the neoliberalism that characterises public policy in Scotland. Yet, there are some differences between Scotland and the rest of the UK, both in policies and in the ways in which those policies are constructed and presented. However, appeals to social inclusion, to community, to opportunity, to closing 'gaps' of assorted and varied kinds, to greater choice as well as to social justice characterise New Labour both north and south of the border. Any differences that exist do so primarily at the level of rhetoric, underpinned by a shared allegiance to the social inclusion through work discourse (see Mooney and Johnstone, 2000; Cultural Policy Collective, 2004). And the failure to address the inequalities that so blight Scottish and UK society today also reflects the priorities of New Labour across the UK to maintain fiscal 'prudence', to pursue economic competitiveness and to continue with a low taxation policy, priorities that underpin the Scottish Executive's entire agenda. The result is that Scotland remains a deeply unequal and deeply divided Society (Brown et al, 2002; Kenway et al, 2002; Hassan and Rawcliffe, 2003; McCormick et al, 2004).

Stewart (2004) suggests that we are in the early throes of devolution, but already this involves significantly greater consultation and a changed democratic process. Can it really be said that social policy post-devolution has been a 'success' in these terms, even a 'qualified' one? And if so, a success for whom? In different chapters, the repeated claims of the greater collectiveness and social inclusiveness of the 'Scots' have been subjected to critical scrutiny. These claims were mobilised to legitimate the devolved Parliament's commitment to openness. To quote First Minister McConnell:

> Devolution is not just about transferring power from Westminster to Holyrood, but about changing the essential nature of the processes of government. So the success of devolution must be assessed not just in terms of the output of policy, legislation and services, but in how far and how effectively people are engaged with government. (McConnell, 2003, quoted in People and Parliament Trust, 2004)

A number of the chapters of this book suggest that, on these criteria alone, Scottish devolution would be deemed to be a miserable failure. One of the key themes to emerge from several of the chapters relates to the 'hidden voices' of Scottish devolution. Where are the voices of minority ethnic groups, working-class women, the low paid, the homeless, ordinary workers in the policies that have been enacted since 1999? Where is the participation, the involvement of the marginalised? Yes, Scottish devolution has provided opportunities for smaller parties to enter Parliament, the Greens and Scottish Socialist Party the most notable, and there have been successes for candidates standing on specific platforms, for instance in relation to defending health services and on promoting the needs of Scotland's pensioners. But as yet, this has made little significant difference in shifting the focus of the Parliament and the Scottish Executive towards a primary concern with the disadvantaged and marginalised. As we write this in September 2004, there is a growing political debate around the future of health services in Scotland, a debate that is calling into sharp focus not only the prospects for NHS Scotland as a whole, but the Scottish Executive's entire health strategy (see *The Scotsman*, 11 September 2004; *Sunday Herald*, 14 September 2004; *The Herald*, 6 and 17 September 2004). This controversy has been sparked by Scotland-wide protests against hospital closures and centralisation, hospital downgrading and the restructuring of health provision across much of the country, both urban and rural. Claims have been made that the growing tide of resistance against the health reforms will parallel the poll tax rebellion of the late 1980s and early 1990s (McDougall, 2004). It has generated a new round of political spats between New Labour MSPs and Westminster-based Labour MPs, many from West of Scotland constituencies where the protests have been among the most vocal. These MPs have called for the Scottish Executive and the Scottish Health Minister to announce a moratorium on the proposed changes, in the process exacerbating already existing tensions that characterise relations between both sets of Labour politicians. Replying to protestors, the First Minister has been widely quoted as commenting:

> Just because people shout loudly, it does not mean that they are necessarily correct. (McConnell, 16 September 2004, quoted in *The Herald*, 17 September 2004)

In dismissing protests around the centralisation of Scotland's health services, the Scottish Executive is being consistent if nothing else. Since 1999, it has similarly been blind to a series of protests and opposition to the closure and run down of local authority services, community and leisure centres, clinics, community and health centres. It has also been deaf to the pleas of low-paid public sector workers who have been forced into strike action, both in pursuit of better wages and conditions as well as in the defence of hard won terms and conditions from the past. Since devolution, council librarians, social workers, nurses, hospital ancillary staff, teachers and lecturers have all been forced into industrial action of one kind or another, in addition to UK-wide disputes involving fire fighters, among others. That many of these groups of workers are at the forefront in the delivery of social policies brings into sharp focus the reality of New Labour's welfare 'reform' and 'modernisation' agenda. Nursery nurses, health protestors, opponents of housing stock transfer, campaigners defending public services (such as notable protests to save swimming pools from closure in both Glasgow and the Borders), have all been marginalised voices in the period since Scottish devolution. For us, the significance of such protests is that they highlight not only the contested, and highly inequitable, reality of Scottish social and public policy but that they seriously undermine any pretence to social justice or to a 'new politics' in the 'new Scotland'.

There are two key issues emerging for us from this discussion. First, that there are few signs that the devolved Scotland is heading in a direction where we can begin to see the development of an equal citizenship, an inclusive citizenship. And second, the examination of social policy in Scotland cannot be divorced from wider UK and indeed global structures. A question we have been forced to ask is, 'What should be the starting point for policy analysis as a result?'. From the perspective of institutions, policy makers, politicians or from the vantage point of service users, public sector and welfare workers, the marginalised and disadvantaged. In other words we need to continually highlight and locate these debates within the wider social relations and social divisions of welfare? Here we have argued that it is only by exploring this wider context that we can even begin to make sense of social policy developments and outcomes. What then of 'Scottish solutions for Scottish problems'? What are 'Scottish' problems and what are 'Scottish' solutions? Whose 'Scottish' and which 'problems' and 'solutions' and for whom are they being constructed and defined here?

The social relations, the industrial relations, workplace relations, service user-provider relations that govern and characterise welfare in Scotland today are also those that shape UK-wide social policy. It is in this context that we must locate questions about the distinctiveness of Scottish social policy.

What is to be done?

So, finally, in conclusion, what would a radically different Scottish social policy look like? All the contributors to this book believe that another Scottish social policy is possible. Here we speak for ourselves, reflecting on the arguments presented by the chapter authors, but who may not share our 'vision'. Let us start by acknowledging something that all contributors to this book agree upon: that ideas matter, and matter a lot. In the drive under New Labour toward evidence-based social policy, often arguably based on rather spurious evidence, ideas have tended to be marginalised in the uncritical acceptance of a neoliberal common sense. One of the repeated arguments made against the Scottish Executive is that is has been short on ideas. One, albeit ill-defined, idea that it did generate was 'closing the gap'. Presented in terms of narrowing the opportunity gap, arguably this proved a useful way of focusing on the disadvantages that accompany poverty and continues to inform current UK and Scottish policy, as for example in the recent *Breaking the cycle* report from the Social Exclusion Unit in London (SEU, 2004).

However, we would suggest that closing the gap could be reconstructed and imagined in a radically different way:

- by addressing the multiple inequalities that characterise contemporary Scotland;
- by closing the gap between rich and poor through progressive taxation and a commitment to redistribution of wealth and income;
- re-interpreting social inclusion as something much more than paid employment;
- by giving social policy workers a greater say in the delivery of welfare;
- by ending workplace insecurity and low pay;
- by the provision of high-quality, publicly-funded public services; and
- by rethinking what good non-market-based public provision would look like and how this could actively promote *real* social inclusion in ways that do not rely on paid work.

There are limitations to how far the Executive in Scotland can act with a free hand in these areas but one of the most interesting challenges facing social policy makers today in Scotland is to see how far it is possible to *at least* moderate the sharp social divisions and inequalities that characterise the UK as a whole. Such issues are at the core of political debate about the future direction of devolution and territorial justice and therefore key to understanding policy in the UK state as a whole as well as in the devolved Scotland and Wales.

References

Adams, J. and Robinson, P. (eds) (2002) *Devolution in practice: Public policy differences within the UK*, London: IPPR.

Blair, T. (1997) 'The modernisation of Britain', Speech to the 1997 Trades Union Congress, 9 September.

Brown, G. (1975) 'Introduction: the socialist challenge', in G. Brown (ed) *The Red Paper on Scotland*, Edinburgh: Edinburgh University Student Publications Board, pp 7-21.

Brown, G. and Cook, R. (1983) *Scotland: The real divide*, Edinburgh: Mainstream.

Brown, U., Scott, J., Mooney, G. and Duncan, B. (eds) (2002) *Poverty in Scotland 2002: People, places and policies*, London/Glasgow: CPAG/Scottish Poverty Information Unit.

Chaney, P. and Drakeford, M. (2004) 'The primacy of ideology: social policy and the first term of the National Assembly for Wales', in N. Ellison, L. Bauld and M. Powell (eds) *Social Policy Review 16*, Bristol: The Policy Press/Social Policy Association, pp 121-42.

Clarke, J. (2004) *Changing welfare, changing states*, London: Sage Publications.

Cultural Policy Collective (2004) *Beyond social inclusion: Towards cultural democracy*, Aberdeen: The Lemon Tree/Scottish Arts Council.

Curtice, J. (2003) 'Devolution meets the voters: the prospects for 2003', in R. Hazell (ed) *The state of the nations 2003: The third year of devolution in the United Kingdom*, London: Constitution Unit, University College London, pp 263-82.

Ferguson, I., Lavalette, M. and Mooney, G. (2002) *Rethinking welfare: A critical perspective*, London: Sage Publications.

Hassan, G. and Rawcliffe, S. (2003) *Staying human: Respect, values and social justice*, Edinburgh: Scottish Human Services Trust.

Jones, C. and Novak, T. (1999) *Poverty, welfare and the disciplinary state*, London: Routledge.

Kenway, P., Fuller, S., Rahman, M., Street, C. and Palmer, G. (2002) *Monitoring poverty and social exclusion in Scotland*, London: New Policy Institute/Joseph Rowntree Foundation.

McCormick, J., Spencer, F. and Gamble, C. (2004) 'Beyond the bounds: resources for tackling disadvantage', in IPPR, Social Market Foundation, Policy Exchange/Scottish Council Foundation and Institute of Welsh Affairs (eds) *Overcoming disadvantage: An agenda for the next 20 Years*, York: Joseph Rowntree Foundation, pp 84-111.

McDougall, L. (2004) 'Health reform: no pain, no gain?', *Sunday Herald*, 12 September, p 13.

Mooney, G. and Johnstone, C. (2000) 'Scotland divided: poverty, inequality and the Scottish Parliament', *Critical Social Policy*, vol 20, no 2, pp 155-82.

Paterson, L., Bechhofer, F. and McCrone, D. (2004) *Living in Scotland: Social and economic change since 1980*, Edinburgh: Edinburgh University Press.

Paxton, W. and Dixon, M. (2004) *The state of the nation: An audit of injustice in the UK*, London: IPPR.

People and Parliament Trust (2004) *Room for more views? Sharing power, shaping progress*, Edinburgh: Scottish Human Services Trust.

RBS (Royal Bank of Scotland) (2004) *Wealth creation in Scotland*, Edinburgh: RBS.

SEU (Social Exclusion Unit) (2004) *Breaking the cycle: Taking stock of progress and priorities for the future: A report by the Social Exclusion Unit*, London: Office of the Deputy Prime Minister.

Stedward, G. (2003) 'Education as industrial policy: New Labour's marriage of the social and economic', *Policy & Politics*, vol 31, no 2, pp 139-53.

Stewart, J. (2004) *Taking stock: Scottish social welfare after devolution*, Bristol: The Policy Press.

Westergaard, J. (1995) *Who get's what?*, Cambridge: Polity Press.

Index

Page references for notes are followed by n